Everyday Justice

Everyday Justice

A Legal Aid Story

ASHLEY WILTSHIRE

Vanderbilt University Press
NASHVILLE, TENNESSEE

Library of Congress Cataloging-in-Publication Data

Names: Wiltshire, Ashley T., Jr., 1941- author.
Title: Everyday justice : a legal aid story / Ashley T. Wiltshire, Jr.
Description: Nashville, Tennessee : Vanderbilt University Press, 2023. |
   Includes bibliographical references.
Identifiers: LCCN 2022011432 (print) | LCCN 2022011433 (ebook) | ISBN
   9780826505101 (paperback) | ISBN 9780826505118 (epub) | ISBN
   9780826505125 (pdf)
Subjects: LCSH: Legal aid--Tennessee, Middle--History. | Practice of
   law--Tennessee, Middle--History. | Justice, Administration
   of--Tennessee--History. | Law--Tennessee--History.
Classification: LCC KFT84.5.P7 W55 2023 (print) | LCC KFT84.5.P7 (ebook)
   | DDC 347.768/017--dc23/eng/20221031
LC record available at https://lccn.loc.gov/2022011432
LC ebook record available at https://lccn.loc.gov/2022011433

To Callie Mae Newsom, Jean Stacey, Denzil White,
and the thousands of others who trusted their problems to us

and to those good souls in the bar and the community
who helped us along the way

Contents

Introduction

The man in the back of the room stood up and pointed at me, "There he is, boys. I told you this would happen, and there he is . . ."

I had just finished my presentation to the Sumner County Bar Association in its meeting at the Gallatin Country Club, talking about our plan at Legal Services of Nashville to open a legal aid office in their town to serve low-income people in three suburban/rural counties. The man pointing his finger at me, I learned later, was the circuit court judge for that area. Like many lawyers in our state, he was convinced that Legal Services lawyers were a danger to society and to the legal profession. Twelve years earlier, two leaders of the Tennessee Bar Association had written in the association's quarterly journal that Legal Services was a part of "a headlong plunge into socialism." The title of their impassioned article was "Et tu, Brute!"

In 1974, three years before my fateful trip to the country club, a committee appointed by the Nashville Bar Association, after a year-long investigation, found that three of us had committed "unprofessional conduct of the worst sort" by representing people with developmental disabilities against the state, which had been warehousing them without recourse in deplorable conditions. The committee recommended that the bar association board reprimand us for our actions and insisted that the board of our organization should "assure that this sort of thing is discontinued."

As we will see during the progress of our story, each of these venomous confrontations eventually had a positive outcome, emblematic of some of the profound changes that will occur in the bar, as well as in the law and in society, over the course of our time. This is a story about the struggle to establish civil legal aid in one place in the American South, about the early instability of Legal Services of Nashville, and about its evolution into an effective and broadly supported organization that has provided representation to vulnerable people who were, and often still are, disadvantaged by their lack of access to all parts of our legal system. It is a story about the wide variety of civil legal cases we handled for our clients and some of the improvements we were able to obtain through those cases.

The opposition and the backlash that we encountered was not and should not be surprising. Many of our cases challenged societal status quo, racial prejudice, bureaucratic lethargy, and business as usual. They disclosed injustices and called for radical changes. They required thoughtful remedies from courageous judges, responsive legislators, and diligent administrators. And thankfully there is no lack of heroes throughout the story in all three branches of government, judges and other public officials who responded effectively to the plight of our clients.

People living in poverty historically have had at best an uneasy relationship with the law. More commonly, they have seen the law as an instrument of oppression. Lawyers and judges were the men who evicted them from their homes, levied garnishments on their paychecks, repossessed their furniture, and allowed businesses to cheat them out of their wages. A poignant illustration from Nashville, but certainly relevant to other places as well: the bar association established a Legal Aid Bureau in 1914, but the chair of the organizing committee had to report the next year that "not as many poor people have availed themselves of the Bureau as could have been due to a feeling of suspicion."[1] And doubtless his report referred strictly to the suspicions of poor White people. If even considered at all, one can only imagine the suspicions of Black people, who experienced not only the usual deprivations of the poor, but also the oppression of life under Jim Crow laws and economic discrimination.

Courts traditionally have been bastions of conservatism, protecting the status quo. Legislatures traditionally have reflected the interests of those who have the most influence with them, those who have power and stature in the community. With a few exceptions at times of crisis, such as the 1930s, the courts and legislatures during our history for the most part have effectively ignored the plight of the poor and resisted reforms that would improve their plight. For a brief time beginning in the 1950s and 1960s, that pattern changed. The civil rights movement and President

Lyndon Johnson's War on Poverty brought to the fore the issues of the poor and dispossessed. Congress passed laws, and courts began to recognize that civil rights should be accorded to people who previously had no claim on them. The courts momentarily allowed or even led social change. It was a brief window; the progress was uneven, and not without stubborn opposition. That is the setting for quite a bit of our story. As we will see, in a number of the larger cases described in our narrative, our clients' cause benefited from that climate. Indeed, the beginning of federally funded legal services for the poor happened because of that climate. But as we also will see, beginning in the 1980s and profoundly in the 1990s, that window closed. Congress and state legislatures, determined to make America like it was again, rolled back reforms, and an increasingly conservative judiciary reverted to its accustomed role of preserving the hegemony of the dominant culture.

Though this book tells a story about one group of lawyers at one time and in one place who every day engaged in the struggle for equal justice on behalf of their clients, it is not a local story only. Every story is a part of a longer history and a wider context. As the first chapter will describe, the organized effort for legal aid goes back nearly 160 years. Many of the chapters that follow will describe how national debates had an impact on the operation of our local organization and the representation of our clients. The national debate is this: to what extent should we as a nation support full and equal access to justice for those who can least afford it? Because the major funding source for civil legal aid since 1965 has been an office of the federal government, the answers to that question by various presidents and members of Congress over the years has had a profound effect on our work and on the lives of low-income people in our country.

As will be explained briefly in Chapters 1 and 5, federal funding for civil legal aid first was provided through the Office of Economic Opportunity's Office of Legal Services (OEO/OLS) as a part of the War on Poverty. In 1974, however, as OEO was being dismantled by the Nixon administration, Congress, in a rescue action, created the Legal Services Corporation (LSC) and transferred the funding and administration of the program to that entity. It survives, but not without scars.

For reasons of definition and containment, our story-in-chief covers only thirty-three years, 1969 to 2002, though there are pre-histories and many post-scripts. What originated in 1969 as Legal Services of Nashville (LSON), later became the Legal Aid Society, over the years changed its name several times as it expanded geographically, and at the defined end of our narrative, because of our consolidation with Rural Legal Services of Tennessee (Rural) and Legal Services of South Central Tennessee (South Central), took on the long and encompassing name of Legal Aid Society of Middle Tennessee and the Cumberlands. To avoid anachronisms as I tell the story, I will use the name appropriate to the time of the events being described.

Any telling of history has a point of view. It is a narrative in which the author selects, sequences, and interprets in order to suit one's purpose in the telling. Despite those who might pretend otherwise, history never is objective, and that is emphatically the case when the writer is an actor in the story. I began as a law clerk at Legal Services of Nashville in June 1970. I stayed for thirty-seven years until I retired in 2007. For the last thirty-one years I was executive director.

I grew up in the stratified, segregated South in the capital of the Confederacy. After the US Supreme Court decided *Brown v. Board of Education* in 1954, the governor of our proud Commonwealth ordered that the United States flag no longer be flown above the flag of Virginia, but that they be flown at the same level on separate but equal flagpoles. As a teenager, my candidate in the 1956 presidential election was neither Eisenhower nor Stevenson but T. Coleman Andrews, the candidate of the States Rights Party. In time, however, the prophetic words from Amos of Tekoa and Jesus of Nazareth, plus broadening experiences while in college and seminary, weaned me from those Old Dominion dogmas and gave me a different direction.

My second year of college at Washington and Lee in 1960, there came to teach religion a newly minted PhD, Louis Hodges, whose dissertation at Duke had been "A Christian Analysis of Selected Contemporary Theories of Racial Prejudice," and whose examination of many current issues brought new light, and new tensions, to our all-White-male campus.[2] His teaching on Christian ethics influenced not only my thinking but my choice of seminary as well, and it was there at Union Theological Seminary in New York City that I listened to Abraham Heschel, who came across the street from the Jewish seminary to expound on the words of the Hebrew prophets, including Amos's challenging words, "Let justice roll down like waters."[3]

In the summer of 1966, cohorts at seminary persuaded me to go with them as part of the Student Interracial Ministry to work with Charlie Sherrod in his Southwest Georgia Project. The charismatic Sherrod, one of the founders of the Student Nonviolent Coordinating Committee (SNCC), had parted ways with SNCC after his colleague John Lewis was ousted from the chairmanship by those who rejected nonviolence and rejected the involvement of Whites in the Movement. Sherrod, who had come to Albany with SNCC in 1961, had twenty White seminarians coming that summer to help with various community projects, and he was not going to reject the help.[4] One of my assignments, in addition to teaching in a Head Start program, was to try to find a way to help Black farmers get a fair peanut allotment from the US Department of Agriculture, which, guided by a local committee of White farmers, had shortchanged the Black farmers every year. I was ill-equipped for the task, lost in the Code of Federal Regulations, and profoundly ineffective.[5]

It was a revealing experience. It demonstrated vividly the connection between race and poverty, the economic oppression that was a part of everyday life for the people I was living with. I also came to appreciate, perhaps for the first time, the everyday importance of law and constitutional principles. That same summer we seminarians were in Southwest Georgia, there were three law students working on other matters with the legendary Black attorney, C. B. King. It seemed to me that they were a much more immediate and practical help than we were. I began to see the efficacy of law in bringing about ethical social change. At the same time, I began to see the futility of waiting for a change of heart from those who benefited so easily from unfair social and economic arrangements.

Nevertheless, I returned to finish seminary and went the next year to teach at a mission school in Thailand, though still with Georgia on my mind. While there, one connection I had with the States was the international edition of *Time* magazine, which arrived by airmail. On the tissue-thin pages of one issue, I read about lawyers at California Rural Legal Assistance representing low-income people there, including migrant farmworkers. That story convinced me to return to the South and to law school.

During my first year at Vanderbilt, convinced I wanted to do poverty law in a rural area, I applied for summer jobs with legal aid programs in Appalachia. Not only did I receive no offers, I received no replies, even when I wrote and said I would work for free. Finally, as the end of the spring semester approached, still without a job, I ventured downtown to the one-year-old Legal Services of Nashville, and one of the attorneys, Jerry Black, hired me.

STAFF CULTURE

The lawyers in this story came not only from Tennessee but also from New York, North Carolina, the state of Washington, Iowa, Illinois, Texas, and elsewhere. They came because of a common commitment to our cause. A good number of us were here already because of Vanderbilt Law School. Others were recruited in. We had come of age in a nation where inspiring leaders had inaugurated an excitement about public service. "Ask not what your country can do for you—ask what you can do for your country" (JFK). "Injustice anywhere is a threat to justice everywhere" (MLK). "Each time a man stands up for an ideal, or acts to improve the lot of others, or strikes out against injustice, he sends forth a ripple of hope." (RFK). Michael Harrington, writing in *The Other America: Poverty in America*, had exposed the extent of poverty in our rich country and its detrimental ramifications in the lives of so many people. Thurgood Marshall and other lawyers at the NAACP Legal Defense and Education Fund (LDF) had demonstrated that principles in our jurisprudence could be employed to benefit those who suffer, that the law was not entirely for the benefit of the powerful. These were motivators for us.

Entirely untrained though I was in motivational science or any psychology, as time went on, I observed an additional and yet more basic motivation among many of my colleagues. In 1996 I was asked to contribute an article to a symposium on "Faith and the Law" to be published in the *Texas Tech Law Review*, and to support the thesis I developed in the article, I interviewed several lawyers on our staff and a few elsewhere in legal aid.[6] Conducting a woefully unscientific survey, I asked each one to talk about "what your religion has to do with your practice of law." I then qualified my question, "If that sounds like an inappropriate question, for instance, if you choke on the phrase 'your religion,' make up your own question and answer it, but tell me something about religion and what you do."

Among those interviewed and recorded in the article, Kevin Fowler, a young lawyer who had worked previously for an insurance defense firm, reminded me of his answer to our question at his job interview: "Why do you want to work here?" He repeated that though he had never been religious, he did go to Sunday school as a child and was sure that his reasons for wanting to work at Legal Services had a lot do with things he heard there. Kitty Calhoon, a legal aid lawyer for more than fifteen years at that point, demurred initially and then recalled growing up in Chapel Hill, "I got the sense of being responsible for making wrongs right . . . from my family" when they started a new Presbyterian congregation after their minister "was kicked out because of his stand on civil rights." The connection became more explicit when she converted to Judaism and was reminded in the liturgy of God's concern for the downtrodden: "Religion keeps me focused . . . it is a frequent reminder." Pat Mock, who was manager of the Clarksville office, reflecting on her life in the Black church said right away, "It is impossible to separate religion from anything you do."

Neil McBride, the executive director at Rural, properly cautioned, "We need to avoid giving anyone the sense that just because we are in this work we are better people. Doing a work doesn't make you a better person. That is theological, too." Gordon Bonnyman, with another caveat, marked my question as "elitist." Mindful that most people do not have the choices or opportunities for work that we have had, he pointed out how fortunate we are to be able to choose work that seems to us to have a connection to faith.

Regardless of how the motivation is characterized, when hiring lawyers and paralegals, we looked for people who were motivated to do legal aid work, who recognized the problems of our clients and wanted to help. And we wanted them to stay with it for a good long while. I remember Russ Overby coming back from a recruiting trip reporting on a candidate who had all the right credentials, plus, "She's a lifer."

Recruiting and retaining Black lawyers was always a concern. In the early years, OEO/OLS was especially helpful. It funded a program at Howard University's law school that recruited principally Black lawyers and assigned them to LSC grantees that requested them. Though at one point in the late 1970s there were six Black lawyers, males and females, on our staff out of a total of thirty lawyers, we did not maintain that number as time went on. At various times during our story, Black lawyers were the managing attorneys in the Clarksville and Murfreesboro offices and were on hiring committees for other offices as well. We provided opportunities for Black lawyers long before most law firms in our area, and we benefited from that. It was a serious concern for us, while other concerns of our staff often were not taken so seriously.

Our life together as a staff was characterized by a certain irreverence. For whatever reason, in the early 1990s, the health and benefits section in the Nashville office self-identified as "The Elvis Section." Beginning after the Gallatin office opened in 1977 and continuing sporadically until 1990, there occasionally would appear a scandal sheet with mischievously doctored photographs and concocted stories about various targets inside and outside the organization. The *Gallatin Gazette* would be distributed most often at staff parties, but also could appear at quite inopportune times, such as just before an LSC monitoring visit. The outrageous articles spared no one. Surprisingly, there were no libel suits, and thankfully, I was able to keep copies of the *Gazette* out of the hands of the auditors and monitors.

There was very little hierarchy in our organization, even when the staff grew to eighty people. There was no assistant director. There were managing attorneys for substantive law sections in Nashville and for the branch offices, but they were in no sense "the boss." That applied to the executive director as well, which was illustrated after a troublemaker in the waiting room questioned my authority to tell him to leave. I answered him, "I can tell you to leave because I'm the boss," and that worked for him. Not so much for longtime staff assistant Melba McNairy who overheard the confrontation. Unaccustomed to hearing anyone on the staff try to pull rank, she for years afterwards laughingly mocked me and my Virginia accent with the greeting, "I'm the boose."

There were monthly managing attorney meetings, but they were open to all, and there were few, if any, recorded votes. We operated by the sense of the meeting and the sense of the staff. At one point, a friendly consultant sent from LSC's Atlanta regional office told me, "You've got to stop running this place like a mom-and-pop grocery store." I took some steps, but it never really happened. Later, a consultant sent by LSC in Washington came as a part of his study of strategic planning in five of what LSC considered its better grantees. After spending three days with us and finding no plan or process but only a common understanding of purpose among the staff, he simply concluded that we did "implicit planning." Ours may not have been the most efficient corporate culture, but it built trust and a collegial basis for our work together.

Though some lawyers inevitably got into more complicated cases and temporarily went off intake, unlike many other legal aid organizations, no one was exempt. We never had an elite unit, or an appellate section, or, except for a brief period in 1972, a law reform office. At one point a couple of young lawyers in the Clarksville office, despite their own paltry salaries, earnestly proposed to me that we pay Gordon a bonus beyond our salary scale because of the extraordinary work he was doing on healthcare cases. I was moved by their generosity but reminded them that we did not do things like that, we did not have a star system, we just all did our work, and furthermore, Gordon would not stand for it. They recognized all of that immediately and withdrew their proposal without debate, but once again expressed their appreciation for Gordon's work.

EVERYDAY, BUT . . .

The title of this book was chosen because the cases described here, like the other tens of thousands we handled, dealt with the everyday problems of people living in poverty: housing, income, food, safety, financial security, and healthcare. Though the problems are routine, as will be obvious to the reader, the impact of many cases described here was not routine, not an everyday occurrence. In many cases the results achieved were transformative. In them we were able to address not only the specific problems of the client or clients who had come to see us, but also frame the problems in a broader context so that in the process of helping those named clients, we were able to bring about systemic changes, such as services for domestic violence victims, wage assignments to ensure child support payments, a reformed prison system, a reformed insurance product, better procedures for determining Social

Security disability, slightly better interest rates, safer nursing homes, and expanded healthcare.

As sweeping as some of those changes may have been, however, the key was that it all started with intake, the people who came in the door every day. That was not widely understood, particularly by people whose inclinations would tend to make them skeptical of our work. In 1979 local investors bought Nashville's afternoon newspaper, the *Banner*, from Gannett, which had owned it only briefly. The new owners were conservative, but much more progressive than the earlier longtime publisher who a few short years before had sold the paper to Gannett and whose legacy still hung over the paper.[7] After seeing a change in the newspaper's approach, looking for support, I went to meet with the new publisher, Irby Simpkins Jr., and the colorful general manager, Jack Gunter.

During our conversation, in a voice that seemed to be not as much an accusation as an inquiry from a skeptical police reporter, Jack, who had been with the paper for decades, asked me about some of our more controversial cases. He wanted to know how we got the idea to bring them, "How do you decide you want to bring a lawsuit saying the stripe down the middle of the road has to be purple rather than yellow?" Appreciative of such a revealing question, I explained that we were not an issue-oriented organization but a law office. We did not come up with ideas about causes. We represented clients who came to us with serious problems, and if in the process of helping them, we could bring about changes in the systems that were adversely affecting not only them but also people similarly situated, we wanted to do that too. It was a matter of economy. There were very few Legal Services lawyers in the state for the number of poor people, and if we could help more people at one time, then we were making better use of our limited resources. Both men seemed to understand, and in the future, both the newspaper and the owners were supportive on several occasions.

Understanding our class action lawsuits was one thing, but understanding our legislative and administrative representation was another, and, as we will note several times in our story, many people, especially those on the other side of an issue, objected to that aspect of our practice. They did not appreciate that justice in the American legal system involves decisions in all three branches of governments, not only court rulings.

Decisions in all three branches impact the everyday lives of low-income people, and when our clients had an issue that could only be dealt with effectively by one of the other branches, it was important that their lawyers represent their interests there.

ADDRESSING RACIAL DISCRIMINATION

Though the majority of poor people in this nation are White, the problems of the poor appear most dramatically when compounded with issues of racial discrimination. While less than half of our clients were racial minorities, issues of race were embedded in many of our cases. Jim Crow may no longer be the law, but practices remain, both the apparent practices and the subtle. In housing cases there were the obvious, like the fair housing class action Bill West won in Nashville that is described in Chapter 11. Also there were the not so obvious, though nevertheless real, racial disparities in a number of public housing cases in towns outside Nashville. In some of these we raised specific claims of racial discrimination; in others we let other claims carry the weight.

Racial discrimination was not a litigated issue in the 1971 cases that challenged the jailing of indigents who could not pay Metro fines, but it was obvious to anyone sitting in a general sessions courtroom that the unconstitutional practice had a disparate impact on minorities. That reality was emphasized dramatically when a federal judge ordered one of our clients freed and she emerged from the jail with a clenched fist Black Power salute.

We had several healthcare cases over the years where it was obvious to us that racial discrimination often affected the treatment patients received, or did not receive. Proving racial discrimination in Medicaid and Medicare cases, however, was a persistent problem because of the US Department of Health and Human Services' (HHS) failure to keep essential data by race, even though the 1964 Civil Rights Act required it. When Gordon raised that on behalf of a client in a 1993 lawsuit, joined by the LDF and nearly thirty other civil rights groups, both the district court and the appellate court declined to order HHS to produce the necessary data. Instead, the courts deferred to the department's administrative discretion as to what data was sufficient to satisfy the requirements of the

Act. All was not lost, however. Despite the courts' decisions, it turned out to be one of the most significant cases in our efforts for racial justice.

As detailed in Chapter 17, a few years later, Gordon learned that the claims of the case had moved people in leadership at HHS to re-examine their responsibility and exercise their administrative discretion differently. They began to make available to health researchers data on race that could be crossmatched with patient treatment records. The work of those researchers then has had the effect of advancing research and understanding of both racial disparities in health status and racial discrimination in patient care. That in turn influenced these issues being addressed with stronger civil rights provisions in the 2010 Affordable Care Act.

SOURCES

A bibliography and acknowledgments follow at the end of the book, but two sources important for context bear mention here because they will be relied on early and often. In 1919, Reginald Heber Smith wrote *Justice and the Poor: A Study of the Present Denial of Justice to the Poor and of the Agencies Making More Equal Their Position Before the Law . . .*, which was the first history of legal aid in this country and a manifesto for the cause. Smith, who first was general counsel for the Boston Legal Aid Society and later managing partner at the law firm of Hale and Dorr, remained a leader in the field for nearly fifty years. His book became the Bible of the movement, and quoting Smith became tantamount to quoting Moses. Smith, it has been shown recently, was not without his faults. Like Moses, he was a product of his time and station. He voiced no concern for the problems of racial minorities and by one analysis purposely wrote women out of the early history of legal aid.[8] Both his tailored message and his limited account of the history now evoke justifiable criticism, but his manifesto and his leadership changed legal aid from the concern of scattered well-meaning groups to a recognized national issue, and I will rely on his words a number of times, particularly in the first chapter.

In 2014, nearly a hundred years after Smith's book, Earl Johnson Jr. published a three-volume treatise, *To Establish Justice for All: The Past and Future of Civil Legal Aid in the United States*. Johnson, now a retired justice of the California Court of Appeals, in 1965 at the age of thirty-two was the first deputy director of the OEO legal services program (OEO/OLS).

As such, he will figure prominently in Chapter 2, while his treatise will provide context throughout.

OVERVIEW AND GUIDE

Here is a guide to the content and sequence of the chapters that follow.

Chapter 1 gives background to our story with an abbreviated history of civil legal aid in the US and then an account of legal aid in Nashville before 1965. Chapter 2 details the extended debate in Nashville beginning in 1965 over whether to accept federal funding from OEO to establish a Legal Services program. After that controversial matter was settled by an extraordinary referendum in the bar association, Legal Services of Nashville finally opened its doors in February 1969.

Chapter 3 is a narrative of the chaotic early years when the fledgling organization had seriatim three executive directors in four years, but woven in with that saga are descriptions of some dramatic cases filed by young lawyers who had joined the staff. In 1973 Walter Kurtz became director, bringing for the first time cohesiveness and direction; Chapter 4 describes his tenure, including accounts of our wide-ranging advocacy during that time.

With Chapter 5, which takes up the story in 1976, the content and arrangement of the chapters change. From this point forward, rather than combining advocacy and administration in the same chapter, there will be topical chapters that discuss the life of the organization and separate chapters that describe our casework. There is a reason for this division, an historical reason. Prior to this time, all the lawyers had handled whatever came in the door on one's intake day, and Walt had carried a full caseload. Administration had not been a major impediment for him. Now, with the events described in Chapter 5, the end of OEO Legal Services and the beginning of the Legal Services Corporation, my becoming director, our opening new offices to represent people in counties beyond Nashville, more grants, more staff, more opposition—the life of the organization becomes more complicated. At the same time, staff lawyers had begun gravitating toward specialization, so it becomes appropriate to devote individual chapters to each of our practice areas.

Though the trials of the institution and the triumphs of the advocacy are treated in different chapters from this point on in the text, it is important that they not be seen as separate. That is why the institutional chapters and the substantive law chapters are interwoven in the book. They belong in tandem. They both are necessarily part of one story. In fact, the only purpose of the institution is to make the advocacy possible. This arrangement corresponds with my understanding of my responsibility as executive director of the organization. My responsibility was to be the janitor. The concept had come to me in a conversation with my spouse, a professor of Classics. She pointed out that the word "janitor" came from the name of the Roman god Janus, the god of doors. (Look it up some January.) The literal job of a janitor is to keep the doors open. Following that two-faced god who looks both ways, my ungodlike job was to do the work both inside and outside the organization necessary to keep the doors open and support my colleagues as they were doing the work essential to our mission.

The seven chapters covering primarily institutional matters are in chronological order according to when the matter first came to the fore. Chapter 7 describes our expansion in the late 1970s and gives an insight into the character of the staff. Chapter 14 deals with a local effort in 1979 to have the United Way defund us. Chapter 15 chronicles the effort by the Reagan administration (1981–1989) to abolish LSC and put us out of business. Chapters 16 and 19 each describe a happy outcome of those troubles; first, the development of pro bono programs beginning in 1982; second, a dynamic local fundraising campaign beginning in 1987. Chapter 20, however, returns to doom and gloom with the sad tale of Congressional hostility in 1995 and its results. That chapter also describes our merger with Rural and our taking over the service area of South Central, effective January 1, 2002, a transformative date and the putative end of this history. That end date is not stringent, however. For clarification and perspective, and in a few cases to complete a story, some narratives in these chapters, as well in the substantive law chapters, will extend beyond that date.

The substantive law chapters—prisons and jails (6); family law (8 and 9); juvenile law (10); housing law (11); consumer law (12 and 13); health law (17); Social Security (18); and welfare law (21)—describe some of the more outstanding cases we handled in those subject areas. There is no chronological significance in the placement of these chapters. Some are placed in proximity to a chapter covering administrative matters because of a connection, for example, *those* cases got us into *that* trouble. Other chapters are grouped because of some similarity, or contrast, stated in the text.

The stories in these chapters recall how a few good lawyers and their staff with passion and persistence over several decades through these cases improved the lives of thousands of low-income people who otherwise would have had no access to our systems of law and justice. There were setbacks and disappointments, but it is an account of how the legal profession and the wider community over time joined together to draw all of us closer to the American ideal of equal justice under law.

The epilogue comments on some of what has happened with legal aid since 2002 and gives brief updates on the Legal Aid Society, the Tennessee Alliance for Legal Services, and the Tennessee Justice Center.

Now, we turn first to the backstory beginning in the late 1800s, and those who went before us.

CHAPTER 1

Early Legal Aid, National and Nashville

1863–1965

> Nothing rankles more in the human heart
> than a brooding sense of injustice.
>
> —REGINALD HEBER SMITH, 1919

It began with immigrants who could not speak English. It was paternalistic and judgmental, but it met a need.

The first legal aid society in this country was founded in New York City in 1876 explicitly to protect new immigrants from those who would prey upon them. Initially it had a German name and was established (translation) "to render legal aid and assistance gratuitously to those of German birth who may appear worthy thereof but who from poverty are unable to procure it." Within a few years, its parochial limitations were relaxed and the organization began accepting non-Germans, but it was not until 1896 that it formally dropped the German language from its name and became in English the Legal Aid Society.

Although the German-American group was the first to organize what we would call a legal aid society, as law professor Felice Batlan and others recently have shown, it was not the first organization in the country to deliver legal assistance to low-income people.[1] The Freedmen's Bureau, the short-lived and hamstrung effort by the federal government to help emancipated people after the Civil War, for a brief time offered legal aid as one of its services. Even before that, in 1863, the Working Women's Protective Union (WWPU) was established in New York to provide aid to women who were laboring in the sweatshops of that city. In addition to other assistance, the volunteer female staff, whom Batlan describes as "lay lawyers," would send demand letters and would attempt to work out agreements when employers failed to pay wages that were due to the working women. They called in their part-time male lawyer only if a lawsuit was indicated.

There were similar aid organizations founded by women in other cities, including the Chicago Women's Club, which established the Protective Agency for Women and Children (PAWC) in 1885 and among other services provided volunteer lawyers. Going beyond the limited clientele of the women's group, three years later, the Ethical Culture Society in that city established the Legal Aid Bureau, the first non-exclusive legal aid project in this country, "to supply legal services in all cases to all persons, regardless of nationality, race, or sex." After nearly twenty years operating separately, the PAWC and the Bureau merged in 1905 to become the Legal Aid Society of Chicago.[2] Meanwhile, well after other organizations had done the initial work, local bar associations stepped up and began sponsoring legal aid organizations; the first was in Boston in 1900. Another significant milestone came in 1910 with the first publicly funded legal aid organization established in Kansas City, Missouri, an undertaking Reginald Heber Smith hailed as a "step of profound importance" because this challenged the notion that "the state's duty ends when it has provided judge and courthouse."[3] It was the first casting of legal aid as not only a charity, but also an essential component in the administration of justice in our nation.

The founding of these and other legal aid organizations in the late nineteenth and early twentieth centuries did not happen in isolation. It was a time of great social change and many organizations were formed to help the disadvantaged.[4] The anti-slavery movement, temperance crusade, and women's suffrage campaign had formed voluntary associations before the Civil War, and during the war, societies were formed to take care of wounded soldiers and their families. These provided precedent for the flowering of charitable organizations that followed.

After the war, industrialization, urbanization, and European immigrants brought a whole new set of social issues to the fore in the booming

Northern states, resulting in associations being founded to deal with them. Northern philanthropists, some with religious impetus and some without, contributed to many efforts both in the North and in the devastated South. Business and professional people encouraged welfare assistance, often for their own self-interest in preserving the social order and preventing uprisings among the more discontented poor. Working class people saw some hope in mutual aid societies, and in some places labor unions struggled into existence. There was widespread social activism and pressure for political reform, ushering in what has been labeled the Progressive Era, which lasted by most accounts until World War I.[5]

Legal aid organizations participated in that activism and pressure. Very early, the Legal Aid Society of New York supported legislation to regulate small loans and installment sales. It sought better conditions for seamen and exposed corruption in the city marshal's office that led to reforms there.[6] The legal aid organizations in Chicago lobbied for legislation raising the age of consent for girls, punishing seducers of young girls, reforming chattel mortgage laws, and limiting employer appeals of wage claim cases.[7] Later they pled with the Illinois bar association to address problems in the justice of the peace courts where many of the problems of the poor were heard, and handled corruptly.[8] The Boston Legal Aid Society successfully lobbied for a limit on the interest rates charged on small loans. In a 1916 speech before the National Alliance of Legal Aid Societies, which had been formed five years earlier, Smith urged "preventive law." By this he meant that the lawyers should ascertain the cause of the clients' problems and if the cause might be preventable by law, then work to secure prevention through appellate decisions, remedial legislation, and education of the public. He counseled that a good result of these efforts "may prevent the happening of a thousand future abuses."[9]

Good counsel, but unfortunately the world was changing. The World War had a devastating effect on legal aid, a talent drain as staff and volunteers enlisted, a loss of funding, and a loss of nerve. Some organizations closed altogether or turned over their operation to other charities.[10] Smith's *Justice and the Poor*, the Carnegie Foundation funded study of legal aid and call to action, came out in 1919, but it reported on a more hopeful and robust time. Now Smith and others turned to the American Bar Association (ABA) for support. The ABA, which had been established in 1878, until this time had no connection with or even any demonstrated interest in legal aid, but Smith and others were able to convince the conservative association to support the progressive cause. In 1920 the ABA created a standing committee on legal aid and in 1922 facilitated the founding of the National Association of Legal Aid Organizations (NALAO), which later was renamed the National Legal Aid and Defender Association (NLADA).

The motives for this connection and the wisdom of it can be debated, but one outcome is obvious: the legal aid movement, with rare exceptions, moved into a forty-year period of relative quiescence.[11] Whatever the impetus, the reformist spirit of the previous fifty years vanished. There is little talk of "preventive law." There were few appellate court cases, and virtually no administrative advocacy or legislative advocacy. While the lions of the ABA and other first-rate lawyers devised sophisticated legal theories and creative solutions to advance the interests of their clients, "legal aid programs generally gave only perfunctory service."[12]

Two additional failings of this period have been highlighted recently. In her illuminating history, *Women and Justice for the Poor: A History of Legal Aid 1863–1945*, Felice Batlan makes the case that male lawyers in legal aid, dating back to the first involvement of local bar associations, and beyond, attempted to masculinize and professionalize the movement. Seeking to curry favor with the established bar, Smith and others, she maintains, dismissed or ignored the efforts of non-lawyer women and the few women lawyers who were so vital to the movement. Though she notes some change in attitude during the Depression and thereafter, the overall indictment remains.

Batlan and others make reference to early legal aid's inattention to racial minorities, but now extensive examination is being conducted by Professor Shaun Ossei-Owusu, who in a forthcoming book and several forthcoming articles is writing about race in both civil legal aid and criminal defense. In one as yet unpublished article entitled "Racial Discounting and Self-Help: Blacks, Americanization, and the Early Twentieth Century Legal Aid," he shows how race shaped the development of legal aid. The focus of those early organizations on assimilating European immigrants and dealing with their problems, plus the predominant racial views of the time, truncated their vision and caused them "to neglect the well-documented needs of African-Americans."[13]

Predictably, in many instances, the treatment of racial issues by White legal aid lawyers went beyond indifference and neglect to utter rejection.

The long-time executive director of the national organization NALAO in the late 1920s, when Jim Crow laws were in full force in the South and few laws prohibited discrimination elsewhere, proclaimed in a speech, "There is no fault to find in the laws of this country. They are remarkably fair and are designed to operate with absolute equality on all classes of persons in our community."[14] The next year he wrote, "It does not seem to me that social rights for colored people have anything to do with legal aid."[15]

THE SIXTIES

The whole attitude and approach of legal aid began to change with the ignition of the New Frontier in the early 1960s. The Ford Foundation funded experimental legal aid efforts in New Haven, New York City, and Washington, DC, entirely separate from the NLADA affiliated groups, and lawyers in those new organizations began to develop a different model that prized aggressive advocacy. When Lyndon Johnson was thrust into the presidency, he declared the War on Poverty, established the Office of Economic Opportunity (OEO), and put Sargent Shriver in charge, the lawyers who had been involved with those three innovative projects fatefully were in a position to propose that lawyers also be soldiers in that War. Plus, these pioneers had a strategy for how these troops could best be deployed. That strategy was based not only on their recent everyday experience in low-income neighborhoods, but also on the example of how the NAACP Legal Defense Fund had been able to improve the position of Black people in the few years preceding. They proposed that lawyers could do the same for the poor. Shriver was convinced.

When word got out that Legal Services had become a part of the OEO plan, there was consternation among many lawyers and at the ABA and NLADA. Lawyers from across the country claimed that Shriver's plan of offering legal services as a part of "supermarkets of services" in low-income neighborhoods was a denigration of the profession and would undermine professional standards. NLADA feared that traditional legal aid societies would be bypassed in this bold approach and squeezed out by the new, aggressive federally funded Legal Services offices. Stuck in quiescence, its executive committee voted to oppose the OEO program unless it funded only the traditional societies. That was not going to happen. Shriver was headed in a different direction. NLADA was on the wrong side of history, a position it had to recover from soon or be left behind.

The ABA was savvier and more strategic, thanks to the leadership of its president that year, Lewis Powell, the conservative lawyer from Virginia and later US Supreme Court justice. Powell, who in his inaugural address a few months earlier had stressed the urgency of making legal services available to low-income people, deftly persuaded the ABA House of Delegates to pass a resolution in support of the OEO program. The resolution pledged the ABA's cooperation with OEO in the "development and implementation of the program," and at the same time staked out two significant expectations: one, a firm requirement that the services should "be performed by lawyers in accordance with ethical standards of the profession"; and the second, somewhat qualified, that the program "utilize to the maximum extent deemed feasible the experience and facilities of the organized bar, such as legal aid." Shriver was delighted with the action of the ABA, and as Earl Johnson assesses the moment, "A partnership had been forged."[16] The ABA and the OEO Office of Legal Services (OLS) proceeded to work together to design the Legal Services Program.

The grants from OEO that began going out soon thereafter went both to selected legal aid societies and to new organizations, including many in places where there had been no legal aid before. By the fall of 1966, 130 local organizations had been funded from the $25 million OLS annual budget. Nashville was not one of them. The reasons for Nashville's unfortunate absence from that early list of 130 grantees will unfold in the difficult story that is the next chapter. For now let us leave the national story and turn back the calendar to the early part of the century to trace what had happened in Nashville up to this time.

MEANWHILE BACK IN NASHVILLE

At its annual dinner and meeting on November 2, 1914, the Nashville Bar and Library Association (now NBA) voted to organize a legal aid bureau, which it then did with financial assistance from the Commercial Club (now Chamber of Commerce). The bureau opened an office in the Commercial Club building and assigned cases to bar members who volunteered to help. Though, like many others, the operation was disbanded with the entry of the United States into World War I, it was reorganized in the early 1920s at the Commercial Club with financial support from the Community Chest (now United Way). The financial support enabled the bureau to hire a staff member who not only referred cases to bar members, but also handled cases himself. Though several men came and went from that position in the 1920s, there was one, William Chester Bowen, who seems to have been involved consistently from late in that decade until the mid-1940s.

Despite the best efforts of those who carried on the work of the bureau, it does not appear to have made much of an impact in the community. In 1937, the Davidson County Bar Association, a second White bar association in town, resolved at its annual meeting in the Hermitage Hotel to establish a legal aid organization.[17] Though there were 125 lawyers at the meeting, no one flagged the duplication. Within a few days, however, the president of that association, Thomas A. Shriver, with some embarrassment, announced that the action had been taken without knowledge that the Community Chest was operating a legal aid bureau already, and he pledged that his association would join that effort. In his letter to the manager of the Community Chest, he excused the mistake saying, "Your work has been done so quietly and with such little display that few of us were aware of its extent and usefulness."[18]

During World War II the NBA operated its own legal aid. The National Defense Committee of the association established a clinic to render legal services to armed services personnel and their families, and to assist civilians who needed to get birth certificates that were required for defense industry jobs. William Bowen of the Legal Aid Bureau also coordinated that clinic, which relied on volunteers from the bar and served more than a thousand people during the war with such issues as wills, family matters, and landlord-tenant problems.

In light of the success of the defense committee's clinic, after the war, the chair of that committee, Louis Farrell Jr., proposed that the NBA establish a clinic "to furnish legal aid to all indigent persons without regard to their military or civil status," but the NBA board was hesitant and asked him instead to "investigate what legal aid the Chamber of Commerce and other organizations were furnishing." Since 1939, the Legal Aid Bureau had been operated neither by the chamber nor by the Community Chest, but by the Council of Community Services (CCS), which at this point was reexamining its roles and responsibility. Skeptical about the propriety of its operating the bureau and the effectiveness of its services given that it was a non-lawyer organization, the CCS had commissioned a study by an NLADA consultant who confirmed those reservations. Thus in March 1947, the council closed the bureau and wrote to the NBA asking the bar to assume responsibility.

Farrell, with CCS endorsement, now recommended to the bar that it establish an independent, staffed legal aid society, but again the NBA declined. Instead, in March 1948 the bar instituted a volunteer clinic. On Wednesday afternoons between 2:30 and 4:00, a lawyer would be in the NBA assembly room on the fourth floor of the courthouse and give advice to any "worthy indigent citizen of the community. . . found to be entitled to any assistance." If the matter required court action, the lawyer on duty would refer it to a lawyer on a list of volunteers. That hour and a half per week procedure remained in effect for the next twenty years until Legal Services of Nashville was founded.

As is often the case in such endeavors, there were gaps with the clinic. Whitworth Stokes Jr., who was a young lawyer at the time and who frequently filled in beyond his turn, recalls that "the clinic was a hit or miss affair and often no one showed up or there was no attorney available (or willing) to participate." Joe Lackey Jr., who was a law student at Vanderbilt in the late 1950s, remembers that by then the venue was the NBA library in the Stahlman Building and that he and other members of the law school legal aid society often would go there on Wednesday afternoon to conduct the interviews and give advice.

In 1956, CCS, as a part of its annual review of social services in the community, renewed its call for a proper legal aid society. In 1961, the NBA Lawyers Referral and Legal Aid Committee headed by George Barrett and including two future judges, Shelton Luton and Richard Jenkins, issued its report for the year with a scathing assessment of the clinic, noting that less than one-tenth of the NBA membership participated and calling for the bar to hire a full-time attorney to operate the clinic.[19] There is no record of any response to either the CCS's renewed call or the bar committee's report.

Nor is there any record of who brought in the heavyweights from Chicago. The most likely suspect is Vanderbilt Law Dean John Wade, who had many national connections because of his prominence in the field of torts law. In August 1963, Charlie Morgan, a member of the ABA

Standing Committee on Legal Aid and Indigent Defenders (SCLAID) and John Irving from NLADA came to Nashville to encourage establishing a staffed legal aid program. They met with Dick Lansden, the NBA president; and several board members; as well as with Mayor Beverly Briley; Judge Benson Trimble, who heard domestic relations matters; and Dean Wade. In his presentation urging a staffed program with at least a lawyer and a secretary, Irving opined that in complex modern society, an entirely volunteer legal aid organization was as outmoded as an entirely volunteer fire department.[20] A few days after the visit, there was a discussion in the NBA board meeting about legal aid, moving Lansden to appoint yet another committee, but there is no subsequent mention in the association's minutes of any report or follow-through. The record is silent until 1965, when there arose the dreadful specter of federal government funding for legal aid.

A WORD ABOUT WORTHINESS

On the first page of this chapter we are reminded of an unfortunate qualifier that has been popular in society since time immemorial. The original charter of the first legal aid society in 1876 announced that it would "render legal aid . . . to those . . . who may appear *worthy* thereof" (emphasis added). Likewise, to be eligible for assistance from the NBA clinic as stated in its 1948 resolution, one must first have been deemed a *"worthy* indigent citizen" before the lawyer determined whether or not she was entitled to any assistance for her legal problem. Distinguishing between the worthy poor and those who are not, between the deserving poor and those who are not, of course, is in the eye of the beholder. The determination most often is filtered through our discomfort with poverty itself and with those who are living in poverty. We have a tendency to blame the poor for their own unfortunate condition. The standards are fluid; I have heard disparaging remarks about a variety of people we have represented who I thought would pass the test: the single mother hospital worker, the disabled steel worker, the battered wife, the pretrial detainee sitting in a filthy jail, the legal immigrant laborer with a tax problem. No one is immune.

It is not within the scope of this book to consider the morality of distinguishing between the worthy poor and the unworthy when one is engaged in acts of benevolence, when one is dispensing food or shelter or blankets for a church or private charity. That is for another day and involves important ethical and religious considerations. Within the context of legal aid, however, such a judgment about the worthiness of the person has no place. We can and must make decisions on the merits of the person's case, not on the worthiness of the person. Access to justice in the United States is not a benevolence. The American ideal of "Equal justice under law" by definition and logic cannot have a means test, and likewise, access to our legal forums cannot be based on tests of personal worthiness. In matters of justice, we cannot evade the fact that here, under our flag, we are pledged to a nation "with . . . justice for all."

It should be noted that later leaders of the New York Legal Aid Society, just as they had removed the national limitation, removed the worthiness language from its charter, and Reginald Heber Smith in 1919 praised it and other existing organizations that had "wisely refrained from erecting any moral standard which applicants must satisfy before being entitled to assistance. The only test is the intrinsic merit of the claim plus a due regard for those restrictions which good [legal] ethics impose on all members of the bar."[21] Regrettably, not all who came after him were as lawyerly as Smith, and we will see the moralistic standard and its implications crop up from time to time as we proceed with our story.

CHAPTER 2

Establishing Legal Services of Nashville

1965-1969

> I have been preaching all over the country
> that I thought it was much wiser for the
> organized bar to handle these matters, but
> we will have very little to stand on if we
> continue to drag our feet.
>
> —LEWIS PRIDE, MAY 1967

Establishing a staffed Legal Services program in Nashville was a long and tortuous struggle. There were many fits and starts and sometimes inexplicable delays. The Nashville Bar Association (NBA) was expected to do it, but its leadership was extremely hesitant, if not subtly hostile. Even after the organization finally was approved by the bar, it took another year before it opened its doors at last on February 3, 1969.

Money was available to begin a program in 1965. The funding would have come from the Office of Legal Services (OLS) at the Office of Economic Opportunity (OEO), which had been created in 1964 as a part of President Lyndon Johnson's Great Society to administer federal monies targeted to help people who were living in poverty. And that was the problem. The funds came with expectations that were difficult for many members of the still all-White NBA to accept.

One expectation of OEO for all of its programs was that low-income people would have a voice in identifying their own problems and developing solutions to them. This would not be an entirely top-down effort. Low-income people would, for instance, have seats on the board of a legal aid organization. This radical idea raised insoluble issues for many lawyers. It was important to the profession that lawyers be independent of the control of others, and the inclusion of lay people on a board that could determine operating policy for lawyers was a serious problem.

Even more radical was the expectation that any program OEO funded would be an integrated effort, bringing together both Black and White people in the same organizations. It would bridge the traditional divides between poor Whites and poor Blacks, and between low-income people and others in the community, threatening the hierarchies of race and culture. Empowering low-income people and uniting the races in a common effort had not been tried previously in many places in our country, and certainly was not a part of the Southern way of life.

In the South, more profoundly than in other parts of the country, there were important cultural and religious countervailing forces arrayed against these new ideas. The poor were expected to be humble and appreciative. Any assertion of any rights on their part was regarded as the rumbling of the rabble and a threat to genteel stability. Helping the poor traditionally had been a matter of charity, and conditional at that. Any effort by "good people of the community" to give aid to the poor was with the reservation of helping only the "deserving" poor. That's the way it always had been. There was no need for any social changes or government programs for the poor. "The poor you have with you always" had become a convenient excuse, a selective solace from Scripture for those who were content to dismiss the problems of the poor.[1]

As with poverty, so with race. The cultural and racial values of the post-Reconstruction South were persistent. Nashville had been an epicenter of the civil rights movement in the early 1960s, with the leadership of James Lawson and Kelly Miller Smith and the brave students who made the sit-ins and freedom rides such successful nonviolent tactics. After the home of local civil rights lawyer Z. Alexander Looby was bombed in April 1960, Diane Nash, James Bevel, and about 1,500 other people had confronted Mayor Ben West on the courthouse steps. They evoked from him the admission that "it is wrong and immoral to discriminate," and he appealed "to all citizens to end discrimination, to have no bigotry, no hatred."[2]

Such admissions helped create in Nashville an environment more moderate than many other places in the South. The city was fortunate in having four prominent institutions of higher education for Black people and something of a Black middle class with respected doctors, lawyers, religious leaders, educators, funeral directors, bankers, publishers, and other businesspeople committed to the betterment of the community. Despite all that, in the four years that are the subject of this chapter, and beyond, Nashville remained a segregated society. The systemic de facto racism was everywhere.

In 1969 when I came to town, high up on the four-story building at Fourth Avenue North and Charlotte one could see the large letters that had been stenciled on the brick façade years before spelling out "Colored YMCA." The remains of the stenciled signs in the courthouse plainly marked where until recently there had been separate restrooms for "colored men" and "white men." Despite perfunctory efforts to remove these persistent courthouse signs and other evidence of the *de jure* segregation, long-engrained attitudes endured, and the past remained.

In the almost universally segregated churches of the time, White clergy and laity alike could cite multiple Bible verses, beginning with the curse of Ham in Genesis and right on through the Christian Scriptures, proving that God meant for the races to be separate and wanted them to remain separate. White ministers like Sam Dodson at Calvary Methodist Church in Green Hills, who did speak up for integration and social justice, were in danger of losing their churches, or worse.

Dodson, a native of Hampshire, Tennessee, a graduate of Hume-Fogg High School in Nashville, Vanderbilt, and Yale Divinity School, was appointed in 1964 by his friend, Governor Frank Clement, to be head of the Tennessee Commission on Human Relations, a biracial group that called for an end to racial discrimination and exclusion. From the time of his appointment, there was opposition to Dodson's involvement from members of his congregation, as well as from many outside. There were threatening phone calls to his home and hate letters; a cross was burned on his lawn in Forest Hills. Finally, because of the opposition to him, less than a year after the Governor had appointed him, and in the first year of our story in this chapter, his bishop declined to reassign him to Calvary or any other church in the district and strongly suggested instead that he take a church in the country of Greece, nearly six thousand miles away, where he went with his wife and three children. He and those who shared his commitment were seen as troublemakers. They were disturbing the established social order. They were part of the problem.

The prospect of having a Legal Services program also was a problem. At the July 19, 1965, meeting of the board of directors of the NBA, the minutes recount that the president, J. B. Lackey Jr., "reported on the problem arising with the War on Poverty matters." The problem as he recounted it to the board was "what was being done in St. Louis County, Missouri, in setting up a staff of attorneys to provide legal services for the indigent, the federal government paying 90 percent of the cost . . . and the remainder coming from any other source." After what is described in the minutes as "a lengthy discussion of this problem, . . . the president was authorized to appoint a committee to make a thorough study of this matter and report to the board."

In his appointment letter to the members and Reber Boult, its chair, Lackey asked the committee to consider "the possibility of the Association sponsoring a civil legal aid association . . . as a part of the Community Action Program which in turn is a part of the War on Poverty." He suggested that the committee consult in the process with the legal advisor to the local Community Action Program and with "one or more representatives of the J. C. Napier Bar Association, because Negroes of our community would constitute a substantial number of beneficiaries of any such program." The NBA, which up until this time had dealt only with White lawyers' issues and had denied membership to Black lawyers, now was faced with the fact that it would be put in the position of dealing with "a substantial number" of Black people and with Black lawyers. For many, whether stated or not, that would be a poison pill for the project.

The president of the NBA was not the only bar official who saw federally subsidized legal aid as a problem. The next month the president of the Tennessee Bar Association (TBA), Robert Kirk Walker of Chattanooga, and its executive director, Billie Bethel, published in the *Tennessee Bar Journal* a call to alarm entitled "Et tu, Brute!" excoriating the OEO Legal Services program.[3] They reasoned that its implementation would undermine one's right to select his own counsel and amounted to "government competition with the independent practicing lawyer." While recognizing that the stated purpose of the program was to serve the poor, the writers feared that "nothing prevents all-encompassing federalism from embracing all [people] within its grasp as 'poor' in its headlong plunge into socialism." With double exclamation marks, they concluded that "Independence of the legal profession cannot survive the program!!" And the legal profession was not the only institution whose prospects were threatened by Legal Services according to Mr. Walker; his concerns went much broader into society as we shall see in his later, more expansive alarm.

In that atmosphere, over the next few weeks the NBA committee met four times and consulted variously with representatives of the Metropolitan Action Commission (MAC), the local community action program; the state administrator for OEO; and with Nashville attorney B. B. Gullett, the president-elect of the TBA. Following Lackey's suggestion, the committee extended an invitation to the Napier Bar Association to send a consultant, and it sent R. B. J. Campbelle Jr.

It did not take long for the committee to reach its conclusion. Its negative report to the September 1965 meeting of the NBA board reflects its understanding, mistaken though it was, that according to its reading of OEO guidelines, "any entity organized to supervise and administer such a federally subsidized legal aid program could not thereafter remain under the supervision of the Nashville Bar Association as such, nor even of a board consisting wholly or even of a majority of lawyers." Though the report notes that the committee reviewed "various types of written material" and plans from other cities, the members missed or ignored the important statement of Sargent Shriver at the ABA convention the previous month, which then had been reported on in the *Tennessean*.[4]

Shriver's remarks reinforced the design that lawyers would be in the majority on a Legal Services board. He even allowed that while OEO wanted one-third of the members of a Legal Services board to be "representatives of the poor," the requirements of one-third and the identity of the representatives both were flexible. As to who could be a representative of the poor, Shriver said it might even be a lawyer, though that seems to be a bit of a stretch. His only insistence was that because the enabling statute for OEO called for "maximum feasible participation of the poor," while he believed in flexibility, "flexibility cannot become a euphemism for evasion of our statutory duty." That story in the *Tennessean*, a month before the committee's report was finished, should have carried some weight. It had been written by the legal affairs correspondent of the *New York Times* News Service, Fred Graham, a graduate of Nashville's West End High School and Vanderbilt Law School, a person well known to members of the committee, but they paid no heed.

The committee also was concerned that the work of attorneys employed by such an entity would result in violations of the ABA Canons of Professional Ethics, even though the ABA had not found that to be a problem. The canons that particularly concerned the committee were those regarding advertising, stirring up litigation, the use of intermediaries, confidences of clients, and aiding in the unauthorized practice of law. In light of all these projected problems, the committee reported that it could not recommend the NBA sponsor or cosponsor such an entity. The NBA board followed suit and unanimously voted against sponsorship. If Nashville were going to have a Legal Services program, it would be up to MAC, the community action agency, to organize it and apply for OEO funding.

ENTER: LEWIS PRIDE

Lewis Pride was an attorney and a member of a prominent Nashville family, a state legislator from Belle Meade and active in many areas of community life. He also was on a committee of the ABA Young Lawyers Section that had been promoting federally funded legal aid. The ABA had sponsored his speaking at a meeting in Denver on the necessity of bar associations participating in the Legal Services Program, and he was on good terms with Clint Bamberger, the director of the OEO Office of Legal Services. Despite all of this, he had been completely unaware of the actions of his own bar association right in his own backyard. In December 1965, he by chance read about it in the outgoing NBA president's report, and he immediately took up the cause. He wrote a letter to the new president, Wilson "Woody" Sims, asking for a reconsideration and offering his counsel from the perspective of his national involvement. He made it clear that he did not want to be appointed to any committee, but he closed his letter with an offer that if Sims and the board would reconsider, "I will do all I can to whip up some enthusiasm among the committee."

Pride also was alarmed that since the NBA had dropped the ball, MAC reportedly was looking into its starting a Legal Services program. The new chair of MAC was J. Paschall Davis, for twenty-five years a practicing lawyer, now an Episcopal priest, who undoubtedly was cognizant of the prevailing opposition in the bar, and he had decided that if it were to get done, MAC must do it. Pride wanted the bar to take the lead and saw MAC's initiative as a threat to be countered, whereas the bar committee had seen MAC's interest as a reason for doing nothing. The *Tennessean* was alerted. Just a few days after Pride's letter to Sims, it ran an editorial that opined on the bar's reticence, "For a group that needs to improve its public image, this is unfortunate."[5]

Woody Sims, two months after Pride's letter, wrote to Boult asking the committee to consider reexamining the matter in light of new information, "and make a report only if your collective opinions differ from your report previously filed." In April 1966, now more than four months after Pride's letter, Boult wrote to the committee, calling a meeting for May 10. He cited five points as reasons for reconsideration. Revealing some skepticism, he first said there had been "a change of attitude on the part of the administrators of the so-called poverty program." Next, he illustrates what a shrewd decision Shriver had made when he persuaded corporate lawyer Clint Bamberger to take a leave from the law firm of Piper & Marbury for this job at OEO. Boult, now with reassurance, wrote to his committee that "a Baltimore lawyer of recognized standing took a leave of absence from his law practice" to be national director of the Legal Services Program. Third, he said that the ABA was giving attention to the application of the Canons of Ethics to Legal Services programs. Fourth, Memphis was doing it, and the new ABA president lived there. Fifth, Paschall Davis had visited Boult to express his hope that the NBA would either sponsor the local Legal Services program or at least act in an advisory capacity to MAC. Clearly, MAC was anxious for the bar to act. At Davis's direction, the MAC staff had developed a draft plan and budget for a Legal Services program to be operated under the bar association's direction. They supplied this to the bar committee, as well an example of a plan developed in another city and a copy of the eligibility guidelines recommended by OEO.

The Tennessee Bar Association, meanwhile, continued on its path of opposition. In February, its president, Mr. Walker, at the national conference of bar presidents in Chicago, rose up in a meeting and accused the OEO Legal Services Program of "fomenting social unrest" and inciting social revolution.[6] It was not only the legal profession that had been stabbed in the back, but for him and those who applauded him in that meeting, the whole of their stratified society was being assaulted. On April 30, the TBA Board of Governors passed a resolution condemning the OEO Legal Services Program and urging local bars not to sponsor programs and not even to participate by appointing members to grantee boards. Thankfully, the TBA did not go as far as the North Carolina Bar Association, which stood in its own schoolhouse door and threatened to disbar any lawyer who went to work for an OEO grantee.

Fortunately, this negative reaction all around did not dissuade the Nashville bar committee from meeting on May 10 and proceeding with its work. As a follow-up to that meeting, MAC's legal counsel, I. T. "Tony" Creswell Jr., sent a letter to Reber Boult making it clear that in the plan MAC was proposing to the bar, the Legal Services program should be a freestanding nonprofit corporation and at least 75 percent of the board should be lawyers. When the committee raised a question about the Legal Services program taking business away from what it termed "marginal" lawyers, Creswell sent inquires to several organizations around the country asking for data or examples, but in the end was not able to answer the questions.

This persistent issue about the livelihood of marginal lawyers is ironic as one looks back over the years. The fact is that because there is so much demand for legal assistance from low-income people, legal aid offices routinely turn away many more cases than they accept, leaving a large population needing private attorneys and plenty of work for the sorely lamented marginal lawyer. Not only is there plenty of work to go around, in many cases lawyers generate business for each other. The testimony of many lawyers over the years is that having a legal aid lawyer on the other side contesting a case, or even the possibility of having a legal aid lawyer on the other side, actually increases their own business. This reflects that old adage: "If there is only one lawyer in a town, he will starve; but if there are two, they will thrive."

The NBA committee was getting lots of help in its deliberations. Most likely at Lewis Pride's initiative, Phillip Murphy, representing both NLADA and SCLAID, wrote to Boult offering consultative services. Boult wrote back with but one concern and asked for no further help. He wanted to know about the progress of SCLAID in dealing with the Canons of Ethics "as it relates to this problem." No specific ethical issue is mentioned in his letter, but Creswell's previous letter to Boult had proposed a grievance committee made up entirely of lawyers to deal with issues of advertising, soliciting, client confidences, intermediaries, unprofessional conduct, and other grievances should they arise, so these must have been the issues on Boult's mind as he wrote to Murphy. We have no record of the SCLAID reply, but we can assume that the reply was, "there is no problem." Certainly, SCLAID was on record as wholeheartedly supporting Legal Services programs.

Help also came from another Nashville lawyer, Whit Stokes, who had been quite active with the NBA clinic. Stokes, whose practice included handling cases for the American Civil Liberties Union and the Tennessee Council on Human Relations, made frequent trips to Atlanta for meetings associated with the work of those organizations. Thomas O. H. "Tommy" Smith Jr., secretary of Boult's committee, learned that Stokes would be in Atlanta at the same time as an informational meeting sponsored by the OEO and NLADA and asked him to attend on behalf of the committee. The meeting in July 1966 had been put together "in an attempt to quell the incipient revolt in the southern states . . . based on erroneous rumors."[7] Two hundred bar leaders and other lawyers from across the South attended. According to Stokes's thorough four-page report to the committee, Smith had asked him especially "to look into" four areas of concern: (1) "the question of local control of the OEO programs by existing bar associations"; (2) "the effect of such a program on the currently existing Canons of Ethics"; (3) "the effect of the program on 'marginal attorneys'"; and (4) "the problem of financing when the government withdraws from such a program (if it does)."

In response, Stokes reported that Earl Johnson had assured the Atlanta meeting that OEO would give local bar associations every opportunity to develop the programs and only in rare instances where the bar association failed to act would OEO fund a program sponsored by another group. Johnson did make it clear, however, that a Legal Services program board must have some members who represented the people to be served. As for the question about the Canons of Ethics, Stokes came back with a copy of a recent Pennsylvania court's decision declaring that the OEO Legal Services Program organized in Philadelphia did not violate the Canons. On the "marginal attorney" question, Stokes simply reported, "no one really knows what effect such a program will have on those . . . we refer to as marginal attorneys." He pointed out that there actually "appears to be no agreement as to what a marginal attorney is" and suggested that if the bar association wanted to pursue this question, it would have to "define what they are talking about . . . and . . . make some independent study on their own." As to Smith's final inquiry, Stokes brought back no wisdom on future funding.

Three representatives of the TBA also attended the Atlanta conference, as well as representatives of other local bars in the state and Vanderbilt Law School. The meeting and other events of the summer, including a change in TBA leadership, had a salutary effect on the state bar association's position on Legal Services. A special committee chaired by B. B. Gullett, the new TBA president, considered the information from that conference, prior resolutions of the ABA, and reports from SCLAID and OEO at the ABA Annual Convention, then unanimously recommended that the TBA Board of Governors adopt a resolution supporting the Legal Services programs and rescinding its resolution of April 30. That resolution was adopted by the TBA Board of Governors in November.

Meantime, others in the Nashville community were urging that a Legal Services program be established. In early November, the Middle Tennessee Chapter of the National Association of Social Workers sent its resolutions to Boult, along with a statement from Mayor Beverly Briley assuring that association of his support for a Legal Services program. The Council of Community Services earlier in the year had voiced its support. In late November 1966, Boult's committee reached it unanimous decision and Tommy Smith drafted its report.

The committee reported to the NBA on December 5 that "the requirements set out by the government agency had been revised so as to eliminate many of the objections noted in the 1965 report of this committee," though it cited no specifics. Grudging to the end, the report of the Boult committee was not without a note of resignation, concluding that "it is inevitable that a federally subsidized legal aid program will be authorized in the near future." It recommended that the bar association go on and establish it "rather than a welfare organization or pressure group" and that the bar association take the responsibility for appointing the majority of the board.

Others were making a more positive push. Dean Wade and attorney George Cate Jr., who was president of CCS, invited Orison Marden, the president of the ABA, to come speak at the law school in early December. Strategically, they asked the NBA to cosponsor the event. Marden came for the occasion on December 8 and spoke about "Legal Aid–Issues and Answers," followed by a panel discussion. Three days later, the *Tennessean*, which had covered the event and had obtained a copy of the NBA committee report, added its editorial encouragement and praised the committee for its recommendation.

The NBA, however, was in no hurry. The committee's report finally was brought before the NBA board for discussion on March 28, 1967, after inexplicably being passed over for three previous meetings. Even then, the board still had concerns. Apparently not confident that the committee had turned over every rock and explored every fault, the board wanted to see for itself OEO guidelines and sample copies of proposed plans, and the board wanted a more detailed description of a projected Nashville operation. Then it would consider holding a referendum for the entire NBA membership to vote on the project, yet another hurdle.

Lewis Pride, when he learned about the board's actions, or inaction, recognized right away the tactics of delay. On May 3, he wrote to Ed Herod, NBA president, with copies to Tommy Smith and Reber Boult, urging the bar association to act. He knew from his involvement on the national level that within a few months Nashville would be the largest city in the country not to have a Legal Services program. He pointed out that he was "on very good terms with Earl Johnson, the director of the Legal Services program for the OEO," and he offered to get any information the bar association needed. Presciently, he was frustrated that the NBA's delay would open the door for another group to make the application for the Nashville program: "I have been preaching all over the country that I thought it was much wiser for the organized bar to handle these matters, but we will have very little to stand on if we continue to drag our feet."

Pride's letter now stirred some action. Without consulting the NBA board, Herod appointed Pride, Tommy Smith, and Karl Warden of Vanderbilt Law School, a committee of focused advocates, to prepare a plan "within the required guidelines of the OEO" and submit it to the bar board. He appointed Pride to chair the committee. Despite his protest of a year and a half earlier that he did not want to be appointed to any committee, Pride now saw that if it were going to get done, he would have to do it, and he accepted that responsibility.

MAC by this time had tired of the bar association's delay and doubted its ability to carry through. MAC had been offering assistance, actually spoon-feeding the bar, and urging action for nearly two years. It had sent numerous samples and draft plans to the bar without any good result. Consequently, on June 9, 1967, MAC sent to Ed Herod a copy of its own application for a Legal Services grant. The deadline for submitting applications to OEO was July 1, and the NBA clearly would not meet it, so MAC had pushed forward. Under OEO guidelines, MAC was required to give twenty days' notice to the principal local bar association if that association were not joining in the proposal, and its mailing to Herod fulfilled that requirement. There was no requirement that the local bar approve the plan, just that it have notice.

On June 12, Herod forwarded the MAC proposal to Pride, Smith, and Warden and cluelessly asked to be advised "what, if anything, needs to be done." Yes, something needed to be done, and quickly. Lewis Pride immediately had Herod send a telegram to Jim Cordell, OEO regional director for Legal Services. The telegram, meant to encumber MAC's move, conveyed unjustified optimism about the bar's trajectory and gave more credit to the bar's process than was due. With lawyerly bluster, undoubtedly written by Pride, the telegram confidently informed Cordell that the NBA board "is diligently attempting to devise a program for legal aid to the poor that will be workable in this community, will conform with the guidelines of OEO, and will be approved by the general membership of the Association." In an obvious effort to piggyback on the MAC proposal that, unlike any bar proposal, would meet the filing deadline, the telegram continues, "It is our sincere hope that such a plan will enable us to cooperate fully with the Metropolitan Action Commission within its present application for funding of neighborhood legal services."

Cordell, surely based not at all on the NBA's purported diligence but rather on Lewis Pride's national reputation, quickly scheduled a meeting in Nashville for July 13. On June 19, Pride followed up with a letter to NLADA Executive Director Junius Allison, asking that he send a representative to the meeting. Astonishingly, the bar association board minutes for June 26 state merely that the president announced he had appointed a committee of Pride, Warden, and Smith "to assist in planning a program of legal aid to the poor in conjunction with the OEO programs." No mention at all of the mess the board's delay had created, and no mention of Pride's incisive remedial action or the upcoming grand meeting Pride had arranged to save the project.

The July 13 meeting was organized and chaired by Lewis Pride. He invited MAC representatives and proposed it as an opportunity to sit down with Jim Cordell and Phil Murphy to work on the MAC proposal and improve it. In anticipation of the meeting, a MAC internal memo reported that "It is the NBA committee's feeling that this [the MAC] proposal is probably deficient in a number of respects, and before modifying or submitting a new one, they would like to have the benefit of the NLADA recommendations." Paschall Davis, Tony Creswell, and others attended the meeting representing MAC. Unfortunately, after that meeting in July the paper trail for this joint endeavor is lost until October.

A RIVAL PLAY

In the meantime, another set of actors appear, with three familiar faces and two additions. George Barrett, who previously appeared in our story as chair of the 1961 NBA legal aid committee, was a politically connected labor lawyer who also had handled a number of civil rights cases. With his fiery temperament, he saw himself as something of a gadfly, referred to himself as "Citizen Barrett," and relished the chance to poke the establishment in the eye, except, of course, when his political faction was in power. Barrett, together with Tony Creswell and Whit Stokes, at some point during this time had formed the first integrated law firm in Nashville. Creswell was Black, from a prominent North Nashville family. After Reber Boult's son, Reber Boult Jr., gained some notoriety representing an anti-Vietnam War protester and a local civil rights leader, he no longer was a good fit with his father's white-shoe law firm, and he moved in for a while with Barrett, Stokes, and Creswell before going to Atlanta as a lawyer with the ACLU.

On September 14, 1967, these four lawyers and their clerk, John Mitchell, became the incorporators and filed in the Secretary of State's office a charter for "Target Area Services, Incorporated." The purposes of this not-for-profit corporation, distilled from the convoluted legal language of the charter, included "to secure funds from sources both public and private . . . to provide . . . advocacy of lawyers for people in poverty"; and "to work with any and all agencies or groups having the same . . . purposes." In other words, they were forming the kind of corporation that could apply to OEO and receive a grant for a Legal Services program. They never filed an application, but with the corporation formed, they were poised.

Barrett, in later years, enjoyed recounting that they founded the first legal aid organization incorporated in Nashville, and he maintained that at the time he had let the word out that they were doing it on behalf of some of his labor clients, including the Teamsters Union, because he thought that the prospect of the Teamsters controlling the Legal Services program would finally spur the bar association and MAC to action. Whit Stokes later cautiously confirmed, "George's claim is not totally far-fetched."

THE FINAL PUSH

After some further delays that were not entirely its fault, Pride's committee adopted a plan on October 26 and sent it to the NBA board. The committee was invited to attend the November 16 board meeting, where Pride presented an outline of the plan and answered questions for an hour and forty-five minutes, an unusual length of time for any one item on the agenda, eliciting a special note in the minutes. Then he, Smith, and Warden were "excused . . . from the meeting." The board went on to other business.

Judging from an interview Pride gave to the *Tennessean* a few days later, one of the issues for the NBA board must have been the involvement of MAC in the operation. Though Tony Creswell and others at MAC had been involved in developing the plan Pride's committee submitted, Pride is quoted as saying, "I don't feel the bar association would approve a plan which they thought was in any way connected with the Metro Action Commission." For the better part of a year MAC had been plagued by an internal dispute that undoubtedly had made a bad impression on the bar board and added to any other prejudices members may have had about this interracial group. Recognizing that and looking for alternative approaches, it sounds like Pride after the NBA board meeting had been in touch with his friends in high places at OEO. He told the reporter, "I've been assured it would be possible for us to get direct funding. There would be certain coordination, but we'd deal directly with the Office of Economic Opportunity."[8]

The committee was asked to come back to a called NBA board meeting on December 4, where Pride presented "an addendum to the program, prepared as result of suggestions made at the last Board meeting" and spent the next hour answering questions, again the unusual amount of time specifically noted in the minutes. Again the committee was "excused" from this meeting, and the board "undertook a further discussion." Finally, the board unanimously adopted a resolution graciously acknowledging the work of the committee, calling for copies of the plan to be printed and placed in the bar library with notice to the membership of their availability, and providing for a mail ballot vote of the membership to be held on or before February 1, 1968.

The decision to submit the matter to a vote of the entire NBA membership was extraordinary, unprecedented in modern times except on one other occasion. In fact, the practice of the NBA board had been to conduct its business and make its decisions in closed sessions only. Not even other members of the association were allowed to be present for its deliberations, as illustrated by the fact that Pride, Smith, and Warden had been "excused" from the board meeting each time after making their presentation.

The only other time since World War II that a matter had been submitted to the membership in a referendum had been the equally controversial question in late 1965 as to whether or not the association should abandon its Whites-only practice and admit Black lawyers to its membership. That vote had been spurred by a letter to the board from Gilbert Merritt, later judge on the US Court of Appeals for the Sixth Circuit. Merritt's concern had been referred to a study committee that struggled with it for nearly a year. Then it was put to a vote of the entire NBA membership, and finally it was approved by a vote of 260 for admission of Black lawyers with 175 against.

The question of whether or not to sponsor a Legal Services program had not only racial issues, but specific practice and political implications as well. For many, as we have seen, federally funded free Legal Services smacked of socialism, which was the next thing to communism. Plus, there were the persistent suspicions about the effects this might have on the profession and the "marginal lawyers." As with the racial member-ship question, the board clearly was not willing to take responsibility, step out on its own, and make the decision. It was not willing to assert any leadership or give any guidance. The matter simply was too controver-sial in this time and place. Less than a year later, in the 1968 presidential election, Davidson County went not for the Republican or Democratic candidate, but for the segregationist Alabama governor George Wallace, whose campaign was "a reaction against the racial changes associated with the Great Society."[9]

Others in the city were decidedly less tentative than the NBA board and more willing to be advocates for Legal Services. The Council of Com-munity Services welcomed the plan, and on behalf of its Executive Com-mittee, George Cate sent a letter of endorsement to William F. "Billy" Howard, the new NBA president. In addition, at its winter membership meeting, which was open to the public, CCS featured a panel discussion on "The Challenge of Equal Justice" moderated by former US Attorney James F. Neal that included the district attorney, public defender, and juvenile judge, as well as Lewis Pride, all of whom spoke in favor of the plan. Between January 18 and the vote on February 1, the *Tennessean* ran seven articles about the vote, mostly written by Rob Elder, including one reporting on the annual meeting of the United Givers Fund (later United Way) where Dan May, a respected civic leader, urged the group of two hundred people to encourage the lawyers to vote for the program. May, who had recently been installed as chairman of MAC in order to stabi-lize that organization, said that if the lawyers would not do it, he was afraid MAC would have to do it. "I'd much rather see the lawyers do it."[10]

There was vocal opposition in the bar. The most strident was Dick Lansden, who had been president of the NBA a few years earlier. He sent a letter to all its members charging that "the proposal . . . is illegal, conflicts with the statutes of our state regulating the practice of law, and could subject the lawyers participating in the program to charges of unprofessional conduct." In its article reporting on Lansden's letter, the *Tennessean* quoted Whit Stokes in rebuttal and referred the reader to its editorial that day, "City Needs Legal Aid for the Poor."[11] For the next three days, the *Tennessean* ran more rebuttals seriatim from Pride, Warden, and Smith.

Predictably, the proposal needed all the support it could get. In the end, when all the ballots were counted, it did pass, but by a vote of only 206 in favor with 171 against, a five-point narrower margin than the integration vote three years earlier. In its lead editorial the next Sunday, the *Tennessean* did not comment on the narrow margin, but rather congratulated the bar association and its leaders "on this step toward meeting a big responsibility of legal profession–and the community." The editorial properly singled out Lewis Pride: "The affirmative vote is a tribute to the efforts of Mr. Lewis D. Pride, chairman of the NBA committee which prepared the proposal. Mr. Pride waged a strong campaign in behalf of the proposal which he had written along with Smith and Warden."[12]

At a special NBA board meeting on February 5, 1968, Harris Gilbert moved that the president be authorized to file a charter incorporating Legal Services of Nashville, Inc. The motion passed, and the charter was filed, with the NBA board members as incorporators. Five days later, Billy Howard and Lewis Pride submitted the application for $190,000 to OEO. At the regular board meeting on February 23, Howard offered a slate of directors for the new corporation that was approved unanimously, and Harris Gilbert was elected president. Within three days the CCS had appointed its Executive Director, William F. Moynihan, to the Legal Services board and Dan May had agreed to appoint MAC representatives.

FAILURE AND DETERMINATION

Alas, it was too late. On April 18, the Chief of Operations for the OEO Legal Services Program wrote back to Billy Howard with a copy to Lewis Pride saying that because the Bureau of the Budget had drastically cut the OEO budget, there was no more money for funding new Legal Services programs during the fiscal year 1968. Lewis Pride clearly was unhappy about the consequence of the bar association's long-drawn-out reticence. In an article in the *Tennessean* on April 24, he was quoted, "the only thing I can say now is that those people who were against using federal funds to do this can now use private funds for it."[13] But he said he knew of no private fund immediately available to replace the $190,000 annual grant that had been requested. The article goes on to state that at one time federal money had been appropriated by OEO for Nashville and designated for a potential MAC plan, but had been withdrawn when no program was begun.

Billy Howard was not deterred. He took the lead in responding to the disappointing news from OEO, calling "an informal meeting" in his office on May 16 that was attended by Harris Gilbert, Karl Warden, Lewis Pride, and four representatives of the MAC target areas. Gilbert and Warden proposed launching a fundraising effort for LSON, which the meeting approved. With this plan in place, Gilbert called the first meeting of the LSON board for May 29, at which the board discussed several ways of raising money for "a voluntary legal aid program to supplement the legal aid program of the NBA and the charitable services rendered by private attorneys," including community contributions, voluntary contributions by lawyers, and a dues assessment on NBA members. Gilbert suggested a budget of $22,000. The first pledge of monetary support came from board member Thomas Wardlaw Steele, who pledged $1,000 on behalf of the firm of Gullett Steele Sanford and Robinson. Karl Warden pledged $500 on behalf of his wife and himself.

Gilbert prepared a "general outline of the proposed project" with details for a full-time staff attorney, a secretary, "a large number" of junior and senior Vanderbilt law students, and volunteer help from private attorneys that was adopted by the LSON board. In July the NBA board unanimously approved a resolution supporting the program, endorsing a fundraising campaign among members of the bar "and the community at large," and recommending "to each of its members who have been practicing for ten years or less that they give freely of their time and talent . . . when called on." Evincing a sad assessment of the bar, the LSON board had concluded that asking older lawyers would not be productive.

By September the LSON fundraising committee, led by board member John Tune, was up and running. Back-to-back articles in the *Tennessean* on September 16 and 17 described a community committee that was co-chaired by Dr. Henry H. Hill, President Emeritus of Peabody College, and The Reverend Dogan Williams, pastor of Gordon Memorial Methodist Church, which was located in one of the target areas. The members of the committee listed in the September 16 article were an impressive cross section of the Nashville community.[14] A later LSON treasurer's report reflects early major gifts from Amon Carter Evans, the publisher of the *Tennessean*; Lewis Pride; The Werthan Foundation; David K. Wilson; National Life and Accident Insurance Company; Life and Casualty Insurance Company; the H.G. Hill Company; John J. Hooker Jr.; and the firm of Hooker, Hooker and Willis.

By the time of its September 27 meeting, the LSON board had begun considering candidates for the position of executive director and at that meeting adopted bylaws. In October, the Chamber of Commerce endorsed the fundraising campaign, as did the Metro Human Relations Commission and Church Women United. The stalwart *Tennessean* added its editorial support, and volunteers from MAC's East Nashville neighborhood service center organized a two-day rummage sale to raise funds for the cause. By November, LSON had raised $14,500, and the board determined that it had enough to begin operation, so it hired an executive director, John C. Corbitt. In December, dramatically came the news that in the new federal fiscal year that had begun in October, funds had become available for OEO to make grants to new Legal Services programs and LSON would receive a grant after all in the amount of $95,000, half the amount Lewis Pride had requested, but with great relief the board voted to accept it.[15]

It happened just in time. The next month in Washington came the inauguration of a new president, Richard Nixon, and the advent of an administration that would stop making new grants and, on the contrary, set about trying to dismantle the Great Society and its programs, including Legal Services. One of the chief assets in Mr. Nixon's 1968 campaign for the presidency had been his "Southern Strategy," which successfully undercut Governor Wallace's attraction in many places by appealing to the same base racial and antigovernment sentiments Wallace espoused.[16] Because Legal Services and other programs benefitted Blacks as well as Whites, they were perceived as Black programs, and by cutting them during his presidency, Mr. Nixon could continue that successful strategy, satisfy embittered Southern Whites, enhance the position of the Republican party in the South, and strengthen his prospects for reelection in 1972.[17]

That was the world as it was, and as it was to be. The struggling board of LSON, with its much-welcomed new federal grant, had embarked on what was to become something akin to the board game of Chutes and Ladders, as one presidential administration after another redefined its position on whether or not our government should financially support equal access for all to its legal system. For now, the new grant allowed the board to roll the dice and begin to move along that perilous game board.

John C. Corbitt, a colonel in the Army Reserve and a former assistant district attorney general, had been practicing law in Nashville for nearly twenty-five years; he was in private practice sharing an office with another lawyer when he was hired by LSON. It was not clear to some on the board whether he had been hired as executive director or acting executive director and, predictably, that later became an issue, but for now, he got right to work. Reflecting his military experience, and perhaps the nervousness of the board, Corbitt regularly detailed to Harris Gilbert his progress: leasing an office from the Metropolitan Government at 615 Stahlman Building; purchasing office furniture and equipment, and loaning some of his own; interviewing secretarial candidates; notifying social agencies about the services to be offered; contacting NLADA for client application forms; preparing an office manual; applying for sales tax exemption; receiving donations of books; and receiving inquiries from attorneys seeking employment. He sought approval from Harris Gilbert for the most mundane matters, such as hiring a part-time secretary and purchasing "a rebuilt, guaranteed Royal electric typewriter."

Having accomplished all this preparatory work, Corbitt opened the office for business on Monday, February 3, 1969.

CHAPTER 3

Conflicts Inside and Out

1969–1973

I'm tired of these outsiders coming in
here and trying to run my court. I think
they ought to go back where they
came from.

—Judge Andrew Doyle, January 1971

We are fortunate that most of John Corbitt's excruciatingly detailed monthly reports to Harris Gilbert have been preserved; regrettably, early 1969 board minutes have not. From one of Corbitt's reports we learn that an elderly lawyer named Alfred Taylor had been working full-time in the office uncompensated, and in April, Corbitt recommended that he be employed as a staff attorney, which was approved. Vanderbilt law students were an important part of the service from the beginning, conducting initial interviews and assisting the lawyers with the cases they accepted. In the first two months of operation, 334 people applied for assistance: sixty-one with garnishment and attachment issues and seventy-seven seeking divorce. Of the 334 applicants, 103 were not eligible for services.

In August, R. B. J. Campbelle Jr. was hired, whether by Corbitt or by the board we do not know. Campbelle had graduated from law school at the University of Tennessee in 1956, the first African American graduate of that school, had practiced law in Nashville, and had been active in the community. As recounted in the previous chapter, he was the Napier Bar Association member who had been invited to consult with the first NBA committee looking into establishing a Legal Services program. Several months after he was hired, Campbelle was assigned to open a branch office in a converted house on Seventeenth Avenue South near Edgehill Avenue, an urban renewal area. It was an area Campbelle knew well. Along with the pastor Bill Barnes, he was one of the founding members of the controversial Edgehill United Methodist Church, which in 1966 had been organized in the neighborhood between the Edgehill housing project and Vanderbilt University specifically as an interracial congregation. Initially at OEO Legal Services there was a great emphasis on having neighborhood offices in urban "target areas," convenient to the homes of potential clients. LSON's following of that strategy will ebb and flow with funding and other factors during the early part of our story, later to be resolved by the necessity of concentrating resources in one place.

At its beginning and for the first few months, LSON was a traditional legal aid program, handling each case as it presented itself, not alert to systemic issues, not posing any challenges to the status quo. The three lawyers at LSON were veteran practitioners, familiar with the informal relationships of bench and bar and used to the social mores in a southern town of that day. They knew well the procedures and practices an attorney should follow if he wanted to "get along" in the bar. That conventional consensus was not to last long, however. It was about to be challenged and then change as younger lawyers joined the staff with ideas more in tune with the ideals of the War on Poverty.

The first young lawyer to appear was Jerry Black, a Vanderbilt Law graduate who had joined the Peace Corps with his wife, but they had left after she became pregnant. Back home, he contacted his former teacher, Karl Warden, looking for other challenging work, and Warden contacted Tommy Smith, who had followed Harris Gilbert as president of the LSON board in July 1969. Corbitt later complained that Black was "employed by the Board, reported and assumed his duties" while he, Corbitt, was absent from the office on active duty with the Army Reserve. In September, Karen Ennis was hired as a staff attorney. A Stanford Law graduate, she previously had been the poorly paid staff attorney for the ACLU in Tennessee. In September, LSON also received two Reginald Heber Smith Fellows, Grayfred Gray and Sara Green. Gray, a Vanderbilt Law graduate, had clerked for Judge Harry Phillips on the Sixth Circuit Court of Appeals.

The Smith Fellowship Program was a national initiative by OEO designed to recruit top law students, federal court law clerks, and promising young lawyers into Legal Services. Those selected as "Reggies" were given intensive training during a summer program operated by the University of Pennsylvania Law School with some of the leading lawyers and law professors in the country as faculty. They had a renewable one-year stipend to work in a local legal services program and were charged with making an impact on behalf of their clients. Rather than just taking routine cases that would benefit only one person, they were encouraged to take cases that would benefit a large number of people and/or make the law more congenial than it had been for their clients. The program had been inspired in part by a suggestion from Howard Westbrook, a partner at the law firm of Covington and Burling who was on the board of one of those pre-OEO, foundation-funded projects. He envisioned that the project lawyers "should offer the poor what his corporate clients wanted most from his firm's lawyers, forms of representation that would shape the law in ways favorable to them."[1] That would mean class action lawsuits, appellate litigation, advocacy before administrative and legislative bodies. It was what Reginald Heber Smith himself had urged in 1916, when he spoke of "preventive law."

Clearly, the concept of the Smith Fellowship and the management of the Reggies was a mystery to John Corbitt: "Their status in the office has never been fully explained to me nor have I seen anything written except a few items of correspondence from the Foundation." The tension between the work of seeing individual clients on the one hand, and dealing with high impact issues on the other, was to be repeated in many places and in national discussions for years to come. Legal Services attorneys, faced with so much demand and so few resources, had to determine how best to prioritize and deal with the overwhelming problems of their clients, and how to allocate their time. It was a tension between the approach of traditional legal aid organizations and the newer vision of OEO. One of the themes of this story will be how we dealt with that enduring tension.

Within months of arriving in Nashville, Sara Green filed a class action lawsuit in federal district court on behalf of Bettie Brooks, asking that the State be required to pay cost of living increases to recipients of Aid to Families with Dependent Children (AFDC) that had been due July 1. A three-judge panel heard oral argument on January 20, 1970, and as reported by the *Tennessean*, "in a rare oral ruling from the bench" unanimously granted the relief Green sought.[2] The newspaper article concluded its report noting that Judge Phillips, who had presided at the hearing, "told Miss Green the court wanted to compliment her on the excellent brief she had filed in the case." The case helped thirty-two thousand people get their delinquent cost of living increase.

Grayfred Gray determined that the best way to fulfill his responsibility as a Reggie would be to act principally as "corporate counsel" to community groups, one of which was the West Nashville Cherokee Citizens Organization. He originally had been asked to attend a meeting of the organization to talk about the new free school lunch program, but the meeting soon evolved into a discussion about the drainage ditches in their neighborhood that at times, especially when it rained, carried wastes and spills from several nearby industrial plants. One neighbor reported that he had tried to clean up some of the mess that was coming down the ditch in front of his house and had been burned in the process by the acid in the water. Others reported similar experiences.

After several discussions, Gray was trying to figure out whether he could file a lawsuit to stop the careless polluting. His clients, however, were not interested in a lawsuit; they wanted help in publicizing their problems and persuading city officials to remedy the hazard. Gray enlisted a lab assistant and a chemistry professor at Vanderbilt to come show residents how to take samples from the flow when there was a rain, which would be tested for chemical content at Vanderbilt. A newscaster from a local TV station came and did a piece on the situation. The Metro Council member from the area for whatever reason was not helpful, but the group persisted. Gray drafted an ordinance and helped the group get it before the Council, and by the beginning of the next fiscal year the health department had new enforcement powers, and there was an appropriation in the Metro budget for clean-up and new storm sewers.

Despite his principal role acting as corporate counsel and dealing with wider issues, Gray did get involved in some individual cases. Both he and Jerry Black remember being in the office late one Friday afternoon when a man came in whose furniture was due to be repossessed the next day. In dealing with a furniture store, the man had signed a "roll-over security interest" agreement, a device commonly used by small loan companies of the day and furniture stores that sold to low-income people. When a person bought an additional piece of furniture on credit while still paying for previously purchased furniture, instead of making a new loan, the creditor merely enlarged the old loan, and as a consequence all of the previously purchased furniture became collateral in the revised loan. Until the whole loan was paid in full, regardless of whether or not the person had paid enough to cover the earlier purchases, all of his furniture was subject to repossession. The man's last purchase had been a baby bed and because he had fallen behind paying that off, the furniture company had obtained a writ to repossess all the furniture he had bought from it, and that would happen the next day.

Black and Gray, fresh from a seminar at Vanderbilt on the relatively new "Truth-in-Lending" regulations, recognized a problem with the loan papers and quickly drafted a complaint with a request for a temporary restraining order. They then went to the home of one of the chancellors and caught him as he was headed out the door to go to a basketball game.[3] The chancellor signed the restraining order, a clerk met them at the courthouse to file the papers, and they delivered them to the sheriff's office that night to stop the repossession scheduled for the next morning. The baby's crib and the rest of the furniture were saved, and at a later hearing the chancellor penalized the lender for its violation of the Truth-in-Lending provisions.

THE ROCKY ROAD

Back in the LSON office, all was not well. After only a few months on the job, Black and most other lawyers in the office had come to the conclusion that John Corbitt was not providing the kind of leadership and administrative sensitivity that the operation of an effective Legal Services office required. They sent a memo to the board signed by Black, Campbelle, Gray, Ennis, and Green detailing some specific concerns about support staff hired and retained by Corbitt despite the staff attorneys' complaints. The receptionist, the first person clients saw coming into the office, had a "poor attitude toward clients." They went on to say "she is at times outright discourteous and at other times makes snide remarks about either them or their problems." One of the part-time secretaries was "extremely hard of hearing. Thus, she cannot answer the telephone, take dictation, nor use the Dictaphone." Finally, they complained that a previously authorized and much needed investigator had not been hired.

While these legitimate complaints do not appear to be the stuff of great revolutions, and while there were no additional details in the memo of complaint, it signaled a much deeper problem. Corbitt simply did not have the same sense of urgency and scope of vision shared by these lawyers. Understandably for a White southern man of his era and experience, the impatience of these staff lawyers and their idealism was perplexing, if not impudent. They wanted "a legal services program which will provide effective advocacy for the poor to the greatest extent possible," and they certainly anticipated testing the limits of what was possible.

The alacrity of the board suggests there must have been further communication from the staff with more serious complaints. Two days later, on October 24, after what the secretary of the board, Lewis Pride, described in the minutes as "an extremely in-depth discussion concerning the deficiencies in administration of the program," the board unanimously passed a motion providing that the president and two board members meet with Corbitt "to inform him that the Board would be agreeable to accepting his letter of resignation," that if he refused, he should be given thirty days' notice to vacate the office, and that Jerry Black be appointed acting director when Corbitt vacated the office.

Not surprisingly, Corbitt, who had not been at the meeting, was shocked when the president and two board members met with him and delivered the news. On November 5, he wrote a two-and-a-half-page single-spaced letter refusing to submit his resignation, laying out a defense, rightly stating that "in all fairness and justice" he should have been given "some opportunity to be advised of the Board's dissatisfaction and an opportunity to be heard before such action was taken." The board, then recognizing its procedural mistake, was quick to grant his reasonable request and scheduled a meeting for November 14, with the five attorneys who had signed the complaint and Corbitt present. At that meeting, after hearing from all the lawyers, the board voted to reconsider its previous action and clarified that Corbitt was acting director "until such time as the Board has hired a Director." Lewis Pride voted no.

On a "Technical Assistance Visit" in January 1970, Dan Bradley and Hugh MacMillan of the Atlanta regional office of the Legal Services Program became aware of the "extreme frustration" of the younger lawyers "with regard to the aimless and inefficient management," and they highlighted that deficit in their report to the LSON board sometime in February. The board had already begun its search for a new executive director and by April was ready to make an offer to David Candish, a Texas lawyer who had been a Reggie in South Carolina. Candish began June 15. At its July meeting, the board thanked Corbitt for his services as acting director and recorded that it looked forward to his continuing as senior staff attorney.

All of this was too late for the four younger lawyers who had signed the complaint to the board. Impatient and discouraged after the November board reversal, Gray began looking for other work. He left in the spring to become Executive Director of the Tennessee Law Revision Commission before moving on to a faculty position at the University of Tennessee College of Law. Green also left in the spring. Black left July 15 to become interim director of the legal clinic at Vanderbilt while Karl Warden was on sabbatical. Ironically, he then was appointed by Dean Wade to temporarily replace Warden on the LSON board. Ennis left in the fall.

The lawyers remaining then were Candish, Corbitt, and Taylor in the Stahlman Building office, and Campbelle in the South Nashville office. For a time, some of the gap left by the departures of the younger lawyers was filled by law students. In addition to clinic students, a number of Vanderbilt law students were hired to work full-time during the summer and part-time during the school year. Under the third year practice rule adopted by the Tennessee Supreme Court, after two years of law school, a student in a public interest position could be admitted to practice provisionally, though any appearance in court would have to be under the direct supervision of an attorney.

David Tarpley had been interviewing clients and working on cases as a legal clinic student during his second year at Vanderbilt. In June 1970, he and two other rising third year students were hired as clerks full-time for the summer, and they continued to work part-time during the following academic year. Two students in the class behind them, Tom Daniel and I, were hired to work full-time in the summer, and we too continued part-time during the school year. In September, we were joined by our classmate, Walter Kurtz.

THE GEIERS

The most significant arrival of the summer was another Reggie, Rita Sanders. A native of Memphis, she spent her high school years in the Methodist church where James Lawson was pastor. Lawson had been the spiritual leader and trainer for the successful Nashville sit-in movement of 1960, for which the Vanderbilt Board of Trust expelled him from its Divinity School.[4] Imbued with Lawson's daring advocacy, six years later Rita followed him at Vanderbilt by enrolling in the law school, the second Black female to attend, and for a while one of only two Black students at the school. She previously had graduated from Fisk and earned a master's degree in history at the University of Chicago. In 1966 she had returned to Nashville to teach at Tennessee State, but soon felt she could contribute more as a lawyer. When she graduated law school in 1970, she was awarded a Reggie to work at Legal Services of Nashville.

Even though she was only on the staff for a couple of years, Rita would become one of the most significant lawyers ever to work for LSON. As a Black woman, she helped bring down the barriers to Black people and women entering law school. She with others began a demographic shift that was slow but persistent as more women and more Black students were able to enter law school in the years after her and then enter the practice of law. As one might expect was the case with such a pioneer, Rita was fearless, and along with that, she had the advantage of being a first-rate lawyer, as the cases in this section and her later career will reveal. She inspired all of us on the staff to be more aggressive advocates on behalf of our clients, to get it right.

Shortly before she started at LSON, Rita married Paul Geier, who was in the class behind her at Vanderbilt. Three years earlier their marriage in Tennessee would have been illegal because Paul was White and a Tennessee statute prohibited interracial marriage, but in the aptly named 1967 case of *Loving v. Virginia*, the US Supreme Court had declared such laws unconstitutional throughout our country. When Rita began working in the South Nashville office, Paul came as a third-year clerk, and LSON got a twofer.

The September 1970 board minutes reflect some concern about Rita's having drawn up a charter for a daycare center in Edgehill: "Several members of the Board questioned the propriety of such an action, however, after discussing the issue, the general consensus was that this was a proper activity." Their concerns were only about to begin. In the October meeting, Tommy Smith reported on a conversation with the attorney for the local housing authority "concerning our relationship to the Nashville Housing Authority." No case is mentioned in the minutes, but probably this had to do with an administrative complaint, followed by a class action lawsuit that Karen Ennis had filed on behalf of tenants questioning hiring practices at the housing authority; Rita had taken over that case when Karen left.

Being a new organization highly sensitive to criticism, the board wanted to avoid any controversy, and it had not yet come to appreciate the admonition of the Code of Professional Responsibility's requirement that a lawyer must exercise independent judgment on behalf of a client and could not be directed in that representation by a third party.[5] That meant that the board of a Legal Services program should set policy and manage the affairs of the corporation, but must not interfere with the lawyer's representation of her client. The board's acceptance of that admonition would come gradually and would be tested often during the time the Geiers were at LSON, and beyond.

On the national level, things were becoming quite unsettled for Legal Services. After he took office in 1969, President Nixon placed Donald Rumsfeld in charge of OEO. In the summer of 1970, Rumsfeld announced that the Legal Services Program (LSP) would be "decentralized." Under this plan LSP would be under the control of OEO's non-lawyer regional directors around the country. This was anathema. One of the agreements between Sargent Shriver and Lewis Powell when they established the program in 1965 had been that it would be managed by lawyers, not lay people, and that the Canons of Ethics would be enforced. The ABA had resisted the "regionalization" when it had been proposed in 1967, and now the association rose to the occasion again when it was floated once more.

The LSON board was remarkably well-informed about the issue, probably because of Lewis Pride's national involvement, and joined the fray in October, sending its own objections to the Senate committee that would hold hearings on the matter. The *Tennessean* editorialized that Rumsfeld's "attempted crippling of the legal aid program" was "a shocking display of callousness by an administration which asks to be judged by its deeds."[6] The regionalization ultimately failed, but that failure was not the end of hostile actions that only increased in intensity and continued over the next four years.

—————

The LSON board in early 1972, again in a financial crunch, made another push to raise money from law firms for the struggling organization. Lewis Pride, who was by this time Secretary-Treasurer of the board, sent a letter in January to board members Tommy Smith, Billy Howard, Joe Cummings (who had joined the board the previous August), and John Tune assigning each of them eight to ten firms to contact. By the February meeting, they had $1,600 in hand with "the possibility of another $1,000 being collected." In March, some relief came with word that OEO had approved another year of funding, a grant of $103,000. The money had not arrived, however, and the board voted to borrow $22,000 from the Nashville City Bank to meet expenses in the meantime. In May, LSON entered into a contract with the local arm of the Model Cities Program that would fund two attorneys at the LSON office in the Matthew Walker Health Center. One of those lawyers would be David Tarpley, who had been staffing the office first as a student nominally supervised by R. B. J. Campbelle in the South Nashville office and then as an attorney after graduation.

The Model Cities grant did nothing to improve the overall finances of LSON. It was not fungible, but rather required specific staffing and specific work in the Model Cities target area that included the Matthew Walker Health Center. Candish was still projecting a $19,000 deficit for the year. He and the board began trimming expenses. They eliminated staff raises and the attorney position held by Alfred Taylor. Candish asked the board to seek a donation of an "electric typewriter" and "any form books or . . . other legal supplies." In October, after discussion of many financial issues, the board reached a consensus decision to "keep operating on a month to month basis."

The South Nashville office was closed, and Campbelle moved to open a specially funded Legal Services office at Juvenile Court, beginning a new career there that eventually would lead to a position teaching juvenile law at Middle Tennessee State University in its criminal justice program. Paul Geier graduated from law school and also received a Reggie. He and Rita moved a few blocks east into a building adjacent to the Edgehill housing project on Fourteenth Avenue South. They designated it the "law reform office," the first and only time we ever had such a segregation either of location or responsibility.

The Geiers, with after-hours assistance from David Tarpley and law student Walter Kurtz, began filing a series of administrative complaints and federal lawsuits that would have a significant impact on the application of due process and equal protection not only in Nashville but across Tennessee. Their productivity, the quality of their work, and the success of their efforts set a high standard for those lawyers who would follow them, and of course, their actions were not without controversy.

In September, Rita filed an administrative complaint with the US Department of Education on behalf of low-income parents of school children in Nashville who should have been the beneficiaries of Title I of the Elementary and Secondary Education Act of 1965. The complaint pointed out that the funds, which by law should have been spent on programs to address the needs of educationally disadvantaged students, had been spent instead on projects and administrative needs of the whole school system, including the data processing division. In response to her complaint, a federal project review team visited the school district in January 1972 and substantiated the complaints of the Nashville parents. Unfortunately, the enforcement actions of the Office of Education were not as precise as the review, and many of the practices continued, but the flag had been planted by the parents.

In November 1971, the Geiers filed a class action lawsuit in federal court on behalf of Alice Brandon and others against the Tennessee Department of Employment Security alleging that its appeals process violated due process. The department had determined Ms. Brandon to be eligible for $27 a week in benefits, but stopped those benefits without notice or a hearing when the employer appealed its decision to a hearing examiner. The US Supreme Court had ruled for the employee in a similar case from California earlier that year, but the Tennessee department had delayed complying with that ruling. The Attorney General agreed that the department should have complied and did not object when District Judge L. Clure Morton entered an injunction in Ms. Brandon's favor one month after the lawsuit had been filed, restoring benefits for her and more than fifty other people in a similar situation.

One week after the Brandon case, the Geiers, assisted by Walt, filed another federal class action lawsuit, again a due process claim, this time against the Tennessee Department of Safety. Billie Joyce Fell, a University of Tennessee student, had been driving her 1968 Opel station wagon down a street in Knoxville when she was stopped by a police officer who ordered her out of the car, seized the car, and gave her a piece of notebook paper as a receipt. She was not told why it was seized or how to reclaim it or that it would be sold within ten days if she did not file a claim and post a $250 bond with the Department of Safety. It turned out that the car was seized under a section of the new 1971 Tennessee Drug Control Act, though Ms. Fell was not arrested or accused of any crime related to narcotics. In fact, the reason for the stop was this: One day the previous month her boyfriend had borrowed her car, and while he had it, he had sold some marijuana to an undercover police officer. The car then had been put on a "pick up list" pursuant to the new Act.

Ms. Fell learned of the Act's procedure and was allowed to request a hearing *in forma pauperis* without posting the bond, but the department refused to issue the subpoenas she requested. The hearing was scheduled to be held in Nashville, not Knoxville, and that brought her to seek the assistance of the Geiers. The lawsuit was filed before the hearing but did not stop the administrative procedure. At the hearing, the commissioner's representative ordered her car returned, but because the potential impact of the Act was still an issue for Fell and others in the class, the lawsuit went forward. At a preliminary hearing in July, the court issued a temporary restraining order enjoining the State from selling vehicles that had been or would be seized pursuant to the Act.

After a later hearing before a three-judge court, the court issued an opinion holding that the Act violated the Due Process Clause in that it failed to provide the owners sufficient notice after the seizure, placed no burden on the state to prove that the vehicle was used in a violation of the Act, and imposed a cost bond on indigent owners. "The Act thus contains no constitutionally sufficient procedure whereby notice and meaningful opportunity to be heard are afforded owners of seized conveyances."[7] The court ordered the state to return all vehicles still in its possession pursuant to the Act and not to seize any more.

In December 1971, only a month after filing the Fell case, Paul, Rita, and David Tarpley filed the most controversial case yet. In March of that year, the US Supreme Court had ruled unanimously that it is a denial of equal protection for an indigent person to be jailed for not being able to pay a traffic fine. In *Tate v. Short*, the court held that since the traffic law in that Texas case said that the punishment for the offense was a fine, the traffic court could not "convert the fine into a prison term for an indigent defendant without the means to pay his fine."[8] Nevertheless, the general sessions court judges in Nashville who heard traffic cases had persisted in that same practice of jailing indigent defendants, a large number of whom were Black. These were some of the same judges who only a few years earlier had filled the jail with Black students who had participated in the sit-ins and other protests against segregation. There had been discussions between the Legal Services lawyers and the judges about *Tate v. Short* and articles in the morning newspaper critical of the judges' practice, but they continued in their defiance of the Supreme Court ruling. On December 8, the Legal Services lawyers filed a class action case in federal court on behalf of their clients, William Harding and Clarence Lytle.

Judge Morton declined to issue a temporary restraining order releasing the approximately eighty people who were being held in Metro jail, but while doing so, he set a hearing on a preliminary injunction for December 20 and told the lawyers for the State and the lawyer for the Metropolitan Government, "I want to know what your excuse is, or what your justification is for incarcerating these people." Indicative of where he was headed, Morton brushed aside the request for a three-judge panel to rule on the constitutionality of the state statute that authorized the judges' practice. Citing the fact that the Supreme Court had ruled already on the practice, he quipped, "Since that is the situation, one judge can do as much damage as three."[9]

The lawyers got the picture. On the twentieth John McLemore, then a reporter for the afternoon *Banner*, later a prominent Nashville lawyer, wrote that the hearing had been postponed after an early morning meeting between the attorneys and Judge Morton, at which the attorneys told the judge that they anticipated coming to an agreement that would settle the matter. By the next day, the agreement had been reached binding the general sessions judges to compliance with *Tate v. Short*, and Judge Morton signed the agreed-upon order that included a procedure for immediately beginning to implement the order. That should have ended the matter. It did not.

There was a lull over the end of the year holidays, but not for long after. On January 12, Judge Dennis Summers found Jacqueline Parrish guilty of violating two Metro ordinances, fined her $100, and when she said she did not have $100, he sentenced her to jail. He made no effort to ascertain whether the young woman was able to pay her fines, and he did not offer her any time to pay them. Within an hour after this happened, Jacqueline Parrish's mother came to the Legal Services office and asked for help.

Walt, still a third-year law student, was on intake. He talked to the mother and then went to the jail to interview the daughter. When he got back to the office, he called Paul in the Edgehill office, prepared a motion asking that Parrish be released pending a hearing on her ability to pay the fines, as provided in the *Harding* agreed order, then went immediately to find Judge Summers. The judge had taken a recess from hearing cases on his morning docket but was still on the bench talking with several attorneys who were waiting for court to resume when Walt approached the bench and presented his motion. Summers read the motion, balled it up, threw it back at Walt, and told him he was well aware of the federal court ruling, but that Judge Morton was not running his court and that he was going to keep Ms. Parrish jailed.

Later that morning, Rita, Paul, and David filed with the clerk of the federal district court a motion for a temporary restraining order to release Parrish from jail and a petition for a show cause hearing to determine whether Judge Summers, the sheriff, and the warden of the Metro jail, who was holding Ms. Parrish, should be held in contempt of court. Judge Morton was on vacation, so the clerk called Judge Frank Gray Jr., who was at his home in Franklin. Judge Gray told the clerk to give the case file to the Legal Services lawyers to bring to Franklin and to issue a show cause order for the federal marshals to serve on Judge Summers ordering him to come to Franklin for the hearing right away.

David Tarpley describes Judge Gray's home on Lewisburg Pike as "palatial." When everyone arrived, they were ushered into the huge library. Judge Summers was accompanied by Larry Snedeker, the attorney for the Metropolitan Government who had participated in the settlement of the case just a few weeks earlier. Rita gave the file to Judge Gray and they all sat down. Judge Gray began reading the file and said not a word. The silence lasted about fifteen minutes. Finally, Judge Gray looked up at Judge Summers and asked, "Do you have anything to say?" A nervous and perspiring Judge Summers, clearly now impressed with the seriousness of the matter, including the possibility of facing jailtime himself, wisely replied, "Judge Gray, if you let me go, nothing like this will ever happen again."

Judge Gray, a spirited man who on occasion in his courtroom also was known to have thrown things in disgust, including his eyeglasses, and who could scold miscreants with the best of them, merely said the Temporary Restraining Order would issue releasing Jacqueline Parrish. He signed it, telephoned the clerk to record the time of the signing, and gave the signed order to Rita to take back to Nashville for filing. After the deputy clerk certified the order, she gave a certified copy to Rita, who in turn handed it to Walt, giving him the honor of taking it to the jail for his client's release. The jail superintendent obviously had been alerted to the result of the encounter in Franklin, and when Walt arrived with the order in his hand, immediately greeted him, "She's coming right up." One of the local TV stations captured the moment as she emerged from the jail with Walt and raised her fist in the Black Power salute. Several days later, Walt accompanied her to a hearing at which she was allowed to pay off her fine at five dollars a week.

Billy Howard, now president of the LSON board, clearly was disturbed by the situation of having Legal Services lawyers and law students going to war against the judges. The three-year-old organization's support had been tenuous from the beginning, and this would not help win friends. He arranged a meeting the next morning between the judges and the young lawyers, wisely bringing along John Corbitt, who was a long-time good friend of all the judges and was still on the Legal Services staff as senior attorney. Howard wanted to prevent such a conflict from ever happening again.

The meeting did not go well. At one point, Presiding Judge Gale Robinson and Judge Andrew Doyle entered into a colloquy about how proud they were of Judge Summers for saying what he did about federal judges. Judge Doyle asserted, "Nobody's going to run my court either." He softened momentarily, "I'm going to try to do what they want me to do," and then he stiffened again, "but if I don't, then they can just go to hell." Summers, who had made the trip to Judge Gray's library and faced the consequences up close, now with the voice of experience, tried to caution Judge Doyle, but he was not successful.[10]

Doyle continued with a common theme of that day and time: attacking lawyers not from Nashville, "I'm tired of these outsiders coming in here and trying to run my court. I think they ought to go back where they came from." A few months later an opposing lawyer in another case came before the Legal Services board to complain about Rita and Paul. He said he understood they got instructions to cause all this trouble from a secret source in Arkansas, of all places, and he referred to the Reginald Heber Smith lawyers by substituting "Hebrew" for Heber. The implication, of course, being that they must be Jews because no one from around here of our Christian faith would engage in such a troubling practice.

Judge Doyle repeatedly lamented that the General Sessions judges were being "harassed" by Legal Services attorneys. Billy Howard, trying to bring peace and avoid further acrimony, finally asked his charges, "What can the judges do to keep from being harassed by federal courts, Legal Services or whatever?" Though he was searching for reconciliation with the judges, by adopting Judge Doyle's language, he clearly had identified with the traditional White Southern attitude of the time that any effort to enforce constitutionally guaranteed rights constituted harassment. Rita, more the lawyer than either the seasoned judge or the veteran Howard at this moment, pounced on Howard's characterization, "I object to the use of the word harassment. . . . When a person is being represented to obtain his full legal rights, I don't see how that can be harassment."[11] The meeting ended in a standoff.

The *Tennessean* reporter, Tom Ingram, in the same story reported that after the meeting Howard said the Legal Services board "may consider some action at its next meeting to restrict the activities of the agency's attorneys." Ingram stayed with his story and attended the board meeting on the afternoon of January 18. That morning the *Tennessean* ran an editorial, "Legal Services Efforts Merit Support of Public," explaining Jacqueline Parrish's case and praising the lawyers at Legal Services, who the editorial said "recently managed to chip away at the notion that justice must continue to be a heavier burden on the indigent." The board minutes of the meeting that afternoon simply record that there were forty-five minutes of discussion and a motion passed unanimously authorizing the president to "appoint a committee to see if lines of communication and discussion could be reopened with the Judges." Ingram reported the next day that the "board upheld . . . the action its staff took against Metro General Sessions Court judges last week," though "some of the board members were guarded in their support." He observed that "the closest any board member came to such drastic steps [as restricting the attorneys' activities] was expressing concern about the 'finesse' with which last week's action was handled."[12]

The next month Howard reported to the board that "the attempts to establish further meetings with the General Sessions judges have been unproductive as the judges do not seem to feel that further meetings would be useful." Then Candish reported that relations between the office and judges Doyle and Washburn "are very satisfactory at this point." Walt recalled years later, "Judge Summers afterwards always liked me and treated me well as a Legal Services lawyer and when I was Public Defender." A truce, even if uneasy, had been reached after all.

It was more than a benign truce, however. Each set of actors emerged from the fracas with an altered standing. Certainly the young lawyers and law students were emboldened. It is not a small matter for a lawyer to sue a judge, much less a group of judges. Though some of their fellow lawyers may have criticized their effrontery and scoffed at their "lack of finesse," none could doubt their fearlessness nor dispute their complete success for their clients.

One must admire also the support of the board and the executive director. David Candish wanted to be conciliatory, but he never backed down and never failed to take the side of the young lawyers. The board members who were present at the January 18 meeting to consider restricting the activities of the young lawyers were an all-star cast, some of whom had been stalwarts in the effort already: Lewis Pride, Jerry Black, and Harris Gilbert. Other lawyers there were new to the board, but not averse to taking strong stands: Brad Reed and Bob Ziegler, who both would take leadership roles later. The two non-lawyer board members present both had a commitment to zealous advocacy: Mildred Bradford was a leader in the West Nashville Cherokee Citizens Organization that Grayfred Gray had represented earlier and I was representing at the time; Ray Thombs represented the Council of Community Services on the board and was involved in a number of organizations in town trying to improve the lot of low-income people. Though the minutes of the meeting record only the length of the discussion and the motion to form a committee, with this cast of members present, it is not surprising that Tom Ingram could conclude that the sense of the meeting was one of support upholding the actions of the young lawyers.

This whole affair was significant too because of the coverage and editorializing of the *Tennessean*. The coverage of the *Banner* by John McLemore was excellent, and in some cases McLemore got the scoop ahead of Ingram, but the *Tennessean* added the support of its editorial page, which would not happen at the *Banner*, given its longtime ownership and editorial stance.[13] Though the morning paper had run editorials of support for our organization many times before, this was the first time it had editorialized about a specific case, and it had done so strategically on the morning of the board meeting.

For the general sessions judges, it was a bitter pill and an affront to their fiefdoms, but it did not end their sense of proprietary entitlement. Each one continued to use the possessive pronoun to refer to the court over which he presided: "*my* court." And each had a sense of independence that came from the fact that he had been elected, seeing his responsibility as being to the people who elected him, not to the decision of a federal court, not even the Supreme Court. For all the bluster, however, the die had been cast, and little by little, pieces of the parochial system would be chipped away and constitutional principles would be injected into the practice of those courts.[14]

Rita and Paul would be at LSON only a few months after *Harding v. Doyle*. Friends in the Pacific Northwest persuaded them that it was a more congenial place for a married interracial couple, whereas in Nashville they were the only married interracial couple in town and possibly in the state. Many people here had a hard time accepting departure from what had been very strong Southern tradition and law. These people felt that in striking down the miscegenation laws, the Supreme Court had violated God's law that had separated the races since the time of Noah. It would be several more years before Nashville would become the mostly cosmopolitan place it is today.

In the years that followed their departure, Rita quite naturally maintained contacts in Tennessee with family in Memphis and a brother, Ed Sanders, who is a prominent minister in Nashville. She also continued to be involved in the lawsuit George Barrett filed on her behalf in 1968 when she was teaching at TSU seeking the desegregation and equitable funding of higher education in Tennessee, a case that finally was settled with a consent decree in 2001. Rita returned to Tennessee for a time after her retirement in 2007 when she was invited to be a Senior Fellow in the Howard H. Baker Jr. Center for Public Policy at the University of Tennessee, and while here she served on the board of the Tennessee Justice Center. Her varied career before that had included Executive Director of Evergreen Legal Services in Seattle, General Counsel for the Appalachian Regional Council, and Associate General Counsel for Hearings and Appeals at the Social Security Administration.

CASES AND CONTROVERSIES

With the Geiers gone, the one-year veteran Tarpley became the lead lawyer in several more federal cases. Just after I finished law school, I had a divorce client, Lovie Jean Brown, who could not file a divorce action against her estranged, unemployed, non-supporting husband because even when filing under a pauper's oath, a Tennessee statute required that when a woman filed a divorce, she had to pay a $10 filing fee, and Mrs. Brown did not have $10. Her only income for herself and her children was a welfare check of $46 per month. The US Supreme Court the year before in the case of *Bodie v. Connecticut* had ruled that a state could not deny a person access to court to dissolve a marriage simply because of that person's inability to pay court costs, but Tennessee had persisted nevertheless, and the local clerk felt obligated to follow the state's statute.[15]

A few weeks before that, Walt had faced the same barrier with one of his divorce clients. When the circuit court clerk refused to accept his client's divorce petition, he filed a complaint in chancery court seeking to enforce the ruling in *Bodie*. At the preliminary injunction hearing before Chancellor Ned Lentz, Walt got nowhere with his citation to the Supreme Court case. The chancellor denied his motion and sternly informed him, "Mr. Kurtz, Justice Burger can run his court up there and rule however he wants to, but I'm running my court down here." With that warning, when Walt returned to the office, we decided he should nonsuit the case and that we would go instead to federal court the next time we faced that issue. The day would come when Chancery Court would be a friendlier forum for constitutional issues, but in 1972 it was not there yet.[16]

My client, Lovie Jean Brown, was the next case presenting the issue. When the clerk refused to accept her divorce petition, David and I prepared the federal complaint, and the week I was taking the bar exam, David filed a class action lawsuit on her behalf in federal district court, asking the court to declare the Tennessee statute unconstitutional and order the clerk to allow our client to file. Judge Gray on reviewing the case pronounced that it would be superfluous to have a hearing because the defendants could not deny that the statute was unconstitutional. In his final order, he rejected the state's contention that the class should be limited to women. Under the statute, men had been prohibited entirely from using the pauper's oath when filing a divorce action. They had to pay the complete filing fee and did not get the special $10 deal women had. When the State asked for time to work out the implementation, Judge Gray refused, saying the State had dragged its feet for over a year and that was enough.

Hospitals were next. In the fall of 1972, Tarpley, this time with newly admitted lawyers Walt, Tom Daniel, and me, filed another federal class action lawsuit. This one challenged the refusal of Hubbard Hospital and General Hospital to accept indigents as patients unless they had resided in Davidson County for at least six months. The Metropolitan Government granted funding to both hospitals to provide care to indigents but added as a condition the six-month residency requirement. The fact that there were two hospitals funded for this purpose was a holdover from the days, not far distant in the past, when one hospital was for "whites" and the other for "coloreds." The complaint in this case did not have to do with racial segregation, but addressed another civil rights issue: the right to travel and move about the country. It relied on *Shapiro v. Thompson*, a US Supreme Court case prohibiting durational residency requirements for welfare recipients, and on a federal district court case in Arizona that had enjoined a durational residency requirement in the provision of healthcare.[17] Our complaint requested a temporary restraining order (TRO) so that the named plaintiff could get prenatal and birthing care.

Ironically, our named plaintiff in the class action lawsuit, Pavana Kodali, was a woman who had moved to Davidson County two months earlier to take a job as a nurse at Hubbard Hospital. Since she was pregnant when she arrived, Hubbard, reflecting the practice of many employers in those days, had prohibited her from beginning work until after the birth of her child, which was imminent by the time she came to us. Because she did not have her job yet and had no other support, she was indigent and could not pay. Because she had not lived in the county for six months, Metro would not pay Hubbard for her care, so her future employer would not accept her as a patient.

Judge Morton solved the problem for Mrs. Kodali right away by granting the TRO, and after the final hearing two weeks later, he solved the problem for other people who might be in the same situation. He found that the Metro residency requirement for an indigent's healthcare at Hubbard or General violated the Equal Protection Clause, and he permanently enjoined its enforcement.

The welfare department was a constant problem in those days. During the same month we were admitted to practice, Walt and I filed another federal class action lawsuit, the first of several we would file against the Tennessee Department of Welfare and its commissioner, Fred Friend, because of illegal delays in determining eligibility for much needed grants to people who applied for them. The state received funding from the federal government for the program, Aid to the Permanently and Totally Disabled (APTD). One of the requirements in the federal regulations governing the program was that decisions on eligibility be made in a reasonable time, no more than sixty days from the date of application. The department consistently violated the regulations and took much longer than sixty days to process applications.

One of our named plaintiffs was Elizabeth Frierson, a disabled widow who had waited 124 days for her application to be processed, with no action. For a while she had received temporary assistance from Metro, but that was time-limited and the time had expired. She had no income, was behind on her rent, and depended on charity for food. Walt and I asserted in the complaint that Commissioner Friend and his deputies had a surplus of money in the department and could hire sufficient staff to operate the program legally and efficiently, but instead had "chosen to operate said department in a penurious and inefficient manner which prevents them from complying with their own standards" and with the mandatory federal regulations.

Judge Gray did not sign the temporary restraining order we submitted, but he did set a hearing for four days later and ordered the welfare department to appear and show cause why it should not be enjoined from violating the federal regulations. Before the appointed day, Assistant State Attorney General Bart Durham was quoted in the *Tennessean* as saying, "I think we're going to settle. . . . The department couldn't defend the lawsuit," and sure enough that happened by an agreed order.[18] The state was given ten days to act on Mrs. Frierson's case and forty-five days to get its house in order and begin processing all applications on time. The order further provided that future applicants be informed of the time limit when they applied and advised of their right to a hearing if the standards were not met. For class members whose cases had not been acted on promptly, the state was required to pay benefits retroactively to the date of any successful application. The indefensible Commissioner Friend was not happy, and he later would strike back at us.

———————

The commissioner was not the only person unhappy. In the early 1970s many complaints came from our brethren at the bar as reflected in the board minutes. A lawyer in an office by himself complained that one of the law students at Legal Services "may be involved in handling a case which has the possibility of a contingent fee." Another attorney complained about a Legal Services lawyer filing "cross actions on behalf of defendants in automobile accident cases." A collections lawyer questioned the eligibility of a Legal Services client represented by John Corbitt; he was objecting to the fact that Corbitt had filed a slow-pay motion so that the certifiably poor client could pay the judgement by installments. In a divorce case, the opposing lawyers asked that the Legal Services attorney not be allowed to represent a poor woman because she owned five acres of unimproved scrub land in a rural county.

As the complaints mounted, the Nashville Bar Association became involved on behalf of the complainers. The chair of the association's domestic relations court committee wrote complaining about a special non-contested divorce docket that had been set up to handle the numerous cases brought by Legal Services attorneys. The purpose of the docket had been "to be sure that the other members of the bar were not kept waiting while large numbers of Legal Services cases were tried." The non-contested cases were heard by a special judge, not the regular domestic relations judges, "to keep from inconveniencing lawyers with fee-paying clients and to keep from holding them up," but many of the very lawyers the process was meant to help resented what they perceived to be special treatment for the Legal Services lawyers, and they were afraid it would hurt their own business.

The president of the bar association, Thomas Higgins, attended the Legal Services board meeting, and, in an effort to head off some of the complaints, suggested that the board "attempt to give information to members of the Bar as to the [income and case-type] guidelines under which the organization operated." He agreed to try to have this information sent out to the entire membership in one of the bar association's regular mailings. The hope was that this would quell some of the misunderstandings and the suspicion that Legal Services was taking away paying business from lawyers who relied on the small fees the Legal Services cases may have generated. It did not.

———————

In April 1972, John Corbitt submitted his resignation to LSON and accepted a position as an administrative law judge with the Social Security Administration. He had been executive director, or acting director, it had not always been clear, for twenty months and then senior attorney for the rest of the time. In spite of policy disagreements, he had been a helpful mentor and valuable interpreter. When board members and lawyers met with the general sessions judges in an effort to calm the situation after *Harding v. Doyle*, Corbitt was the one who could speak to Judge Doyle as an old friend ("Come on, Andy, you know you can't do that.") and try to explain to him that Legal Services lawyers were simply representing qualified clients with legitimate constitutional claims and were not there to harass the judges. Those of us who were new lawyers or clerks relied on Corbitt for direction in state court cases. I remember his sitting with me when as a third-year student I was trying a case in chancery court. A man of experience, at one point he told me to sit down and shut up when he saw that the Chancellor was going to rule in our favor. Several months after he had left Legal Services and Walt and I had passed the bar examination, we asked John Corbitt to introduce us to the Tennessee Supreme Court.

———————

With the money saved from no longer having the expense of Corbitt's salary, Candish was able to hire Walt and Tom Daniel as staff attorneys, each at a salary of $850 per month. I had received a Reggie for 1972 through 1974 so my salary was paid by that grant. The transition from third-year clerk to attorney was almost seamless. We just kept doing the same things, like Tarpley the year before us. The difference was that now we could sign our own pleadings and go to courts of record without accompaniment.

In addition to new lawyers, LSON now had a new location for its downtown office. Metro government had notified the board some months before that it would not renew our lease for space in the Stahlman Building. We never knew definitely whether or not our eviction was related to the *Kodali* case, *Harding v. Doyle*, or any other cases we had brought against Metro officials. The coincidence certainly was there. We would be allowed back in the building later under a different administration, but for now we were out. After several dead ends, Candish obtained space in the Sudekum Building at the corner of Sixth Avenue and Church Street, an art deco relic still with elevator operators and antiquated accommodations, later demolished for modern condominiums.

In the sixth-floor space LSON rented, one window would have an air conditioning unit in it and under the next window would be a radiator. When the space was remodeled for LSON and carved up into offices, that meant that one office would have only air conditioning and the next would have only heat. The remedy for this impediment was that between such offices the separating wall was not built all the way to the ceiling. Needless to say, this two-foot gap did not solve the problem. It afforded little warmth in winter to the lawyer with the air conditioner and vice versa for the neighbor in the next office during the heat of the summer. An additional problem was that the only way to ensure client confidentiality was to be sure that lawyers in adjoining offices did not have client interviews at the same time. And anyone who needed to concentrate on anything had to retreat to the library.

The library. Here begins a saga that will take us to yet another transition for the young organization and bring yet more instability. LSON had very few law books of its own, but the Nashville Bar Association maintained a library on the third floor of the Stahlman Building, and while LSON was in that building, access to a library was not an issue. When LSON moved to the Sudekum Building, however, convenient access became an issue, at least in David Candish's mind, and he determined to build a library there. Never mind that to this point most of the major litigation and legal research had been handled by lawyers in the Edgehill and North Nashville offices and by third-year law students with easy access to the Vanderbilt library. He wanted a proper library at our downtown office.

Candish sought and received a special grant of $5,000 from the Atlanta OEO office to buy books, but in May and June of 1972 he purchased more than the $5,000 would buy. He spent about $11,000 with West Publishing Company and more with the Lawyers Co-op. He set aside one room of the Sudekum Building office with a plaque that read "State Library" and another room was designated "Federal Library." The staff was appalled at the allocation of resources.

In September, the board learned about the purchases. This was after it had spent a good part of its August meeting trying to deal with how to reduce a projected deficit of between $23,000 and $31,000 for the year. Bob Ziegler, the crusty collections lawyer who was treasurer of the board, after "considerable discussion . . . moved that LSON return the entire federal library to West Publishing Company and the American Law Reports series to Lawyers Cooperative Publishing Company and make no more installment payments." The motion carried unanimously, and Ziegler told both publishers in no uncertain terms that they should come get their books. West Publishing Company hired Vanderbilt law professor Harold "Hal" Bigham to represent its interest, and he came to the next board meeting in October. Bigham insisted that "Candish had at least apparent authority to make the purchases and [LSON] is therefore bound on the purchase contracts." The board "after considerable discussion" decided to take no action on Bigham's request, thus leaving in effect its previous position, "and Mr. Bigham left the meeting."

After more financial discussion, Candish was asked to leave the meeting. The president, Billy Howard, reported to the board "that there had come to his attention certain apparent serious deficiencies in Mr. Candish's discharging of his responsibilities." He laid out several particulars, including "allegations by members of the staff that Mr. Candish is simply not working." Again "after substantial discussion," Howard was authorized to investigate and was given "sole authority to make any change in personnel."

Howard did not have a report for the board at the November meeting because he was waiting for an evaluation from the Atlanta regional office of OLS. Candish was present and brought several funding items for the board to consider as it continued to wrestle with the precarious financial situation. The battle of the books escalated as the board voted to notify Hal Bigham and notify the moving and storage company holding the books that LSON would no longer be responsible for the moving and storage charges. With that, any record of the books matter or Candish's status is lost for three months. There are no board minutes preserved for what must have been pivotal meetings (executive sessions?) in December and January. My memory is that Dan Bradley, the skillful OLS regional director, who later would be named president of the Legal Services Corporation, came to Nashville, had lunch with Hal Bigham, worked out and funded a compromise, and we kept the books.

We did not keep Candish. The next written record is board minutes of the February 14, 1973, meeting at which Billy Howard announced that he had hired Thomas Warren, a lawyer from Dallas, as executive director of LSON. The board accepted David Candish's resignation effective February 28 and voted to give Warren a contract through December 31 of that year. He lasted through May.

Warren was a strange choice. Candish, who at that point did not have the confidence of the board, nevertheless was the person who recommended Warren and vouched for him. Warren had practiced law in Dallas for ten years and then worked at the Legal Services program there, where he and Candish had been colleagues. In his first meeting with the staff, Warren introduced himself to us by saying "some people say I am a little Napoleon . . ." Things went downhill from there.

Warren said he still had law practice matters and personal domestic issues that required him to fly back to Dallas for several days at a time, and consequently he often was not in the office. He did not apply for admission to the Tennessee Bar. The staff saw him as an impediment to its work. The relationship became hostile. One day when he had come back to the office from a trip to Dallas, Warren put out a memo to the staff saying that his briefcase was missing and that the unfriendly staff member who took it must return it immediately or the whole staff would face the consequences. Later that day the receptionist took a phone call from the airport reporting that his briefcase had been left at the Delta ticket counter that morning.

Sometime before its May meeting, the Board must have become aware of the problems. There is no mention of any concerns about Warren in the April minutes, but at a special meeting on May 21, the Board received reports from two people who had looked into the matter. Harris Gilbert reported on discussions with members of the staff about Warren's performance. In addition, Junius Allison, now a professor and head of the legal clinic at Vanderbilt, who was not a member of the board, was in attendance, and he was asked by the board to give his insights and impressions. Allison had come to the law school in 1971, after retiring from his position as executive director of NLADA. He had been involved with legal aid work since 1945, first with the Legal Aid Bureau in Chicago and then with NLADA. He had attended several meetings of the LSON board as an interested observer since coming to Nashville, and as elder statesman and mentor, he was influential and had a good working relationship with the staff. Just that spring he had hired Gordon Bonnyman to supervise Vanderbilt law students at LSON.

It is not clear whether Allison had acted on his own because of his concern about the situation or acted at the request of the board, but he informed the board that "morale at the downtown office had not improved and was not improving." Allison had in fact "confronted Mr. Warren," who assured him that his performance would improve, but Allison concluded that it did not. Soon after that, Warren told Allison that he planned to resign. After what the minutes describe as "a detailed discussion," board members Harris Gilbert, Brad Reed, and Lionel Barrett were appointed, together with Allison, to meet with Warren and if appropriate, to terminate his employment. In case of termination, they were further empowered to hire an interim director. Warren resigned, but the committee instead of naming an interim director, for the time being gave Walt responsibility for the downtown office and Tarpley responsibility for the North Nashville office.

The winter of our discontent was over. Things got better right away with David and Walt managing things, and in the late summer the board named Walt director. A new era had begun.

CHAPTER 4

Wide-Ranging Advocacy

1973-1976

> If we are to keep our democracy, there
> must be one commandment: Thou shalt
> not ration justice.
>
> —JUDGE LEARNED HAND, 1951

Walter Cotton Kurtz had been a lawyer for nine months when he became
executive director, but despite his lack of experience as a lawyer, the board
recognized his leadership, courage, and commitment. They may have
missed with Candish and then Warren, but this time they got it right.

Walt had graduated from The Citadel and studied political science
at the University of Tennessee before accepting a commission in the US
Army as a second lieutenant. He had been awarded four bronze stars for
his meritorious service, achievement, and "heroism in ground combat"
in Vietnam. Coupled with his valor was a commitment to high ideals of
civil liberties, leading him to designate one-half of his combat pay to his
family and the other half to the American Civil Liberties Union. After
his return from Vietnam, during his first year of law school, he traveled
to Washington with other veterans and threw his medals over a fence at
the Capitol in protest against the war.

We all were young, it was a time of tension in our country, and in
most cases our parents were not entirely comfortable with what we were

doing. We had attached ourselves to a different view of social and political responsibility from theirs. In Walt's case, the difference was illustrated by a story he told us about a jocular encounter with his father during a trip back home to Elmira, New York, after he began working at LSON. His father was an engineer with General Electric, and his mother was the chairwoman of the Chemung County Republican Party. One day during the visit, some of his father's buddies had gathered in the family's den before going to play golf. When Walt, who while growing up had been known by his middle name, walked into the room to say hello to these old friends, his father mockingly reintroduced him to the guys, "This is my son Cotton; he works for Roosevelt."

Walt's becoming director at Legal Services was a New Deal of its own for all of us, and it did not take one hundred days. Brad Reed, who was president of the board when Walt was named director, was interviewed in the next month by Kenneth Jost of the *Tennessean* for an article that ran on September 21, 1973. The article first walks through the administrative turmoil and staff discontent that had plagued LSON earlier in the year. Then Jost reports on the changes since Walt took over, particularly the improved relations with the NBA. Reed is quoted as saying that LSON "is in the best shape it's ever been in" and that the board was "really pleased" with Walt's administration.[1]

At the August 1973 meeting of the board of directors, Walt had introduced to the board Randall Hylton, whom he had hired as the accountant for LSON. For the first time the organization had an accountant on staff. The finances no longer would be managed out of the executive director's desk drawer by him and an untrained secretary. Hylton, who had come to Nashville like so many others to pursue a music career, remained on the staff for several years, brought financial stability, and provided great entertainment at staff events before going on to become a nationally known bluegrass singer and writer. Randall also functioned as office manager and having him on staff had the added benefit of freeing Walt from many administrative tasks, allowing him to spend more time on cases.

THE SAVILLE CASE

In 1973, as had been the case for many years, more than a thousand people with varying kinds of developmental disabilities were confined at Clover

Bottom Hospital for the Mentally Retarded in Nashville. One person described it as a "custodial warehouse." The patients received little or no rehabilitative services. Most of them had been committed to the institution without anything more than the word of a family member or county worker, no hearing, no consideration of their needs, no consideration of their rights. A former staff psychologist at Clover Bottom, hoping something could be done to remedy this horrible situation, contacted NLADA. He was particularly concerned about one young child there, Amy Lynn Saville, and wanted to see if legal action could be brought to establish her right to treatment. NLADA referred him to us, and Walt agreed to visit her.

This was a new and developing area of the law and it would be difficult to bring a case that would convince a court to order remedies. It was uncharted territory. It was obvious to Walt from his first visit to Clover Bottom that this would be a difficult case in other ways as well. He saw scores of people milling about in open areas, sleeping in beds a mere two feet apart, many of the patients with vomit and fecal matter on them. To clean the patients, the staff sometimes would just hose them down. Some of the residents were kept in cages. Others were chained to radiators and still others just sat rocking back and forth for hours on end. Reflecting back more than forty years later, Walt concludes, "Outside of my experiences in Vietnam, the conditions in there were the most disturbing thing I have seen in my life."

In the course of his visits, several present and former employees of the institution approached Walt, stated they had personal knowledge of deplorable conditions, and asked to act as next friends of other residents they knew were suffering special deprivation. The staff members who came to Walt were putting their employment in jeopardy, but some of them were risking even more. Several were conscientious objectors doing alternative service as orderlies, and if they were fired, their CO status could have been jeopardized, and they might end up in jail. They nevertheless had the courage to step up.

Next friends were necessary for two reasons. One, because of the incompetence or disability of the resident, and two, because in this case the residents' interests were adverse to that of their normal guardians or family members. Amy Lynn Saville was an orphan minor ward of the state. Since the complaint about her treatment would be against the state, there would have been a legal conflict, as well as a logical contradiction, to having the state purport to represent her interest. Other patients who would become plaintiffs were minors or adults whose families had placed them in Clover Bottom and despite the horrible conditions wanted them to remain: again, a conflict of interest.

In April, Walt and I, together with private attorney Larry Woods, filed a class action lawsuit in federal district court alleging that the patients' constitutional rights had been violated in their commitment to the institution and were being violated further by the state's failure to provide adequate care and training while they were there. Soon after the suit was filed, Gordon Bonnyman was hired and joined us as counsel. Walt and Gordon did almost all the work on the case. As they conducted their investigation and developed the case, they were aided in great part by Floyd Dennis, Director of the Institute on Youth and Social Development at Peabody College's Kennedy Center and longtime advocate for people with disabilities. Floyd met with them numerous times, guided them along in this field that was new to them, introduced them to people at the Association for Retarded Citizens (ARC), and helped them round up experts. But there was more to the case than the lawsuit.

Although we recognized the precarious position of the social workers and orderlies who bravely had come forward as next friends, we did not realize then that by filing the lawsuit, we, too, were putting our professional standing in jeopardy. Within days of our filing the lawsuit, Hayes Cooney, the assistant attorney general handling the case, began filing motions seeking to disqualify the next friends and thus undermine the lawsuit on the grounds that the residents already had guardians or family members who (with one exception) did not want the lawsuit to go forward. When the court did not rule on these motions, Cooney picked up another stick. On July 20, he filed a complaint with the NBA charging us with misconduct for representing the residents without permission of their guardians or family members.

Strange as it seems now when such complaints are handled at the state level by the Board of Professional Responsibility, the local bars were the initial arbiters then. Following the usual procedure, the president of the NBA, Louis Farrell, appointed a committee made up of Leon Ruben, Mitch Grissim, and chaired by Dick Lansden to investigate Cooney's complaint. The choice of Dick Lansden to lead the investigation was not a casual selection. It will be recalled from Chapter 2 that he was the lawyer who in 1968 had sent a letter to every member of the NBA urging them to vote against the Legal Services program and asserting that lawyers participating in the program could be "subject . . . to charges of unprofessional conduct." Now he had an opportunity to prove the truth of his prophesy, and he would do it.

When we, the charged lawyers, sought to learn the charges against us and the specific allegations of misconduct, Lansden sent a curt nine-line letter back to us citing no section of the Code of Professional Responsibility. He wrote that our misconduct was "disclosed" in the affidavits Cooney had filed in federal court to support his pending motions to disqualify the next friends. Lansden's statement was curt, but the process was not. The bar association investigation and deliberation would drag on for more than a year. The federal lawsuit, however, went on apace. On September 18, Judge Morton issued a one-word ruling in answer to Cooney's several motions to disqualify the next friends: "Denied."

On December 18, a three-judge court consisting of district judges Morton and Gray and court of appeals judge Harry Phillips heard arguments on that part of the complaint challenging the constitutionality of the state statute governing admissions. Walt told the court that while the state claimed that all 1,100 residents were there "voluntarily," the claim was "an utter fiction." He argued that before admission there needed to be a meaningful hearing with an effective advocate for the perspective admittee. Though their parents or guardians may not want to care for them, they should not be sentenced "to a lifetime of incarceration" without due process protections.[2]

Walt and Gordon cited numerous examples from the state's own records in which the justifications for admission seemed more like "the shunting aside of those who are deemed misfits." The justification for the "voluntary" admission of a thirty-six-year-old woman was her husband's statement that she was "fighting, stubborn and uncooperative." A boy was accused of fighting with his brothers. A twenty-three-month-old girl was described by her father in the admission record as "tending to violence." Walt and Gordon argued that there needed to be some protection from unwarranted institutionalization, some process that would provide an independent check on the decision to commit the unfortunate child or adult.

Less than three months later, the three-judge panel issued a short *per curiam* decision finding that under the state's statute a person could be committed to Clover Bottom "without restriction" and that the commitment "is potentially of lifelong duration." The court held that "where individual liberty is at stake to the extent it is in the present case, it is absolutely essential that such confinement be preceded by adequate procedural safeguards," yet it was "obvious that the 'voluntary' commitment procedures of T.C.A. 33–501 fall far short of those required by due process." The court held the statute unconstitutional and enjoined further admission pursuant to it.[3] It was a monumental decision, the first of its kind in the nation. The first round was over.

In May 1974, Dick Lansden's committee finally made its report. Whether the committee was negligently ignorant of Judge Morton's denial and the three judges' decision or deliberately chose to ignore them, we do not know. The committee members righteously came to their own conclusion, finding that "The bringing of such litigation . . . without being properly employed so to do . . . constitutes . . . unprofessional conduct of the worst sort." Careless of the law, the committee cited as applicable a provision of the Canons of Ethics that had been replaced in Tennessee four years earlier by the adoption of the Code of Professional Responsibility, and it proceeded to recommend that the NBA reprimand us for our actions. Then it paternalistically opined that the board of Legal Services "should exercise a greater supervision . . . and assure that this sort of thing is discontinued and does not happen again."

On receiving the committee's report, John Hollins, president of the NBA, forwarded a copy to LSON board president Brad Reed. Reed, a brilliant corporate lawyer, was not shy about expressing himself. He did not wait to consult with other LSON board members but immediately fired back a letter with his own views: "The only printable response to the Report and the recommendation contained therein is one of incredulity." He sent Hollins a copy of the *per curiam* decision of the three-judge federal court and averred, "the attorneys who were the object of the special committee's investigation are deserving of commendation, not condemnation." Signaling his resolve, he warned, "the last thing in the world I desire is a fight with the Bar Association."

After that, there was radio silence from the NBA for more than three months. Then in August the NBA board voted unanimously, with three abstentions, to approve a resolution stating, "The complaint was found to be without merit and it was decided that no action should be taken thereon." Round Two was over.

Back to the case. The significance of the *Saville* case was underlined during the summer of 1974 when the US Department of Justice (DOJ) sought permission of the court to participate as *amicus curiae* "with the right to conduct discovery, call witnesses, file motions and briefs and present evidence and arguments." The department deemed it potentially a landmark case, "The U.S. believes this case offers a unique opportunity to establish and define the constitutional rights of mentally retarded individuals, and that the interests of the U.S. and the public interest should be represented." In a hearing on August 22, Walt, with barely concealed relief, told Judge Morton that he and other plaintiffs' lawyers would welcome the assistance of the Justice Department. Dashing our hopes, Judge Morton was not persuaded. It was too late. The case had been going on for more than a year, and he did not want to start over. He ruled against the *amicus* intervention, stating that he had utmost confidence in Mr. Kurtz and Mr. Bonnyman and that they did not need the assistance of the US Justice Department. After that unwelcomed praise, when they got out in the hall, Walt and Gordon, only two years out of law school and never having undertaken any case approaching the complexity of this one, looked at each other and broke down laughing, though they felt like crying.

With the application of the DOJ, however, the state realized it was in the crosshairs of the federal government, and the plaintiffs' lawyers realized they would have to go it alone in a very complex case. It was in the interest of both sides to settle the case, and they did within a month. The comprehensive agreement reflected the good influence of Floyd Dennis and his years of advocacy. The parties submitted a proposed order to Judge Morton establishing for all the residents of Clover Bottom a right to habilitative services and a right to receive those services in the least restrictive alternative environment possible. Judge Morton signed the order on September 18 and gave the state four months to submit a plan implementing the order. When the plan was completed, the judge approved it and incorporated it into his order.[4] Within months the case had been cited in law review articles and in the decisions of other courts around the country. It was a significant influence in the transformation of care for people with developmental disabilities in our society. It meant the beginning of a new life for many of the people in Clover Bottom, and it meant a much different system would emerge for many who came after them.

Over the next couple of years, Walt and Gordon handled more than thirty cases for people with intellectual disabilities or mental health issues. Some were commitment cases, others were habeas corpus actions to get the person out of an inappropriate institution. Some were to stop inappropriate and unwanted mental health treatments such as electroshock therapy. They educated judges about the rights of the mentally ill and infuriated a number of doctors who had no appreciation for due process and the legal principle that there are civil liberties issues involved when you lock up a person for mental health treatment. One doctor, who with his son owned a mental health hospital in a neighboring county, was so outraged when Walt filed suit on behalf of one of his patients, that he made a diagnosis of Walt over the telephone, "Young man, you are the one with the problem here. This compulsion you have about the legal rights of the mentally ill is so obsessive and unbalanced that you are the one who ought to get treatment."

Not everyone agreed. The persuasiveness of Walt and Gordon's cases led to the state's rewriting of the mental health statutes and a revolution in the rights of people with mental health problems in Tennessee. As results of their groundbreaking work, they were asked to teach a seminar at Vanderbilt Law School on mental health law, which they did, Walt for one year and Gordon for two. Because the developments in this area of the law were so new, there was no textbook, so they developed the course from scratch. To help doctors adjust to the new interaction between the legal model and the medical model, Walt was asked to be a consultant on medical ethics at Vanderbilt Medical School, which he did for a year. They both were doing what Legal Services was designed to do, giving voice to the forgotten and the powerless. Their impact was significant, and others took up the cause behind them.

Ten years after the Saville case, the *Tennessean* ran a follow-up feature article on Amy Lynn, by then a young woman of twenty-two, "the young woman who has become an integral part of the history of mentally retarded people in Tennessee." Jan Shoemaker, who had become Amy Lynn's foster mother, recalled the day in 1976 when she first met

Amy Lynn at Clover Bottom, "She cried and begged 'please take me home.'" Now things were different. At the time of the feature article, Amy Lynn was in a day program at New Horizons, a workshop for people with developmental disabilities, but she was preparing to move up yet another step to a group home. Her case had opened the door to a plethora of programs. Charles McLeroy of Residential Services, Inc., noted in the story that whereas before Amy Lynn's federal lawsuit there were only six community programs in Tennessee, ten years later there were a hundred.[5]

BACK AT THE OFFICE

One would think that while conducting such a massive federal class action lawsuit as *Saville*, the young lawyers involved would have had time for nothing else. Perhaps that should have been the case, but it was not. For one thing there was ongoing intake and the demands that came every day. The phone calls from new people did not stop and each day more people would show up at the office in distress. Walt even established Thursday night intake for people who could not come to the office during the day. The lawyers continued to take on the usual divorce cases, detainer warrants, juvenile court matters, and that was not all. This was before the days of case priorities. We took whatever came in the door, as long as it was a legitimate case. Poor Gordon suffered the consequences of the Thursday night intake and the open-door practice in two cases back-to-back. In one, however, he got his revenge on Walt. In the other he helped us see the light.

Because of family commitments and other involvements, scheduling staff to cover the Thursday night intake sometimes was a problem. There was much trading back and forth. Late one afternoon, Walt, who had been scheduled to be the lawyer on duty that night, remembered that he had a softball game, and he did not want to let the team down, so he asked Gordon to fill in for him, which Gordon did, not wanting to let the LSON team down. As it happened, one of the people who came in that night seeking help was a young man who wanted a name change. We long ago had agreed that handling matters like name changes was not the best use of our time given the other demands, but with our open door policy, Gordon felt obligated to proceed. He interviewed the young man, got the necessary preliminary information, and then asked him what he would like his new name to be. The young man earnestly gave the whimsical title and name of a small furry animal. Too far in to stop now, Gordon drew up the petition and told him to be at Probate Court the next morning at 9:00 for his hearing.

Gordon would have his revenge: he listed Walter C. Kurtz as the attorney on the petition. Knowing the convenient procedure that Probate Court had established for name change petitions, he duly filed it the next morning as soon as the clerk's office opened, asked for a hearing at the top of the docket that morning, hurried back the six blocks to our office in the Sudekum Building, presented the file to Walt, and told him his client was waiting for him in front of Judge Luton. Not surprisingly, the young man with the whimsical identifier got one of the last name changes of that sort we handled. We still did not develop a priorities statement, and we still had an open door policy, but we made a rule that we would not handle name changes, except in connection with another case or for very serious reasons.

Filing name change cases had been common for us in those days. Filing replevins was not, but it fell to Gordon's lot to be asked to replevy a mule.[6] An elderly man living in Northwest Davidson County had a mule he kept in a shed on his property. He used it to plow gardens and do odd jobs in the neighborhood, but unfortunately the mule had a habit of getting out and making a meal out of some of those same gardens. In retaliation one neighbor locked the mule in his garage and refused to give him back, at which point the mule owner came to see us for help. Unaccustomed as he was, Gordon filed a replevin action for the return of the mule, and he was successful. Case closed.

Not so fast. This was a persistent animal, stubborn as a mule. He got out again, and again a neighbor caught him, locked him up, and refused to return him. The mule owner came back to the smart young lawyer who had done such a good job for him before. This time, after a few moments of soul searching, Gordon decided he was going to make his own policy about case acceptance: we would replevy a mule once, but we would not replevy the same mule twice. He turned down the mule owner's request. Gordon's stubborn stand against taking the case would lead to some thoughtful consideration about priorities and case acceptance, not only at home, but also in the broader legal aid network where demand was great and "what case to take" was a common issue. Soon after his experience, Gordon wrote an article for an NLADA journal entitled, "How many times must we replevy a mule?" pleading for case acceptance policies with strategic direction. The mule became a rather homely part of the serious national discussion that eventually led to more legal aid organizations adopting case priorities.

Mules aside, there were larger issues for all of us to deal with, including housing for low-income people. In July 1973, Tom Daniel, Tarpley, and I filed a federal class action on behalf of people who had been denied public housing because they were too poor. The local housing authority had adopted a quota system known as "rent ranges" in response to a 1971 directive from the US Department of Housing and Urban Development (HUD). The aim of HUD was a commendable one: to get a more diverse population in public housing. The problem was that because there was no "maintenance of effort" requirement in the directive, no requirement that the same number of poor people be housed under the new plan as there had been before, it meant that the result was defeating the primary purpose for which Congress had established public housing: to provide housing for *low*-income people. The case lasted nearly three years until the court ruled in 1976 that HUD had not legally initiated the rent range policy at the time of our class members' applications and therefore the policy could not be used to exclude them from housing. In the interim, however, HUD had corrected its administrative mistakes, and the court found that the formulation of the rent ranges plan was within the discretion of HUD under the Housing Act. We had won the battle for our clients, but going forward, the scheme would stand.

COMMISSIONER FRIEND'S DEPARTMENT

In August 1973, Walt and I filed another lawsuit in federal court against Fred Friend, the commissioner of welfare, because of illegal delays in processing applications for aid. Two previous cases had been successful in bringing relief first to the elderly and then to the disabled. This one came because of the department's failures in administering Aid to Families with Dependent Children (AFDC). The commissioner had attempted to avoid the obligation to make prompt decisions by maliciously requiring applicants to sign a waiver of the time limit. Our client, Carol

Newsome, had refused to sign, and in response the department simply denied her application—within the thirty-day limit, thus deviously in compliance with the promptness regulation. As before, the attorney general had no defense for the actions of the commissioner. An agreed order was entered prohibiting the use of waivers and mandating compliance with the federal regulation requiring a prompt decision on AFDC applications.

In January 1974, Commissioner Friend announced a plan to require all recipients of AFDC to come to a central place in each county to pick up their February check, instead of having it mailed to them as was the normal practice. His stated purpose for this unprecedented practice of gathering all recipients into one place was "weeding out ineligibles." Most recipients and many welfare department workers more accurately saw this as calculated harassment, an attempt to stigmatize and intimidate recipients. There also was a great deal of opposition to the plan from social welfare organizations in the community, including the Council of Community Services, Church Women United, and the Council of Jewish Women. Someone dubbed it a "Welfare Roundup," and there were charges that Friend was using the draconian maneuver to further his personal political ambitions. He objected to that charge but would not deny that he might be running for public office later that year.[7]

LSON lawyers filed a class action lawsuit on behalf of several named clients in an attempt to stop the "roundup." Friend, in turn, went to the Board of Trustees of the United Givers Fund (UGF) and threatened to withdraw his support for the UGF if that board did not intervene and stop LSON attorneys from filing class action suits against him. It was a common ploy that other disgruntled opponents had tried, and more would try in the future with some success, but Commissioner Friend was not successful. When he attended the UGF board meeting and presented his case, he was opposed by Joe Cummings, a member of our board, who appeared at the meeting with Walt. Joe was the epitome of an establishment lawyer, from an old Nashville family, a named partner in the second largest law firm in town, and an imposing figure. Walt recalls his standing there "like a rock" before the UGF board "in his expensive suit" speaking forcefully on our behalf, saying, "We should be proud of what they are doing, standing up for the rights of the beleaguered. That's what they are supposed to do." After Joe's statement, one UGF board member, Nashville Bank and Trust president Joe Howell, opined, "I don't believe this group [the UGF board] has jurisdiction over this question [stopping the lawsuits]. The board of directors for Legal Services dictates the policies [of LSON] and I don't think it appropriate for this board to tell that board what to do."[8] The rest of the UGF board looked at Joe Cummings, the personification of the LSON board, and agreed.

When the "roundup" lawsuit was tried before Judge Gray on February 2, for the first time against Commissioner Friend, we were not successful. Despite recipients' testimony about the embarrassment and humiliation of the process and about the lack of transportation to the roundup site, and despite a former welfare department supervisor's testimony about the ineffectiveness of the plan and its burden on department's workers, Judge Gray found that Friend's plan was "a viable method of at least some utility in eliminating errors and fraud." He expressed in his ruling that he was "disturbed" by some aspects of the commissioner's plan but found no statutory or constitutional violations. "The purpose of this hearing is not for me to pass on the wisdom of the scheme. I have no authority to do that."[9] There have been no more roundups since then.

In another case against the department later that month, Judge Morton ruled for our clients, holding that in AFDC cases when there had been a mistake in past payments, whether made by the welfare department or the recipient, the department could not strip or reduce future payments without first looking at the current needs of the recipient. In May, in yet another case of ours, Judge Morton ruled the department's "arbitrary, mechanical deductions from grants to needy children" to recover past overpayments was a violation of federal regulations. Commissioner Friend resisted compliance with rules at every turn and continued complaining about Legal Services filing lawsuits.

On May 4, 1974, the *Tennessean* editorialized that the way for Commissioner Friend to stop the lawsuits would be to have his department "act responsibly in the interest of the State as well as the poor who need public assistance," in a word "to do his job properly." This prompted Friend to call a press conference attempting to defend his record. He said he felt like LSON lawyers were "picking on" him and added, "I really have no respect for legal aid."[10] Friend claimed that "they have won one time" of the six cases brought against him and the department. His general counsel Aubrey Blankenship would not back him up, however, and "agreed with Legal Services' version of the score." Blankenship is quoted as saying

"Obviously, there was some merit to most of the suits," and added, "I'm not really interested in a won and lost record," but he did go on to voice concern about the "tremendous amount of time" he had to spend defending Friend.[11] Surprisingly, despite his candor, Blankenship, a longtime state lawyer, kept his job and was still there when Friend left with the change in the governor's office later that year.

It was not over yet, however. In September it was back to federal court to contest the department's failure to follow an eligibility provision for AFDC. The federal regulation, in effect since 1946, provided that "when the mother's pregnancy has been determined by medical diagnosis," the mother could begin receiving benefits for that child. After 1964 and the introduction of Medicaid, the policy made even more sense because with AFDC, the expectant mother also would be covered by Medicaid and thus have access to prenatal care, yet under Commissioner Friend the department refused. One of our clients had been told by a doctor that she would have a difficult pregnancy. Another had been told that her "continued malnutrition" threatened the health of the baby.

Judge Frank Gray granted a temporary restraining order requiring the department to accept applications from the three named plaintiffs, but benefits for other members of the class would have to await a hearing in court. Commissioner Friend dug in his heels, but eventually after further proceedings, Judge Gray, citing numerous federal court decisions, enjoined him and the department from withholding benefits from women with "medically determined pregnancies who are otherwise eligible for the program."

Two days later, the *Commercial Appeal* in Memphis reported that the state planned to appeal the case. The press secretary for Commissioner Friend informed the newspaper, "We are going to appeal that case because we find no basis in law for the judge's ruling." He claimed that several similar cases were pending in other states and that Tennessee would join in an appeal and go all the way to the US Supreme Court, if necessary.[12] Soon cooler heads prevailed. Guided by its lawyers, rather than the press secretary, before the end of the month the department issued guidelines implementing Judge Gray's ruling. There was no appeal.

In his complaints at the press conference about the cases brought by LSON lawyers against him and his department, Commissioner Friend specifically objected that they had been class action cases, ignoring the fact that the injustices alleged, and proven in all but one, were common to a great number of people across the state. He had his own vision of LSON, "I think it's supposed to take individual cases." Pat Welch from the *Tennessean* must have called Walt and me after the press conference for a response. I am quoted in her story as saying, "We've opened 1,100 new cases since January 1. I have 370 divorce cases myself."[13] Walt pointed out "that despite the newspaper headlines about important cases, the bulk of the work is still individual cases" and he gave several examples. Pat Welch did not report which ones he mentioned, but one might have been the case he was handling about the same time for an elderly widow in Old Hickory. He says now that it was one of the most satisfying of all his cases at Legal Services.

CASES, CONTROVERSIES, AND CONFIRMATIONS

Mrs. Cole was in her early eighties. She and her late husband had moved into a small house in Old Hickory more than forty years before. She thought they owned it, but they did not. They were renting it. The house had been owned by a man who had died years before, and his distant heirs, probably not knowing about the property, had neither collected rent nor paid the property tax on it since his death. Assistant Metropolitan Attorney, Jag Annam, as he would do each year, filed suit against a whole list of properties with delinquent taxes, including this one, and when no one came forward to pay, a judgment went down. He then auctioned it off on the courthouse steps to satisfy the judgment. The new owner brought a detainer action to remove Mrs. Cole. Since she had no legal title to the property, she had received no notice of any of these procedures and was caught completely by surprise when the deputy sheriff appeared and served the warrant. She did not understand how anyone could evict her from the home she thought her husband had bought, and where she had lived for much of her life.

Somehow she learned about Legal Services and called our office. She had no way to get to us, so Walt went to see her. After hearing her story, the only possible remedy he could figure was to file a bill in Chancery Court to set aside the sale and quiet title based on adverse possession, but he knew it would be difficult to set aside the sale because even if she had any claim to the property, the fact remained that no one had paid the taxes.

He filed the lawsuit anyway against Metro and the new owner, hoping for some break. At that point Walt did not appreciate the significance of the fact that the new owner was Jag Annam, the Metro lawyer who had conducted the sale and sold it to himself. Annam hired attorney Leon Ruben to represent him, and Ruben, the same lawyer who had been on the NBA disciplinary committee that accused us of "unprofessional conduct of the worst sort," called Walt to accuse him this time of bringing a frivolous lawsuit. We heard that often in those days.

Concerned but undeterred, Walt doubled down on his research about tax sales, and in doing so, found the break he had been hoping for. He discovered the statute that prohibited any employee of an entity conducting a tax sale from purchasing property at that sale. Annam must have known about this prohibition, and his accusing lawyer, too. They had been caught red-handed. Now with the upper hand, it was Walt's turn to call Ruben. In a few moments, Ruben called back to say that Annam would deed the property at no cost to Mrs. Cole free and clear of any past tax obligation. She paid nothing. She kept her home.

━━━━━━━━━

Walt seemed to have an eye for newsworthy cases, or at least that was the accusation of his colleagues and the subject of much banter in the office. One of his cases and his comments on it found their way onto the pages of the *National Enquirer*, an achievement he proudly proclaimed to all who would listen. His boast was bolstered by the headline of the story that identified him as an "expert" on Social Security. On the other hand, the derision of his colleagues was fortified by the fact that the story was buried on page 52, and it was, after all, in a publication sold at the checkout line of a grocery store, not exactly on a par with *Law Week*.

Banter aside, it was in fact a serious case with dire consequence for low-income disabled people. Oscar and Leona Miller were both blind, and she required "expensive kidney machine treatments." They each received a small monthly check from the Social Security Administration's Supplemental Security Income (SSI) Bureau for the Aged, Blind, and Disabled. That federal bureau only recently had taken over the administration of the program from the states, and it had a new computer system. Those statements alone, "recently taken over the administration" and "new computer system," in those early years of computers routinely constituted a recipe for disaster. And the Millers were the unfortunate victims of this disaster.

Though he was blind, Mr. Miller did what he could by working as a snack bar vendor in the basement hall of the Metro Courthouse. In the months before the federal government took over the administration of SSI, the state agency responsible for the program had calculated Mr. Miller's snack bar income and expenses incorrectly. That was one of the problems. There was another. Inexplicably, the state incorrectly listed the Millers as two individuals, instead of as a couple, which also had an effect on the calculation.

When all this incorrect information had been fed into the Social Security Administration's newly installed computers, "several additional errors were made in computing the Millers' SSI benefits," and the calculations kept changing during this transition process. As a result, the Millers received a different amount in their grant checks each month for four months straight. They tried telephoning the local Social Security office each month to get an explanation, but they could not get through. Finally, Mrs. Miller went to the office, taking her last check with her to show what was happening. Compounding the bureaucratic horror, during the interview the worker at the office took her check from her to look at it and then refused to give it back. Accusing Ms. Miller of cheating, the worker told her she and her husband had been overpaid and consequently they now were not eligible for any assistance: no SSI; no Medicaid; nothing.

Walt's filing the federal class action lawsuit on behalf of the Millers immediately got the attention of the administrators of the SSI program and their lawyers. Assistant US Attorney Martha Johnson quickly responded and at the hearing candidly told the court that the allegations in the Millers' suit "were essentially correct." She described it as "a morass of confusion and ineptitude," but promised that it was in the process of being fixed, that the Millers would be reinstated on SSI and Medicaid, and that they would be afforded a hearing if and when their benefits were ever to be reduced in the future.[14]

Pushing the bounds of credulity, one of the Social Security administrators testified that the Millers' situation "is factually unique and is certainly not representative of a class," buttressing Johnson's request that the case not be certified as a class action. Even more astounding than the bureaucrat's allegation and Johnson's argument was the fact that Judge

Morton, a known skeptic of bureaucratic promises, bought their plea, did not certify the class, and as soon as the Millers got their grants, he dismissed the case as moot.

Not surprisingly, that dispatch lasted only a few weeks. Not long after the dismissal, Gordon and Russ Overby sought to reopen the case. They filed affidavits from seven other SSI recipients who also had their benefits delayed or denied because of issues with the switch-over from state to federal administration. In each case, the federal defendants corrected the mistakes, the judge refused to certify the class, and the many snafued people who did not find their ways to our office received no relief from the "morass of confusion and ineptitude."

Over the five years of LSON's existence at this point, a frequent suspicion of opponents and skeptics had been that unworthy people who they thought could have scraped up enough money to pay a lawyer would instead go to LSON. Even in the years before Legal Services, when the only legal aid was the Wednesday afternoon clinic, several NBA presidents in their annual reports on the clinic voiced this suspicion about "that type of person." One president reassured his hearers that "it is not intended that this service [the NBA clinic] render legal services to that type of person who is always seeking something for nothing."[15] As illustrated in Chapter 3, the LSON board in the early days received a steady stream of complaints from lawyers about the eligibility of individual clients, and the staff often heard gripes from lawyers on the other side of their cases. It came up both in informal discussions and in negotiations. It just went with the territory. Every LSON lawyer came to expect it and developed various ways to respond, or not, depending on the circumstances.

What had not happened, surprisingly enough, was that no attorney had raised the matter formally in court. That changed in the fall of 1974. Harry Lester, an attorney, had an automobile accident with an elderly man named Henry Gray, and he sued Mr. Gray in general sessions court. The case was heard by Judge Gale Robinson, resulting in a $1,000 judgment for Lester, despite the fact that Lester's Cadillac struck Gray's old car from the rear when Lester could not stop it on the wet pavement.

Gray, who had represented himself in general sessions, came to LSON after that debacle and requested help. Carol McCoy accepted his case and appealed it to circuit court.

Harry Lester was a vocal opponent of Legal Services and in circuit court he filed a motion questioning "the right of the federally funded agency to represent Gray." At the hearing on the motion, Judge William Rutherford allowed Lester to testify as to what he knew about Gray's finances, which was that he had a car and therefore was not poor. Carol declined to present any testimony as to Gray's eligibility and maintained that the court did not have the authority to interfere with her representation of her client. The judge felt otherwise; he agreed with Lester, ruled that Gray could not be represented by a Legal Services lawyer, and prohibited Carol from proceeding. A federal statute provided that no question of client financial eligibility for representation could "be considered in, or affect the final deposition of, any proceeding in which a person is represented by [a Legal Services lawyer]" but that was not persuasive to the judge, who let other instincts and loyalties rule.[16]

Fortunately, it was not necessary for Carol to file a federal lawsuit over the matter. She was able to get relief by filing a petition for a Writ of Certiorari and Supersedeas in the Tennessee Court of Appeals. The writ was issued and the case was heard on January 3, 1975. That same day, not leaving a moment of doubt, the court issued a one-page *per curiam* order finding that "The trial judge was without authority to remove counsel of record on grounds that the defendant is not indigent and does not qualify for free legal services." The court vacated Rutherford's ruling and remanded the case.[17]

Because Carol was leaving Legal Services for another position, David Tarpley took over the case at that point and filed a counterclaim in circuit court. With that, Harry Lester dropped his lawsuit, and it was over. The *per curiam* order of the court of appeals became our talisman for years after that, and it was particularly effective because it had been a ruling of a *state* court, not the much-maligned-by-then federal judiciary. That mattered. A few years later, after Lester had been elected as circuit court judge in Davidson County, Russ Overby remembers appearing before him and having him "question my reliance on federal law because we were in state court," as if federal law did not apply in Tennessee.

The LSON board was focused on finances. Money is always a concern with any nonprofit, but the end of 1974 and beginning of 1975 was a particularly trying time for LSON. There was constant discussion about possible grants from UGF, Metro Government, the Commission on Aging, and other sources that did not pan out. The board discussed staff cuts and a proposal to close the North Nashville office. Walt was directed to submit "a plan for reducing expenditures sufficiently to avoid a deficit in the event that increased funds were not forthcoming in time." Board treasurer Bob Ziegler at one point stopped Randall from paying any bills except salaries.

Junius Allison, who had joined the board after helping with the executive director transition, wrote a fulsome three-page letter to Dan Bradley in Atlanta touting the record of the staff since Walt had become director and pleading for financial help to prevent "the loss of two or more staff members." From his experienced perspective, Allison hit all the right notes. He highlighted the support in the bar, the strong board of directors, a constantly increasing caseload, and "a phenomenal record in the area of law reform matters." Dan came through with a device called "short funding," giving twelve months' worth of funding in eleven months' time. Full relief did not come until late spring, however, when we received funding from two new sources. The new commissioner of welfare for Tennessee, Horace Bass, a 180 degree change from his predecessor, approved a Title IV-A grant to us, and the Metro Council approved a contract for services sponsored by then councilman, later general sessions judge, William "Bill" Higgins. At the July board meeting, with renewed optimism, Randall projected that LSON would run a $4,000 surplus for the year.

Federal funding for any operation brings with it not only standards and requirements, but also audits and evaluations. In May 1975, the Community Services Administration (CSA), the Nixon administration name for what was left of OEO, sent a three-person team to evaluate LSON. Their report followed in October, and it reflected the progress that had been made under Walt's leadership.

The evaluation properly cited a characteristic in the management of the organization that had evolved during Walt's tenure and became a hallmark going forward—participatory decision making: "Staff morale is one of the greatest assets of the program. This most probably results from high individual motivation and the success of the director's efforts to have total involvement [of the staff] in decision making." While the report was critical of a lack of supervision in the staff and found "no formal articulation of program goals and priorities," it did recognize that "the management plan that exists has evolved through an informal process and while flexible, it is well understood by the staff." Translation: we were flying by the seat of our pants, but like birds in migration, we all intuitively knew where we were going.

We all knew we were supposed to be helping all manner of poor and dispossessed people, and we were doing it in concert together. That year we opened 3,258 new cases and closed 3,391. Almost all of them mattered only to the people involved. More than 40 percent of our cases involved family problems. Nearly four hundred dealt with individual consumer and finance issues. On the other hand, some of our cases mattered to lots of people.

———————

Some cases were controversial because our clients were in the criminal justice system, but in each one of those cases, the clients had a civil rights claim, legitimate issues not involving a conviction. Gordon, Walt, and Russ brought a case in chancery court seeking reform of the bail bond system. After the case went through several hearings, Chancellor Ben Cantrell, who had been appointed in 1973, wrote in his memorandum opinion, "The great weight of the evidence shows that bail bonding breeds corruption, is ineffective for purpose of criminal justice, and serves no useful function that could not otherwise be attained."[18] Nevertheless, he had to conclude that it was up to the legislature to decide whether or not to make the changes being sought. Later, the court of appeals likewise recognized "the distressing inadequacies of the present system," but agreed that the remedy must come from the legislature.[19] In another case, this one involving the revocation of parole, I was able to convince the court of appeals that my client had been entitled to a hearing and other due process requirements before he was returned to jail. More common was our handling of cases attacking jail conditions.

In June 1975, Walt filed a jail conditions suit on behalf of a pretrial detainee who had been in the Metro jail for three-and-a-half months awaiting a hearing in his case. He was poor and had not been able to make bail. His complaint alleged that the cells were dirty, overcrowded, and unhealthy. It listed poor ventilation, filth, insects, no fire extinguishers, no evacuation plan in the case of fire, inadequate bedding, and broken shower facilities among the problems in the jail. It alleged that the facility had inadequate healthcare services, limited exercise facilities, and no appropriate accommodations for inmates to confer with their attorneys. The defendants, Metro Sheriff Fate Thomas and State Corrections Commissioner Herman Yeatman, were charged with failing to enforce Tennessee's "Minimum Standards for Local Correction Facilities."

Suits like this raised the ire of many people and led to criticism of Legal Services for "coddling criminals." Those offended by these suits maintained that people in jail were not worthy and did not deserve to be treated with such care. Even those who were pretrial detainees like our client who had not been found guilty of anything, should just endure the lack of health services, exercise, and cleanliness. Many public officials resented having the courts looking over their shoulders and telling them how to run their institutions. That was not the case with the sheriff in this case. Fate Thomas welcomed it. Within a few weeks after the case was filed, Chancellor Cantrell held a preliminary hearing that lasted only ninety minutes. Lawyers for both sides all agreed on the need for improvement at the jail. The chancellor ruled that "based on the allegations made in the complaint and the admissions made here in court there is probable cause to believe that overcrowded, unsanitary and unsafe" conditions at the Metro jail violated the constitutional rights of the inmates. He ordered the sheriff to submit within thirty days a plan to alleviate the conditions.

The sheriff's lawyer, William Willis, responded that the ruling "came as no surprise" and that Sheriff Thomas "is very happy to comply."[20] He was quick to point out the obvious, "The council and the Metro government have to come to grips with the problem that they have an inadequate facility." Thomas was quoted afterward as saying, "I told them this is what would happen" and volunteered that in anticipation of the ruling he had already asked the Tennessee Law Enforcement Planning Association for help in drafting the plan the chancellor required. The result of the case was that the sheriff got the new jail he had been pleading for since he was first elected. When the building was completed, he presented to Walt a key to the jail.

". . . THE PEOPLE'S THANKS"

In December 1975, Walt concluded that he loved the law but did not love management. He submitted his resignation as executive director and stated his intention "to devote more time to the legal aspects of Legal Services." A five-person committee of the board was appointed to select a new director. One month later, the committee reported that I was its choice and at the same time recommended that Walt be given the title of general counsel. After the report and recommendations were accepted by the board, Walt, seeing daylight, suggested that I begin my duties as executive director four days later on February 1, and the board accepted that suggestion as well.

A couple months later, Walt left for what would be an eighteen-month sojourn in Knoxville where he would be an attorney and instructor in the University of Tennessee Legal Clinic. As he was leaving, the *Tennessean* published an editorial entitled "Mr. Kurtz Did His Job Well" that concluded, "There is no doubt that Mr. Kurtz has served this community well and deserves the people's thanks."[21] A few days earlier, the newspaper had quoted LSON board president Gareth Aden's assessment, "Under his direction, Legal Services has become a sound, respected, and vital organization." In the same story, it reported that Walt had been honored at a reception and especially noted that in attendance were "several Metro judges and the current and two former presidents of the NBA."[22] More remarkable than those notables, only appearing briefly at the occasion and consequently missed by the reporter, was one who rarely if ever attended a social function in Nashville, having been ostracized after stubbornly doing his duty by following a Supreme Court ruling in the school busing case. Federal District Judge L. Clure Morton, a man who knew about courage, made this unusual appearance to show his respect for Walt.

Walt's passion for the law and his interest in constitutional issues made the opportunity to work at the UT Clinic particularly attractive because it would give him a chance to expand his experience into criminal law.

The experience served him well. He tried several major criminal cases in Knox County before returning to Legal Services in December 1977. This time he worked in the Gallatin office for a few months while looking for the right opportunity in criminal law. In March 1978, he announced his intention to run for the office of public defender in Davidson County.

By all rights Walt should not have won a political election in Nashville. In the old-time established politics of the city, he was an outsider running against a native son, an incumbent whose father also was a Nashville lawyer. Walt was a Yankee from New York. He had been a Vietnam War protestor in a pro-war town. And he had worked at Legal Services, still regarded by many as part of a socialist plot to take over the legal profession and then the nation. But he campaigned hard, promised that all his assistants would be full-time, promised that he would walk through the jail every week to be sure no one was neglected, and in the end, with devoted campaign work by many of his colleagues from Legal Services, and with a campaign slogan that Harlan Dodson brought to life from Joseph Conrad, "Kurtz, he works," Walt won fifty out of fifty-four precincts. Four years later, now despite the added deficit of having been an effective defender of the accused, he was elected judge of the Fifth Circuit Court for Davidson County, where he served, with a picture of Clure Morton on his courtroom wall, for twenty-six years before retiring and being appointed a senior judge by the Tennessee Supreme Court.

With Walt's tenure, there had been four executive directors of LSON in seven short years, three less than successful and one tremendously successful. Now began a director who would serve for more than thirty years, during which time legal services for the poor would be significantly expanded and transformed.

CHAPTER 5

We Grow

1976-1980

> For many of our citizens, the availability
> of legal services has reaffirmed faith in
> our government and laws.
>
> —LEGAL SERVICES CORPORATION ACT,
> SECTION 1001, 1974

I was fortunate to begin as executive director of Legal Services of Nashville at an opportune time, with the good will generated by Walt at the bench and bar, the increasingly sophisticated lawyering by our staff, and a new day for Legal Services on the national level.

In 1974, Congress had adopted the Legal Services Corporation Act, taking the administration of federal funding for civil legal aid out of the Community Services Administration and placing it in a new freestanding federal corporation. The American Bar Association for many years had been advocating this structure, thinking that separating civil legal aid from the administration of other poverty programs would make it less political. A bill had passed Congress in 1971 that would have established the structure, but it had been vetoed by President Nixon who wanted more control over appointments to the board. By 1974, after the forced resignation of Vice President Spiro Agnew, an outspoken opponent of Legal Services, and during the turmoil of Watergate, Nixon's resistance finally wore down, and he signed new legislation two weeks before he too resigned. Because of struggles in the early months of President Gerald Ford's administration, it was still more than a year before the Legal Services Corporation (LSC) board members were named and the corporation began operation.

Had it not been for the efforts of the ABA and other advocates who lobbied for the independent corporation, it is likely that federal funding for civil legal aid would have been terminated eventually, if not immediately. The opposition was persistent and, for us, close to home. Senators Bill Brock of Tennessee and Jesse Helms of North Carolina had offered numerous amendments to the Act in an unsuccessful effort to weaken it. For one, as an alternative to the corporation, they proposed offering a limited amount of money to the states in a social services block grant and allowing the states to decide if and how the program would operate. When all their proposed amendments failed, they conducted a filibuster against the Act but that was stopped by cloture vote, and only then had the bill passed.

Even with that survival, the hope of making Legal Services less political was not ever to be fulfilled, and the political struggles would continue, but the independent corporation would provide something of a shield. In the battles to come, supporters could rally behind a singular theme: access to justice. For better or worse, Legal Services no longer would be lumped with other "poverty programs." This was a justice program. It was anchored in the foundational ideals of our nation.

In November 1975, before becoming director, at Walt's behest I had been to an NLADA meeting in Seattle and then had reported to the LSON board on initiatives to come at the new LSC, including the prospects for increased funding for us. One of the aims of the corporation was "equalization" to correct inequities in grants to the various grant recipients around the country. In the early years of OEO, because of the reluctance of southern and rural areas to accept federal funds for Legal Services, the bulk of the grants had gone to other parts of the country, with lesser amounts remaining for places like Nashville that came late to the table. After 1968, OEO and CSA did not receive funding sufficient to correct the imbalances, and they remained. Now with increased funding from Congress, that inequity would be fixed, and we would benefit.

The new corporation encouraged cooperation among its grantees in a state. In February 1976, LSON received a $25,000 grant from LSC to fund an office that would carry out that purpose. The four grantees in the state formed an organization with the rather unwieldy name of Tennessee Association of Legal Services, Legal Aid Programs (TALSLAP; later Tennessee Alliance for Legal Services, TALS). With the new federal funding, the directors of the four grantees hired a state coordinator whose job included "to act as a clearing house, backup person, and monitor . . . the legislature." Though the first coordinator was not particularly successful, it was a beginning, and TALSLAP was to become in the future an effective institution, particularly as a brief bank and training center, and for legislative and administrative advocacy. This also relieved a burden on LSON. Previously, when another legal aid provider in the state had a matter before the legislature or an administrative agency or when one had a case that had to be filed in Nashville, we often would be called on to be local counsel. Now, in many cases, the TALSLAP staff could fill that function.

With the formation of LSC came also a feeling of permanence and a consequent realization that we must pay attention to administration and to strategies appropriate for an organization with a future. At an all-day meeting for staff, board, and community members, we identified three strategies reflecting concerns that had been brewing for some time, and would continue for years to come. First, we had to deal with the fact that we could not represent everyone who requested our help, and consequently, we needed a reasonable standard for case acceptance decisions. We agreed to make case acceptance decisions based on "whether the case involved a necessity (food, shelter, income, custody, support) and whether interventions by the attorney would make a significant difference in the quality of the person's life." The second strategy adopted at the meeting was related to the first: "to make quality a high priority at the expense of volume." And the third was related to the second: to develop what now would be called a continuing legal education program, complete with manuals, training sessions, and a "buddy system." This resolve was remarkable because we were ahead of the times. The legal profession in Tennessee then had no continuing education requirements.

━━━━━━━━━━━━━━━━

Another goal of the Legal Services Corporation was the expansion of services to areas with no legal aid. As of 1976 in Tennessee, there was free civil legal aid available in only four counties, the four major cities. Having more than enough to do helping low-income people in Davidson County, we at LSON routinely declined to represent anyone in another county and rarely made exceptions. Tom Ehrlich, the former Stanford Law dean and first president of LSC, set a goal of "minimum access," making Legal Services available to eligible people in every county of the country; the LSC board adopted it, and Ehrlich began incremental approaches to Congress. An increase in the LSC appropriation followed in late 1976 that enabled the first step. LSON applied for some of the expansion funding to begin serving four more counties: Sumner, Trousdale, Wilson, and Rutherford. LSC awarded the grant and in January 1977, the Board of Directors amended our charter to reflect the broader area and changed our name to Legal Services of Nashville and Middle Tennessee, the first of several name changes to come. We proceeded to eventually hire five new lawyers and open offices in Gallatin and Murfreesboro.

We were not welcomed universally. Preparatory to opening the new offices, I set out to meet with each of the local bar associations in the counties we would serve. Fortunately, on the recommendation of someone on our board, before I went to meet with the Sumner County Bar Association, I contacted Charles Bone, a young lawyer practicing in Gallatin who was known to be sympathetic to our cause. We agreed that I would come to his office on the day of the meeting and we would ride together to the country club where the bar met for lunch and its monthly programs.

After lunch, I gave my presentation describing the work we would do. I tried to assure the lawyers that we were not there to take paying business away from them, that we would serve only very low-income people who could not afford to pay a fee, and that we would not accept, for example, tort cases that might generate a fee from the recovery. I left time at the end for questions. The first person up was a man in the back of the room, who stood, pointed his finger at me and barked, "There he is, boys. I told you this would happen, and there he is." It had been twelve years since the "Et tu, Brute!" article in the *Tennessee Bar Journal* asserting that federally funded legal aid for the poor would lead to socialism and government control of the profession, but the gentleman recounted faithfully all the fears and predictions of that day, plus some more, and his jeremiad inspired a chorus of nods and amens.

I do not remember my response. I do remember the two people who immediately came to my defense and the defense of Legal Services: Charles Bone and Ernest Pellegrin. I do not remember what they said, but I do remember the temperate and lawyerly way they said it. They calmed the charged atmosphere so that the question-and-answer time could continue, and I proceeded to respond to a few specific inquiries before the hour was over.

Charles reassured me as we drove back from the country club to his office on the square. He agreed to be on our board, and in the weeks and months that followed, he helped us find an office and begin our work there. More than thirty years later, well after he had moved his practice to Nashville and established one of the larger firms in town, he once again was our champion, leading the 2010 annual fundraising campaign. Ernest Pellegrin was a state court judge, so his defense had been particularly effective. Twenty-five years later, his son John was elected president of our board of directors, the first lawyer from outside of Nashville to hold that position. Likewise, there is a follow-up story concerning the man with the accusing finger.

When we opened the office in Gallatin in the fall of 1977, fitting in with the community was not one of the criteria for our selection of lawyers. We wanted the best lawyers we could find who would zealously represent low-income people in Sumner, Wilson, and Trousdale counties. As it turned out, the three lawyers we selected for these three counties in the Bible Belt were all Jewish and all from the Northeast. Steve Palevitz and Andy Shookhoff both had just finished Vanderbilt Law School. Steve was from Washington, DC, and Andy was from New York City. Deborah Kane Dickinson was from New Hampshire and had graduated from Franklin Pierce Law School there.

After they settled in and began going to court, some of the other lawyers and judges in Gallatin referred to them as "those Russian lawyers." How much of that was due to their names and heritage, how much was due to their use of arcane legal points, and how much was due to Legal Services being perceived as a harbinger of socialism/communism, we do not know. It is true that they introduced new ideas into the legal practice of the three then-rural counties. They invoked seldom-used defenses available under the new Landlord Tenant Act that Walt had helped draft just a few years earlier. They challenged decisions by political appointees in the local office of the welfare department. They were aggressive in seeking child support for their clients.

Palevitz's forte was commercial law. He in particular, and the others as well, raised defenses under the federal Truth-In-Lending Act in collection cases, much to the frustration of banks, collection agencies, used car dealers, and their lawyers. Local lawyers had been accustomed to going into general sessions court and taking their judgments against low-income people without opposition. When Steve found defects in the loan documents or violations of the repossession process, he would mount a vigorous defense and in some cases file a counterclaim for penalties because of a violation of the commercial code or a federal statute. General sessions practitioners were not accustomed to arguing intricate legal issues, and they did not like this complication to their well-greased practices.

Hal Bigham, who by that time had left his position teaching at Vanderbilt and joined the Gullet law firm in Nashville, had been appointed to our board. Before a board meeting one day, he told me he had been in Gallatin a few days earlier handling one of his cases and had struck up a conversation with some local lawyers while waiting for court to start. During the course of the conversation, apparently not knowing he was on the board, they began complaining about the disruptive Legal Services lawyers coming into general sessions court to defend collection cases and citing all these arcane statutes and regulations. Bigham reported to me that his response was not sympathetic: "I told them I taught those guys the Uniform Commercial Code in law school and they damn well better be using it."

Even though they were good students of the law and certainly zealous advocates, each of the three new lawyers was also personable, and each had a special charm that eventually won friends in the three counties they served, so much so that after a couple years they decided to have an open house at the office and a reception for members of the local bench and bar. They told me about their plans and invited me to attend. I was pleased with their progress and looked forward to meeting their guests. There was one person I did not expect to meet. After the luncheon two years earlier at the county club, I had learned from Charles Bone that the person who stood up in the back of the room and pointed at me was Circuit Judge Thomas Boyers III, so I was somewhat surprised to see Judge Boyers at the reception, but I soon was even more surprised. He came right up to me and told me what an asset the office had been and how happy he was to have Legal Services in town, and he credited the success, "It's all because of these fine young lawyers you sent up here." Steve, Andy, and Deborah were doing their jobs well, working their charms, and succeeding beyond all expectations.

———————

At the same time plans were being made to open new offices in Gallatin and Murfreesboro, we moved the Nashville office from the soon to be demolished Sudekum Building to much more commodious space in Parkway Towers. For the first time we were in space designed for a modern law office and in a building with modern elevators. We could not afford new furniture, however, and brought with us the much used, scarred, broken desks and chairs that had been accumulated as hand-me-downs during the preceding eight years. When the movers began unloading it, the building manager at Parkway Towers, not an otherwise fussy person, was visibly shaken. His only comment was that he never before had seen such "ratty" furniture. Beyond the detriment to the reputation of the building, he probably was thinking that if he had known about this before, he would not have rented to us: how could any organization with furniture this distressed ever afford to pay the rent?

Thankfully, we never missed a payment, and as we expanded our staff in the late 1970s and then reduced the staff in the tumultuous 1980s, the building manager was able to work with us and meet our varying needs for space. At one point we rented nearly the entire fifteenth floor and part of the sixteenth before shrinking back to the original footprint. It was an efficient space.

In the interest of efficiency in May 1977, we made yet another office change. For seven years we had maintained an office in North Nashville, first in the basement of the Matthew Walker Health Center and then in the former Pearl Elementary School building. In this latter location, we were the tenants of the local Model Cities Program, a not very well-managed remnant of the War on Poverty. It had not been a cordial relationship, particularly after we threatened to sue Model Cities because of its failures in the operation of one of its projects. When Model Cities substantially raised the rent and the two lawyers in the office asked to be moved downtown, we closed the office.

This ended our experiments with neighborhood law offices in Nashville, which signaled our abandonment of one of the guiding principles of the original OEO Legal Services, to take the service into the neighborhoods where low-income people lived. We had closed our South Nashville office several years earlier and had declined requests that we open offices in West Nashville and East Nashville. For better or worse, we decided that concentrating our Nashville resources in one place to facilitate developing the best law practice possible took precedent over having a neighborhood presence and being more accessible. To compensate for our abandonment, we had good intentions of developing "a method for doing intake on an outreach basis in the various poverty communities of the city." That is recorded in the board minutes of March 15, 1977, but it never really happened.

We did not treat the consolidation into one office as a philosophical stance. We did not advertise the decision. We simply closed the North Nashville office. We did continue to emphasize our mantra that had been developing over the past couple of years, and certainly since the all-day meeting in May 1976: I am quoted in a *Tennessean* article in July 1977, "Our job is to provide the highest quality legal services to people who cannot afford to hire private lawyers."[1] In the interview, I went on to explain further our understanding of quality legal services. I compared our practice to that of corporate counsel who must stay on top of issues and anticipate problems for their clients.

That comparison may have sounded presumptuous to some people or signaled to them that we were overstepping our boundary and duty. It derived from our sense that we had a wider responsibility to low-income people as a group, not a corporation of course, but as a group. We certainly had no attorney/client relationship with low-income people as a group, and no *legal* responsibility to low-income people as a whole, but by default we were the only lawyers who were handling every day the wide range of issues that affect most low-income people, and therefore we had a professional obligation to pay attention to their interests.

The staff had initiated several strategies in an effort to fulfill this wider responsibility. First, we would pay attention to "issue spotting." At intake we would ask the applicant not only about the presenting problem, but also would probe for other possible issues she might be facing, whether related to the presenting problem or not. From time-to-time we developed formal checklists, and we would go down the list of potential problems in housing, home repairs, health access/billings, consumer, food stamps, child support, and other areas. When that became too cumbersome or time consuming, we resorted to a more informal practice, but the idea was the same, to be a counselor to the client, identify potential problems, and prevent further difficulties. Sometimes that resulted also in a certain amount of what some would characterize as social work, assisting the client in getting other kinds of help, but that too was part of our responsibility. Several of our paralegals, particularly in later years Janet Rosenberg, had special talents for doing this.

The second strategy was to improve community education so that we could inform low-income people who were not actual clients about potential issues, their rights and responsibilities. The hope was that through information and education we could prevent problems before they occurred. Failing that, we hoped to alert people to possible remedies and suggest they seek counsel. Especially after Adinah Robertson joined our staff, this developed into an extremely effective part of our service, as will be documented several times in our story.

The third strategy was to address clients' problems that were common to a large number of people, not only by individual litigation, but also, when appropriate, by class action lawsuits. This was not a new or unusual process. Class actions have been a part of American jurisprudence since 1842 and are provided for in both the federal and state rules of civil procedure. The whole purpose of the class action procedure is to address the common problems of a large number of people in one case and thus avoid a multiplicity of lawsuits. It was an efficient means for us to represent more people in the low-income community, some of whom were our actual face-to-face clients and others whom we never met. By the early 1990s we had been counsel or co-counsel in nearly seventy class action lawsuits.

The fourth strategy was advocacy in legislative and administrative matters. We did not have a separate "government relations" section like so many large law firms do, but we did share with the other legal services organizations in the state the assistance of TALSLAP. Like attentive corporate counsel, we knew that if we could achieve a good result for our clients in an administrative agency or legislative body, it would be a lot better than trying to deal with a bad result in court. From time to time, also, legislators or administrators would call on us to give a perspective on matters pending before them because of our unique situation representing low-income clients every day.

It is fair to say that not every member of the board was comfortable with this expansive interpretation of our community responsibility, and not every member of the board was comfortable with the rapid expansion of our services to other counties and the increase in staff. Though the board in November 1977 approved further expansion of services to Williamson, Cheatham, and Robertson counties, it was hesitant and the vote was not unanimous. There was a feeling we were going too far, too fast. At the urging of members, the president requested that Bucky Askew in the Atlanta Regional Office of LSC come to a meeting of the board and discuss the whys and wherefores of expansion. Bucky came in March and explained the "minimum access" goal of LSC to make Legal Services available to low-income people in every county of the country by 1980. He explained that LSC recognized it would not have enough money to establish an office in every county, so for ease of administration, it would prefer to give additional funding to current grantees to extend their service areas, provided the current grantee were well managed and doing a good job delivering services already. He expressed confidence in our organization and urged the Board to continue expansion as funds became available.

In November 1978, I put it on the agenda again, this time proposing an expansion to Montgomery, Dickson, Humphrey, Houston, and Stewart counties with an office in Clarksville. The board deferred it for one meeting, but in December approved it unanimously. At the same time, recognizing the wider area, it voted to drop the Nashville identifier and change the name of the organization to simply Legal Services of Middle Tennessee. There was no appetite for any further expansion, however. TALSLAP worked with local people to establish a new organization in the southern part of Middle Tennessee that would become Legal Services of South Central Tennessee with offices in Columbia and Tullahoma. And that is the way it stayed for a little more than twenty years.

The discomfort of some board members with our case selection and case handling procedures came to the fore in the fall of 1977 with yet another appearance of the unpredictable Louis Farrell, who had been appointed to our board by the president of the NBA. We had established a contract attorney program in which we would screen selected cases and send them to private attorneys we had recruited to handle them for the handsome fee of $25 per hour—actually a thinly disguised pro bono service. In the September board meeting, Farrell noted that according to our case statistics and financial report, the cost for our contract attorney cases appeared to be $108 per case, whereas for staff-handled cases it was $220. In light of that, he proposed that the staff program be cashed in, the attorneys laid off, and all cases referred out to private attorneys. He followed that up the next month with a more detailed letter to the board president.

In the first sentence of that letter, Farrell announced, "I am becoming increasingly disturbed over the inept manner in which Legal Services is handling its volume of cases." He was concerned that though the staff was growing each month, we had by the end of August closed only 1,340 cases. He concluded that the problem was a lack of experience: "To put it bluntly, these youngsters are not dry behind their ears, and they consume an enormous amount of time uselessly, even though the results of their work are reasonably good." In December, Farrell raised the ante. He brought to the board meeting a reporter from the *Nashville Banner* and a two-paragraph written motion that the president appoint a committee to study the operation of LSON. The motion, after some modification, passed unanimously. After the meeting, Gareth Aden appointed five members to the committee, including Farrell, and named Joe Cummings chair.

Cummings had been on the board for several years at that point, had been president, and had helped us through several controversies in addition to the United Givers Fund matter described in the last chapter. He was a thorough lawyer and could be every bit as irascible as Farrell. Some in the bar referred to him, though not to his face, as "Vinegar Joe." He held five meetings of the committee, reviewed regulations governing Legal Services, reviewed the recent LSC monitoring report, interviewed several staff members, considered the goals and priorities that had resulted from the May 1976 meeting, and reviewed financial reports and case statistics. Joe presented the committee's four-page report at the February 1978 meeting of the board. It reflected a remarkable understanding of the case acceptance policies, client eligibility issues, case handling, supervision, attorney hiring, and the need for outreach. He found that "we have competent staff, and efficient operation, and that the morale of the staff attorneys and employees is at an all-time high." He thanked "the entire staff for its commitment, dedication, and hard work." The next month, Louis Farrell resigned from the board.

The concerns Farrell had raised were not inappropriate, but his conclusions and accusations had been off the mark. His concern about the inexperienced young lawyers was legitimate, and in an ideal world all our staff would have been seasoned veterans ready to go to work with a full caseload on the first day. We had looked for experienced lawyers and would have hired them, but there were two big issues that impeded us. The first was money. We could not pay competitive salaries. The second issue was motivation. Lawyers can gain experience after a while, but if they are not committed to representing low-income people and dealing with their particular problems, they will not be happy doing this work and will not stay long. We wanted people who wanted to do this work, not regard it as a second choice or just a job. Joe Cummings appreciated that and had written in his report, "It is hard to find an experienced attorney who has the dedication and commitment to do a good job at Legal Services." We did find some as the years went on, but it was a rare find.

Farrell's cost per case comparison failed to appreciate that the cases referred to contract attorneys were by design routine matters that we had screened and assessed beforehand. The staff cases, on the other hand, included a number of larger cases, some of which were stretching over several years involving multiple hearings and requiring expenditures for depositions, expert witnesses, and other litigation expenses. One of those cases, admittedly an extreme example, is the subject of the next chapter.

CHAPTER 6

Nasty, Brutish, and Long

I was in prison and you came to me.
—MATTHEW 25:36 (RSV)

This is the story of a Legal Services lawsuit that began a year-and-a-half before Louis Farrell's negative assessment about our $220 cost per case and lasted in its two iterations for seventeen years, first in the state court system, then in federal district court. It dealt with the problems of a particularly unsympathetic group of people, the majority of whom are poor: prisoners in the custody of the Tennessee Department of Correction. Gordon Bonnyman was lead counsel in the case, but in various ways and at various times Walt Kurtz, Drake Holliday, Russ Overby, Kitty Calhoon, and Juliet Griffin from LSON played important parts. It was a cooperative effort involving lawyers from other organizations as well: David Kozlowski, first at the Vanderbilt Legal Clinic and later at Legal Services of South Central Tennessee; Lenny Croce at Rural Legal Services of Tennessee; Susan Kay at Vanderbilt Legal Clinic; Dale Grimes and Cliff Knowles in the firm of Bass, Berry & Sims; plus Al Bronstein, Nan Aron, and Matthew Myers at the National Prison Project of the American Civil Liberties Union.

The pendency of the case spanned the administrations of three governors and seven commissioners of correction. Governors would come and go, commissioners would come and go, attorneys general would come and go, but the efforts of the plaintiffs' lawyers persisted. As the case progressed, it was said that Gordon became the institutional memory of the

Tennessee Department of Correction; no one else had the consistency of experience, perspective, and knowledge gained over those years about the operations of the system. And by the end of the two cases, the system had been brought from being one of the most violent and dysfunctional in the nation to being the first state system fully accredited by the American Correctional Association.

———————

Gordon had decided he wanted to be a legal aid lawyer during his junior year at Princeton when a lawyer from Alaska Legal Aid came to speak about his representation of indigenous people there. Inspired to help, Gordon applied for a summer job with the group, but since he was not even a law student, much less a lawyer, Alaska Legal Aid was not moved by his inspiration. Undaunted, after college he went back home to Knoxville and enrolled at UT Law School, worked at the UT Clinic, and helped with a bail bond reform project of the ACLU. He also got involved in a prison project and went to visit prisoners at the infamous Brushy Mountain State Prison. He remembers that the first inmate he ever met was a "check-in," an inmate who voluntarily had asked to be put in solitary confinement to escape the violence in the general population. Gordon was puzzled as to why the guards could not have protected the man in the general population, and furthermore why he was complaining about the conditions in "protective custody." Within a few years Gordon was to learn a lot more about "check-ins," about violence in prison, and about prison guards.

First he needed to get a job. During his last year of law school, he sent applications once again to Alaska and to every other Legal Services program he could identify as a possibility from Alaska to Florida. He even flew a plane to Texas, taking his new spouse Claudia, and they looked for jobs for him as a legal aid lawyer and for her as a schoolteacher in several towns there, but it was a time of stagnant funding for Legal Services and no one was hiring. All his mailings and all his travels were to no avail. Idaho Legal Services replied that there were no jobs, but if he came to the state, took the bar exam and was successful, then they would talk to him. That did not seem like a likely prospect. Then in the late spring of 1972, he heard there might be something in Nashville, and sure enough, he managed to get an interview with the person at LSON who seemed to be in charge of hiring, a "Mr. Kurtz." It was an uncertain time at LSON, one of several such times in those days, and it was hard to tell who was in charge, but Walt, with his bushy mustache, did look older than most.

"Mr. Kurtz" impressed Gordon with his descriptions of the impact cases we were handling and the commitment of the staff, even if it was a bit disconcerting during the interview to watch Mr. Kurtz eat peanut butter out of a jar using his index finger for a spoon. Mr. Kurtz offered him a job, or at least that's what Gordon understood, and told him he could start in August. It was only later that Gordon learned that "Mr. Kurtz" was just a third year law student like himself.

Based on the "offer," Gordon and Claudia rented an apartment in Nashville and she enrolled in law school at Vanderbilt, but when Gordon showed up at Legal Services, there was no job. The funding had not come through, and Gordon was left to pound the hot pavements of August looking for employment. Finally he found a position at the Department of Mental Health, where he stayed until December when he left for several months of Army Reserve duty driving big trucks. Gordon remembers that a couple of weeks before his tour was over, either Walt or I called to say that Junius Allison at Vanderbilt had snagged a Ford Foundation grant to hire an assistant for three months who would be stationed at Legal Services to supervise clinic students. Gordon applied on faith that there might be time to do more than supervise students. He was hired, and his faith was rewarded. He remembers the thrill of his first day on the job, walking into the office and Walt giving him a motion to file in the Clover Bottom case at federal court. His first day and already involved in a federal class action. Little did he realize what a significant case it would become and how significant his role would become, but for now, as soon as he returned from the filing, he was plunged right into the regular intake of landlord-tenant cases, collection defenses, divorce cases, and juvenile court matters that he would handle with assistance from his students.

At some point in 1975, Gordon, now a regular staff attorney, having passed the clinic supervision job on to Russ, was contacted by some "check-ins" at the main prison in West Nashville seeking protection from the rampant violence and miserable conditions there. About the same time, Joe Ingle, with the Southern Prison Ministry, began referring prisoners to him who reinforced and added to the complaints of the check-ins. Gordon and other lawyers who would be involved in the case spent the next several months investigating the stories told by the inmates and consulting with the National Prison Project, which soon was persuaded to assist.

Despite the fact that the Tennessee Constitution called for "the erection of safe and comfortable prisons, the inspection of prisons, and the humane treatment of prisoners," none of those ideals was a reality. The system was a mess and its failings were not new. A state-initiated report in 1937 had catalogued the dangers of overcrowding, cited boredom and inactivity as leading to violence, lamented the failure to separate the more violent prisoners from the more vulnerable, recognized that people were coming out of prison worse than they went in, and concluded, "We are now reaping a bitter harvest."

By the 1970s, things had only gotten worse. The main prison in Nashville, where the maximum capacity according to national prison guidelines and public health standards was eight hundred, had 2,300 prisoners crammed within its walls. A sustained epidemic of hepatitis there and at the Fort Pillow Prison Farm had been attributed principally to overcrowding by both state and federal public health investigators. The Department of Correction had failed to cooperate with state public health officials to establish an effective program of tuberculosis control in the system. There had been numerous other critical reports from outside experts and professionals, but in each case the department had been unable or unwilling to make the corrections necessary.

In 1972, the department came up with yet another plan to address some of the issues, including a proposal to build more regional prisons, a benefit that not only would reduce overcrowding, but also would keep prisoners closer to their families, helping maintain those important connections. In 1973, Governor Winfield Dunn approved plans to build a regional prison in Morristown, but local opposition, including the Ku Klux Klan, quickly squashed that, and the whole plan was scrapped by the next administration. The state once again had failed.

By February 1976, the preliminary investigation done, Walt recalls that he and Drake Holliday, a third-year law student, spent a weekend in a seminar room at Vanderbilt drafting the complaint. After only a few revisions, it was filed in the Chancery Court of Davidson County on behalf of eight named plaintiffs, a twenty-four-page class action complaint that amounted to a sixty-three-count indictment of the Department of Correction. It was styled as an Intervenors' Complaint because the court already had several handwritten *pro se* petitions, the earliest of which had been filed by an inmate named William Trigg. Thus the case became known as *Trigg v. Blanton,* Ray Blanton being governor at that time.

Al Bronstein, head of the National Prison Project, was accustomed to trying cases in federal courts, relying on the Eighth Amendment. When Gordon asked him to help here, chauvinistically touting his home state, he convinced Bronstein that Tennessee's Constitution was even stronger than the Eighth Amendment, that Article I, Section 32 went a step further when it specified "safe and comfortable prisons" and "the humane treatment of prisoners," and that they should file for their clients in Chancery Court. Bronstein surprisingly went along with the novelty and it proved to be the right call, at least in the trial court; not so much on appeal. The case landed on the docket of Chancellor Ben Cantrell, the first Republican judge ever elected in Davidson County. He had been appointed three years earlier by Governor Dunn, and because he was greatly respected by the bar, had then handily won election in the otherwise Democratic county.

After the filing, there followed nearly two years of depositions, interrogatories, and the footwork of interviewing prisoners in the various facilities. Then came the trial. Beginning January 9, 1978, it lasted three weeks. The plaintiffs' lawyers decided that the out-of-towner, the Brooklyn-born Bronstein, would give the opening statement. On the face of it, this may have seemed like a foolish selection in a local Tennessee court, but the lawyers had confidence in the chancellor's fairness, and Al Bronstein was not just any out-of-town lawyer. Four times he would be named one of the one hundred most influential lawyers in America by the *National Law Journal* and in 1989 he would be given a MacArthur Fellowship, "the genius award." More than forty years after Al's opening statement, Gordon still recalls the setting. "We were expecting, and probably the court and the media were expecting, a real stem-winder of a peroration from this nationally

famous attorney. We figured it would be fiery and aggressive in attacking the defendant state officials. Instead he started by saying something
to the effect of:

> May it please the Court, the defendants preside over an unconstitution-
> ally cruel prison system that destroys lives and endangers the public by
> the way it treats prisoners. But, although the system is evil, the defen-
> dants are not. They are decent, honorable people who strive to achieve
> a constitutional system. It is a measure of the unconstitutionality of
> the system that, even under the management of decent officials like the
> defendants, it remains so destructive and depraved. Their best efforts
> cannot redeem or reform the system. The inability of the good people
> who are defendants, and the inability of other good people in the same
> positions of responsibility over many decades to bring Tennessee's pris-
> ons into conformity with the Constitution, attest to the urgent need for
> judicial intervention. The Court must act, because the defendants are
> otherwise powerless to reform the system.

During the trial, among the many witnesses was a twenty-five-year-old
ex-inmate who had been sexually assaulted by five prisoners while serving
his sentence at the main prison. "It happened while I was taking a shower."[1]
An eighteen-year-old sentenced to prison for third-degree burglary testified he was gang-raped on his third night at the penitentiary. There was
testimony about a twenty-one-year-old who had been sentenced for joy-
riding and was found dead at the penitentiary lying in his own blood.[2]

An expert witness testified "the transient building at the Nashville
prison is a disgrace to the state and to the nation. I wouldn't be responsible for that building. It is one of the most horrible things I have seen
in thirty-nine years of working in corrections." When the court took
a recess from the hearing, out in the hall reporters questioned Department of Correction officials about the expert's testimony. They admitted
that the prisons were overcrowded and that the transient building was "a
shame," but they said that rather than having the chancellor order changes,
they would prefer to make the changes by implementing their "master
plan."[3] They had not bought Al Bronstein's opening argument, but even
more astounding, they had not learned the lesson of the wily Falstaffian
sheriff Fate Thomas who three years earlier had been happy to have the

court's intervention. It had enabled him to get the new jail he knew the city needed.

The state actors in this drama, however, would fight in court long and hard, and would resist the courts' help for as far as they dared, and for years to come. In this case they lost the first round. Immediately after the conclusion of the trial, Chancellor Cantrell, without waiting for anything more, ordered the department not to house prisoners "in any quarters which were not constructed for the purpose of human habitation." This meant the transient building had to close right away. The chancellor took the rest of the case under advisement and set a post-trial briefing schedule that concluded in April.

Then in August, with remarkable speed, sorting through nearly two years' worth of discovery and three weeks of trial testimony plus voluminous briefs, the chancellor produced a sweeping sixty-three-page memorandum opinion. The product reflects the chancellor's previous training as a mechanical engineer in its attention to physical details about each correctional facility in the state. He devoted a section of his memorandum to each of the seven facilities and in some sections described specific conditions in the individual buildings.

In the second part of his memorandum, the chancellor found that the classification system failed to segregate predators from others in the population and failed to identify important individual needs for medical and psychological treatment. The staff was unqualified; the systems and procedures were deficient. There was no dispute that the facilities were overcrowded, a situation the chancellor found to produce violence and the spread of disease. Other defects included no provision for fire safety, not even evacuation plans. The fire safety issue was especially poignant in light of the fact that the year before there had been a fire at the Maury County jail resulting in the deaths of forty-two people, including eight visitors. As one expert witness for the plaintiffs had said at trial when the state defendants excused their failures by lack of funding, "Money isn't the total problem. It doesn't take money to come up with a good fire evacuation plan."

One of the most glaring pitfalls of the prison system was healthcare for the prisoners, or the lack there of: no full-time licensed physician anywhere in the entire system; untrained, unqualified staff; inmates caring for cardiac patients though they had not been taught even the basics of cardiopulmonary resuscitation; inmates with access to medical records who then would go back into the general population with that sensitive personal information; untrained inmates dangerously operating medical equipment; inmates even working in the pharmacies handling drugs.

Whether from the unsupervised pharmacies or outside sources, the chancellor found that there were plenty of drugs both licit and illicit available in the population. There were, however, no drug treatment programs available, even when an inmate had the presence of mind to request treatment. There was a pretense of a system for mental health treatments with confinement at some of the facilities, and a separate unit in Nashville, but it was abjectly inhumane. The testimony of one of the state's own witnesses was that the "system . . . fosters mental illness rather than treats it."[4]

The overcrowding in the prisons was compounded by the idleness. The department's statistics showed that a large number of inmates had jobs, but in truth even menial tasks were overstaffed so that several men were assigned to a job that "would not keep even a single worker busy." Idleness and conflicts led to frustration and then to violence. The "check-ins" system was an attempt to avoid violence, but the chancellor found it to be "a horror in itself." Taken all together, he found that the failure of the department "contributes to the unnecessary debilitation of inmates."

One marvels at Chancellor Cantrell's comprehensive grasp of the intricacies of the system and the dangerous situations produced by its failures, but at the same time, his understanding also is a testimony to the thorough presentations of the plaintiffs' attorneys. Finally, after wading through all the evidence and all the particulars, the chancellor found that the Tennessee correctional system did not comport with the requirements of the Tennessee Constitution, or even the US Constitution's lesser standards.

Seeing the handwriting on the wall, the state had asked again in its post-trial brief for time to make the necessary changes and implement a "master plan" to correct the deficiencies rather than having to follow a court's orders. The chancellor recited in his memorandum reasons for not buying that pie in the sky: previous plans had not been implemented; the department had not made much progress on its present plan, even in the two-and-a-half years *Trigg* had been pending; the General Assembly had not signed on to any plan; and there was no assurance that the next governor and his commissioner would follow through on anything started by the current administration. The chancellor saw no alternative to judicial intervention. He determined that he needed to appoint a special master to help him shape the order and to assure follow-through with the remedy.

Rather than acquiescing and doing what it ultimately would have to do, the state appealed to the court of appeals, and here it would gain respite, while the prisons seethed. Over the next nearly year and a half during the pendency of the appeal, all efforts of the plaintiffs' attorneys to get relief for their clients were frustrated, and portending rulings to come, the court even blocked the chancellor from enforcing his post-trial order prohibiting the department from housing prisoners in buildings not designed for human habitation. Despite the state's admission that it was violating that order and despite the fact that at one point the state had 206 prisoners housed in what had been an auditorium/gymnasium at the main prison with access to only two commodes, one shower, one sink, and a urinal, the court of appeals let it continue.

In May 1980, in an opinion written by Judge Henry Todd, the court issued its decision completely eviscerating Chancellor Cantrell's monumental work. Judge Todd labeled Cantrell's order "inappropriate," found that the record was "stale," and sent the case back to the chancellor to determine the current situation and consider the steps taken by the state since his order, which were minimal. The chancellor could take proof about individual events, but he was prohibited from considering "findings or conclusions with respect to the entire state correctional system as a whole." Judge Todd wanted "narrow" findings, drawn "as narrowly as the nature of the subject matter will permit." In other words, the chancellor could not regard the defendants as operating a correctional system, a system with policies and procedures and administrative decisions that controlled the living conditions of nearly eight thousand people. He could hear individual complaints, but he was not to find any commonality. Despite Rule 23 of the Tennessee Rules of Civil Procedure, Judge Todd and his colleagues essentially undermined the efficacy and economy of a class action lawsuit. Plaintiffs' lawyers saw the futility of going back to Chancery and within the month filed an appeal to the Tennessee Supreme Court.

———

Then, with a federal court decision in Cincinnati, things got really complicated. Though *Trigg* was a class action, some rogue class members had chosen to go it alone in another forum, filing *pro se* complaints in the federal district court in Nashville. Traditionally, that court had tried to respond to each such complaint from a prisoner in an appropriate manner, but after the strong opinion by Chancellor Cantrell, seeing that most of the same issues raised in the *pro se* complaints were being addressed in *Trigg*, Chief Judge Morton began placing the *pro se* filings on the "retired" docket, to wait and see whether the state appellate courts would indeed follow through.

In September 1980, however, three months after the court of appeals decision in *Trigg* had been appealed to the Tennessee Supreme Court, the Sixth Circuit, in a case from Ohio, held that abstention by the federal courts was inappropriate in cases challenging institutional violations of rights guaranteed by the Constitution. It ruled that federal courts must hear those challenges without delay.[5] In dutiful response to that ruling by the appellate court above him, Judge Morton took the *pro se* cases off the retired docket, placed them on the active docket, consolidated them all, and appointed Gordon as the lawyer in all of them. Morton still hoped the Tennessee Supreme Court would act and solve the problem, but that was not to happen. The surprise appointment was a bolt out of the blue for Gordon, but not entirely unwelcomed given the mess created by the Tennessee Court of Appeals.

The first thing Gordon had to do was figure out how to solve a sticky ethical issue. One of the *pro se* plaintiffs he had been appointed to represent was an inmate he knew all too well from past unpleasant encounters, and one of that man's complaints in his *pro se* petition was that the named plaintiffs in *Trigg*, also Gordon's clients, were not adequately representing the class. This created a conflict. A second man was only asking for money damages and Legal Services lawyers were not supposed to handle damages cases if that could be avoided. After consulting with disciplinary counsel, Gordon filed a motion to withdraw from representing them.

On December 4, 1980, Judge Morton granted his motion and promptly appointed the firm of Bass, Berry & Sims to represent those two men, but despite Gordon's request, he refused to sever their cases from those of Gordon's remaining clients. They would all stay in the stew together. It was a disparate mixture indeed, not only of clients, but also of lawyers, knowingly concocted by the judge, who at the same time was presiding over another contentious class action lawsuit in which Legal Services and

Bass lawyers were on opposite sides. As it turned out, in the best tradition of the bar, and given the ability of both sets of lawyers to compartmentalize, the mixture worked well. The young Bass lawyers who were assigned to the case and the Legal Services lawyers formed an extremely effective team.

Very quickly, the Legal Services lawyers, joined once again by the Prison Project lawyers, filed an amended complaint on behalf of the two remaining inmates Gordon had been appointed to represent, Scotty Grubbs and Elbert Thompson. It was a class action styled as an "amended complaint" since it amended and greatly expanded the *pro se* complaints previously filed by those two prisoners, essentially a reprise of *Trigg,* alleging all the familiar and still uncorrected problems at the prisons.

The next month, Cliff Knowles and Dale Grimes, young associates who had been assigned the case by the Bass firm, filed an amended complaint in the case on behalf of their clients. Cliff and Dale had a particularly difficult job. As Gordon recounted it, one of their clients enjoyed considerable notoriety in both state and federal courts as a jailhouse lawyer. He distrusted any appointed counsel and had an inflated idea of his own legal ability. Gordon, Drake, and Russ had dealt extensively with him in previous years "and none of us had ever succeeded in earning his trust." For several months, Cliff and Dale vigorously pursued the claims of their clients, in the process earning the respect and trust of both. Consequently, when they sat down and talked with them in late March about the futility of their claims for damages, armed with Judge Morton's skepticism expressed in a status conference a few days earlier, their clients listened and gave up their insistence. They dropped their claims against the individual corrections officials they had sued, the court approved, and the several lawyers who had been employed by those individual defendants were allowed to withdraw. Cliff and Dale were not so lucky. Judge Morton kept them in, and Gordon quickly assigned each one responsibilities in the ongoing discovery efforts.

Judge Morton had to deal with countless preliminary matters while the case was pending, including the state's motion asking him to abstain in deference to the state courts. Gordon opposed the motion, still stung by the treatment in the court of appeals and not at all confident as to what might happen next in the state system. Judge Morton had not changed his reading of *Hanna* since October, and he had come to his own conclusion that the state courts had been playing politics with the case, which then had been pending before the Tennessee Supreme Court for nearly a year. The legislature was about to adjourn for the year, which meant that even if the state court were to order some remedy, any funding necessary would have to wait until the next session. Furthermore, the legislature had done nothing to make any improvements during the years since the *Trigg* order in chancery court, so there was no sense waiting any longer. He felt he had no option but to proceed, do his duty, and dispose of the case forthwith. He denied the state's motion, and a week later, set *Grubbs* for trial in November.

Finally, on June 18, 1981, the Tennessee Supreme Court heard arguments in *Trigg*, a full year and twelve days after this extraordinary case had been appealed to that court. It was not a happy occasion for anyone. Right afterwards, Gordon reported to his co-counsel, "I had only gotten a short way into my argument when all five of the judges went into a twenty-minute tirade, interrupting me and even each other expressing their anger at us for litigating the same claims in federal court and their anger against the federal court for accepting jurisdiction of those claims."

Two weeks later, wasting no time now, the Tennessee Supreme Court "abstained" from the case altogether and "retired" it until after any final order in the federal case. That court's decision later was ridiculed mercilessly by Judge Morton in his *Grubbs* memorandum opinion. The idea of a state court abstaining in deference to a federal court stood the abstention doctrine on its head, and "in so far as this court is aware is wholly unprecedented in the annals of our federal system." He called it "an unfortunate curiosity" and expressed hope that it "will remain an aberration."[6] It was for the best, however. The appellate courts of Tennessee, much more sensitive politically and much less willing to apply constitutional protections than the brave chancellor had been, never would have acted to remedy the situation, and Clure Morton, the savvy East Tennessee Republican, knew that very well.

The discovery and the pretrial wrangling shifted into high gear after Judge Morton's scheduling order of June 11. Gordon further specified and refined areas of responsibility for plaintiffs' lawyers. Kozlowski would be responsible for psychological, psychiatric, and counselling services for mentally disturbed, intellectually disabled, or drug-dependent inmates. Gordon, in addition to managing the case, had overall responsibility for medical and health services. Cliff and Kitty were responsible for the classification system, which the state had made some inadequate effort to improve after Chancellor Cantrell's ruling. Sue Kay and Russ would develop proof on the violence at the facilities, including the accuracy or, as it turned out, the woeful inaccuracy of the department's statistics and its lack of awareness of what was going on "inside the walls." Kitty was responsible for development of documentary exhibits, and did that with a great deal of help from Cliff's law firm that had developed a much more sophisticated indexing system than Gordon and Drake had devised for *Trigg*. This proved essential in the management of the case, the development of proof, the presentation of evidence at trial, and the filing of a highly organized trove of documentary material at the conclusion of the trial.

After months of preparation, the case was tried in only three days during late November and early December 1981, in contrast to the three-week trial in *Trigg*. One of the reasons for the brevity was the plaintiffs' extensive use of Requests for Admissions. The state could not contest the obvious and take a chance on incurring Judge Morton's wrath by needlessly prolonging the plaintiffs' proof. In an extraordinary compliment to Chancellor Cantrell's work, Judge Morton had indicated before the trial his intent to essentially begin with the chancellor's findings and come forward; and later in his memorandum opinion, several times he employed the findings in *Trigg*. Morton recognized that the chancellor's conclusion had been supported by "extensive factual findings, the accuracy of which has been admitted by the present defendants."

The short trial was not without its drama. At one point in Gordon's cross- examination of then Commissioner Harold Bradley, it became obvious that the commissioner had no idea of the extent of violence in some of the facilities. The department's official "incident reports" failed to record what happened in the dark corners, the tiny cells, and even what happened in plain view but went unreported by the guards. Russ and Sue had reviewed the incident reports that were supposed to register any instances of violence in a facility, and then they had compared them with the medical records of the infirmary in that facility. What they found in many cases was that there would be in the medical records a report of treatment for a stab wound, but there would be no corresponding incident report on any stabbing. This omission made it appear that there was much less violence in the system than actually existed. When confronted with this on the witness stand, the commissioner had no explanation.

An expert witness hired by the state glowingly testified as to the cleanliness of the food preparation area at the Fort Pillow facility and then was confronted by evidence that in the short time while he was in the kitchen on his visit, he, like the others with him, saw a rat run across the floor. Another witness for the department testified that overcrowding was as much a state of mind as a physical condition. William Nagel, a consultant to the National Commission on Crime, put on by the plaintiffs, was asked to respond to that assessment. He said simply, "It's not a state of mind to be [in a small cell] three feet from someone defecating or urinating."[7]

Nine inmates were called as witnesses. One told of sitting on his bunk in his cell doing a flowchart for a computer class and asking his cellmate to turn down the radio. In response, his cellmate threw disinfectant in his eyes and beat him mercilessly. It took ten minutes for the guards to respond to the attack, leaving him with multiple injuries in addition to temporary blindness.

One important inmate witness, a named plaintiff in the lawsuit, almost did not testify. By the time of the trial, his sentence was almost over and in preparation for release he was transferred from the main prison in Nashville to Fort Pillow in West Tennessee. Russ was at a loss as to how they would ever persuade Scotty Grubbs to come back to Nashville now that he had done his time and, if they could persuade him, how they would get him back in time to testify. Russ and the other lawyers responsible for the case were frantically preparing other testimony for the next day. Drake, who had become managing attorney in Clarksville and consequently had not been as involved in *Grubbs* as he had been in *Trigg*, happened to be at the Nashville office on the afternoon the panic arose. He volunteered, "I'll go get him." And as Russ tells it, Drake got in his ratty old faded green '66 Chevy that looked and drove like a tank, made the four-hour trip to Fort Pillow, got there in time, and persuaded Scotty Grubbs to come back to Nashville with him instead of going home. As Drake drove Grubbs back to Nashville, he did witness prep and got him ready to testify the next day. He got him a hotel room for the night and in the morning picked him up to go to court, where Drake smoothly conducted the direct examination. After Grubbs testified, Drake took him to the bus depot and gave him a bus ticket home.

Drake could do all this so easily because of the good relationships he had built with prisoners and prison officials during his work on *Trigg*. He had spent countless hours in those years interviewing inmates and taking depositions of prison officials at the various facilities. He knew them well. Many years later after the prison litigation was just a memory, Adinah Robertson, as part of our community education program, asked Drake to speak in a prerelease class at the main prison. As she tells the story, Drake said yes he would do it, but only if whoever introduced him to the group would tell the men that he had "spent more time in prison than most of you."

Following the trial, the plaintiffs' lawyers, according to the judge's later memorandum, filed "some 20,000 to 30,000 pages of evidentiary material." The defendants objected to some of it, but with a couple of exceptions noted in a footnote, all the objections were overruled.[8] The evidence filed was accompanied by a 435-page post-trial brief, plus twenty-seven pages of proposed findings of facts and conclusions of law. The state made a similar filing in late May. Obviously, the judge and his clerks had not been sitting around waiting in the interim. Within seventy-five days, the judge issued his Memorandum and Order, 171 pages long.

The court specified and declared that multiple conditions and practices in various facilities amounted to cruel and unusual punishment in violation of both the federal and state constitutions. He ordered the parties to submit together a nominee for a special master, just as Chancellor Cantrell had four years before, and if they could not agree, he would choose one. In an attempt to get the state to take responsibility for its problems and come up with the solutions, he ordered the defendants to submit to the special master within specific deadlines plans to remedy the constitutional violations he had declared. The special master would evaluate the defendants' plans, monitor their progress in carrying them out, and report to the court.

Five days later Gordon wrote a memo to his co-counsel, "On balance, I think there is much to be grateful for in the decision, given the post-*Chapman* times in which we live." *Rhodes v. Chapman* was a ruling just one year earlier by the US Supreme Court that narrowed the conditions of confinement that might be found unconstitutional.[9] The specificity of Judge Morton's order—his failure to find systemic connections and declare other egregious practices unconstitutional—explicitly reflected his understanding of that ruling.

The question for the lawyers was whether or not to appeal, and that depended in part on what the reaction of the state would be to the ruling. Already, Gordon had the sense that, despite his initial assumption, it seemed the state might not appeal. Both the governor's office and Commissioner Bradley had made comments indicating they might finally have learned the Fate Thomas lesson and were ready to take advantage of the court's leverage. The Democratic leadership in the legislature, however, appeared to be trying to make a political issue out of the situation, and they urged appeal.

Among the plaintiffs' lawyers, the one most disappointed and perplexed by Judge Morton's memorandum was David Kozlowski, who had been responsible for the mental health proof. The judge had cited with concurrence Chancellor Cantrell's finding that the mental health unit at the main prison was "not much more than a medieval dungeon out of the dark ages," and he cited one expert witness's opinion that it bordered on the inhumane, but because of *Chapman* he drew no conclusion and issued no order.[10] David reviewed the evidence, read several cases from other circuits, and optimistically assessed in a memo to Gordon the chances of success on appeal. Then, however, in a bow to the greater good, he reluctantly concluded that "plaintiffs should not institute the appeal." With characteristic understatement, he noted, "Overall, we obtained some fairly impressive relief." As it turned out, thanks to the work of the special master, in the end significant improvements were made in several areas not specified in the order, and mental health was one of those.

Thanks to Attorney General William Leech's influence with the legislature, the state did not appeal. There was no appeal by either side and the attorneys for each side moved on to the process of selecting a nominee for special master. The national reputation of Commissioner Bradley and the wide network of the National Prison Project helped the process along considerably, and despite some disagreements between the parties, Judge Morton on November 12 appointed Patrick McManus, a widely recognized expert in the field who at that time was Secretary of Corrections for Kansas. It was not a short-term assignment; the case would go on for ten more years.

In February 1983, the state submitted to the special master a "Correction Plan for the '80s" that purported to address the problems listed in the court's order. It did not. It was product of Governor Lamar Alexander's office, a political document drafted with limited or no input from the Department of Correction, or the Attorney General, or the legislature. Among other defects, it contemplated no new funding for the department. McManus pronounced it totally flawed. The administration tried again, but what they produced three months later had few changes. Commissioner Bradley resigned.

For the rest of 1983 and into 1984, McManus cajoled and negotiated, hoping to avoid a showdown. One ray of hope: during this time, legislative leaders were persuaded to tour some of the prisons, and after seeing for themselves the deplorable conditions, they grudgingly began to accept the need to act. The governor, who needed to take the initiative, however, continued to offer ineffectual solutions that lacked a comprehensive approach and were doomed to failure. Finally, in April 1984, Judge Morton threw down the gauntlet. He entered a terse order rejecting the latest lame version of the "Correction Plan for the '80s" and gave the defendants until July to come up with a realistic plan. In frustration, he directed plaintiffs' lawyers to submit their own plan in the meantime, an unwelcomed assignment but one that would have some salutary influence on negotiations in the months to come. The judge in his charge to the defendants addressed the ongoing and ever-increasing violence in the system and implied that if they were unable to curb it, in July he would begin releasing enough prisoners to achieve single-celling and would order a lockdown of those inmates remaining in the system.

As July drew near, still the defendants produced no plan, but a combination of factors was focusing their attention. The judge's threat of a mass release, the increasing media criticism of the Alexander administration's mishandling of the chaos, and the plaintiffs' completed plan proposing that the department be placed in receivership, led to some serious discussions between the lawyers in late June and then a request for a status conference. Present at the conference with the judge and special master five days before the deadline were not only the familiar faces, Gordon, Kitty, Cliff, and soon-to-be-retiring Bill Leech, but also the incoming attorney general, W. J. Michael "Mike" Cody, and even more significant, the governor's new counsel, William Inman, a longtime friend of Morton's and a former judge himself. Morton expressed his frustration to his old friend and pronounced apocalyptically, "The hour is now." Inman got the message.

Within the week, the lawyers for the parties sequestered themselves in Bass, Berry & Sims' conference room, away from the scrutiny of the press. Their nonstop discussions were mediated by the special master and after three days resulted in an agreed order that provided for outside "evaluators" to examine all aspects of the prison system and make "recommendations" to the defendants, which the defendants were bound to follow unless they had an alternative proposal that was approved by the special master. This profound breakthrough, which for the first time committed the state to much needed outside guidance, preserved the politically necessary appearance that the state was in control of the solutions. The evaluators were selected in the next few months, of course after some wrangling about the scope of their examination, and they began their arduous work in November 1984.

Unfortunately, the state did not abandon its foot dragging. Though it remained under the court's order to reduce overcrowding, the population numbers were going the other way, and the department made every effort to hide the failure. In March 1985, McManus discovered the state's ruse to prevent his learning the extent to which individual facilities were still overcrowded: When the department was informed he would be visiting a facility, it would move a large group of inmates by bus to another facility just ahead of his visits, "midnight transfers," and then when the visits were over, the department would move them right back. He reported this to the court. In response, Judge Morton threatened to release three thousand prisoners in order to bring the facilities in compliance with recommended capacity. He relented only with the state's repentance and renewed assurances. Soon after, having reached the appropriate age, Morton, with great relief, took senior status and happily transferred the case to his most junior colleague, Judge Thomas Aquinas Higgins, recently appointed by President Ronald Reagan.

If the parties thought the enforcement would relax with the new judge, they soon were corrected. In June 1985, Judge Higgins, made aware by Gordon and the special master that the state still was dragging its feet, summarily ordered that the total prison population be reduced from its current 10,000 to 7,019 by December of that year. When in October it became obvious that the state would not or could not do it, he took matters in his own hands and ordered that, with rare exceptions, no new inmates be admitted until the total population was reduced to the "designated capacity."

The state began complying. At last state leaders were getting religion. After nine years of avoidance, resistance, and abdication by its appellate courts, administration, and legislature, the conditions in the prisons were only getting worse. Then came destructive prison riots in July 1985.[11] The whole mess had become a political liability for the governor. Finally, he called the General Assembly into a special session to be held in November, devoted exclusively to the corrections crisis. This was the key. Despite the usual demagogy and vilification of federal courts, in the end the session produced a historic commitment to reforming the state's troubled prison system.

The legislative process was aided immeasurably by resources Pat McManus brought to the table. The evaluators he had assembled with the agreement of the state, all nationally known experts, had assessed the system and come up with a reasonable blueprint for reform. At the same time, McManus had established a relationship of mutual trust with prison administrators. They came together to the legislature with a program that convinced key legislators of the need for genuine reform, not just to satisfy the court but to better serve Tennessee.

The process was also aided at a key moment by a tragic figure we will meet again in the chapter on health care, the brilliant and passionate legislator Tommy Burnett. On a day when resistance had reemerged in the House and a majority of that body clamored for defiance of the federal court, Burnett arose. Invoking his own prison experience to which he had been sentenced by that same federal court, and appealing to the memory of Confederate forbearers who had suffered in Yankee prisons, he pled for reform. His extemporaneous eloquence turned the tide. The legislature stayed in session, adopted the plan, and, over the course of the next few years, appropriated an additional $300 million to improve the prisons.

The special session also created a sentence revision commission that would be headed by Circuit Judge Barbara Haynes, one of the state's first female trial judges. The commission spent years comprehensively revising Tennessee's criminal code and sentencing laws, which had never undergone such a rewrite in the state's two-hundred-year history.

It was one of the most significant reforms achieved by the litigation, not because it had been ordered by the federal court, but because the special master and evaluators had persuaded state officials that true criminal justice reform could not be achieved by simply fixing the prisons but must include reform of the criminal legal system itself.

After many more battles, the case at last was concluded in 1993. In the course of it, the special master and evaluators had made more than 1,500 specific "recommendations" for remedial action, and for the most part, the state had complied. Sometimes that compliance came only after failures to comply had been exposed by plaintiffs' counsel. Sometimes that compliance required pressure from McManus and/or intervention by the judge, but finally, more than ten years after Judge Morton's order, the enforcement of that order had accomplished a reformation that, with one exception, satisfied Judge Higgins. When he closed the case, the judge in his concluding memorandum harkened back once again to the origin of the case in Chancellor Cantrell's court: "There can be no doubt that the shocking conditions which existed at . . . the time this litigation was first instituted in state court and later in this Court, do not exist today. The Tennessee prison system today is an altogether new and completely rehabilitated system."[12]

Many years before, Higgins had been the president of the Nashville Bar Association. A highly respected lawyer throughout his career, he appreciated good lawyering and collegiality. When as a judge he closed the book on this case, he graciously concluded with a nod to the lawyers, "The Court compliments the attorneys for the lawyer-like fashion, in the highest and best tradition of the Bar, in which this litigation has been conducted." He named specifically Gordon and the two most recent attorneys general, Mike Cody and Charles Burson. He recognized "their respective colleagues." He thanked Pat McManus and named him "the father of the new Tennessee prison system."[13]

———————

Ironically, as this case was winding down, legal standards were changing, and federal legislation was enacted that would have made the case and its advances impossible. In 1991, the US Supreme Court in *Wilson v. Seiter* limited the causes of action for cruel and unusual punishment and required that to maintain his case, a prisoner would have to prove that the prison official had acted "deliberately indifferent." Four years later the court held in *Sandin v. Conner* that to constitute a violation of the Eighth Amendment, the action or condition suffered by the prisoner must have been "atypical and a significant hardship in relation to the ordinary incidents of prison life."

At the same time, the US Congress underwent a profound change in 1994, following Representative Newt Gingrich's "Contract with America." The Prison Reform Litigation Act of 1996 was not an act to encourage prison reform—just the opposite. It restricted both an inmate's right to sue in federal court, and echoing the pinched ruling of the Tennessee Court of Appeals thirteen years before, provided that "relief in any civil action with respect to prison conditions shall extend no further than necessary to correct the violation of the federal right of a particular plaintiff or plaintiffs." Longtime advocates for civil rights and good government, both Bill Leech and Mike Cody went to Washington to testify against the bill as it was being considered. They frankly conceded that but for the federal court's ruling the state never could have achieved the much-needed reforms. Congress, however, was not so much interested in their experience as in its own ideology. The bill passed. Not content with that, as will be discussed more fully in Chapter 20, that same Congress in another legislative move placed numerous restrictions on any organization that accepted any funding from the Legal Services Corporation, including prohibitions against handling class action lawsuits or any lawsuits at all on behalf of prisoners.

And with that this chapter ends.

The progress of this seventeen-year-long lawsuit has taken us chronologically far ahead of our story. We need to go back now to the time long before Judge Higgins's benediction, back to when *Trigg* was pending before Chancellor Cantrell, when Louis Farrell opined about our lawyers being wet behind the ears and our $220 cost per case being out of line.

CHAPTER 7

Mostly Drake

The Saviors come not home tonight;
Themselves they could not save.

—A. E. HOUSMAN, "A SHROPSHIRE LAD," 1887

Even back in 1978, there were others with a better opinion of our practice. After a two-day custody trial in Third Circuit Court, Judge Joseph Loser Jr., chatting informally, surprised me by saying, "You know, I think Legal Services is getting to be one of the better law firms in town." Our client in that case, a few days later, sent a dear note to Gayle Squires and me thanking us "for working so hard for me." She wrote that even if she could have afforded to pay a lawyer, "he and his assistant could not have given me better service." She thanked Gayle for her patience "and for being so understanding. I got a lot strength from you."

We were also developing a national reputation among Legal Services people thanks to David Tarpley's work on consumer issues, Drake and Gordon on prisons, Russ and Andy Shookhoff on juvenile issues, and Gordon on healthcare. As a result, we were able to recruit from all over the country excellent candidates for attorney jobs that came with our opening new offices.

We sent lawyers to recruit at job fairs, such as those sponsored by the National Association for Public Interest Law, and to law schools, not only those in Tennessee, but also to Howard, Northeastern, and others that emphasized public service. We were looking for people who were committed to this kind of practice, and we were seeking diversity. Our recruitment of Black lawyers was helped in some measure by the Reggie program, which in the early 1970s had been moved from Penn to Howard's law school with a new priority of selecting Black and other minority fellows.

To fill the new positions in the Clarksville office and other openings in 1979, we had more than two hundred applications. In the end, we chose eight, a diverse group: graduates of Duke, Northeastern, Georgetown, Vanderbilt, Boston University, the University of San Francisco, and the University of Tennessee law schools. They were not experienced lawyers; they were recent graduates. But they were highly motivated and had proven already their strong commitment to the work by their previous experience in poverty law or similar service. Gordon set up a training program for all the new lawyers. Drake volunteered to go to Clarksville as the managing attorney and supervise the new lawyers there.

Drake's going to Clarksville is a story in itself. Several months earlier, when we learned we would receive the expansion grant from LSC and open an office there, we knew we would have to have an experienced lawyer manage the office. Certainly, we could not send our new recruits up there to manage on their own; that would be too much like Nashville in 1973. Despite our large applicant pool, we had not found or been able to hire any experienced lawyers who were committed to legal aid work. For a while it looked bleak. Then one day Drake came to me and asked to have lunch together. Our lunch date consisted of taking our brown bags across the street from Parkway Towers to the crumbling concrete plaza beside the Metropolitan Auditorium.

Drake was then all of twenty-eight years old, but he had worked with us as a law student and had been a lawyer for three years, which made him a real veteran at Legal Services in those days. He looked at me across that little concrete table and, as he often did, began with some self-deprecation. "Now forgive me if I'm out of line or you think this is a crazy idea," his voice faded away, and then he jumped to the point, "I think I could open and manage that office in Clarksville if you're willing to trust me with it. I really like working on these big cases with Gordon and Russ, and I do want to come back to Nashville in a couple of years, but I think I could do this." I summoned all my acting skills from my high school senior play, tried to be coy, and deadpanned, "Well, I think it might work." I did not say what I was thinking, that a couple of years would not be enough, so I am going to try to play him in now and later try to get him to stay longer. The hook was set, and that was enough.

Drake was not by nature a small town guy. Though he had gone to college in Iowa at Grinnell, he grew up in Washington, DC, and was proud to say that one of his summer jobs while in college had been helping dig the trench for the new Metro DC subway. Careful not to dampen his newfound rural enthusiasm, I did not remind him of the provincial greeting I had received that past fall when I went to talk to the bar association in Clarksville about our opening an office there. I was walking down the sidewalk with several lawyers on our way to the lunchtime meeting of the bar when an older lawyer, prominent in state bar activities, a person I assumed would have a wider view, came up beside me and casually said, as if it were just a matter-of-fact part of a friendly conversation, "You know, we really don't think much about your opening an office here. In fact, we don't want *anything* up here that comes from Nashville. We don't want any Nashville banks up here; we don't want any Nashville businesses; we don't want any Nashville lawyers; nothing from Nashville. For example, if they were giving away ice cream at a Fourth of July picnic up here and we found out it had come from Nashville, we would not eat it."

Drake moved to Clarksville and did much better at community relations than I had done. He cultivated relationships in the bar. He played on softball teams. He became a part of the community, and he stayed twice as long as he meant to originally. His perseverance and success were helped after a while by the fact that he met Lynne Marrale there. Their relationship survived her experience on arriving at her first Legal Services party. Every woman there had on a badge that proclaimed, "I dated Drake." They married near the end of his time in Clarksville. And he was not without "big cases" while there. In addition to handling individual cases, supervising the five new lawyers handling cases in seven rural counties, and staying somewhat involved in the prison case, Drake filed several federal lawsuits.

Any motor vehicle one might see by the side of the road today that has a florescent orange or other color sticker on the back window is a testament to a federal class action suit brought by Drake and one of his young mentees, Marty Brigham. Before their lawsuit, if a person had a breakdown or ran out of gas and left his car on the apron beside the road to go get help, no matter how short a time he might be gone, a police officer who happened by, not knowing the circumstances, might consider the vehicle abandoned and have it towed away. The owner then, of course, would incur towing and storage fees, in addition to the shock and inconvenience he would experience upon his return. What then would be a major inconvenience for a person who could afford to pay would become a major catastrophe for a poor person who could not.

A man to whom this had happened came into the Clarksville office one day and asked for help. Because of his low income, he could not afford to pay the bills for towing and storage and thus could not get his car back. To compound it all, he was incurring more storage fees every day. The tow-in lot would not relent. Marty and Drake filed a federal class action lawsuit alleging that the whole procedure was a violation of due process. The court agreed with them and ordered the state to come up with a procedure that warned the vehicle owner and gave him a certain amount of time to remove the vehicle from the side of the road before it would be towed. The notice to the motorist that the state devised was printed on the florescent sticker affixed to the back window of the vehicle. Because the prior practice was declared a violation of due process, the court ordered that Drake and Marty's client could get his car back without having to pay the fees.

With another of his new lawyers, Michael Pruden, Drake filed a federal class action lawsuit challenging the conditions in the Montgomery County jail. Among other complaints, the lawsuit cited that in some situations up to four people would be housed in an eight-foot by nine-foot cell. Like Walt's case ten years earlier in Davidson County, this case, though tried for a couple of days, finally was resolved mostly by a settlement and resulted in a modern jail being built in Clarksville. Despite the settlement, unlike Walt's case, this result was not met with general approbation in the community. Drake was not an entirely popular figure for having brought the case on behalf of his poor imprisoned clients, but this did not bother him a bit.

Sometime later he came across a speech by a federal judge in Texas that articulated his motivation in this case and many others. The federal judge, appropriately named, was William Wayne Justice. The speech, entitled "Burrs under a Saddle," had been given before a group of Legal Services lawyers in Texas. In his first sentence, Judge Justice recognized

that the lawyers he was addressing were "sometimes attacked as dangerous nuisances." He went on to detail the accusation:

> There would be no problems—no homelessness, no hunger, no under-
> class—if only you would stop bringing them up, as you do, unavoidably,
> with every case you handle. And even if your clients didn't go away,
> they would then be easier to ignore, through comfortable, well-worn
> abstractions that efface their individuality.

The judge encouraged the Legal Services lawyers to be persistent in
the "reiteration of the facts, your highly specific, personal, individuated
reminders of the world beyond the hallucinatory domain of privilege."
Then in the last paragraph of the speech, he applied the title: "In your
truth-telling role, you are like burrs under a saddle."

Drake kept a copy of the speech taped to the wall above his desk, and
he gave a copy of it to each of us and to every new lawyer who came
to work with us. It was a part of his ritual of orientation, his passion for
the work, and his concern that we all stay focused with mutual support.
That concern went beyond the office he happened to be in at the time.

In 1980, we thought we were going to have enough money to hire
another lawyer in Nashville, and we had the perfect candidate. Juliet Griffin had worked with us on numerous cases when she had been a social
worker in Nashville several years before, and she had clerked with us
while in law school at UT, where she was editor of the law review. After
law school, she clerked with Federal District Judge Thomas Wiseman Jr.,
and now she was ready to come be a lawyer with us. We offered her the
job and she accepted. Then, shades of Gordon's experience with Walt, a
couple of months before she was to start, I discovered to my great embarrassment that we were not going to have enough money to pay her and
would not be able to fill the position. Her salary would have been $15,000
a year. Drake decided we could not let her down and could not miss this
opportunity to have her join us.

He came to see me after the managing attorney meeting in which we
had discussed the problem and said he wanted to go talk to each of the
lawyers in the Nashville office who had been with us more than three or
four years and thus made more than the $15,000 we needed. He would
ask them to take a salary cut to help raise enough money to fund Juliet's

salary. We had done this before a couple of times. Several years earlier Dot Dobbins and Carol McCoy volunteered to take a salary cut in order to increase the salary of their secretary. Russ remembers that when he began working full-time with us but was only being paid a partial salary by Vanderbilt for supervising clinic students, Carol, Gordon, and Lucy Honey had taken a salary cut that enabled us to supplement his pay. I had decided sometime before that given my position I could not be the person to ask something like this of anyone on the staff. I did not want them to feel any pressure from me, but I certainly did not mind Drake doing it.

Drake and I each made our financial commitments, and he went off to talk with others. A few days later, he let me know that he had enough pledges to almost cover it, pledges even from attorneys who had argued that we should bite the bullet and renege on our offer. As it turned out in the topsy-turvy world of a nonprofit organization's financials, soon after Juliet started, because of changes in funding, we saw that we were going to have enough money for the salary, and we never had to collect on the pledges. It had been a powerful statement of commitment, however.

Just as Drake's commitment went beyond his local office, it went beyond our organization to others in the state. Because he later developed a specialty of sorts in housing law, others could call on him for help. Lenny Croce remembers that shortly after he had started at Rural, he had some clients who wanted to stop the Oak Ridge Housing Authority from perpetuating segregation by building new units only in a Black section of town. Not knowing where to start, he called Drake. "He not only was familiar with the case law on breaking up segregated housing patterns, he connected us with an expert from Chicago who did an 'impact' study. He also knew of some friendly official in HUD."

Lenny "used all of Drake's suggestions to get HUD first to disapprove the proposed site," then to be an ally in a lawsuit that followed. After several years of ligation, he won that lawsuit in the Sixth Circuit Court of Appeals, resulting in public housing being built on scattered sites in non-minority communities for the first time in Tennessee, a project that later was "held up as a model for other communities." And he concludes, "The smartest thing I did was call Drake."

Other people called Drake on non-Legal Services-related business, but that too had some impact on his effectiveness for his clients. He was active in several organizations in the community, but his main forte was his (after hours) involvement in politics. It was a materialistic involvement: yard signs. For twenty-seven years beginning with Walt's campaign for public defender in 1978, Drake was the person many candidates in Davidson County called on for yard signs. They had to meet his good government standards, but those candidates were plentiful after Walt's groundbreaking campaign. Drake organized platoons of workers, but he also did the work himself. Gayle Squires recalled waking up "very early one weekend morning . . . before it was yet full daylight" looking out her kitchen window and seeing Drake "twenty miles from his home . . . hammering up the yard sign I had requested." Former mayor of Nashville Bill Purcell nailed it: "Drake was always there with help for all good political causes, and I think it is fair to say we all depended on him as a force for good, house by house by house."

There were occasional specific benefits for our clients, as well, from Drake's seasonal after-hours job. One day, probably in the late 1980s after he had developed his reputation in the field, I happened to meet him when he came back from general sessions court after handling a more difficult-than-usual detainer warrant. "How did you do?" Rather sheepishly he told me, "I had a real bad case, but I knew things were looking up when I walked into the courtroom and the judge announced, 'Here comes Drake Holliday, the yard sign king.'"

There is much more about Drake's advocacy in the previous chapter covering the prison cases and a later chapter on housing law, but this chapter is simply about him as a person. He was a mainstay of our staff for more than thirty years, and it was the greatest tragedy of our life together as a staff that in 2006, a few months after he left to be a part of a bankruptcy law firm, this passionate soul took his own life. Sharmila Murthy, a Skadden Fellow with us and a talented artist as well as an excellent lawyer who had worked closely with Drake, painted a haunting portrait of him that hangs in the Nashville office today, a tribute to his commitment and collegial spirit.[1]

CHAPTER 8

Women Lawyers Challenge Domestic Violence

> Legal Services has given me a chance to begin picking up the pieces of my life and putting it together again. You've given me Hope. Thanks. Thanks so much.
>
> —ANN F., NASHVILLE, 1988

This is a story of an awakening in the law brought about by the women's movement of the 1960s and 1970s.

Until the 1970s, women had been a rarity in law schools. Even as their numbers began to increase in that decade, there remained few opportunities for them in the practice. Hardly any firms would hire them. One of the opportunities that was available was work in the new Legal Services offices. These women pioneers, who in many cases had been through mistreatment and discrimination themselves, brought a heightened sensitivity to other people's problems, particularly women's problems. They opened our eyes and profoundly changed our approach to family law.

What we had missed came through vividly to Gordon and me in the late 1980s when we resolved to go through the closed files accumulated over the preceding two decades to assess which ones we could destroy or edit responsibly. We had carried those hundreds of banker's boxes

from the Stahlman Building to the Sudekum Building to Parkway Towers and back to the Stahlman Building again, where they now lay jum-
bled in a basement storeroom. One afternoon we bravely descended into
that dark, dimly lit cavern and began looking through what we had. It
was an overwhelming task and we did not get far. After a couple more
trips down there, spread over the next few weeks, the frustrations of the
task and the demands upstairs brought the whole quixotic endeavor to
a whimpering end.

In the process of examining even the small number of files we got
through, there were embarrassing revelations about our early practice
in family law. We were appalled as the files revealed our ignorance back
then about the seriousness and implications of domestic violence. We,
like most lawyers in those days, had taken it for granted, just one of those
unfortunate things that happens in some marriages, part of the culture. I
remembered with chagrin a man (whose case we did not take) once plain-
tively questioning me, "If you can't beat your wife, who can you beat?"

As we went through those files, we shuddered seeing the number of
times we had advised an abused woman that she and her husband should
go to counseling to see if they could work it out before we would file
anything for her. We had no appreciation of the danger we were leaving her in by not taking immediate action to stop the abuse. As we sat
there in the basement with files on our laps, that past flashing through
our minds, we recognized also the world we had been living in then, the
practice we had been a part of when almost all the lawyers, and certainly
all the judges, were men, before the women, liberated by the spirit of the
1960s, had come to the practice, had seen the problems, and had begun
formulating solutions.

Dot Dobbins began working at Legal Services in the summer of 1972,
between her first and second years of law school at Vanderbilt, clerking
with R. B. J. Campbelle in what was for a short time our office at Juvenile Court. When Campbelle went to teach at MTSU and that office was
closed, Dot moved to the downtown office where during her last year as
a clerk she was able to go to court under the third-year practice rule, and
reflecting the plurality of our cases, that meant mostly handling family
matters: divorce, custody, child support. Consistent with how a number of us got our jobs at Legal Services in those days, after graduation

Dot stayed on as a lawyer and began practicing at our Matthew Walker Health Center office in North Nashville.

While in college at Southern Methodist University during the late 1960s, Dot was active in the student YWCA, was president of the YW on her campus, and was a member of a national advocacy committee, "Young Women Committed to Action." This involvement raised her awareness of many women's issues coming to the fore in those days, including issues around domestic violence. During her first year at Vanderbilt, Dot helped start a women's center across the street from the law school at Scarritt College, a more welcoming campus than Vanderbilt in those days. The YWCA downtown recognized her leadership and asked her to join its board. There she began working with other board members to raise awareness about domestic violence and look for ways to deal with the problem in the community.

The other lawyer in our Matthew Walker office was Carol McCoy, who had finished law school the year before. Dot and Carol had become friends in law school, being two of only twenty-two women in the student body of 450. Carol remembers that Dot "told me about the women's movement, about NOW [National Organization for Women], about the ERA [Equal Rights Amendment], about the women suffragettes." Dot also invited her to a NOW meeting, "and I was enthused by the energy and drive that the women showed for improving the lot of other women, not just themselves." Carol joined NOW; she read books Dot recommended to her; she became active in the YWCA and lobbied for the ERA. Soon, like Dot, she was invited to join the YW board where in years to come they were able to work with others in that organization to make real differences in the lives of many women in Nashville. First, however, they struggled together in the basement of Matthew Walker adjacent to the railroad tracks in North Nashville, learning to practice law and trying to figure out how to help their clients.

Nearly 60 percent of the cases Carol and Dot handled in their office concerned family law issues, many with domestic violence. One disappointing case Carol recalls vividly even more than forty years later. A woman in her forties appeared in the office early one morning without an appointment, her clothes and appearance in disarray, desperate and afraid. She asked to see a lawyer right away, and Carol listened to her story.

The woman had been attacked by her husband the night before, and this was not the first time. He had knifed her previously and she showed Carol the scars on her arm, midriff, and abdomen. Carol had been in discussions about domestic violence, but "this was a first for me. I did not know that men knifed women (or that a woman would survive such a knifing)." Despite that attack, the woman had continued to live with him.

This time she ran. He chased her with the knife, threatening to kill her. When she ran across the railroad tracks, she fell on the tracks, but managed to get up and keep running. Finally, she managed to lose him, probably because he was drunk. When Carol saw her that morning "she was truly panic-stricken and scared to death that he would kill her. I told her that I would immediately seek a restraining order and protect her." Carol had the woman stay in her office while she typed up the summons, complaint, affidavit, pauper's oath, and proposed order. She drove her to the courthouse, filed the papers, presented them to a judge, and got the restraining order signed. A court date was set for the following week. In those days, Carol had nothing further to offer. All she could do was give the client a copy of the order, trust that the husband would obey, and send her back home. There were no support groups, no shelters, no social workers trained in the dynamics of domestic violence, and little enforcement by the police.

The next week, the client did not show up for the hearing: "I never saw her again. I tried to reach her repeatedly. I never found out what happened to her, although I did watch the papers for news of any deaths." Carol, who recently retired after twenty years as a chancellor in Davidson County, reflects back now on her experience with that client and our limitations then: "I realize how useless I had been. The reality of her fear, her helplessness, the likelihood that she would suffer serious physical injury or death, and the lack of any real options for her only became apparent to me over time." We all had to learn, and for a while our progress was slow.

In 1974, we formed the family law section in the downtown office. The motivation was simply to make our practice more efficient. Nearly half of all our cases were family law matters, and with no specialization it meant that all our lawyers were handling family cases. On a given morning of a motion docket or show cause docket in Fourth Circuit or Probate Court, we would have three or four of our lawyers sitting there for a good part of the morning, each one waiting for his or her one case to be called. By funneling all the family law cases to one lawyer, just one of us could handle them all, preventing downtime and duplication. It worked well, and I got to spend a lot of time in court, which I enjoyed.

In the nearly two years I managed the family law section, 1974 to 1976, I cannot remember any progress on the issue of domestic violence beyond our increasing lack of hesitancy in the use of restraining orders. The judges who heard the cases were elderly men whose traditional world-views included male prerogative and control. Good men, but of another era. They had not been educated about the issue, and if they had any awareness of NOW, they probably regarded its concerns as the rantings of bra-burning radical feminists. When I moved over to become executive director, Dot left North Nashville and came downtown to head the section. Then things began to change.

Dot inherited from me two outstanding support staff, Pat Maynard (later Hylton—she married our accountant, Randall) as secretary and Gayle Jennings, later Squires, as paralegal. Gayle had been the courtroom clerk in the Fourth Circuit Court where the majority of our domestic relations cases were heard. Over several years she had come to appreciate our work in that court and had become attracted to our mission. She had talked about that many times with her friend, Pat Maynard, and when our paralegal position opened up, Pat recruited her. Gayle left the certain security of that very comfortable government position to take the decidedly insecure position with our ragtag group in the Sudekum Building, and her bravery in making that move became a blessing to many.

For nearly thirty-five years thereafter, Gayle was a kind and sympathetic help to thousands of women. She was often the first person applicants would talk to about their problems. They would comment on how understanding and reassuring she was at that traumatic time. She was a persistent advocate in case acceptance conferences where decisions had to be made about how many and which cases we could reasonably accept that week. She literally as well as figuratively often held the hand of the client through the progress of the case. And, given her intimate knowledge about East Nashville politics, about the personalities in the courthouse, and about the practices of a wide swath of the lawyers in town, she helped us become more effective. She was our guide: she told us who was trustworthy, who was not; who to see; where to file it; why you can't do that. And because of her family's political connections—her father, Robert Jennings, had been the Nashville city attorney under a former mayor and her mother had been a deputy circuit court clerk—she gave us a creditability in the Davidson County courthouse we had not had before.

The first lawyer to join Dot in the family law section was Margaret Behm, who, though fresh out of law school, brought her own considerable energy and savvy. When Margaret transferred to the consumer law section, Jimmie Lynn Ramsaur and Floyd Price joined Dot. These three lawyers handled hundreds of cases at a time, and they drew on their clients' experiences to raise awareness of domestic violence. Jimmie Lynn and Dot were involved in numerous organizations and activities that were helping victims and educating the public. At the same time, they were attending conferences and training programs sponsored by LSC, the YWCA, and others, learning about the dynamics of domestic violence and "victims' mentality." They learned that the frustrating experience Carol had, and they themselves had many times, of the client not following through was not unusual. They learned that on average a victim will go back seven times because economically and/or emotionally there were no alternatives. They learned that the violence gets worse every time. But they also learned not to get frustrated and not to threaten "Don't call me back" when the client did not follow through. They learned about the pathetic, persistent patterns.

A November 1977 newspaper article quotes Dot shedding light on one part of the problem, "Often women won't report that their husbands have beaten them or won't even seek medical care. They are embarrassed or feel they must have deserved it."[1] She appeared on panels at the Vanderbilt Women's Center and many times on radio programs talking about the issue. On one panel discussion, Dot reflected that her clients who had been beaten often would not mention it at first in an interview; they just did not think it was relevant. "Too many people still believe that it is a rite of marriage for husband and wife to knock each other around," she said, and she quoted research showing that there is violence in 60 percent of marriages and in 10 percent of them the wife requires medical treatment as a result. Being on the board of the YWCA, Dot and Carol helped start the first local organization devoted exclusively to dealing with these issues, a YWCA project called "Services to Wo/men in Crisis."

Soon after that, the YWCA opened the first local domestic violence shelter in Nashville.

In the summer of 1978, Dot received a grant from LSC to hire three law students to work on domestic violence issues. Mary Walker and Abby Rubenfeld were assigned to do court watching and to document the difficulties victims of domestic violence encountered dealing with the court system. Based on their observations and research, they and Dot drafted Order of Protection legislation for Tennessee. Ann Young, the third student, drafted an adaptation of the Uniform Custody Jurisdiction Act to address other problems experienced by some of our clients. The next year Dot worked with Allan Ramsaur at TALS to get the legislation passed. Jimmie Lynn was instrumental in compiling a report by the Tennessee Commission on the Status of Women in 1979 that called for state funding of shelters for victims of domestic violence, an education program, and increased cooperation within the criminal justice system to address the problem.

In 1985, the lawyers in the family law section—working with Adinah Robertson, our community education coordinator—developed a handbook, *The Legal Rights of Battered Women*. They wanted to inform women about the protections that now had become available to them if they found themselves in an abusive relationship. They covered details of divorce, police assistance, warrants, child custody, shelters, and counseling, all written in "plain language," either avoiding or explaining legal terms. As was the case with many of our community education publications, other groups were anxious to see this information disseminated widely, and in this case, the Young Lawyers Conference of the Tennessee Bar Association and the Nashville YWCA funded the printing and distribution.

Dot was the managing attorney of the family law section for eleven years until she left to become general counsel at the Tennessee Department of Human Services, formerly the welfare department. The irony of a Legal Services attorney being appointed to that position was not lost on those of us who in the previous decade had, in a way of speaking, made a career out of filing lawsuits against that department, and who had been around when the commissioner of that department tried to persuade the United Way to stop us from filing class action lawsuits against him and the department. Many relationships had changed for the better in the intervening years and a new respect for law and order had evolved in that department.

Lucinda Smith became the managing attorney of the family law section following Dot and continued her work, but Nashville was not the only office where staff attorneys were doing good work in this field and coordinating with other community groups. Judy Bond-McKissack in our Clarksville office was an advisory board member of Safehouse, a shelter for abused women that served the same seven counties covered by that office. Pat Mock in the same office was on the Domestic Violence State Coordinating Council and chaired the Montgomery County Foster Care Review Board. Donna Sonner in our Murfreesboro office chaired the Rutherford County Domestic Violence Program.

Kathy Skaggs came to the Gallatin office in 1982 after receiving her law degree from New York University where she had been a Root-Tilden Scholar. She had grown up in Kentucky, graduated from Western Kentucky University, and one of the reasons she wanted to be a legal aid lawyer was "because I grew up in a working-class family and we experienced some of the same problems that many clients have to deal with."[2] In Gallatin more than 60 percent of her cases involved domestic violence, and early on, in addition to representing individual clients, she cofounded the Sumner County Coalition Against Domestic Violence. She helped draft and pass legislation to provide state funding for domestic violence shelters and additional legislation to make it easier for police officers to make arrests in domestic violence cases. She later wrote grant proposals that brought in over $100,000 in funding to the local coalition, and Legal Services provided space to the group in our Gallatin office until it could secure its own place. Thanks to those grants, Legal Services lawyers in the Gallatin office were now able not only to represent domestic violence victims in court, but also help them secure support services, shelter, and financial support they needed in their time of crisis. The name of their project was "HomeSafe."

The staff in all our offices came to see that comprehensive support was essential for women trying to escape domestic violence, that they needed more than just a lawyer. It would take a holistic approach to stabilize her life, help her feel empowered, and help her break the cycle of violence. Our lawyers became very resourceful, as illustrated in a case Jean Crowe handled several years later for Jill, a young woman with four small children and an abusive husband. She wanted to go to a vocational school so she could get a job that would improve the family's financial situation, but her husband, who belittled and opposed everything she wanted to do, opposed this. He threatened her life and on one occasion slammed her headfirst into a wall, saying he would not stop until she was braindead. She went to court and got an Order of Protection, but it didn't work. The violence continued. Her husband hired an attorney and filed for divorce, but that did not calm his cruelty and coercion. The Domestic Violence Unit of the Metro Police Department referred Jill to Legal Aid. Jean countersued and represented her in multiple hearings, including contempt proceedings for the husband's violations of orders. Finally, the divorce was granted, with orders that provided effective protection for Jill and her children.

In the meantime, of course, Jill had many other problems. Jean, paralegal Maria Arvizu, and an intern from Vanderbilt Divinity School helped Jill get counseling for depression, which is often triggered by domestic violence. They helped her get financial assistance from the Department of Human Services. They gave her bus passes when her car was repossessed. They helped her get a grant to pay her school tuition, and a church in Brentwood paid for her books. After the case was over, Jill wrote an account of her experience and said that at one point

> I didn't know or care what the future held for me . . . I was feeling alone and abandoned the world . . . but it appeared to me that Legal Aid [cared], especially Jean Crowe and Maria. . . . They not only helped me get back on my feet, but they gave me the love and support that I needed to build my self-esteem.

The multiple problems associated with domestic violence of course are compounded when the victim is a person from another culture who has limited or no ability to communicate in the English language and is unfamiliar with the legal system. She is even more lost and confused. As this became more apparent, we applied for grants to hire bilingual paralegals. In an interview with the *Tennessean*, one of those paralegals, Grace Guerra, pointed out that in addition to the issues of child custody, housing, finances, and employment, there was the issue of immigration. And there is a twist on that: "abusers often tell their victims they will be deported if they call the police."[3] In a later interview, Grace expanded on the power play of the abusers, "the level of violence I see is very high, and often weapons are involved."[4]

Very early in her career at Legal Services, Jean began looking beyond the individual cases she was handling for ways to improve the legal systems and support systems that dealt with family law. By 1989, she had become so prominent in her advocacy that the Tennessee Supreme Court appointed her to a state Child Support Guidelines Commission that set for the first time a standard for courts to use. In 1994, she cofounded the Nashville Coalition Against Domestic Violence and became a spokesperson for that group, advocating for a domestic violence division in the police department and more prosecutors in the district attorney's office to handle those cases. At one point she was chair of the Davidson County Death Review Team that monitored and publicized the deaths from domestic violence, emphasizing the profound seriousness of the problem.

After Congress in 1996 placed limitations on lawyers employed by an LSC grantee prohibiting legislative and administrative advocacy, Jean advocated for the cause from her positions on various Tennessee and American Bar Association entities. At different times she was on the Executive Council of the TBA Family Law Committee, Chair of the TBA Domestic Violence Committee, on the Governing Council of the ABA Family Law Section, and on at least three other ABA councils, committees, or commissions. These gave her a platform from which she could continue to speak to the issues affecting her clients, even if not in their names.

In mid-2010, the *Tennessean* ran an article detailing the depletion of the Nashville Police Department's Domestic Violence Unit over the past four years, the decrease in the number of assistant district attorneys handling those cases, and the increase in the number of cases they had dropped in that time without prosecution. In response, Jean and Judge Phil Smith, who heard many of the domestic relations cases in Davidson County, went to see Mayor Karl Dean to express their concern about these failings. The mayor later recounted the meeting: "Jean also told me, in no uncertain terms, that she wanted *me* to do something about it—she asked for my office to lead a domestic violence safety and accountability assessment to review the policies and practices of every Metro agency involved in our city's response to domestic violence crimes."

The mayor quickly appointed an assessment team that included representatives of every Metro department dealing with domestic violence along with members of organizations in the community concerned about the issue, and he named Diane Lance in his office to head it. Two years later they released their sweeping assessment that made fifty-five recommendations, and the city was quick to begin implementation. In September 2014, the city opened an advocacy center that addressed fourteen of the recommendations in one package, and at the dedication it was named the Jean Crowe Advocacy Center. Whitney Blanton, who had been a paralegal with Jean at Legal Aid and before that a victim advocate at the district attorney's office, was named manager of the center.

Less than a year later, Jean died, felled by an inoperable brain tumor. After her death, the Family Law Section of the ABA created the Jean Crowe Pro Bono Award, a national recognition to honor each year a lawyer who made significant contributions to family law clients. Jean, Dot, Kathy, and the many others in this field had brought the law and the community a long way from the time of those cases Gordon and I reviewed with shame in the basement of the Stahlman Building. Legal Aid had been an important part of the progress, and that progress had meant a better life for many women in our state and beyond, not just for our clients.

───────────

Of course, not every family law case involved domestic violence. There were many others. So now we leave the legacy of these lawyers and go back in time to recount some of the other dramas of our family practice over the years.

CHAPTER 9

Family Dramas

I would like to thank Mrs. Judy
[Bond-McKissack] and Mrs. JoAnn
[Dupree]. Both were great with me
and the children. God bless you all.

—MS. L. H., CLARKSVILLE

A best estimate is that in the period of time covered by our story, lawyers at this Legal Aid Society handled between sixty thousand and seventy thousand family law cases—child support, visitation, custody, divorce, and adoption. There are many iterations of family dramas, and most of them because of the natural emotions involved are heart-wrenching. In 1977, two women came to see us about their tragic family matter that had tormented a mother for fifty years.

For several decades until shut down finally in 1950, the Tennessee Children's Home Society in Memphis illegally obtained and sold mostly fair-haired children for purpose of adoption.[1] In 1927, Elizabeth Ingram, a young widow in Nashville, trying to support herself and her three sons by doing ironing for other people, one day was away from home when agents came and stole the two younger boys from the care of their thirteen-year-old brother. Despite her frantic efforts, including trips to Memphis, Mrs. Ingram never could get the boys back. She was powerless against the politically connected home and its agents. She was poor and had no advocate, in the same position as thousands of mothers over the years. Meanwhile, the administrators of the home profited handsomely from its heinous operation.

Both boys were sold for adoption, one to a family in Ohio and the other to a family in West Tennessee, all without any notice to Mrs. Ingram or any opportunity to be heard. She never was served any papers alleging she had not cared for the children properly, and she never was notified of any proposed termination of parental rights or adoption. Any court records were sealed by a complicit judge, and all other records remained secret, despite the injustices in them, a brick wall for thousands of mothers and their children.

For fifty years, Mrs. Ingram and her oldest son tried to find the younger boys, but without success. The law was against them. Then, due to an error on the part of a court clerk and a lead they followed from that, they located one of the boys in Ohio, an occasion for a heartfelt reunion. Similar efforts and inquiries in all fifty states, however, failed to turn up the third son. That is when a granddaughter brought Mrs. Ingram to Legal Services. It was 1977, civil rights cases and legislation were still relatively new, due process and equal protection claims of all kinds were fresh in the news, and some people hoped it might truly be a new era for all. The granddaughter's plea to Gordon was couched in the racially two-world vernacular of the day, "The colored people have gotten their rights, and it's time for MawMaw to get her rights, too."

Gordon and Stewart Clifton filed an action in Davidson County Chancery Court seeking to open the records, alleging every constitutional claim they could muster, aptly characterized by one of the attorneys for the state as a "Writ of Desperation." The only relief the chancellor could give under the law at the time was to order the state to disclose to Stewart and Gordon the identity of the court that granted the adoption, but then he forbade them from taking any action until the state had a reasonable time to seek to have the records remain sealed. The chancery court could not give MawMaw her rights, but fortunately that was not the end of the matter.

Thanks to Kirk Loggins's reporting, the sad story of the case was published in the *Tennessean* the next day and seen by a retired social worker who unwittingly had been a part of the Children's Home's corrupt practice.[2] Such had been her innocent devotion to her work and to the children those many years ago that she had kept a scrapbook of clippings and notes about the children whose adoptions she had facilitated, even following them as they grew up. One of the children whose case she handled and whose life she followed afterward was Mrs. Ingram's third son. She first brought her information to the attention of the assistant attorney general, who then offered it to Gordon and Stewart on the condition that they drop the case and not appeal. After consulting with their client, they accepted. The information did not contain good news. The social worker's scrapbook had a clipping about the death of the third son in 1943 on a US Navy ship that was torpedoed, with all hands lost, during the battle for Guadalcanal. The social worker even had a photograph of a memorial marker using his adopted name that had been placed in a West Tennessee cemetery in honor of the young man. Gordon remembers driving out to the housing project to give his client the sad news, "I was an inadequate substitute for a Navy chaplain." He told her what had happened and gave her a picture of her son's memorial marker. "She of course wept as bitterly as if it had all happened that morning."

As one might hope, there was some collateral benefit from Mrs. Ingram's heartbreaking experience. Little consolation for her great loss, but as result of the attendant publicity from this and similar injustices, including a touching first-person account in *Reader's Digest* by a medical doctor describing his search for his birth mother, the public became more aware of the scandal, and eventually the legislature by statute relaxed the strictures of confidentiality surrounding stolen children and what became of them. A sign of some progress in our society, the tragic story began as one of abject class maltreatment and barbarous gender oppression, one more example of the powerlessness of the poor, but now at least and at last, the victims of that vicious scheme had some rights. As the granddaughter in her words recognized, "the coloreds," read Thurgood Marshall, Z. Alexander Looby, Avon Williams, and the NAACP, began the rights transformation in our country and in our state, but now with the advocacy of Legal Services lawyers, it was reaching even wider. Gradually, gradually, despite inevitable setbacks, what Legal Services could do, thanks to the vision of those who established the Legal Services Program at OEO, was to invoke the law *for* the poor, rather than *against* them.

Of course, not all family cruelty is externally imposed. Owing to proximity and human nature, the much more typical scenario is an inside job. One of the most distressing is child snatching by a separated parent, as was the situation in several cases handled by Judy McKissack in Clarksville. Because of the Fort Campbell army base there, many families are transient, stationed there for a while but with homes and family elsewhere, and in the shuttling between places, the tensions between parents are heightened. In one case, the father snatched the daughter as the mother waited in the Greyhound bus station to return to their hometown in Pennsylvania with the daughter by her side and a two-year-old son asleep in her arms. It took three months, court orders in two states, and the intervention of sheriff's deputies to restore the girl to her mother's care. Not only Judy's legal ability, but also her compassion was obvious. She arranged to pay her client's motel bill when she came back for the final hearing, and she later told a newspaper reporter, "I know how I would feel if my child had been snatched away from me."[3]

Family cruelty is not limited to spouses, nor even to current family members, as we found out in a bizarre case of elder abuse where a woman was able to gain the confidence of and control over her former mother-in-law by pretending to act as her protector. The client was referred to us after her former daughter-in-law had placed her in an unlicensed facility, had taken $15,000 out of her bank account, and had convinced her to sign over her interest in her home. Drake took the case and filed an action in chancery court. At the hearing, the ex-daughter-in-law attempted to justify her actions, but Chancellor Robert Brandt found her "credibility and integrity . . . in doubt from the very start."[4] He ordered her to restore the money and real estate, found fraud, and awarded our client $20,000 in punitive damages.

Thankfully, not all family law cases are quite so fraught. From time to time, we also had cases that dealt with changing social conventions or prejudices, but underlying those too were serious concerns for the people involved. Most often they involved the interests or lifestyle of a younger woman in the court of an older male judge, long on the bench, who found it difficult to countenance diversity. Remarkably, the court of appeals, which was similarly composed, often was much more receptive. Perhaps that was the result of more time for reflection, a luxury that on occasion can enable one to reexamine barriers and broaden his views about such things as names and nudity.

Patti George represented a client in what seemed to be a routine divorce case, but for the trial judge in Gallatin, it was not. Her client, a woman married with children, sought a divorce and restoration of her maiden name. The judge readily granted the divorce, but he refused to restore her name because he thought she should have the same last name as her children. He took judicial notice of the proposition that it is not in the best interest of the children for their mother to have a last name different from theirs. Patti appealed that ruling, and the court of appeals reversed, holding that the trial court could not make such a conclusion based on judicial notice. The court allowed that if indeed proof at trial had shown there would have been a detriment to these children from their mother having her name restored, that could have been a basis for denying her request, but in this case no detriment had been shown. The woman could choose her name, an important identifier for any of us.

The social convention Patti dealt with in her court of appeals case concerned a name. The one I dealt with concerned nudity. That episode would have been lost to memory but for a recent revival. In 2018, David Kozlowski compiled a list of significant cases that had been handled by Legal Aid Society lawyers over the years, to be used primarily in new staff orientation sessions introducing them to the heritage of outstanding cases at LAS. When he searched Westlaw for reported cases handled by Rural, Middle, and South Central lawyers before consolidation and LAS lawyers since then, he found more than two hundred federal court and state appellate court cases. From those, he narrowed it down to the twenty-one he judged to be the most significant, and he described each one briefly in a tidy memo. One reported case, however, justifiably not on his list, he felt constrained to mention in a footnote, a 1981 child custody case appropriately named *Moon v. Moon*, "As far as I can tell, this is the only reported opinion in which Ashley Wiltshire argued before the court of appeals, establishing the very important principle that trial courts cannot conclude that a parent is unfit on the sole ground that the parent is a member of a nudist colony." Yes, she met our income guidelines. Yes, she was a nudist, as were her parents. No, there were no pictures.

———————————

In the early days, before state agencies began handling child support cases, a large part of our family law practice had been obtaining and enforcing child support. In Nashville, a family law lawyer would go to Fourth Circuit or Probate Court on the appointed day each week with fifteen or twenty clients for hearings on motions to set support or on petitions for contempt for nonpayment. Even after that responsibility was taken over by the state agencies, however, we continued to handle child support issues related to divorce cases we undertook.

Typical was a case handled by Lucinda Smith during her second tour at Legal Services in 1989: A violent husband left his wife and young child, provided no support for six months; they had no place to live and could not get public housing because husband, who was employed, refused to pay $120 he owed to the housing authority. At the final hearing, wife was awarded divorce, child support by wage assignment, and a protective order. Husband was required to carry insurance on the child and pay the debt to housing authority. This enabled the ex-wife and child to move into affordable housing.

The wage assignment provision for Lucinda's client was in place because of work by Dot Dobbins a few years earlier. Before there was a provision in federal law for this technique, Dot, with help from Allan Ramsaur at TALS, lobbied the Tennessee General Assembly to give judges the power to require employers to withhold from wages the monies owed for court-ordered child support and forward those monies to the court clerk for distribution. This, coupled with the financial guidelines for support that Jean Crowe later helped develop on the Child Support Commission, made child support much more reliable for custodial parents.

The enactment of the Child Support Enforcement Act, Title IV-D of the Social Security Act in 1975, was a great relief to us and led to our gradually getting out of the straight child support business. The Act provided federal funding for states to contract with agencies that would hire lawyers to obtain child support orders and enforce them. We did not apply for the Davidson County contract and were pleased when it went to the District Attorney's office, figuring that office would be especially good at finding absent parents and enforcing the law. For us, it meant our family law attorneys no longer would be handling hundreds of child support cases and spending an inordinate amount of time in Fourth Circuit, Probate, and Juvenile Court every week, but would be freed up to devote more time to other family law cases. Unfortunately, for many mothers and children, IV- D did not turn out to be the panacea we had hoped.

Over the years, because we had many clients in common, our family law attorneys in Davidson County would hear complaints about the service at the DA's office: long waits, no result, little follow-up, ineffective enforcement of orders. They knew that the program had failed multiple audits. The Metropolitan Government, a party to the contract jointly with the DA, was not providing the supplemental funds needed; the program was grossly understaffed as compared with other IV-D programs in the state and was collecting support payments in only 4 percent of its cases. They also knew that Department of Human Services Office of Child Support Services was not doing what it should to ensure that the Davidson County program complied with IV-D requirements. They knew all of this and they heard the complaints from their clients, but they had neither the time, inclination, nor experience to deal with this federal law issue.

Then in the early 1990s, there were changes in our office structure that had the collateral effect of bringing this issue to the fore. Because of the loss of funding and depletion of staff, we temporarily combined the family section and the benefits section of the Nashville office. That meant, among other structural adjustments, that the two remaining family law attorneys would meet each week for case review with the three remaining benefits attorneys, attorneys who were very familiar with the Social Security Act, were used to filing lawsuits under that Act and were accustomed to making claims under "Section 1983," a federal civil rights provision dating back to Reconstruction days that gives a person a cause of action against a state official who has deprived her of her rights under a federal law, such as Title IV-D of the Social Security Act.[5]

David Ettinger heard the frequent laments of the family law attorneys in case review and agreed to help. Jean referred four clients to him, and in November 1992, he filed a class action lawsuit in chancery court against the DA, Metro Government, and the Tennessee Department of Human Services Child Support Services. The filing of the lawsuit had an immediate result. Within a week of the filing, District Attorney Torry Johnson announced that his office would get out of the child support enforcement business altogether when its current contract expired the next June. Johnson is quoted in an article by Kirk Loggins as saying that the lawsuit "probably precipitated a decision that I have been considering for some time." He explained, "It's not a traditional function of a prosecutor's office. There is not a natural fit with other things we do."[6]

When the contract with the DA expired, the state entered into a contract for Davidson County with Maximus, a private firm with similar contracts in several jurisdictions. That ended the case against the DA, but there remained the case against the department for not doing its job enforcing the Act, or so David thought. Chancellor Irvin Kilcrease disagreed and dismissed our clients' case, holding that the women had no right to bring the lawsuit in the first place: they had no private right of action under Section 1983 to enforce any provision of Title IV-D. David appealed and the court of appeals reversed. The department, in turn, appealed to the Tennessee Supreme Court. That turned out to be a mistake on their part. The supreme court, in an opinion written by Justice Frank Drowota, went even further than the court of appeals. The intermediate court had held that the women only had a right to seek the state's "substantial compliance" with Title IV-D, that is, compliance with a *state-wide* standard. The supreme court, in a more precise reading, held that under Section 1983 they were not limited to that, but had a right to bring an action to enforce the department's direct obligation to them *individually* under Title IV-D, whether the state was in "substantial compliance" or not.[7] The state had an obligation to each program participant to see that she got the services she was entitled to.

Asked for a comment after his victory in the supreme court, David understated, "As this case clearly demonstrates, bureaucracies sometimes need the impetus of legal action to move them to do what the law already requires them to do."[8] The case also demonstrated that we could help clients obtain child support even when we did not handle specific child support cases.

Defeated by its own supreme court, the persistent state appealed the case to the US Supreme Court, but it fared no better there. David filed a brief in opposition and the court rejected the state's appeal. The Tennessee Supreme Court's decision had been a profound affirmation of rights for our four named plaintiffs and the hundreds of other custodial parents in the same situation seeking child support. It was not an altogether sweet victory, however. The success of the case coincided with a tragic turn of events that restricted our practice in the future and diminished the cause of everyday justice.

Davis v. McClaran was the last class action case we handled. At the same time in the spring of 1996 that the US Supreme Court was rejecting the state's appeal and reinforcing the rights of those hundreds of parents we represented, Congress was enacting legislation that undercut their access to justice in the future. The legislation, which opponents of Legal Services had sought for thirty years, prohibited lawyers at an organization funded in part by LSC from handling class action cases. The prohibition persists to this day. No longer is it possible for lawyers at Legal Aid to file such a widely beneficial case as this. This case, and many of the others described in our story would be foreclosed by the Congressional restriction.

———————

While child support was always a major concern for us, as a rule we did not get involved in alimony and property settlement matters. We rarely had cases in this area for the simple reason that our clients' ex-spouses usually had very little ability to pay any meaningful alimony, and the parties rarely had any property to divide. This was not the situation in Clarksville, however, where owing to the large number of retired service people, there were reliable government pensions available, even to the lowest-ranking veteran. Chris Church and other lawyers in that office often found themselves dealing with law peculiar to the military, and marriage dissolution was no exception. One of Chris's cases, which she won in the court of appeals, involved the difference between veterans' retirement payments and veterans' disability payments.

When her client and the client's ex-husband had been divorced in 1986, the wife was awarded, *inter alia*, as a part of her marital property, 40 percent of her husband's gross military retirement benefits. Soon thereafter the husband retired, and wife began receiving her portion of the retirement payments, but shortly after that, he qualified for veterans' disability payments and opted to receive them. The problem arose because the law prohibits double-dipping: the pension had to be reduced by the amount of disability payment. In this case, the amount of the disability payment was such that the pension was canceled entirely by it, leaving no share of his retirement benefits for the wife, a slick move on his part.

She went back to the divorce court asking for an award from the disability benefits, but because federal law provides that a court may not diminish a veteran's disability payments by ordering any distribution of them, she was unsuccessful. Following that setback, she came to see us. Chris filed an appeal, and based on a Tennessee Supreme Court decision in a similar case, she was able to argue that the original distribution of the marital assets was for an amount of money and therefore was an obligation of the ex-husband, regardless of the source of his money. The court agreed. The ex-husband could not defeat the marital property distribution obligation by opting to take the disability payments rather than the retirement payments. He had to pay.

Juvenile law often is grouped with family law, for obvious reasons, but there are distinctive issues, as well. In the next chapter, there will be overlaps with the family law issues described here, but the emphasis will be on cases dealing with the rights of the juvenile as an individual and the rights of parents when dealing with the state.

CHAPTER 10

Young Lawyers Change Juvenile Law

Russ Overby . . . was a gift from God.
He made me and my children whole
again. If I need help again, he is the one
I would want to help me out.

—D. TURNER

Russ Overby was a Legal Aid lawyer because in 1968 he met Chuck Hogren at Elm LaSalle Bible Church in Chicago located near the infamous Cabrini Green housing project. As a part of the Christian Service Council at evangelical Wheaton College, Russ and other students would go on Sunday afternoons from their suburban campus into the city to participate in the church's tutoring program for children at Cabrini Green. The tutoring program was not the church's only service for its neighbors. A couple of years earlier, Hogren, a corporate lawyer who was a member of the congregation, had been asked by the pastor to represent various people in the neighborhood. Later he resigned his law firm job to do that full-time at what became Cabrini Green Legal Aid. His work and his challenge inspired Russ.

But Russ did not act on it immediately. He was a math major, and after graduation in 1970, he went to work for International Harvester as a computer programmer, which in those days consisted of manipulating punch cards. After a year of punch cards though, Russ responded to Chuck Hogren's example and enrolled in law school, at Vanderbilt. He joined the legal aid group there his first semester and was assigned to interview people in jail for the public defender's office, all the while making numerous calls to Legal Services asking for a position. His persistence paid off when finally at the beginning of his second year, he was given a position clerking for David Tarpley and Tom Daniel at the Matthew Walker Health Center office. There was no pay, but Russ did get clinic credit at the law school. The next semester he was hired to a paying position as a clerk in the downtown office.

In the tradition of the day, as a third-year law student, Russ began working long hours at Legal Services and handling a large caseload. After graduation in 1974, reflecting our piecemeal funding, he was shoehorned into a position of part-time clinic student supervisor (inherited from Gordon) and part-time staff attorney (funded by staff contributions described in Chapter 7). The continued contact with law students would prove significant. Less than two years later, with student assistance, he would file a major class action lawsuit, the *Doe* case, that transformed the treatment of juveniles in state custody, but before that there were many other cases along the way.

At some point in 1974, Russ and Gordon were contacted by Bart Stokes, who was on the staff of Spencer Youth Center, a Department of Correction facility for juveniles in the Bordeaux area of Nashville. Stokes came to see them on behalf of some boys who felt they had been mistreated by the courts back home that had sent them there. They wanted to talk to a lawyer. Russ began making trips to Spencer to talk with the boys and enlisted the help of a couple of law students, including Lucinda Smith, to help with the interviews. Lucinda initially worked as a volunteer and then was employed as a clerk at LSON, the first of her three tours with us, a record likely never to be broken.

Russ, Lucinda, and others working with them began filing habeas corpus petitions on behalf of students who had not been accorded the rights they were entitled to pursuant to the recent US Supreme Court decision *In re Gault*.[1] Most of the cases involved boys who had not been represented by lawyers at their delinquency hearings and had not "knowingly and intelligently" waived their right to counsel. Inevitably the Davidson County Chancery Court would grant the habeas petitions and release the youths. Another flaw in the system was the competence of the judges who heard the cases and sentenced the children. In many cases they were "county judges," today more appropriately titled "county executives," who might be lawyers, or just as likely would be local politicians, untrained in the law, not careful about such concepts as due process. Again, Gordon and Russ would file a habeas petition challenging the constitutionality of the commitment by non-lawyer officials, the court would hold a hearing, and their client would be released. Later, in response to these successful petitions, the legislature amended the statute to require that the judges be lawyers.

In 1975, David Kozlowski, who had graduated with Russ in 1974, returned to Vanderbilt as a clinic instructor and found a group of students anxious to continue the work at the juvenile institutions that Russ and Lucinda had begun. Andy Shookhoff, who later would be elected juvenile judge in Davidson County, was a second year student. Others included Roy Herron, later a member of the Tennessee Senate; Bill Purcell, later majority leader of the Tennessee House of Representatives and then mayor of Nashville; and Stewart Clifton, later a lawyer at LSON, then TALS, and for eight years a member of the Metropolitan Council. Kozlowski estimates that they were able to secure the release of approximately 175 juveniles. The accompanying excursus, a eulogy for Senator Douglas Henry Jr. written by Stewart Clifton in 2020, describes in its first three paragraphs the surprising involvement of the senator in this juvenile justice issue. The last three paragraphs are included because they describe some of the other ways that classic conservative Southern gentleman, despite some retrograde positions on other matters, advanced the interests of our clients on numerous occasions over the years. Much of this will echo in later chapters.

Excursus: Unforgettable Senator Henry
by Stewart Clifton

I first met Senator Henry when I was a volunteer for Friends of Spencer Youth Center in the mid-70s. I was still in law school. This group focused on legal advice and advocacy for teenage residents of this Davidson County juvenile detention facility. We regularly filed habeas corpus petitions in Davidson County Chancery Court on behalf of juveniles who we thought had been committed illegally. As it turned out, Davidson County chancellors uniformly thought we were right. Most cases were before Chancellor Ben Cantrell.

We were so successful that an assistant attorney general who had been on the other side in many of the cases drafted a bill for state legislators that required post commitment relief actions to be brought in the county of commitment rather than where the juvenile was incarcerated. Our clients had been mostly African American teenage boys from Shelby County who had been convicted by the infamous court of Juvenile Judge Kenneth Turner. I got involved in the lobbying effort against the bill, knowing that our side had no real chance to prevail. But it was closer than we expected: we only lost 30 to 3. We knew we had the vote of Senator Avon Williams, who was an amazing advocate for civil rights and people without power. And we were pretty sure we would get the vote of Senator Bill Boner, but Senator Henry was another matter entirely.

None of us had ever met him, but we got an appointment with him before the vote. He told us, "This doesn't seem fair to me. I don't think your side will win, but you are right. I will speak on the floor." He gave a wonderful argument on the Senate floor about why we have the habeas corpus tradition (to control authoritarian actions of governments particularly in relation to unjust imprisonment). He said it made no sense to forbid a Davidson County Chancellor from ruling on the legality of the government's keeping someone incarcerated in Davidson County based on rulings of juvenile judges with no legal training and no sense of appropriate procedure. Yes, this was a long time ago and before Linda O'Neal, Linda Moynihan, and Debbie Miller, with help in the legislature from Senator Henry, Representative Mike Murphy, Representative Jim Henry, and others in both parties finally got juvenile justice and children's services to a pretty good place in this state.

Through the decades Senator Henry worked successfully with us on many issues. He was a huge supporter of Commissioner Manning's and Governor McWherter's TennCare program; an important force for juvenile justice reform and what later became Adverse Childhood Experiences; a strong environmental advocate; a supporter of disability rights; the Senate sponsor of the Tennessee School Breakfast Law, which resulted in our state's having the highest rate of participation of any state for many years; and about a thousand more good causes. He was an amazing man who never quit surprising me.

The last legislative effort Senator Henry and I worked on together took place over thirty years after our first encounter. It was his last term. He had announced that he was not running again. Russ Overby and I discovered that the Department of Human Services was pushing a bill that would have dramatically harmed many TANF recipients. They would be disqualified from benefits for failing to meet harsh work requirements that went beyond those mandated by federal law. I talked with the commissioner and her legal staff and whomever I could think of. No luck. In a last-gasp effort I met with Senator Henry, who frankly was always known as a supporter of administration initiatives without regard to the political affiliation of the governor.

The senator immediately understood our concern and said he would see what he could do. Five minutes before the Senate committee meeting that we expected would result in an overwhelming vote for this administration bill, he called me up to the front of the committee room. He whispered to me that he had asked the commissioner to drop by his office to discuss the bill. After the discussion the commissioner promised that the bill would not move forward. And it did not. Senator Henry was truly the one person in the state who could have stopped the bill. He had nothing to gain by it. But he thought we were right, so he did it. The bill was never brought forward.

The attorney general's Post-Conviction Procedure Act survived challenges in the courts and ultimately led to the demise of the clinic's project. It was impractical for the students to travel to the various counties from which the juveniles had come. The due process issues that had been raised by the lawyers and students in their many cases, however, had not gone unnoticed by the judiciary. In the early 1980s, the Tennessee

Supreme Court, under the leadership of Justice Frank Drowota who had heard some of those cases as a chancellor, convened a committee that included Andy Shookhoff to develop the first Tennessee Rules of Juvenile Procedure. Those rules, which were promulgated in 1984, were a beginning of the supreme court and the Administrative Office of the Courts' paying serious attention to what was happening in the juvenile courts around the state. Now, with rules, standards, training, and oversight they could take much-needed further steps to improve the practice in those courts.

For lawyers dealing with children, it is not entirely about constitutional procedures and requirements of the law. Sometimes it also is about pediatrics and psychiatry.

In January 1976, Charles and Joanna Batey came to see Russ because their seven-month-old son had been summarily removed from them by the Department of Human Services (DHS) after they had taken him to General Hospital because of problems with the child's digestion. Without an opportunity for the parents to be heard, a DHS worker obtained an order from the juvenile judge removing custody from them and placing the child in a foster home. Russ requested a DHS hearing on behalf of the parents, but the request was denied, following which he filed suit in chancery court challenging not only the lack of due process, but also the lack of appreciation for the effect such an abrupt removal had on the child and the family.

During pretrial discovery, Russ was able to obtain testimony from Albert Solnit, Sterling Professor of Pediatrics and Psychiatry at Yale, author of *Beyond the Best Interest of the Child*, and from Sally Provence, also a professor of pediatrics at Yale, both widely published authorities in the field. They testified as to the adverse effect on children who are summarily or abruptly removed from their parents and from contact with their family. Having that testimony, Russ was able to persuade the state to settle the case on quite favorable terms. A consent decree was entered requiring an adversarial hearing in front of a judge before DHS could remove a child, unless there was an immediate threat to the child or the child was about to be removed from the jurisdiction.

The decree required that if a child had to be removed before a hearing, there first must be sworn testimony as to why the child should be removed and a specific finding in a written removal order; then a hearing must be held within three days after the removal. In his memorandum approving the settlement of the case and its terms, Chancellor C. Allen High recited at length the credentials of both professors Solnit and Provence and approvingly gave a summary of their views and conclusions. The consent decree also set out standards for notice and the conduct of the hearing. It was a comprehensive solution to a traumatic problem.[2]

The case was not entirely the success this suggests, however, and did require remedial action later. It had been filed as a class action with not only a plaintiff class consisting of all parents in the state, but also a defendant class consisting of all juvenile court judges in the state. There was no problem with the plaintiff class. No parents came forward who would not want due process if the state tried to remove their child. The problem was with the defendant class of juvenile court judges.

The certification of the defendant class had been by an agreed order between the plaintiffs and the state without notice to the juvenile court judges, and when they became aware of the chancellor's ruling, that set off a firestorm. Many of the juvenile judges did not fancy having the chancellor in Nashville ordering them to comply with due process. The county/juvenile judge in Roane County was so adamant in his objection that he, on his own motion in the juvenile court that he presided over in that East Tennessee county, issued an *ex parte* restraining order against the Davidson County Chancery Court, the attorney general, and Legal Services, enjoining the court, the lawyers, and the parties from proceeding with the case.

The mouse roared, but not for long. On application by the attorney general, the Tennessee Supreme Court, in an order written by the venerable Justice William J. Harbison, quickly told the Roane County juvenile court judge that he was "wholly without authority or jurisdiction" to issue such an order. The court decreed that his restraining order was "dissolved, superseded and vacated" and that the show cause order issued with it was "in all things quashed, abated and for nothing held." Then the court enjoined him from "issuing any further order which would in any way interfere with the orderly processes of the [*Batey* case]."[3]

Other recalcitrant juvenile court judges, through their association, took a more orderly route and filed their objections with Chancellor High. He ultimately decided that although under the Rules of Civil Procedure the decision to give notice to them had been discretionary, he would set aside his order certifying the defendant class. He issued an amendment to the decree that kept in place all the substantive relief, but he made it effective only against the Davidson County Juvenile Court.[4] Nevertheless, it was a Pyrrhic victory for the complaining juvenile court judges. Because DHS also was a party to the lawsuit, it was bound by the ruling statewide. Regardless of what the local juvenile judge may want to do, or not do, the department could not remove a child without following the procedures Chancellor High had ordered. Thus, the protections were extended to all parents in all counties in Tennessee. Furthermore, within a short time, the requirements of the agreed order were enacted into law by the General Assembly.

———————————

Juvenile law cases seemed to generate a great deal of defiance. That was the case also with staff at Department of Correction (DOC) facilities that confined juveniles. They were accustomed to making up their own rules for what they could do with the kids, regardless of the law or constitutional protections. After Andy graduated and became a lawyer in our Gallatin office, the juvenile court judge in Sumner County asked him to represent two runaway girls who had been in his county but now were being held at Tennessee Preparatory School (TPS), a juvenile facility in Nashville. When Andy tried to contact the girls at TPS, he was told by a counselor that because they were runaways they were being held in the "guardhouse" and could not speak to anyone; furthermore, one of the girls was going to be sent to East Tennessee the next morning. The counselor also informed Andy that her supervisor would have to listen in on any conversation Andy might have with either girl. Andy told her that would not be acceptable because it would violate attorney-client confidentiality. She insisted that those were the rules at TPS.

Andy realized he might need some help and went to talk with Russ. Russ suggested Andy call the assistant attorney general who handled cases for juvenile institutions, a person Russ and Andy had lots of experience with by that time. Surely as a lawyer, he would get the picture and straighten out the people at TPS. After leaving several messages, they got a surprising reply from the lawyer, "Those are the rules. No communication between the student and anyone for a certain period while the student is in detention." Tough luck.

It was tough luck indeed. It was late in the day by then, and Russ and Andy had to stay up late into the night drafting a complaint and putting together a federal lawsuit, which Andy then typed. The next morning, Russ kept his appointment to have two wisdom teeth pulled, and Andy filed the lawsuit asking for a temporary restraining order. The case fell to Judge Thomas Wiseman, who wasted no time scheduling a hearing for that afternoon. Russ, with packed sockets where his teeth had been and still feeling the mouth-altering effects of Novocain, stopped by the office to collect his things, then went off to federal court with Andy for the hearing. Judge Wiseman, who was not impressed by the arbitrary action of the TPS staff in denying the girls access to counsel, was further disturbed by the assistant attorney general's argument: "The whole matter is moot. Both students are no longer at TPS." The judge ordered the assistant attorney general to "bring those two people back to TPS, have them there by Monday morning, and have affidavits to support it."[5] And so Andy got to meet with his clients and their cases proceeded.

There were many other juvenile cases, most brought by Russ and Andy, together with David Kozlowski at the clinic, but Kitty Calhoon, Allston Vander Horst, and Mary Walker also handled cases that made law. One case established the logical rule that the Department of Correction could not hold "unruly children" after they became adults. Another determined the right of a parent to see the DHS file on their child. Another clarified parental visitation rights when their child was in foster care, a case that raised again Professor Solnit's admonition about maintaining parent/child contacts.

It is not surprising that problems like these came up often and that the staff at TPS had not wanted Andy to be able to talk with the two girls he had been appointed to represent. In those days, every part of the system was vulnerable to challenge because of a lack of due process and other legal failings. The constitutional rights of parents and of children, surprisingly enough, hardly ever had been asserted before Legal Services lawyers began raising them here and in other places around the country in the 1960s and 1970s. Staff in the state institutions and departments were used to doing things their own way, regardless. That penchant became most stark in the *Doe* case.

THE DOE CASE

The *Doe* case started because Andy, who was still a law student at that time, had been urging Russ to represent some developmentally disabled children he had encountered during visits to Spencer Youth Center. When finally a staff member from Spencer called Russ with the same plea, Russ relented and agreed to go meet with the children to see if there might be something he could do for them. What he found was exactly what Andy had described. Using labels of that day, developmentally disabled children—some mildly disabled, some moderately, some "truly retarded"—were housed together with other youths in that facility, and, as he learned, in other Department of Correction facilities as well. There were no programs or services available in any of the facilities that would be appropriate to the mental and physical condition of those children. They were in physical danger from bullying by other children. Because of their conditions, they were easily goaded by others to do things that understandably got them into trouble. Then, as a punishment or for protection from others, they spent an inordinate amount of time in isolation cells, not a good situation for anyone, much less for children with developmental disabilities.

By the time the lawsuit was filed on September 10, 1976, the scope of the problems from the lack of treatment in the facilities had broadened beyond those of the developmentally disabled children. The named plaintiffs (their real names were not made public) were two boys and a girl in the custody of the department: a sixteen-year-old boy with developmental disabilities who suffered from epileptic seizures, another boy in need of treatment for drug and alcohol abuse, and a mentally ill thirteen-year-old girl. They were represented by Russ, David, and Mike Engle, who was then in private practice. Andy worked on getting the case ready to file and was listed on the pleadings as a Vanderbilt Legal Aid Society student, along with Juliet Griffin, who was in law school at UT and had worked on the case as a clerk that summer. The plaintiffs asked the court for psychological evaluations and then treatment or habilitation, and they asked that their suit be certified as a class action

so that it would benefit other children in the system who were similarly situated.

The case was filed in the Chancery Court of Davidson County, and,
in the rotational assignment system of that court, it fell on the docket
of Part I, the third major lawsuit challenging system-wide conditions
filed by Legal Services lawyers during that time that had fallen to Chancellor Ben Cantrell. In addition to this one and the adult prison case, the
chancellor also was dealing with the *Rainey* case that sought to enforce
a 1972 state statute regarding education for handicapped children. *Rainey*
had been filed by Don Hollingsworth of Memphis Area Legal Services
and would be inherited by Allston when Don moved to Arkansas Legal
Services. All three cases were so complex that each would require the
appointment of a special master or monitors before it was over. These
cases were in addition to a full docket and the other noteworthy cases
Chancellor Cantrell was handling during this time: telephone company
rate increases, property tax assessment procedures, and election disputes.

Russ's memorandum of law that followed the complaint pointed out
that the legislation dealing with children committed to the DOC required
that they receive a program of treatment, training, and rehabilitation
suited to their individual needs. John Doe 1 had been determined to
be a "retarded child, and in need of care, supervision and treatment."
Nevertheless, the Director of Psychological Services for the department
is quoted in the memorandum as admitting, "Practically speaking, the
only thing the Department of Correction has to offer is custody." Russ's
memorandum also cited the agreed order in *Rainey*, which the state had
signed in 1974 recognizing its obligation to provide special education services for all handicapped children, regardless of location. He reminded
the chancellor that the named plaintiffs in this case were all handicapped
children within the definition of that statute and were entitled to education under that agreed order.

It took more than five years of often contentious discovery, maneu-
vering, inspections, hearings, and sidetracks for the state finally to come
to the place where it would agree to remedies needed in this case. As discovery progressed, the scope of the case got wider and wider. After the
case was certified as a class action, the plaintiffs' counsel hired experts to
tour the facilities and determine the extent of the problems, the impact
on the children, and the potential remedies. The state, in turn, hired its

own experts to tour, evaluate plaintiffs' experts' conclusions, and develop counter testimony.

As it turned out, the experts hired by the state could not save the state's case. Despite their employment, they could not condone much of what they discovered on their tours. For instance, when they discovered that staff at Spencer were using isolation cells in which a boy might be confined "usually for five days," they insisted that the state discontinue the practice. When the morning paper reported that discontinuance, it also reported that following that, officials at Spencer had begun hand-cuffing boys to radiators or other objects.[6] In light of that public knowledge, two weeks later the officials had to announce they had discontinued that practice as well.[7]

In December 1978, the plaintiffs' experts began uncovering even more disturbing abuse. At the end of the month, the Legal Services lawyers (by now Andy had graduated and been admitted to the bar and Allston had joined Legal Services) submitted to the court an affidavit from one of their experts, Harold W. Heller, a professor of education at the University of Alabama and former superintendent of Alabama's largest institution for the mentally ill. He reported that developmentally disabled youths in several facilities, especially Taft Youth Center in Pikeville, were often physically abused by staff members and sexually assaulted by other boys. Further, he reported that many boys were afraid to talk about their problems because of fear of reprisals by staff members. Heller concluded that the staff's actions and attitudes contributed to "an aura of fear among residents" that interfered with whatever meager treatment and education program an institution might have.[8]

As Heller and another expert, Dr. Jerome Miller, visited the various facilities, it became obvious to them that the problems for children in the department's custody went far beyond the lack of appropriate educational program, the absence of services for children with intellectual disabilities, and the absence of treatments for those with addiction or mental illness. They told the plaintiffs' lawyers that those defined issues raised in the original complaint could not be dealt with in isolation and that the scope of the remedies requested needed to be much wider. Allston conveyed this to the chancellor on December 22 in a motion for a temporary restraining order supported by several affidavits describing widespread physical and mental abuse.

The chancellor declined to grant the TRO at the hearing four days later, but implicitly recognizing the wider scope, he did call the allegations in the affidavits "extremely serious" and required the attorneys in the case "to thoroughly investigate all allegations made." He warned officials at Taft, Spencer, and the Tennessee Reception and Guidance Center for Children in Memphis that any interference with the investigation "will be viewed as a contempt of this court's orders and will be dealt with accordingly." To aid the investigation, he ordered officials at those three institutions to give to all residents notices explaining the lawsuit and including this language: "The court is interested in learning about what is going on. . . . No one may punish you for talking to the judge or to the lawyers about what is happening [here]. The court will protect anyone who does provide information."[9]

The staff in the fiefdom that was Taft Youth Center at Pikeville were not used to exercising personal restraint in dealing with the boys there, and, protected by a powerful local legislator, they were not accustomed to taking orders from someone in Nashville. The chancellor's order went down on Monday, December 26. By Friday, plaintiffs' attorneys were back in court with a motion to restrain one staff member from coming on campus and to order staff specifically not to retaliate against students who spoke to experts. The motion was supported by affidavits from students and attorneys about continuing abuse. Cantrell set a hearing for the next Tuesday.[10] On Monday, state corrections officials, on their own, suspended two staff members and two other staff members resigned, one after the superintendent confronted him with allegations he had performed homosexual acts on young boys at the facility.[11]

This time there was a hearing with testimony from students, staff, department officials, and the local district attorney. Robert Delaney, the assistant attorney general handling the case, argued that the chancellor should not order further relief, but allow his office and the local DA to investigate the allegations of abuse. Russ countered by reading an affidavit from a student who had told one of the state's psychological consultants nearly four months earlier about many of the problems just now coming to light in this hearing. Cantrell, consistently cautious and wanting to give the state every chance to clean up its own act, declined Russ's request for additional specific orders at this point. He even declined to issue a restraining order against the suspended staff member who had been most abusive, whose suspension would expire in nine days. Exercising judicial restraint, he reasoned, "That's simply not the job of this court to tell the people who run this institution who they may hire or who they may not hire."[12] He had not told them explicitly how to run their institution, but they got the message, and a few days later the officials extended the staff member's suspension. In one matter, the chancellor was explicit: he ordered staff members at Taft, Spencer, and the Reception and Guidance Center not to quiz students about what they had told attorneys for either side in the case.[13]

The rest of January and most of February were marked by strife and chaos at Taft, with both staff and boys behaving badly. It was not an insignificant factor that while more than a third of the boys were Black kids from Memphis, almost all the guards were local White men from isolated Bledsoe and surrounding counties on the rugged Cumberland Plateau. They were from two different worlds. Two weeks after the hearing in Nashville, five more staff resigned. Staff complained that with the investigations and the new restrictions on them, the boys had become unmanageable. In early February, 180 workers at the facility walked off their jobs without warning. Initially the 212 students were kept in their dormitories by the skeletal staff and things were under control. That night everything broke loose with a full-scale riot and attempted escapes. Calm finally was restored when state troopers arrived. Meanwhile, the lawyers struggled to protect their clients and at the same time prepare for a hearing on the abuse allegations scheduled later in the month, for which plaintiffs' lawyers had issued forty-five subpoenas for students and staff in various facilities. As preparations proceeded, the lawyers for both sides also were doggedly trying to reach an agreement that would settle this part of the case. Finally, over the weekend, hours before the hearing scheduled for Monday, February 26, the parties agreed.

The agreed order, reflecting the degradation that had prevailed in the institutions, prohibited staff from hitting, slapping, shoving, kicking, or throwing juveniles and prohibited the use of humiliating punishments, such as "the dying cockroach" or "standing the wall." It prohibited staff from directing or allowing one juvenile to abuse another. It prohibited the use of mace, except in special circumstances and then only at Taft. It detailed a system for investigation of student complaints of physical or sexual abuse, with a sped-up timetable for investigation of alleged sexual abuse. It required and specified more adequate dormitory, shower, and restroom supervision when more than one student would be present. It ordered that a monitoring team of three people be appointed by the governor to visit regularly, interview students and staff in private, and report findings every six weeks to the court, the governor, and attorneys for both parties. Plaintiffs' attorneys were not able to get an agreement in this order requiring additional training for staff and psychological counseling for children who had been victims of sexual attacks. Those remedies would have to wait for another day and additional proceedings.[14]

The case ground on for over two years more before there was a comprehensive agreement dealing with the heart of the case. By this time Chancellor Cantrell had been elevated to the court of appeals, a well-deserved recognition of his exemplary judicial performance, and Irvin Kilcrease had been appointed in his place. In December 1981, the parties presented to Chancellor Kilcrease an agreed order outlining "an appropriate program of habilitation, care and treatment" for members of the plaintiff class.

The parties agreed that the necessary elements of an appropriate program included individual evaluations, classification, and program plans for each juvenile; behavior management programs for them; a fair disciplinary program; a clear grievance procedure; appropriate medical, dental, and psychological services; adequate staffing; and individualized education plans consistent with state standards. The agreed order provided for monitoring, both independent and by the state, and that the case be continued for five years to ensure compliance in the meantime. The chancellor signed the agreed order and it was entered.[15]

The case was not over. The culture changed slowly. Just before the agreed order was signed, the Tennessee Bureau of Investigation began investigating allegations of physical abuse at Taft, which the following April resulted in disciplinary proceedings against the former director there and the outright firing of six staff members. In September of that year, David Dillingham, a monitor appointed by the court, reported that students at Spencer had been "locked in tiny, stark isolation cells for months at a time." Things like this required constant follow-up and enforcement actions.

There also were good ways in which the case was not over. Here are seven examples. Ten years later, when Andy was juvenile court judge in Davidson County and Mary Walker was a referee in that court, the standards laid out in the *Doe* agreed order still controlled the treatment of minors in state custody and the services they received. Second example: several years after the *Doe* case, the responsibility for juveniles was removed from the Department of Correction altogether and transferred to a new Department of Children's Services (DCS). Third, Mary recalls that when she was general counsel for DCS as late as 2004, the department still had to make *"Doe* reports," long after the five years in the chancellor's order had expired. Fourth, children with more than mild developmental disabilities are no longer committed to the juvenile institutions operated by DCS, but are placed in group homes or mental health facilities. Fifth, when Linda O'Neal was at the Institute for Children's Resources, before she came to TALS, she and others, using the *Doe* orders, helped pass legislation prohibiting the placement of children in adult jails. Sixth, in 2012, finally, Taft was closed as a juvenile institution. Seventh, in 2018, citing the *Doe* case, the Tennessee Justice Center was able to persuade the General Assembly to pass legislation mandating that education funding must follow children while they are in state custody so that they receive the required education and special education services.

———————

In juvenile law, education law, and the due process rights of parents, the court cases handled by Legal Services lawyers across the state made a substantial difference in the law. In addition, the administrative and legislative changes they stimulated improved several of the systems that deal with children. The improvements and structural changes in this area over the years were numerous and substantial.

Unfortunately, in the subject area of our next chapter, not so much. With the exception of a few outstanding court cases that will be described, most of our work on housing cases has been defensive, in what for our clients has been principally a zero-sum struggle.

CHAPTER 11

Bless This House

I was so relieved when I heard from you all
stating that they wasn't going to take my
home because I am by myself and I wouldn't
have nowhere to go.

—Ms. M. C., NASHVILLE

I have five children that I support because
their father has passed away and the help
from the Murfreesboro office has secured
our family and our home. Thank you for all
your help.

—Ms. K. D., SMYRNA

Obtaining and keeping affordable housing is an abiding problem for
low-income people. There are a multitude of barriers: supply, demand,
access, racial discrimination, discrimination against the poor, and the
overriding factor, the lack of ability to pay. Legal Services always has
given priority to handling cases involving housing because it is such
a vital need and so cries out for attention, but it has been difficult and
often frustrating. At root, most housing problems will not be solved by
litigation but by housing policy and, specifically, by affordable housing
policy. That takes political will and concentration, which regrettably has
been an off and on affair in our country and inadequate to meet the need.

Nevertheless, over the years, about 15 percent of the cases we have
accepted involved housing issues, and we have been able to do some good.

This chapter will illustrate some of the problems our clients experienced both as tenants and as tenuous homeowners, and how we have been able to help, sometimes with very creative solutions, more than once with remedies beyond a normal law practice.

The traditional detainer docket in general sessions court is one of the lowest circles of Hell, one of the most depressing scenes in American jurisprudence. The perfunctory clerk calls down the list of delinquent tenants; after each name the landlord's lawyer standing close by answers, "Plaintiff"; there is a pause to see if the defendant is in the court room, which she usually is not, having given up all hope; and after that brief pause, the judge pronounces, "Granted," just before the clerk in rhythm goes on to the next name. It is all over in a few minutes, and another set of families faces homelessness.

The tenant must vacate the apartment or house or house trailer in ten days and will have a judgment against him for whatever back rent he owes, coupled with late fees, court costs, attorney fees, and any other assessment the law and the lease allow. If he does not vacate in ten days, the sheriff's deputies, following a writ of possession awarded to the landlord, will come and clean out the residence, putting all the tenant's furniture and goods off the property on the sidewalk or in the road. As Matthew Desmond details in his Pulitzer Prize winning book *Evicted*, and as any legal aid lawyer can confirm, this can mean for the unfortunate family a cascade of horrors: dislocation, change of schools, instability, scattered families, crashing with relatives, missed appointments, lost or destroyed furniture and clothes and food, loss of job, depression, violence.[1]

In the early 1980s, at the behest of the Reagan administration, Congress drastically reduced federal funding for housing, and a problem that had been severe for low-income people became even worse. Homelessness increased dramatically. More people began sleeping on the streets. Camps appeared under bridges.

At the same time, because of the Reagan administration's opposition to Legal Services and resulting cuts to our funding, we lost about a third of our staff and had to face the fact that we no longer could do all that we had been doing before. We needed to prioritize even further our case acceptance policy and concentrate on those matters where we could be most effective. In considering our work on housing cases, we compared what we had been able to do in private landlord-tenant cases with what we had been able to do for clients in public or subsidized housing. Even though occasionally with a private tenant we had been able to stop an eviction, or get the client more time, or reduce the amount of the money judgment, or get the necessary repairs made, our won-lost record was not encouraging. The law was not with us, plus more often than not, it was just a matter of money, which our client did not have. The few favorable outcomes could not justify our continuing to put significant resources into these cases. We would make exceptions when compelling cases came along, but not as a rule.

With our reduced staff, we would concentrate on government subsidized and public housing, an area where, though the supply is unduly limited, the legal provisions are more generous for tenants. As with any government program, there are remedies for any arbitrary actions of those administering the programs. There are statutory and regulatory provisions governing the programs, and there are constitutional protections available. That gives a lawyer much more material to work with. Case in point: *Ferguson v. Metropolitan Development and Housing Agency*, which held that a tenant with a Section 8 housing voucher had a right to a due process hearing before she could be removed from the program.[2]

Section 8 of the Housing and Community Development Act of 1974, an updating of the federal public housing program, created an alternative to the concentrated housing projects for low-income people that had been built previously. In 1937, Congress had declared it to be a policy of the United States to promote the general welfare by providing decent, safe, and sanitary housing for those who qualified. With Section 8, it asserted an additional goal of economically mixed housing. One of the methods for achieving all these goals was for a local public housing authority, which in Nashville was the Metropolitan Development and Housing Agency (MDHA), to issue certificates to qualified families certifying that MDHA would subsidize what the tenant could pay up to a federally determined fair market value. The family then would go into the private market to find an owner willing to participate in the program with all its requirements for lease approval, inspections, and authorizations.

Louise Ferguson had a Section 8 certificate and had been living in an approved apartment with her two children for several months when MDHA notified her that her certificate would be revoked because of a disputed bill of $228 dating from a couple of years earlier when she had lived in a project. Not having any recourse with MDHA, she came to see Russ. With help from Peter Komlos-Hrobsky at TALS, Russ filed in federal district court to prevent Ms. Ferguson from losing the certificate, and consequently her home. He obtained a temporary restraining order and subsequently a preliminary injunction by agreement with MDHA, which stayed in effect until the case was resolved some twenty-two months later.

This was a case about a public benefit, the housing certificate, and whether or not MDHA could revoke that certificate without providing to Ms. Ferguson procedures such as adequate notice; an opportunity to be heard; and a decision by an impartial decision maker based on evidence at the hearing. In the end, Judge Thomas Wiseman, following the Supreme Court decision in *Goldberg v. Kelly*, and other federal benefits cases, decided the answer was that MDHA as a "state actor" owed her those due process protections.[3] She simply had too much at stake, an essential need, housing. On balance, MDHA would have a "relatively light" administrative burden in giving her notice and conducting such a hearing. Ms. Ferguson and her children kept their apartment.

The Section 8 program's emphasis on scattered sites rather than the concentration of low-income housing in one neighborhood has proven advantageous in several ways, and it helped Drake solve a sticky "not in my backyard" (NIMBY) problem in Gallatin ten years later. The Gallatin Housing Authority, with its three hundred units full and another 282 families on its waiting list, applied for and received a federal grant to build another traditional forty-unit project on Red River Road. The project initially was approved by the city council, but then the neighbors rose up. "We're not against all these people having a place to live, we just don't want them there" was one of the nicer comments by an opponent at a public hearing. A supporter of building the housing, the executive director of the local family shelter, noted in the comments of others at the hearing "a tinge of racism."[4] The council, convinced by the NIMBY neighbors, reversed and voted down the project, a decision that then was challenged in a lawsuit by the housing authority, charging that the council's decision had been arbitrary and capricious.

While that was pending, the housing situation in the low-income community continued to get worse, moving two women to come to our Gallatin office and ask for help. Because we were understaffed in that office at the time, the case ended up being referred to Drake. The two women, like the majority of people on the list, were of a minority race, providing a basis for a suit against the city for violation of the federal Fair Housing Act. With two suits now pending, there began discussions among the parties that took many months but finally resulted in a compromise plan for scattered site housing with eight units in each councilmanic district. The council approved the plan in principle, but of course, the devil was in the details: identifying and obtaining the sites.

One of the solutions to that problem was right in *our* backyard. We owned our office in Gallatin, a former house with a lot behind it that went all the way back to the next street, a vacant area that had been useless to us and required maintenance every year. Drake, looking to help the city and housing authority along to a settlement, came to me with the idea that we sell the back lot to the housing authority for one of its sites. He checked with the Board of Professional Responsibility to be sure there was no ethical problem with our involvement in the substance of the settlement. There was not. We took it to the executive committee of our board. There was no NIMBY problem here. Our backyard was the perfect place for a couple of homes.

It seems that we were involved in non-legal, creative solutions in housing cases more often than in any other type of case. Pat Hylton adopted two cats from an elderly client who could not bear to give them up but could not take them with her into an MDHA high-rise. Drake and Pat had secured a place for her there, away from a violent spouse and a condemned house. Her cats had been the last obstacle to her admission. She gave them up only with the assurance they would have a good home, and they did with Pat, a one-person humane society. After the client was settled in her new apartment, there was a picture in the newspaper of Pat taking the cats to her for a visit.[5]

Sometimes the creative solutions resulted from an imaginative use of the law and came from the bench. As Russ says, Drake communicated well with general sessions judges and often got them to do the right thing. His client, Mrs. Davis, lived in a privately owned apartment complex. Her problem was her violent estranged husband whom she had prosecuted for assault. Sometime after he got out of jail for that, he came back to the apartment complex parking lot and was arrested again, this time for a drug sale. Having had enough of him, the manager filed a detainer warrant against both Mr. and Mrs. Davis because they both were on the lease. When she came to see Drake, he tried to negotiate with the manager and persuade him to simply take the estranged husband off the lease, but he refused. The detainer action went to trial in general sessions; the judge granted judgment for the landlord against both spouses. The law was on the landlord's side. The equities, however, were on the side of Mrs. Davis, so after ruling for the landlord, the judge then turned around, adopted Drake's plea, and ordered the landlord immediately to enter into a lease with Mrs. Davis individually, listing only her and her children as occupants.

Drake did well, but the prize for the most comprehensive landlord-tenant remedy went to Allston Vander Horst. He also had the most unlikely client, the resident manager of a privately owned complex. We certainly were not accustomed to representing managers, but this one was unusual, and principled, and recently fired. The manager had been told by the owner of the complex to evict a tenant the manager knew had done nothing wrong. The tenant simply transgressed one of the owner's prejudices. When the manager would not do his dirty work, the owner fired him and ordered him to vacate the apartment he occupied as part of his compensation.

The ex-resident manager, feeling he had been wronged, dug in his heels and refused to leave. The owner filed a detainer warrant to get him out. Since the man now was unemployed and about to lose his place to live when he came to see us, Allston took his case. Predictably, he lost in general sessions and the owner was awarded possession; but on appeal to circuit court, Allston took the initiative, charging the owner with extortion. After all the proof was in, the judge agreed, denied the detainer warrant and ordered the owner to allow the ex-manager to keep his apartment for the rest of the year without payment, which meant more than six months of free rent.

The imaginative remedies were not all one-shot deals. Kitty Calhoon and Drake were among the pioneers in a far reaching legal remedy for public and subsidized housing tenants who had fallen behind in their rent, even those who had a detainer judgment against them. It was a remedy we and others were able to use multiple times for our clients, and it was fashioned in a surprising place: bankruptcy court. The Bankruptcy Act contains a section providing that in a Chapter XIII bankruptcy a debtor can rehabilitate a lease that is in default. What that means is that the tenant can list the debt, establish with the Trustee a plan to pay it off, and stay in possession of his place for the term of the lease. The landlord cannot evict him before the end of the tenancy as long as the debtor pays the Trustee according to the plan and stays current on subsequent rent. That applies to commercial and residential leases, to private party leases, and most significantly for our clients, it applies to public housing and federally subsidized leases. In fact, that provision's effect can be even more potent in the cases of public and subsidized housing residents because their leases have no termination date. The tenant has a right to continue in possession so long as she continues to be eligible for the housing and is not in default; and if she is paying the Trustee in compliance with her Chapter XIII plan and paying her current rent, she is not in default.

Having seen how our brethren at the bar have been able to enlist the Bankruptcy Act to protect real estate developers, automobile manufacturers, and financial institutions, it was gratifying to see how our lawyers likewise were able to employ it to protect low-income tenants from homelessness. They also were able to use it to protect homeownership, which, though not dependent on an arcane provision like the public housing lease anomaly, still can be a creative and effective remedy.

It was for Mrs. Smith who was about to lose her home of many years through a pending foreclosure. She had worked all her life, but recent health problems prevented her from working any longer. She had two mortgages on her home and although the total payments were not excessive, with her only income being an SSI check, she had fallen behind. Normally, a Chapter XIII bankruptcy would have provided a remedy, but Mrs. Smith did not have enough income to fund a Chapter XIII plan, until Drake came up with an idea: If she could take on a boarder, this should give her enough income to fund a plan. She found a boarder. Drake filed the petition, stopped the sale, and saved her home.

Not all of Drake's housing miracles involved a creative solution; at least one involved speed. Sitting in his office one morning working on another case, he paused to take a call from a friendly social worker with a desperate plea on behalf of a client of hers, an ill seventy-one-year-old man who lived "out in the country" and whose house was about to be foreclosed on. A second mortgage holder, who had bought the mortgage from a home repair contractor (a common scenario), had scheduled a sale that morning at eleven o'clock.

"Bring him in. I'll try to stop it."

By 9:30 the social worker had the man in our office. Drake took enough information to complete an emergency Chapter XIII petition. His paralegal, Janet Rosenberg, filled out the necessary forms. Georgia Byers typed everything up in record time, and the man signed it. Then began the race to the courthouse, or more precisely the race to the courthouses. We needed lawyers in two places at once. Adinah Robertson brought her car down to the front door of our building and was waiting when Drake came out with the signed petition. David Tarpley went across the street to the Metro Courthouse and stationed himself at a payphone on the first floor near the spot where the sale was scheduled to take place. He saw the trustee and the deed of trust holder gathered, waiting for the appointed hour. At a time that David calculated Drake should be close to the bankruptcy court clerk's office, he called that office. A deputy clerk who knew both David and Drake answered and agreed to stay on the phone keeping the line open. Thirty seconds later, Drake ran in.

"Here he is." The deputy clerk put down the phone, gave the petition a docket number and stamped it filed at 10:58. She returned to the phone to read the docket number and stamped time to David, who entered them on the copy he had carried with him. He hung up the phone and hustled over to the trustee, an attorney he knew, who already had started through the litany he was required to recite for the sale.

"I'm here with a bankruptcy petition that stops the sale."

"How do we know you are telling the truth?"

"You don't, but here is a copy of the original that has been filed and stamped, and here is the docket number on this copy I am giving you."

Still not believing that the ill and elderly rural man could have pulled himself together enough to act with that much alacrity, the deed of trust holder quizzed, "So where is your client?"

"He is in our office."

"I want to see him."

David took them both across the street. They saw him, but in that sanctuary with David standing by, there was nothing they could say or do to him, and so they left. Drake came back beaming from the clerk's office, completed a routine XIII plan, filed it, and ultimately had it confirmed. Another home saved.

Losing one's lease or one's property and having to move away was not the only housing problem our clients faced with some regularity. Sometimes the problem was not being able to move, having no place else to go, no options but to stay in a place that was unsafe and uninhabitable. In landlord-tenant law there is an implied warranty of habitability, which requires the landlord to maintain the premises in a condition fit for human habitation, but that warranty has to be enforced. In counties that have housing codes and inspectors, there is some enforcement, but those offices most often have limited staff and are no match for the persistent slumlords. A social worker from Catholic Social Services brought to Drake and Kitty four Cambodian refugee families, "family oriented and dedicated to the American work ethic," living in cold, damp, rat infested apartments on Boscobel Street with leaking roofs and rotting wood floors. The social worker said they could only afford cheap housing, but, "We want to show them [that here in America] they can expect to have more." The landlord, who was well known to codes inspectors, predictably claimed, "The problems are grossly exaggerated," and he opined about Cambodian families, "They don't mind rats at all."[6]

Kitty and Drake filed suit against the landlord, but as with the experience of the codes inspectors, the delay, judicial reluctance, false fixes, and broken promises meant there was no good result. An inspector is quoted in the paper, "He's just a junk landlord. He pays his fines and then goes on."[7] And that was the case in this instance. Several months later fire destroyed the refugees' apartment building, and they were left homeless, a not unprecedented occurrence for that landlord's properties. Fortunately, in this case there was some rescue: Metro Social Services, churches, and other agencies helped resettle the Cambodian refugees, saving them from yet another horror.

There are public housing conditions issues also, but usually those cases are not so intractable. HUD regulations and other legal requirements usually impose reasonable standards on the property and afford some protections for the tenants, except when they don't. Among the many measures advanced during the Reagan administration that were punitive to low-income people, there was a set of HUD regulations instructing local housing authorities to impose a surcharge on any tenant who had installed a window air conditioner in her apartment. HUD determined that air conditioning was a luxury and that people living in the brick and block housing built without air conditioning in the 1950s should pay for the extra electricity needed to operate their luxury. Though the regulations were not yet final, MDHA dutifully followed the HUD instruction and began imposing the fee, which ranged from $9 to $26 per month depending on the size of the apartment.

The reaction among the tenants was quick and desperate. For some of them this represented a substantial percentage of their monthly income, particularly for the elderly and disabled on a fixed income. They turned out in great numbers at tenant meetings to protest. One of them came to Kitty with her complaint. It was still summer, enough time for Kitty to hire a public health environmental expert to measure the heat in a number of the apartments where people had removed their air-conditioners because they could not pay the bill. Kitty recalls, "We had a string of days in the 90s, so the readings he got in those small brick units (where it wasn't safe to leave your windows open, especially at night) were off the charts." He prepared a report showing that air conditioning was not a luxury but was a necessity for health and safety. Kitty sent that report to HUD along with her comments on the pending regulation. She then used it as the basis for a federal class action lawsuit she filed in October 1987 against HUD and MDHA.

The leadership of MDHA was sympathetic to the woes of the tenants and in a couple of months reached a settlement of the lawsuit that brought along HUD as well. HUD agreed to pay MDHA $130,000 to compensate for the extra electricity and MDHA agreed to suspend the surcharge. George Barrett, who represented MDHA, is quoted in the *Tennessean* after the board unanimously adopted the settlement agreement as saying, "We think air conditioners in this area [of the country] are necessities, and therefore, there should not be a surcharge."[8]

The problems with conditions in outdated public housing projects and in substandard private dwellings illustrate why there is such a demand when new housing possibilities come along. In the late 1970s, a new federally subsidized apartment complex, Dellway Villa, came on the market, and more than a thousand low-income people applied for admission. For a good number of those applicants, however, in addition to all the other impediments to decent housing, at Dellway they faced another not uncommon barrier, racial discrimination. Two of the rejected applicants came to us. What follows in the next section is the story of their precedent-setting case and the young lawyer who helped them.

DELLWAY VILLA

Bill West had been on staff for about six months in 1978 working in the Nashville office. A graduate of Tipton County High School in West Tennessee, he had been to Yale for undergraduate and UT for law school, clerked on the Tennessee Court of Appeals, and worked for a year at Memphis Area Legal Services before coming to work with us.

Bill was assigned the intake for Charlie Mai Jordan and Vanessa Bush, two Black women who had been turned down for admission at Dellway Villa even though they understood that they had met all the qualifications for admission. The two women told Bill that they knew from talking with others that the resident manager, Laura Notgrass, routinely favored White applicants over Black. She would tell Black applicants to come back later but would accept applications from Whites. They told him about other people who had been discriminated against and even about some White friends who recognized what was going on at Dellway. Neither we nor they could find a private attorney who would take their case, so Bill did.

Bill talked with other applicants his two clients referred to him and with the White informants as well. He reviewed the HUD files on the Dellway project, part of which had been built already, but with more buildings under construction. He studied the law on housing discrimination, a field not familiar to us. Just ten years before, in the aftermath of Martin Luther King Jr.'s, assassination, Congress had passed the Fair Housing Act of 1968 explicitly prohibiting most private race-based housing discrimination. A couple of months later, the US Supreme Court ruled that a Reconstruction Era civil rights bill, an act that had been on the books but unenforced for a hundred years, actually had banned racial discrimination in the sale or rental of real estate by private as well as public entities.[9] The enforcement of these 1968 developments in the law had been predictably slow and sporadic at best, but Bill was about to become an accelerated part of that creeping enforcement.

He filed the federal class action lawsuit on February 29, 1979, that set out not only the allegations of the two named plaintiffs, but also testimony in an affidavit from a White friend who had worked part-time in the Dellway office where she saw Ms. Notgrass keep separate lists of applications segregated by race. At one point the friend had been assigned to alphabetize a list of five hundred to six hundred Black applicants that had been separated from a stack of fifty to sixty White applicants. Bill had determined that the strongest proof would lie in the numerical disparity between the race of the applicants and the race of those to whom apartments were rented. As of the date the lawsuit was filed, 70.9 percent of the applicant pool had been Black, whereas 82 percent of those admitted were White.

A month after he filed, Bill learned that Dellway had received from HUD permission to begin renting out apartments in additional buildings that recently had been completed. Because he knew members of the class were continuing to be excluded from admission, he filed a motion for a preliminary injunction to stop the process. Judge Morton was not persuaded to hurry; he set the hearing on the motion three weeks off and later continued it another month. When it finally happened, that hearing brought both a blessing and a curse.

The judge granted Bill's motion for class certification, but he declined to grant the motion for a preliminary injunction because Bill's clients could not post a bond sufficient to indemnify potential loss of income to Dellway if admissions were stopped. On the other hand, even as he denied the injunction, the judge was not subtle in his message to the defendants. They had filled fifty-four additional apartments since the time Bill filed his motion, leaving only ninety units that would be subject to the court's control for initial rental. After having commented earlier on the 71 percent Black applicant pool and 82 percent White tenant body, the judge turned to the Dellway lawyer and said, as Bill recalls, "I'm not going to enter a formal injunction at this point, but after the hearings in this matter, if I rule against the defendants and find out you have rented these apartments in the meantime, I'm going to hold it against you." Enough said. Then, to hurry things along for everyone, the judge set the trial to begin June 12, one week off. Bill now was in a position to get quick relief for his clients, but at the price of having one week to prepare a major class action lawsuit for trial. He returned to the office in shock and started looking for help.

Margaret Behm and Robert Greene signed on immediately and would play major roles in the trial. Margaret agreed to locate witnesses and handle witness preparation for most of the plaintiffs' witnesses. Robert had experience in statistical analysis for discrimination cases from his education at Howard University's law school, and he agreed to handle that part of the evidence. Bill drafted and served motions for expedited production of documents and for leave to inspect tenant files, which the court promptly granted. Tom Grooms and Allston, along with five new law graduates who were waiting to take the bar exam, helped go through the more than 1,500 applications. Bill defended a number of class members during their depositions by Dellway lawyers, and he conducted depositions of Ms. Notgrass and other defendants. At several points, when the swamped team had difficulty gaining access to essential files, Bill submitted motions for a continuance, each of which was denied, but there was some breathing room when the father of a Dellway lawyer died and the judge granted a continuance of two days.

The trial commenced on June 14 and was held off and on for four days, ending on July 19. Despite the defendants' denials that they had discriminated, the testimony at the trial brought out more damning stories from Black applicants and White residents as well. Another White resident who had worked part-time in the office testified that she had watched Ms. Notgrass discard freshly completed applications from Black people on several occasions. Drawing on their discovery, Bill and Robert were able to prove the statistical allegations in the complaint, and more. The numbers were dramatic, but real bombshells were the revealing notations in the application files: "old, but nice looking"; "gray eyes and light skin"; "she begged for it humbly." And then there was one that became the mantra for the trial, "Black, but nice."

Judge Morton's decision came down on September 10, finding that there was a "calculated course of conduct" that constituted a pattern or practice of discrimination, a violation of the 1868 Civil Rights Act and the 1968 Fair Housing Act. He enjoined the defendants from leasing the remaining apartments at the complex until the new manager (Ms. Notgrass had left soon after the suit was filed.) classified all applicants according to a HUD established procedure and submitted the list to the court for approval. This meant that Bill and Margaret spent an enormous amount of time that fall reviewing applications, credit reports, and rating forms as they monitored the process. For whatever reason, the defendants could not get it right. After numerous conversations with defendants' lawyers, continuations, and conferences with the judge, Bill and Margaret on November 15 filed detailed objections to the classification process used by the defendants, including the forms they had developed to determine eligibility for admission, which had a discriminatory impact on Black applicants, especially Black public assistance recipients.

At a hearing on December 27, Judge Morton upheld the objections and directed that the process be conducted in his presence in the courtroom in Cookeville. The process commenced there and continued in meetings later that week in Nashville until the decisions were made as to which applicants would be offered the remaining ninety apartments in the complex, and the judge on January 3, 1980, entered an agreed order mandating it done. Continuing the good news, bad news tradition of the case, however, during the same chambers conference where he approved the agreed order on admissions, Judge Morton indicated to Bill that he intended to limit the number of class members who could recover damages. Bill tried to persuade him otherwise in a motion and extensive brief, but at the February hearing on that motion, the judge ruled that "only those qualified Black applicants who were *rejected* can recover" (emphasis added), dismissing and disregarding all those whose applications had been trashed or merely filed away. When Bill followed up with a motion to either reconsider or certify the issue for interlocutory appeal, Judge Morton would do neither, but rather further limited the class that could recover. Now it included only "any applicant who was discriminated against by the defendant and who was qualified at the time of the discrimination *but limited to the total number of apartments available*" (emphasis added). With every ruling, the class that could recover was shrinking smaller and smaller.

In an effort to get a decision the court would certify for appeal, Bill tried several other approaches, but the judge was unpersuaded at each turn. Finally, Bill argued that class members who had been excluded from recovery were being denied access to the court to claim damages, thereby having their rights under the Fair Housing Act diminished. He filed a motion asking that their claims be heard, and though Judge Morton denied that motion, the specificity and finality of his order gave Bill a stronger basis for appeal. In early October, based on a six-month-old decision of the US Supreme Court clarifying the use of the federal rule on interlocutory appeals, Bill followed up with another motion asking for certification of an appeal. Finally, the judge was persuaded.

Lots of balls were in the air at the same time. Bill and Robert were busy contacting members of the constricted class that the judge had defined as a recovering group, those who were entitled to claim damages. Each one had to prove her own monetary damages. With the hearings on those claims scheduled to begin in November, Bill and Robert had to prepare them to testify, subpoena supporting documents, and interview collaborating witnesses. The initial hearings stretched over two weeks in Nashville and Cookeville. In each case, there would be cross-examination and pushback on many issues from the defendants who were trying to limit the damages payments. They demanded documents and conducted extensive discovery between the initial and the later set of hearings.

At the same time all this was going on, Bill had one eye on Cincinnati and the Sixth Circuit Court of Appeals, but he had good assistance on that phase of the case, as well. Waverly Crenshaw, a Vanderbilt law student, was clerking with us, and Bill enlisted him to help with the research and writing involved in developing the appeal of Judge Morton's rulings. In that enlistment, Bill was more prescient than he could have guessed. As this is being written forty years later, the Honorable Waverly Crenshaw is the chief judge of the US District Court for the Middle District of Tennessee, the same position Judge Morton held during the *Dellway* case. With Waverly's help, Bill filed the necessary brief and documents to perfect the appeal and then filed a motion for an expedited hearing, which was granted.[10]

The appeal was argued before the Sixth Circuit on June 17, 1981, two years after the trial, and the decision came down in October.[11] In an expansive ruling, the court found that all qualified Black applicants for an apartment at Dellway who applied anytime there was an apartment available would be eligible to recover damages. It reasoned that because the district court had found a "pattern or practice" of discrimination, any decision the defendants had made during the time of that pattern or practice was by definition discriminatory. As to each claim for damages, rather than the plaintiffs' having the burden of proof, the defendants would have the burden of proving that the class member applicant had *not* been qualified and therefore was not a victim of discrimination, or that no apartment had been available at the time of the application. The court then ruled that proving no apartments were available at the time of an application would be impossible because the defendants were still building new units at Dellway when the plaintiffs filed suit.

One of the defendants' fallback positions had been that recovery should be limited to 244 applicants, at most, because that was the number of units finally built at Dellway, so therefore no more than that number of applicants ever could have been harmed. The court of appeals refused this limitation, as well. Citing other housing cases, the court concluded "discrimination is discrimination." Citing common sense, the court ruled that there can be emotional suffering when one is the victim of discrimination, regardless of the situation. Following legal precedent, it reiterated that even where there are no demonstrable damages, victims of such violations are still entitled to a nominal recovery.

The defendants petitioned the US Supreme Court for *certiorari*; Bill opposed it; and it was denied. Then the focus went back to damages, but now with a much larger recovering group. Judge Morton issued decisions on the claims for damages he had heard, and he referred to the magistrate the remaining claims that Legal Services had filed on behalf of two hundred others who had come forward in response to class notices. The case would go on for another two years with hearings and disputes about discovery, requiring Bill to file numerous objections and motions for protective orders, which usually were granted. Kitty joined Bill in this phase of the case, preparing class members for testimony and conducting some of the hearings. When Bill went part-time with us and began working part-time at the Housing Opportunities Corporation in Memphis, Kitty assumed the day-to-day responsibility for the case. There were partial settlements from time to time regarding damages payments to defined groups, a class settlement for nominal damages claims in the summer of 1984, and finally a settlement for attorney fees, negotiated for us by Vanderbilt law professor and former civil rights attorney Robert Belton.

After more than six years, it was over, the first fair housing class action case for damages ever to be fully litigated. It had established law on discrimination in the Sixth Circuit. It obtained a significant award for the class, one of the largest at the time. It protected our clients against discrimination with sweeping declaratory and injunctive relief, and for many of them, it obtained a place to live in new housing.

WHERRY HOUSING

This last story has to do with preserving the supply of affordable housing. Greg Sperry in our Murfreesboro office, with some creative lawyering, helped save 228 units that were about to be destroyed.

When the US government closed the Seward Air Force Base in 1971, it sold the land and buildings to Rutherford County, which developed a good portion of the base into a new industrial park. The former Wherry housing on the base was rented out by the county, providing homes for several hundred low-income families.[12] When the city of Smyrna, in a suspect move, evicted all the tenants from its city-owned apartments and razed the buildings, Wherry became the only low-income housing available in that town. The county, too, had its reservations about providing housing and was not an attentive landlord. It maintained Wherry, but not very well, and when units became vacant, they often were demolished, leaving scars and vacant lots scattered throughout the neighborhood.

In June 1980, a group of the tenants got together to talk about the deteriorating condition of their neighborhood, named themselves the Wherry Housing Action Committee (WHAC), and set as their purposes to improve their housing and preserve their racially integrated community. One of their first actions was to have some members meet with the county Economic Development Committee, which was responsible for the former base. They asked the committee to make repairs and improvements in the housing, roads, and sewerage system. Instead, the committee punitively voted to demolish all the houses and add the land to the industrial park. It sent notices to the remaining tenants informing them that they would have to leave by June 1, 1981.

Two members of WHAC, Judy and Andy Fabri, came to our Murfreesboro office within days after that action, met with Greg, and told him of their woes. They had lived at Wherry seven years and could not afford to live anywhere else. A number of the other residents had moved there when Smyrna closed its housing project, and now they would be displaced again. When the county bought the property, there had been

546 homes; now there were only 228 left. The Fabris were White, but in the interest of their neighbors, they pointed out that more than half the remaining residents were Black, and the closing of this project after closing the other seemed like a systematic effort to eliminate low-income Black residents from Smyrna.

A week and a day after his first meeting with the Fabris, Greg filed for them and WHAC a class action lawsuit in federal district court against Rutherford County, the county Board of Commissioners, the Economic Development Committee and its executive director, the de facto manager of Wherry, asking for a temporary restraining order to stop the demolition of thirty-six units the county planned to tear down immediately and for preliminary injunctions requiring maintenance of the remaining houses. Judge John Nixon granted the TRO and later granted preliminary injunctions extending the prohibition and requiring maintenance.

Having deterred the destructive designs of the county, Greg then had to figure out what might be the solution for his clients in the long run. In the meantime, however, there were several interim crises that he met with amended complaints and more preliminary injunctions. There were issues with the sewerage system and other maintenance failures. WHAC needed an office, but the county would not allow them to use a vacant unit. WHAC moved in anyway. The county threatened to evict, but Judge Nixon enjoined the eviction. There was conflict at every turn.

Even more problematic: Greg needed to figure out what his clients might do if they actually won the lawsuit. They would be stuck in housing the county clearly did not want to exist and did not want to maintain. At first he explored resources the county might be persuaded to use to maintain the housing. He looked at Community Development Block Grants and had several meetings with officials. He looked at weatherization grants from the Tennessee Valley Authority to fix up the uninsulated units. All the resources he could muster, however, would require action from the owner, the county, and the county wanted no part of these solutions. It just wanted to tear the houses down.

Then, in early January 1981, just after Judge Nixon had declared the case a class action, at the suggestion of the National Housing Law Project in Berkeley, Greg got in touch with Jaime Bordenave at Cooperative Housing Foundation in Washington. Two days after they talked, Jaime flew to Nashville and was in Smyrna to tour Wherry housing and meet with WHAC. The next day he spent more than twelve hours consulting with Greg, meeting with the Economic Development Committee, and that night with WHAC again. Jaime was floating the idea of the parties' settling the case by having the county sell the houses and land to a cooperative formed by the residents. He offered to consult with WHAC in forming the coop and to help apply for loans and grants to finance the purchase.

Over the next two years Greg proceeded on the two tracks with this case, while also handling the regular load of cases that a lawyer in a small office would see each week. One track was preparation for trial, with all the depositions and other preliminary work that required; the other track was the groundwork for and the formation of a coop. There was no assurance their ownership would ever come to fruition, but with Jaime's assistance, he wanted to be sure his clients were equipped and ready if it did.

As often happens when a trial is imminent, the looming date will focus the mind and lead to more serious discussions. That is what happened after the filing of the pretrial order and then the pretrial briefs in the late summer of 1982. The negotiations lasted through the winter with many ups and downs, but finally the parties reached an agreement that was approved by the court in February 1983. The county would sell the property to Wherry Housing Cooperative, Inc., (WHC) for $1,250,000, financed by the county over twenty-five years, if the coop could raise a down payment of $125,000 by March 1984.

With this, Greg felt his work here was done, and he left to follow his calling, taking a position with the new National Christian Foundation in Georgia. The rest of the story for the Wherry Housing Cooperative was a stormy one. Susan Garner, who had worked on the original federal complaint with Greg and who had been involved tangentially during the process, assumed responsibility for the case and attempted to represent the interests of WHAC and WHC as they moved forward to the completion of the deal. Jaime Bordenave also continued to work closely with the groups, bringing multiple resources to aid them in the process.

Regrettably, there developed dissention in the group of residents that was trying to manage the transition, and there was opposition from some of the other residents who were opposed to the change altogether. Like the complaining Children of Israel in the Sinai wilderness, the opposing residents wanted to go back to Egypt and continue as renters, not realizing that the alternative was not that they could continue to rent, but that the county would demolish their houses. Susan tried to explain that to them, but to no avail, and when they wanted to take their complaints to the court, she tried to explain to them that the time for opting out of the class was long past. They filed a pro se pleading anyway. Their request to opt out was denied.

During all of 1983, WHAC sponsored community dinners, published a regular newsletter, had bake sales, and even had a yard-beautiful contest in an effort to reinforce a sense of community and encourage residents to buy-in to the coop. The buy-ins were slow, and some of the opposition turned ugly. The county dropped all pretense of maintenance, and when its onsite manager left, it did not replace him. Even with that, the county continued to rent units to new tenants, people who were not familiar with the coop process and had no commitment to the program, making it even more difficult for WHAC to achieve its goal of signing up the majority of the residents for the coop.

Despite all those discouraging difficulties, in January 1984, just two months before the deadline for closing, the National Consumer Cooperative Bank, again thanks to Jaime Bordenave's advocacy, made a loan of $200,000 to WHC, a portion to be used for rehabilitation of the units and a portion to help with the down payment. As result of that, WHC was able to reduce the initial buy-in from $600 to $300 and allow the buyer to pay the other $300 in installments over the next year. This was designed to meet one of the complaints from many of the dissenters: they could not come up with the initial payment. The loan also made it possible for WHC to close the deal on time, and the coop was established. Now the hard part began.

Sorry to report, things did not get better with the operation of the coop. The internal disputes intensified every month. Alex Hurder, who assumed responsibility for the case and represented the coop at the closing, tried to help bring people together, but finally we had to withdraw because of the divisions among the people we originally represented. Alex had to inform the different groups that they each would have to get other counsel, which they did. Eight years later the coop filed for bankruptcy.

The rest of the story is not part of the Legal Aid narrative, but it is worth bringing it up-to-date so that we do not end this episode on such a sad note. Miraculously, thanks to good lawyering by a bankruptcy attorney, Marilee McWilliams, forbearance from the county, new outside management, and the vision of a local pastor, Wherry survived. The same manager has been in charge for more than twenty years, and the vision of the pastor has blossomed into a ministry named Community Servants that has brought stability, care, and thousands of college-age volunteers over the years to help the people at Wherry. A couple of the units are used as housing for missionaries on furlough, and there is a dormitory for young volunteers who come from afar. A number of the residents at Wherry have been refugees, principally from Myanmar and Honduras. Community Servants has operated English-language classes and citizenship instruction for residents and others in the area nearby. The staff and volunteers provide tutoring for school children living at Wherry and were encouraged in their work when the county recently invested $20 million in an elementary school adjacent to the property.

So the early hopes of the original organizers of WHAC and WHC, the hundreds of hours of work by Greg, Susan, and Alex, and the essential support by Jaime Bordenave, were not in vain. Though most of the houses are now rentals, the houses are still there, and grateful people are living there. The Wherry of today is not the strong coop that was intended, but it is appropriately providing affordable housing that would not be available otherwise. As a bonus, the services now being provided there to immigrants in the area are appropriately reminiscent of the purpose for which the first legal aid society in New York was established nearly 150 years ago, to help assimilate recent immigrants to this country.

───────────

Among the ills from which the founders of that legal aid society in New York wanted to protect their clients, they listed, "the rapacity of runners . . . and a miscellaneous coterie of sharpers."[13] These ills were what we today less colorfully call "consumer problems." The next two chapters will describe some modern versions of those problems and the variety of ways we have addressed them.

CHAPTER 12

Caveat Emptor

The help of your services are greatly
appreciated especially when you feel
there's no one to help you when you've
been taken advantage of.

—A. C. P., NASHVILLE, 1990

David Tarpley is a musician as well as a lawyer. For years he has played French horn in the Trevecca Symphony Orchestra. He pays attention to notes, pitches, and counterpoints. Very early on at Legal Services he gravitated toward commercial and consumer cases, the intricacies of the Uniform Commercial Code, Regulation Z of the Truth in Lending Act, and other such compositions that brought a dull glaze to the eyes of the rest of us. If a client's consumer case seemed in the least bit complicated, the common mantra became, "Let Tarpley do it." And he accepted that. He even delighted in it. He would gleefully rub his hands together and start talking gibberish none of the rest of us even vaguely understood. It made all the sense in the world then in 1974 to form a one-lawyer "consumer section" and allow him to specialize. By 1986, his mastery in this area of the law brought an invitation to be a part-time instructor in the clinic at Vanderbilt. After five years in that position, he became adjunct faculty, teaching first a seminar and then a regular course at the school for nearly twenty years, while still practicing at Legal Services.

Though the law Tarpley practiced seemed esoteric, the results he obtained were very practical and even heartwarming, especially when he saved a person's paycheck or home. Low-income neighborhoods are particularly fertile ground for home repair rip-offs. Widows and single moms are especially vulnerable to sweet-talking salesmen who promise solutions to their housing problems. Bob Poole, doing business as Colonial Construction Company, was one of those salesman, and while David encountered many others, Poole is especially memorable for the volume: David estimates he must have handled twenty cases against him over the years.

People like Poole who prowl low-income neighborhoods often have outside enablers. In one case, it was an airline pilot. Poole had persuaded Diane Jetton that he could replace the leaking roof on her family home. Anxious to nail the deal, he had the material delivered and began the job before giving her the credit disclosure required by Regulation Z and before she even signed the financing papers, a prohibited practice known in the industry as "credit spiking." To compound his future problems, he began the job before the three days she would have had to rescind this door-to-door sale. He kept the financing papers himself, and for about a year and a half collected payments from Ms. Jetton. Then she fell behind and was in default.

At this point, Poole sold the paper to an airline pilot who as a sideline bought paper like this in order to foreclose and get the property cheap for resale and a quick profit. Without contacting Ms. Jetton to negotiate anything, the airline pilot initiated the foreclosure process and had the sale date set. When Ms. Jetton received the notice of the sale, she came to Legal Services. After looking at the paperwork, David immediately sent a notice of rescission to the pilot, but time was short, so he did not wait long for a reply. He filed a lawsuit in federal court against both the pilot and Poole asking to stop the sale and prevent further foreclosure proceedings.

When the case came to trial, Judge Thomas Higgins rescinded the financing papers and the deed of trust, and he awarded statutory damages to Ms. Jetton because of the pilot's failure to acknowledge her rescission notice and stop the sale immediately on receipt of David's notice. In an effort to cut his losses, Poole tried to show that Ms. Jetton had received reasonable value in that she had a new roof, but David's expert witness, a construction consultant, testified that the work had been grossly overpriced and done so badly that the value at best was $3,700 rather than the

$15,000 charged originally. The judge credited his testimony, not that of Poole's witness, and since Ms. Jetton had made payments to Poole totaling $3,700 before her default, she owed him nothing.

Predatory contractors, small time financers, and a random airline pilot are not the only people seeking to make money off the difficulties of low-income people needing home repairs. The cast of characters also has included a multistate drug dealer and money launderer. Beginning in 1985, people started coming to us who had bought replacement windows from Season Sash, a Kentucky firm owned by Joseph Mohwish that sent door-to-door salesmen into people's homes with misleading sales pitches that resulted in their buying very high-priced windows and incurring oppressive mortgages on their homes. Eventually, David and Drake had eighteen clients they were trying to untangle from the Season Sash web.

After they filed suit in the federal district court in Nashville, a former employee of Season Sash called and offered to tell David about the management of the operation, but only if they could meet secretly, he could remain anonymous, and David promised not to call him as a witness. They met the next night at the rear of a parking lot behind an industrial building off Elm Hill Pike. The man, according to David, was "white as a sheet . . . looked like a ghost." It was a dangerous occasion, if not for David, then clearly for the informant who told David, "If they find out about this, I'm a dead man." He described the intrusive way the company got prospects and the standard procedure on a sales call, which could last up to four hours. People were worn down when the salesman just would not leave, and then there was the paperwork. One client recounted that she and her husband did not have a good education (second grade), were not in good health, and could not see to read, but the salesman persuaded them to sign what David described later as "more paperwork than I've ever seen."

Armed with the informant's information about the management and the financing, David noticed Mohwish and two of his lieutenants for a deposition in Nashville. They arrived in a private jet and looked, as David tells it, like they were "out of the cast of the Sopranos." He remembers that Mohwish, "at 6'8" and over 300 pounds, was the largest person I have ever seen not to be an NFL football player." While David took his deposition, Drake labored through the obfuscation of the two lieutenants.

Both David and Drake emerged unharmed and in the process were able to get admissions of information they had received elsewhere, and they learn about the interplay between the sales outfit of Season Sash, the manufacturing unit, and the financing arm that kept some of the contracts and sold others to cooperating banks in Cincinnati and Knoxville. With all of that background, they were ready to proceed with their cases, but then there were snags.

Both the Tennessee and Kentucky attorneys general were conducting investigations into the consumer practices of Season Sash, while the Kentucky attorney general and the US Attorney for the Eastern District of Kentucky at the same time were looking into possible drug trafficking and money laundering being conducted through the company. When David first contacted the Kentucky attorney general's office about Season Sash, a criminal investigator in that office cautioned David to "be careful, you are litigating with the mob."

As the circle around Mohwish tightened, Season Sash filed for bankruptcy protection in the Eastern District of Kentucky, and while that stopped David from proceeding in court in Tennessee, it did not stop his pursuit. He filed claims on behalf of his existing clients in the bankruptcy court. In a parallel move, when new clients came to us, he filed on their behalf separate actions in Nashville, not against Season Sash, but against the banks that held their mortgages, which were based on defective documents from Season Sash. Three times he went to Lexington for meetings of creditors and other hearings, and though he was not able to recover anything his clients had paid for the windows, the assets of the company having been pledged to the banks, he did get a rescission of all our clients' contracts and release of the mortgages held by the company. In the process, he was able to convince the banks to release all the contracts and all the mortgages they held against our clients in exchange for his dismissing the Nashville cases against them. For our eighteen clients, when it was all over, David could say that their homes were free of the mortgages and that since the day they had become our clients, because of his initial rescission notices, not one of them had paid a dime to Season Sash or a bank. It was a good result for all of our clients. Not so for Mohwish; the next year he was convicted of the federal crimes related to his operations and later sentenced to the penitentiary.

While the need for home repairs seemed to be mostly a problem for the low-income elderly, for younger ones the need for employment was an abiding concern, and here too there were scheming people, perhaps not on the magnitude of Joseph Mohwish, but ruthless nevertheless, ready to take advantage of that anxiety about employment in order to line their own pockets. In the mid-1970s, a group of people represented by Nashville lawyer Robert Polk organized a corporation they called Above the Salt, Inc., which claimed to operate an employment service, International Job Bank, Inc. (IJB). A number of frustrated people who had dealt with IJB came to Legal Services and asked for our help. They had paid in advance "membership fees" of $49 to IJB on the promise that they would get jobs at IJB or receive leads to other jobs. The leads turned out to be nonexistent jobs or jobs that had been listed without the prior approval of the employer. Not one of our clients had secured a job through the employment service. One woman said she had been offered a job at IJB itself distributing posters advertising its services in low-income neighborhoods, but that did not last long.

In June 1976, David and Richard Jackson, who was then a Reggie in our North Nashville office, filed a lawsuit on behalf of our clients in Chancery Court to stop this scam and get the clients' money back. They charged that IJB was a pyramid scheme in violation of the Tennessee Consumer Protection Act, that it was charging fees in advance in violation of the Employment Agency Act, and that it was a fraud. At the same time, the state consumer affairs office was receiving complaints about IJB, leading the attorney general to file suit adding the charge that IJB was operating as an employment agency without the necessary state license. Don Hollingsworth at Legal Services in Memphis filed also on behalf of five people there who had been mistreated in the scheme. The chancellor enjoined the defendants from proceeding as an employment agency and from removing documents from their headquarters, but the case dragged on for nearly three years of contentious wrangling. At one point the chancellor had to appoint a special master to preside at depositions of the defendants because of their evasion or refusal to answer legitimate questions. In the end, the defendants dissolved the corporation and ceased to do business. Regretfully, David concluded that there were no assets to go after and it was not worth it to try to pierce the corporate veil, "It was just one of many cases over the years where I could not get any money for my clients." But he had helped stop yet another pernicious fraud that preyed on anxious unemployed people.

———————

Next scheme: health spas. Everyone wants to be fit and healthy. Poor people are no different, especially when someone offers a way that is both cheap and easy. Cosmopolitan Health Spas was a going concern in the late 1970s, offering lifetime memberships in their spas with financing available and low monthly payments. A quick look through Newspapers.com turns up numerous want ads during that time announcing jobs at Cosmopolitan for "sales counselors" that had "excellent earning potential." These were the people who would do the high-pressure telemarketing for the company. A few months later, there are numerous want ads for "collectors" to work for Brandywine Acceptance Company, a division of Cosmopolitan Health Spas, "background in phone collection necessary." Obviously, there were lots of folks who responded to the calls from the "excellent earning" sales counselors, signed the contracts, but then could not keep up the payments. Thus the need a few months later for the guys with a "background in phone collections." If the phone collector was not successful, then the paper was turned over to a lawyer and the "member for life" was sued. David estimates that thirty to forty of those people ended up in our office. They had been solicited and persuaded to sign up for something they could not afford and now they were being held liable for the total cost of a lifetime of benefits they would never receive.

Two questions might occur to some readers at this point. Why would those people, having limited resources, do something so irrational as to sign a long-term health spa contract? Second, with all the basic problems low-income people encounter (housing, food, health care), why would Legal Services spend some of its limited resources on health spa contracts? Some answers to the first question are suggested by sociologist Matthew Desmond, who lived for a time in 2008 and 2009 with low-income people in Milwaukee before writing *Evicted*. He points out the obvious truth that those of us who are more judgmental often forget: as human beings we are not eternally rational actors. Sometimes, given the right temptation, or, he might have added, the right telephone sales pitch, we do things that in a more rational moment we would resist. More particularly, he observed that his neighbors at the bottom of the economic ladder had little prospect of climbing out of poverty, even if they pinched every penny, so "instead, they tried to survive in color, to season the suffering with pleasure."[1] And so with our clients: even in their poverty they wanted bodies like the pretty people they saw on their color TV, so with the attractive time payment to Cosmopolitan and a small yearly fee thereafter, they thought they might build beautiful bodies, too.

Even granting that, why should Legal Services help them out of this frivolous delusion? Two reasons. One, because of the impact a judgment for $1,500, plus interest, plus attorney fees, plus court costs, would have on their already precarious family finances. A judgment would lead to collection measures against them, including garnishments of wages, which would mean fewer resources for the family, and could even lead to their losing their jobs. Then there would be real disaster. The snowballing effect of such things we had seen before. The other reason to help was simply because we could. David had spotted the vulnerability in Cosmopolitan's cases.

The defense David and others in the consumer section used in general sessions court was keyed on "present value." They argued that the creditor could only recover an amount equal to the present value of what the debtor had received. In most cases, the debtor had never used a spa. In a number of cases, Cosmopolitan was preselling contracts for a spa that was "coming soon." It would then bundle the contracts it had sold, go to a bank, and use them for collateral against a loan to finance building the spa. In many of our cases, the judge agreed with the present value defense we raised and dismissed Cosmopolitan's case, but in others, judges did not, and those David appealed to circuit court where he could file a counterclaim and conduct discovery. Cosmopolitan wanted none of that, and Herman Loewenstein, its lawyer, would take a nonsuit in each case so there would be no discovery about Cosmopolitan's operation, nothing on the record for others to see.

After Cosmopolitan predictably went out of business, defaulting on its loans, its several banks were left only with the lifetime membership contracts they had accepted as collateral. In an attempt to recoup its loss, a bank then would sue the erstwhile lifetime member. The good news is that Herman represented the banks, too, and all David had to do for his client was pick up the phone and call Herman, who very quickly would pronounce, "It's gone," and take a nonsuit, without David ever having to make an appearance in court.

A brief interlude is in order with Herman Loewenstein having made an appearance in our story.

————————

The easy working relationship between David and Herman over the years benefited not only our clients, but in the end benefited our organization as well. In addition to banks and collection agencies, Herman also represented small loan companies and several landlords. David estimates they must have had at least fifty cases against each other. They developed a warm and knowing adversarial relationship. Each one knew when the other guy had the upper hand and usually, though not always, they were able to work out an appropriate solution.

In addition to practicing law, Herman was a sophisticated investor, and later became quite wealthy. In 2006, Gif Thornton, the president of our board, and I took him to lunch and asked him for a sizeable gift to Legal Aid. Herman asked us how much. I told him that if he would give us a $1.5 million, there would always be a David Tarpley at Legal Aid. He said he would put a gift of that amount in his will, and a couple of weeks later, he called me to his office to see his revised will, which included that gift and a like amount for Vanderbilt Law School. He wanted me to know he had kept his word. We did not have any more cases against Herman. He died suddenly a few months later. We received the promised amount, and the earnings from that gift pay a substantial part of David's salary to this day. Herman's gift, the first of that size we ever received, is a testament to collegiality at the bar, a sign of the respect he had for our mission, and a token of gratitude from a man who had escaped the horrors of Nazi Germany for the promises of this country, where he was able to thrive as an immigrant.

————————

Back to consumer law. More common than installment purchases of health spa contracts are installment purchases of furniture and appliances, which often include their own set of problems. In a modern urban society, low-income families, like all other families, need furniture and appliances, and the problems associated with those purchases have been a constant at Legal Aid ever since Jerry Black and Grayfred Gray handled that Friday night case for the man with the baby crib back in 1969.

In 1986, Rosa Atchley purchased, or thought she purchased, a washing machine from Mayfair Furniture, one of many such stores that sold to low-income people on what was then a rough and crumbling Lower Broad, a place very different from the vibrant entertainment district of today. The sales contract she thought she was signing with Mayfair was actually a rent-to-own contract with Consumer Lease Network (CLN). It provided that she would make monthly payments for the $605 washing machine and then in small print noted that to own the machine at the end of the term, she would have to make a balloon payment. The total obligation for her would be $1,150, nearly double the original cost. When she realized that, she came to see us.

David filed suit in chancery court on behalf of Ms. Atchley and another client who had fallen into the same trap, alleging that either this was a disguised credit sale or that CLN actually was a financer. In either case the effective annual percentage rate in the contract was more than 75 percent, far above the rate allowed by statute. David charged that the whole scheme was a violation of either the state Consumer Protection Act (CPA) or the federal Truth in Leasing Act and was usurious. Chancellor Robert Brandt had no hesitancy in holding that the transactions were unfair and deceptive in violation of the CPA. Consequently, he awarded our clients treble damages based on the difference between what they should have paid in a normal credit sale and what the "lease" contract obligated them to pay, and he awarded us attorneys' fees. CLN, a multistate operation, did not appeal, but it did shut down its entire operation in Tennessee.

———————

And always there were the collection agencies. When the in-house debt collectors at the hospital, utility, bank, or other enterprise could not bring in the money, the bill would be farmed out to an outfit that frequently had the soft-toned word "adjustment" in its name. Some agencies were competent and reasonable, others were not. Some skated the edge of the law; that was the case with the Mid Tenn Adjustment Service in Wilson County operated by Yvonne Hunter. A lawyer in Lebanon referred a woman who had been sued by Mid Tenn to Patti George in our Gallatin office. Patti very quickly saw that this matter fell into the category of "Let Tarpley do it," and he took it from there. Before it was over, David had five clients with similar stories.

Hunter, who was not a lawyer, exceeded all bounds of legitimate bill collection procedures. Before she would bundle accounts for her suits in general sessions, she would employ a wide range of harassment and threats to intimidate the debtor. She would make repeated vexatious phone calls or send legal-sounding written notices threatening drastic actions, actions she had absolutely no power to prosecute or conduct. She would threaten eviction without notice, imminent utility cutoff, even incarceration for the nonpayment of a bill. Beyond that, on occasion she would attempt to collect bills for which she had no authorization from the lawful owner of the account. If all that failed, she would file suit in general sessions court, where judges raised no question about her legal standing and routinely entered judgment not only awarding the amount of account, but also including attorney fees for her.

David drafted a federal lawsuit alleging violations of the federal Fair Debt Collection Practices Act, the Tennessee Consumer Protection Act, and the Racketeer Influenced and Corrupt Organizations Act (otherwise known as "federal civil RICO") naming as defendants not only Hunter and Mid Tenn, but also the City of Lebanon, which had engaged her to collect past-due electric bills. As a courtesy, David sent a draft of the complaint to the city attorney with a message that his client would be removed as a defendant if within seventy-two hours the city would cease making any referrals to Mid Tenn and would make available to him all records of accounts previously referred. The city met those conditions well before the deadline and was dropped as a party.

A series of federal lawsuits was filed, one for each client, and discovery began, including the deposition of a local bank president who had used Mid Tenn's service. Now realizing the potential exposure of the bank, the president was equally as cooperative as the city attorney had been. After several months, in an effort to resolve the matter without a trial, Judge John Nixon ordered court-supervised mediation and the lawyers entered into discussions. The lawyer for the insurance company that covered Mid Tenn, like the city attorney and the bank president, fully appreciated the problems for his client and soon a settlement was reached, part of which was confidential. The *Lebanon Democrat* newspaper could only report that there was a "substantial" cash settlement.[2] In addition, the parties agreed to an injunction, which was public, prohibiting all of the bad acts that had been alleged.

David thought the cases were over, and they were, but Ms. Hunter's problems were not over, and several months later, David was dragged into the drama again in a way he had not expected. Following David's thorough exposure of Hunter's predations, the state regulatory board that governed collection agencies filed a notice of its intention to revoke the license of Mid Tenn, and it set a hearing, at which point the attorney for the board called David and asked him to come help present the board's case. When David with the demand of other cases demurred, the attorney responded that if he would not come voluntarily, "I'll subpoena you," and he did. David obeyed the subpoena and showed up for the hearing where he saw his old clients again and assumed he would just sit with the board's attorney and assist him with details of the case, but no, the board's attorney stood up and announced, "Mr. Tarpley will present the state's case." Trapped and resentful of having to do the state's work for it, he proceeded nevertheless, "It was easy. I just put on my old clients and examined them, presented the documents the board's lawyer had assembled, and it was over." This time it was. The board revoked Mid Tenn's license and imposed a fine. David speculated that it may have been the first time that board, being made up mostly of industry representatives, had ever revoked a license for the mistreatment of debtors.

Automobiles: another financial issue for low-income people. In the absence of an efficient mass transit system, for most people automobiles are essential for getting to work and doing many tasks of daily life. Low-income people are no different. What is different, of course, is what they can afford. For that reason, over the years most of our many cases involving automobiles have been against neighborhood used car lots, "we tote the note," and we have encountered all the problems that slogan traditionally has suggested: defective vehicles, bad credit, missed payments, hidden costs, midnight repossessions. In the late 1970s, however, perhaps because of changes in the credit market, perhaps because of more pointed advertising, we began to get cases against franchised dealers. In most instances, whether it was a lot, a dealer, or the financer (e.g., GMAC), we were defending the buyer, usually for nonpayment; and in some cases we had a counterclaim because of some defect in the vehicle or in the finance papers. Departing from this routine, however, in a case in 1979, David and Jimmie Lynn Ramsaur represented a plaintiff.

A couple came in who felt they had been misled by Beaman Pontiac's advertisement that it would sell cars for "one dollar over factory invoice" and by the fact that when they went to Beaman, they were told there were no comparable cars on the lot with a price as low as the price of the car featured in the advertisement. Using Tennessee's Consumer Protection Act, David and Jimmie Lynn filed a lawsuit in chancery court on behalf of the couple seeking to have this practice declared deceptive advertising and enjoined by the court. Since the "invoice" was not the real cost to the dealer, they sought to have the chancellor rule that Beaman Pontiac would have to reveal its real cost of the vehicle rather than touting a questionable "invoice." They also wanted the dealer to be required to list the number of comparable vehicles available for sale at the advertised price.

David asked for a preliminary injunction to stop the practice pending the full trial, but after a hearing at which the dealer disputed some of the allegations, the chancellor declined to do that, and the parties began discovery. David took the deposition of the salesman who had sold the automobile to his clients, the sales manager, and the general manager. It was not a pleasant experience. Nevertheless, David later said, "I got everything I needed." For several weeks after that, there were discussions between David and the attorney for the dealership resulting in a confidential settlement.

There would be repercussions. Not only Beaman, but other franchised dealers were upset that we had questioned their advertising, and there was more. As a result of the revelations from the discovery in our clients' case, Ann Eaden, director of the state's Consumer Affairs Division cautioned the dealers about not making clear in their advertising the extra fees they would charge at a sale, such as "dealer prep" and "document fees." The dealers resented being called on the carpet by the state agency and were upset that our case had led to Eaden's attention. Used car lot owners that we usually encountered typically do not have a lot of influence in a city, but franchised auto dealers are big business, and they do have influence. They would strike back at Legal Services later that year through one of our funding sources, as we will see in Chapter 14.

━━━━━━━━━━━━━

More opprobrium would come from leaders in the financial sector. Our clients often had to borrow money and consequently were severely impacted by interest rates. They generally were charged the highest rates the law would allow, if not more. In the late 1970s, we tried to ameliorate that situation, but with little success and much malediction. In 1977, a constitutional convention eliminated the 10 percent limit on interest rates that had been set in the state's constitution a century before. The amendment allowed the legislature to set the rate from time to time as it deemed appropriate, and in its 1979 session, the newly empowered legislature was considering what the rate would be. The new rate would apply to banks, of course, but also to other financial institutions, including those operating under the Industrial Loan and Thrift Act (ILTA), a strangely misnamed act that had nothing at all to do with loans to industry, but rather governed, very leniently one might add, the small loan companies that made loans to desperate low-income people. David and the other lawyers in the consumer section had considerable experience dealing with small loan companies, their interest rates, and the multiple exorbitant fees that were allowed under the ILTA.

Representative Steve Cobb asked David, Jimmie Lynn, and Joe Dickinson at various times to come testify before the legislative committees considering the matter and to discuss the impact of several of the proposals on their clients. They were not well received. At one hearing, fourteen financial executives and lobbyists spoke on behalf of various financial institutions and associations, while David alone spoke for our clients. The financial people testified that if the legislature did not raise the allowable rate to at least 15.5 percent, the economy of the state would suffer. One ominously warned, "Any lower figure . . . would cause disruption in the steady flow of money." In David's testimony, he pointed out that the legislation before the committee also allowed a 4 percent "service charge" on installment loans, which had the effect of pushing the rate as high as 19.5 percent.

The reaction to David's testimony from the lawmakers was swift, scornful, and imperious. The *Tennessean* reported that Lt. Governor

John Wilder "was upset the most."[3] While Wilder did not question the authority of the financial lobbyists to speculate on the economy of the state, he did question the authority of the poverty lawyer to speak for low-income people in the state. He insisted that providing legal assistance to the poor did not include advising legislators on the impact legislation would have on a poor person, especially when the poor person's lawyer was paid with government funds. And legislators were not the only ones who were upset.

Griffin Boyte, a lawyer from West Tennessee who represented a bank and who that year was immediate past-president of the Tennessee Bar Association, also did not like it that our lawyers were commenting on proposed laws. He was quoted in the newspaper as saying, "If they want to reform society, I don't think they ought to do it under the guise of being lawyers for indigents."[4] With the backing of the executive committee of the TBA, though without talking with me or with the TBA representative on our board, he filed a complaint with LSC alleging we had violated the restrictive lobbying provision in the LSC Act. When LSC investigated the complaint, it found no violation of the Act because David and the others had been responding to a request from a legislator that they testify, which was allowed under the Act.

Needless to say, the financial industry got almost everything it wanted from the pliant legislature on interest rates that year, but the work of our lawyers was not entirely in vain. Representative Cobb was able to use their testimony to convince colleagues of the need for some modifications. He told the *Tennessean*, "As a result of their help, I was able to spot several very unfortunate provisions in the original draft of the interest rate bill, which were then removed." In a calculated understatement, he called the attacks on the Legal Services lawyers "unfortunate."[5]

There are several ironies in the attacks on our lawyers' advocacy. Many of those fourteen lobbyists for the financial industry lined up against David that day were also attorneys. This is what lawyers do: try to advance or defend the interests of their clients. Many law firms the size of Legal Aid or larger have a separate section usually with a name like "government relations and public policy." The specialists in these departments may or may not be lawyers. One large local law firm's website properly boasts, "Our government relations team is a strong lobbying force before Tennessee's executive branch, the Tennessee General

Assembly and the many agencies of the state and local government." It goes on to describe its work before federal decision makers as well.

And it is not only large firms. A recent, not untypical "People on the Move" column in a local newspaper told of a young lawyer who had joined a smaller law firm to do this work after having been in "legislative relations" for a state government agency and then "government relations" for an industry association. Lawyers like that young man provide an effective and essential voice for their clients, but when a Legal Aid lawyer in an organization funded in part by LSC needs to do the same thing, it was deemed improper and, since 1996, illegal.

The final irony is the message it sends to poor people in our nation whose lawyers are attacked or prohibited when their position needs to be presented before a legislative committee or rulemaking body. The poor are expected to abide by the law and play by the rules, but denying them effective advocacy before the bodies that make the rules and enact the laws undermines that expectation. It suggests that their interests are not equal to the interests of others in our democracy. That gradation of access reinforces what one recent writer has called "the precarious trust between low-income Americans and the law."[6] It recalls now one hundred years later what Reginal Heber Smith labeled "a brooding sense of injustice" among the poor.

Griffin Boyte, the TBA leader and bank lawyer, plus others with complaints about our work pressed on. They brought their charges to the Nashville Bar Association, for whatever control that body might have. The NBA board requested that I come to its September meeting to explain our work and answer questions, which I did. Kirk Loggins of the *Tennessean* was there, too, and reported on the free-ranging colloquy. Some questions were about client eligibility. One board member surprisingly insisted that we were "being used" by people who lied about their financial situation in order to get free legal help. I had to explain that we checked that pretty carefully on the front end, and furthermore, that in the course of the representation, particularly with people on a fixed income and especially in cases involving such matters as debt, welfare, or child support, an attorney gets a pretty good sense of a client's finances. I further explained that we did not want to represent over-income people, having quite enough to do already just representing eligible folks, plus we had waiting lists three or four weeks long for initial appointments.

Other questions had to do with the various charges, including those from Boyte, stemming from our legislative, administrative, and class action cases: the charges that we were "social engineers" disguised as lawyers. I acknowledged the accusation but insisted "everything we have gotten into arises out of cases that have come into our office." It was just a consequence of our work: "Representing some of our clients may turn into social reform. If it does and it's needed, so much the better."[7]

The epithet "social engineers" was meant as a condemnation, but actually it was a compliment. Charles Hamilton Houston, the dean of Howard University School of Law and architect of the Legal Defense Fund's strategy to attack Jim Crow, famously said to his students, "A lawyer is either a social engineer or he's a parasite on society."[8] Indeed, any lawyer who takes seriously her role in shaping case law or administrative regulations or legislation on behalf of her client is engineering, for good or ill, the terms of the social contract by which we all live together. Houston charged his students to use their role as lawyers for solving the "problems of . . . local communities" and "bettering conditions of the underprivileged citizens."[9] The same charge is applicable to legal aid lawyers.

———————

The ire of the Lieutenant Governor, the state bar past-president, and other critics who were so offended by David's advocacy, may well have been aroused also by the surprising success of another consumer lawyer in the same session of the legislature. Margaret Behm and four other women had exposed an exploitative scheme and brought about significant reforms in the insurance industry in Tennessee, the subject of the next chapter.

CHAPTER 13

Five Women Reform Industrial Insurance

Lawyers for the indigent tend to be unsettling people, disturbing the arrangements that the powerful create.

—JUDGE WILLIAM WAYNE JUSTICE,
"BURRS UNDER THE SADDLE"

In late 1977, Margaret Behm went to the home of an elderly client who had called and asked her to prepare her will. While they were talking about what should be in the will, the client brought out eleven insurance policies and asked about them. She told Margaret, "I have paid on these for years, but I don't understand them." Margaret was stunned. She asked her client if she could take the policies back to her office and try to figure out what was going on.

Margaret had just encountered the nickel and dime world of industrial insurance. Initially, when she saw that term "industrial insurance" on the policies, she thought they must have been written to cover work-related injuries at a factory or mill. Why would this elderly woman have such a thing? Margaret began trying to learn all she could about the product and this multi-policy phenomenon. She asked colleagues and confirmed that, yes, many of our clients were in the same situation, often spending a considerable portion of their incomes paying the premiums for multiple low-dollar life, health, and disability policies that had very few benefits and that were sold door-to-door exclusively in low-income neighborhoods. She looked at the statutes governing insurance and saw that, curiously, industrial insurance was covered separately from ordinary insurance.

After that, when other clients came in asking for help with their bills, Margaret, now alert to the issue, was able to spot these policies and the premiums as part of the problem. Another elderly woman we will refer to as Ms. M. came to our office seeking help with paying her husband's burial expenses. Although she and her late husband had purchased twenty-eight insurance policies from five different industrial insurance companies, when her husband died and she made claims, she was told she had only $1,000 of insurance on his life. The other policies were on the life, health or disability of various other family members, not on him. This left her $1,200 short of the bill for his funeral. With her monthly income of $214 and still paying $105 per month for the remaining twenty-seven policies, she needed help. She had sought help from the Metropolitan Action Commission to pay her utility bills that she had let slide, but she felt she could not stop paying the insurance premiums because the agents, who came regularly to collect the premiums, had convinced her she had "too much in these policies to let them go." In truth, they were practically worthless.

Ms. M. had life insurance policies on herself, her adult son, a young grandson, and a sister, some with quite limited terms under which they would pay. Some were "death and dismemberment" policies that would pay a small benefit in the case of the loss of a foot or hand or eye. Margaret later was told by a former insurance agent that these limb-specific benefits were a good sales gimmick because of a person's natural fear of losing a hand or a foot, although those losses actually were rare. Some of Ms. M.'s policies were for medical benefits that the insured family member had not used or not qualified for in the ten years they had been in effect.

As Margaret questioned other clients, she came to see how widespread this consumer problem was. It was most concentrated in the housing projects, a "target-rich environment" for the agents, but was endemic throughout low-income communities, where insurance companies and their agents were taking advantage of the fears and apprehensions of low-income people. They capitalized on the desire of poor people of both races to afford for themselves and for their loved ones funerals that would accord them at death a measure of dignity and respect they had been denied in life. Margaret wanted to do something to protect our clients from this scam, but what? Unless the companies themselves could be convinced that the product should be reformed, the remedies would have to come through changes in the statutes and regulations governing insurance. But first she was going to have to learn a lot more about the industry, the products, and the practices. In representing her clients' interests, she would be dealing with some formidable interests and facing knowledgeable people who had a very different take on the situation and a sizeable economic interest in its preservation.

The product had been developed in Britain by the Prudential Assurance Company in the middle of the nineteenth century, capitalizing on the fears of death and dismemberment among the uneducated manual laborers in the expanding mills and mines there. Established insurance companies in the northeastern United States after the Civil War saw the same market emerging with the increasing industrialization there. Though the South lacked much industry at that time, it did have plenty of vulnerable poor people, and at the turn of the twentieth century, two groups of men in Nashville, seeing the opportunity, formed their own companies just three years apart specifically for the purpose of marketing this kind of insurance. As had their predecessors in Britain and the northeast, they touted it as a means for people with limited income to learn the value of saving and thrift, responsible money management. Through their door-to-door agents, they marketed their product throughout the South, and with the premiums they collected, they built substantial financial holdings at home.

The two companies, the National Life and Accident Insurance Company and the Life and Casualty Insurance Company, quickly became dominant forces in the economy of Nashville. In the 1920s each company began operating a radio station, WLAC (Life and Casualty) and WSM ("We Shield Millions"). In the 1950s each was awarded a television license, WSMV (channel 4) and WLAC (channel 5). Both radio stations reached all over the South and beyond, WLAC with rhythm and blues at night appealing mostly to a Black audience and WSM with the Grand Ole Opry targeting Whites, but agents for both companies aggressively sold to anyone, regardless of race. The companies built great wealth for several families and the two tallest office buildings in downtown. By the late 1960s, according to historian Don Doyle, "the future of Nashville's downtown and the vitality of the whole urban economy rested heavily on the insurance industry."[1] And this was the case even more so in the late 1970s when Margaret confronted this phenomenon. The two companies, and others in Chattanooga and Memphis, were rich and powerful players.

Margaret soon saw that she was going to need some help if she were to take this on properly. She was going to have to build a case that would convince the companies, and if not the companies, which was unlikely, then the state. She would have to persuade the Department of Insurance and the legislature to take seriously the problems associated with industrial insurance as it had been sold up to that time, and then convince them to make the changes in the laws, both regulations and statutes, necessary to correct the abuses. She needed to have her facts straight, and lots of substantiation behind them. She needed to do a lot of research on the industry and on laws governing the product in other jurisdictions. She needed to develop realistic remedies. And she had a full caseload, with lots of other issues to tend to in the meantime.

We hired two second year law students from Vanderbilt to help her, Mary Frances Lyle and Beverly Fisher. Beverly had been clerking with David in the consumer section and had some familiarity with the issues; Mary Frances was new, but it did not take her long to get up to speed. In little more than three months, building on what Margaret had learned already, the three women produced a comprehensive study of industrial insurance. The 141-page document, entitled "Poor People and the Insurance Industry in Tennessee," using case studies of five of our clients, first described the problems with the policies. Then it gave a history of the product, described the debit agent marketing system through which the policies were sold, listed the remarkable profits the companies made from the product, and recounted the companies' justifications for the higher premiums. Finally, the study discussed the scant federal and state statutes and regulations governing the product and suggested some remedies for the problems.

First, with polite deference, the writers allowed that "the entity best able to solve the problems . . . is the insurance industry itself," but then they reported that in their discussions with company executives, not only did the executives have "no suggestions for solving the problems," but "many of our suggestions were rejected outright." So much for that admirable gesture. Moving right along, they briefly discussed the possibility of litigation based on the unequal treatment of industrial insurance policyholders under Tennessee law and the disparate impact that unequal treatment had on low-income elderly and minorities, but they quickly dismissed that tack for its lack of potential success and litigation's limited capacity for comprehensive reform that only legislation could bring.

Then began their statutory and regulatory suggestions for the state. Abolish the distinction between industrial insurance and other life and health policies. Regulate them the same. Forbid weekly premium schemes and surcharges: Mary Frances and Bev had found that many policyholders who paid their premiums monthly still had to pay a "collection fee" surcharge of up to 20 percent based on weekly collection. Other suggestions ran the gamut from regulating agent compensation to allowing conversion from industrial insurance to an ordinary policy. The most comprehensive recommendations, however, had to do with enhancing the power and authority of the state Department of Insurance, and they cited various statutory provisions on "deceptive acts" and "unfair discrimination" that the commissioner should employ. These recommendations were accompanied by a strong endorsement, "we have reason to believe that in the future the Department will be receptive to the comments of those concerned about this."

Margaret had cultivated a respectful relationship with the state commissioner of insurance, John Neff, and had confidence in him. She had gone to see him early on in the process, as soon as she had learned enough to be able to talk with some knowledge about the product. He had seemed genuinely interested in her concerns and wanted more information. He introduced her to other people in the department who dealt more directly with the industry and allowed her to talk with them. One key person in the department was aligned with the companies and was openly hostile to her, but among the others there was one who would prove very valuable. "I had someone I called my 'Deep Throat' in the department," she confessed to me nearly forty years after the fact. "He was amazing. When I would get confused, he would get me back on the right track. I've never told anyone. He was very helpful."

As they were finishing the study, Margaret and the students realized that just publishing it, distributing it to the legislators, and hoping someone would notice was not going to help our clients. It needed to be publicized. Mary Frances volunteered that she knew Wayne Whitt, the managing editor of the *Tennessean,* and that she could talk to him. Mary Frances was not a typical law student fresh out of college. She was at that point in her forties, had raised a family, had been a schoolteacher, and had been active in the community. Wayne Whitt was responsive to her call and set up an appointment in early July for her and Margaret to meet with John Seigenthaler, publisher of the paper.

As a result of the meeting, Seigenthaler assigned two young interns, college students Carolyn Shoulders and Linda Solomon, to do their own investigation. On Sunday, August 20, 1978, the newspaper began publishing an eight-part series they wrote that covered many of the same issues as the Legal Services report, but in much more graphic language and personal detail than the measured document from our law office. Their articles had stories, with pictures, portraying low-income people holding multiple policies, some policies with such pinched terms that they had little likelihood of ever paying off. Tellingly, the young interns described the fear-based sales tactics and quoted several former insurance agents saying industrial insurance was a "rip-off," "fraud," "a waste of money." Carolyn and Linda interviewed the insurance commissioner and reported his saying he had no power to deal with the abuses or to regulate the industry without specific enabling legislation. The head actuary for the department was more candid. He told them that the insurance lobby in the state legislature was so strong that "I might have made recommendations to the legislature, but a bill would never have gotten out of committee."[2]

During their investigation, the interns discovered that the department had recently promulgated a rule requiring that there must be a buyer's guide issued to every purchaser of a life insurance policy in Tennessee but had specifically exempted policies with a face value of less than $5,000. How slick was that? That meant no poor person who bought industrial insurance from a door-to-door salesman would get a buyer's guide because industrial insurance policies, by definition, had a face value of less than $5,000. The newspaper followed up the daily series with a front-page article on Sunday, August 27, describing at length the Legal Services report, reciting its findings, and listing its recommendations. On its editorial page that day, the paper called on the legislature to act, and in the days and months that followed, the newspaper continued to cover the story and continued to editorialize in support of reforms.

Four days after the story about the Legal Services study appeared in the Sunday newspaper, the department announced that three investigators would begin looking into industrial insurance abuses in Nashville's housing projects. Commissioner Neff, in making the announcement, explained to the newspaper, "We cannot take action without our own proof of abuse. We must do our own investigation and prove it independently." He urged other consumers with complaints to contact the department. He hedged a bit, expressing his belief that many of the reported abuses were the result of agent improprieties, but regained his authority by saying that the companies were "completely responsible for the actions of their agents" and that if a company were found to be repeatedly abusing consumers, it could lose its license to do business in Tennessee.[3]

In addition to facilitating the department's investigation, the housing authority board set up a consumer education program. In the weeks and months that followed, other community groups, including the local NAACP, applauded the reports and voiced support for reforms. The Consumer Affairs Division of the Department of Agriculture announced that it would investigate complaints about industrial insurance. At a legislative committee hearing, the state Commission on Aging called on the legislature to pass a "truth-in-insurance" law to protect senior citizens. At the same hearing, Margaret emphasized the scope of the matter by noting that in Tennessee there were more industrial insurance policies in force than any other kind, and she echoed the Commission on Aging's call for legislative remedies.

Nearly four years before, in the spring semester of her last year in law school at UT, Margaret had been enrolled in a class on legislation taught by Grayfred Gray. As a part of their course work, the students functioned as interns at the General Assembly in Nashville, learned how to draft legislation, and how to place it in the code. Margaret had made friends in the Legislative Office of Legal Services that drafted legislation for senators and representatives, and she had gained from them valuable insights about how the General Assembly worked. She later said, "If I had not been there in 1975, I would not have known what to do at this point."

What she did in the winter of 1978–1979 was draft the Small Insurance Policy Act. It was not as idealistic as the 141-page study had been, and it did not include provisions that, as it turned out, some friendly members of the legislature would have wanted; it had in it only what Margaret thought might be acceptable to sponsors. She quickly found two sponsors in the House, Representatives Steve Cobb and Bill Nolan. They told her she needed someone in the insurance business. Senator Ben Longley was that person. Not only was he in that business, but he was chair of the Senate Commerce Committee, making him a particularly powerful sponsor. Then began Margaret's arduous task of getting the bill through the legislature, while juggling court appearances and negotiating with creditors for her other clients.

Meanwhile, the scope of interest in industrial insurance was about to get much wider. During the week in late August when the *Tennessean* had run its series of articles, it so happened that the producer and some staff from the CBS program *60 Minutes* were in Nashville filming a piece about fraudulent recording studios here that had been cheating aspiring songwriters and musicians. While they were in town filming, the crew apparently read local newspapers. Several weeks after they returned to New York, Margaret received a telephone call from the producer who said *60 Minutes* wanted to do a story about industrial insurance and wanted her help. Margaret agreed to talk to them, and in January Mike Wallace came to our office to meet with her.

Margaret gave Wallace lots of background information, but she declined to give him any names and contacts of her clients. They had not authorized her to do so, and many were embarrassed because of the unwise decisions they had made in buying the products. Margaret did the same thing with CBS that she had done with the newspaper: she told them to just go to a housing project and start asking around. She figured it had worked well for the newspaper's college interns, so it ought to work for the network's investigative reporters. It did, and a few days later they came back with several people holding multiple policies. They wanted to film Margaret interviewing the policyholders and explaining to them what was in their policies, but again Margaret declined. She figured she was going to be in a very public arena trying to convince the commissioner and the legislature to make changes in the governing of industrial insurance, and she did not want those officials to think she was doing this work for personal attention, to get on television. Plus, we had begun receiving criticism for what she had done already, criticism that would only mount in the months to come.

Finally, however, Margaret relented and allowed the crew to film Beverly and Mary Frances interviewing one of the policyholders the crew had located. As Mary Frances told the woman on camera what was in the policies and what she could expect to receive as benefits under the policies, the woman began to cry. Needless to say, that scene appeared in the story that ran on television, along with a couple of stories the crew had found in other states. Margaret did make one other contribution to the program: it was a visual she had seen several times from the front stoops of some of her clients.

The National Life headquarters at that time was an imposing 452-foot-tall building, now owned by the state, on the western slope of Capitol Hill. It loomed over the gulch below and the entire western part of the city. On the other side of the gulch was, and is, the John Henry Hale housing project, in those days acres of stark regimented brick apartment buildings, much different from the modern homes in the project today. Margaret suggested the crew film a view through a line of stoops in those gruesome projects looking up to the gleaming building on the hill, and she suggested that they use a voice caption: "The people who live here built that." It was the opening shot in the program, which aired January 28, 1979.

The day after the *60 Minutes* program aired, the Federal Trade Commission (FTC) released a staff report that examined industrial insurance and its offshoot, monthly debit ordinary insurance, that also was sold to poor people. The FTC report concluded that the policyholders who bought them would be better off without any insurance at all. It found that "little tangible economic security arises from the meager benefits," and concluded that people who buy them pay "a high cost for low benefits."[4] The report cited both the *Tennessean* series and the Legal Services publication, as well as results of the committee staff's own investigation. The next day the nationally syndicated columnist Jack Anderson wrote a column critical of industrial insurance and gave as an example the case of a seventy-nine-year-old woman described in our publication who had thirty policies.

In February Commissioner Neff held hearings on proposals to tighten requirements on insurance sales in the state, including education for agents. At the hearing, counsel for National Life announced that the company no longer would sell industrial insurance, but he offered no relief to present policyholders and said the company would continue to service the policies it had in effect. He also announced that the company immediately would begin to provide cost disclosure and buyer's guides for policies below $5,000 that had been exempted in the department's previous rule.

In April, the bill Margaret had drafted passed in the House Committee on Labor and Consumer Affairs despite, of all things, opposition from the commissioner. Surprisingly, he voiced the industry's argument that treating industrial insurance like ordinary insurance would mean that many people would have no insurance at all. Paternalistically, he added, "If an agent is not there before Friday night to collect the money, then it might go somewhere else," as if that would have been a bad thing. He even tried to get the committee to postpone consideration for a week. An astute legislator assessed that the delay was designed to give time for the insurance lobby to "descend on the legislature and kill the bill," and the committee refused the commissioner's request. In response, he then set the cost to the department of regulating industrial insurance at $52,000, just enough above a $50,000 legislative threshold to require that the bill be referred to the potentially unfriendly House Finance Ways and Means Committee.[5] Despite intense industry lobbying before that committee, the bill survived. Then it stalled.

As the month wore on, the end of the session was looming and Margaret began to fear that the bill would not get through the remaining committees and onto the floor before time ran out. Then there was a breakthrough. The Speaker of the House, Ned McWherter, had not been involved until this time, but he had been aware of the intense industry lobbying and the drag it was creating on other legislative business. Exasperated, one afternoon late in the month he ordered everyone with anything to do with the bill to come to his large conference room. There were insurance executives from Memphis, lobbyists for several companies, corporate lawyers, and there was Margaret, the only woman, twenty-eight years old and not quite four years out of law school. After all the time that has gone by since, Margaret still remembers the Speaker's charge, "I only have a high school education, and back in the day, I know this insurance had a good purpose, but things are different now, and this product needs to have some changes. I want you to sit here and work it out." And in that long afternoon, they did.

When the negotiated version of the Small Insurance Policy Law of 1979 finally reached the floor, it passed the House ninety-three to zero and the Senate twenty-seven to zero. As with any compromise, each side would have wished for more, or less, but the bill as passed went a long way toward curbing some of the abuses. Margaret's main objective was to have the state treat policies sold to low-income people the same as those sold to everyone else, so the "small policies" were required to have many of the provisions and protections that applied to others. The companies were required to file policy forms with the department that would allow the department to review the benefits, rates, and compliance with new standards. In addition, the company was required to provide a statement to be signed by the applicant and agent disclosing the number of policies the person was carrying and the rates compared with the applicant's income. The policyholder then had ten days to review a policy after the purchase date and revoke it. As an aid to enforcement, the Act included a private right of action giving the policyholder the right to sue the insurer if the company failed to comply with the law. After passage, one senator remarked, "We've done our part. I just hope the commissioner will do his part now."[6]

In an article on May 30, the *Tennessean* reported various assessments of the saga and its outcome. When he signed the legislation, Governor Lamar Alexander called it an "important step forward in protecting consumers" and he added, "The bill is a good example of how the public and political processes work together." Representative Nolan praised the work of Legal Services for its research into the problems and added, "Without their work and perseverance over a year and a half, it wouldn't have happened." Commissioner Neff observed that the legislation already was being regarded as a "model bill throughout the South."[7]

In recognition of their series of articles and the breadth of understanding they revealed, Carolyn Shoulders and Linda Solomon received the United Press International's award that year for the best public service reporting in Tennessee. Beverly and Mary Frances's study received further national attention when a summary of it was published as the lead article in the *Clearinghouse Review*. After graduation from law school, Beverly became one of the five new lawyers in our Clarksville office, where she worked until 1993. Mary Francis entered private practice where she continued to work on public issues, including as lobbyist for the Tennessee Women's Political Caucus.

Margaret stayed with Legal Services until 1980 and then left to found with Marietta Shipley the firm of Shipley and Behm, the first all-women law firm in Nashville. Later they joined Margaret's husband Harlan Dodson III, and others to form what became Dodson Parker Behm & Capparella. Margaret's many political, civic, and professional contributions over the years since then include being appointed by the Speaker of the House to the Tennessee Judicial Selection Commission, which she chaired for several years; being appointed by the Tennessee Supreme Court to chair the Access to Justice Commission in 2009; and heading the Legal Aid Society fundraising campaign in 2015. But of all her accomplishments, none has been more astounding than her taking on the insurance establishment as a twenty-eight-year-old woman lawyer in 1978. With four other women who were all students at the time, she challenged and changed an industry.

Predictably, not everyone was pleased. George Evans, corporate counsel for Interstate Life Insurance Company in Chattanooga, was not at all happy with Margaret's involvement in trying to remedy some of the problems with the product that had been so profitable for his company. He filed a complaint with the Legal Services Corporation alleging that Margaret's work violated the LSC Act, which, as noted in the previous chapter, prohibited staff of an LSC grantee from lobbying, unless it was done on behalf of a client or at the request of a legislator. In fact, we had satisfied thoroughly both tests. The widely published study that Margaret and the students had produced described in its first sixteen pages five of our clients and their insurance policies. It was obvious on the face of the publication that we were lobbying on their behalf, not to mention the numerous other clients whose stories did not make it to the printed page. As to the second test, Representative Cobb had asked for Margaret's help at several points early on and along the way. It did not take long for the compliance people at LSC to clear us of Evans's charges.

───────────

Clearance or no clearance from LSC, there were by this time a number of people and institutions that were unhappy with our representation and wanted to put a stop to our advocacy. Before Legal Services, rarely had the law been employed *for* poor people; more typically it had been used *against* poor people. Never before had large institutions like insurance companies, hospitals, mental health facilities, housing authorities, banks, welfare departments, and franchised automobile dealers been sued by low-income people, much less had to face a class action lawsuit from them or deal with them in the legislature, and they resented these changes. The next two chapters recount some of the efforts in the early 1980s, both locally and nationally, to reverse those changes and make America like it was again. The first thing they sought to do was to get rid of the lawyers.

CHAPTER 14

Hospitals, Banks, Automobile Dealers, and the United Way

Being an advocate for the indigent is no way to
win a popularity contest. . . . Indeed, it is often a
way to get people quite angry at you.

—JUDGE WILLIAM WAYNE JUSTICE,
"BURRS UNDER THE SADDLE"

It is a natural tactic for individuals or institutions that have been challenged by a charitable organization, sooner or later, to try to persuade
funders of that charitable organization to cut off its funds. And there is
a formulaic tactic for arguments in legal disputes that has a similar conclusion: First argue the facts; if you don't have facts, then argue the law;
if you don't have either the facts or the law, then attack the lawyer. Since
Legal Services is a charitable organization that employs lawyers, and its
lawyers often challenge individuals and institutions on behalf of their
clients, both that natural tactic and that formulaic tactic can be applied
conveniently against us at the same time. One of the most dramatic applications was in 1979–1980. The funder was the United Way in Nashville.

The first person that year to voice a formal complaint about us to the
United Way was I. E. Lowrey Jr., senior vice president of Baptist Hospital. We regularly defended clients who had been sued by Baptist and

other hospitals for nonpayment of medical bills. Usually the cases got no further than general sessions court where we would raise some desperate defenses as to the cost of the services or the collection methods, losing many more than we won. We had tried to argue that since Baptist was a tax-exempt charity, it should mark our poor client's charges up to charity care and forgive the debt, but we had not been successful with that argument, yet. We could not use the Hill-Burton Act requirements we had asserted against many hospitals in collection cases (see Chapter 17) because Baptist, on principle, had not accepted that federal funding.

Whatever the particular case or cases may have been that bothered Mr. Lowrey, in June 1979 he wrote to the United Way and said that because they funded Legal Services, he would discontinue his support of the United Way and urge others to do the same. Although the hospital had not been a particularly strong supporter of the United Way over the years, it was a large employer, and its defection would be significant. Even more significant was the fact that a few weeks later the Tennessee Hospital Association added its weight to the Baptist complaint. Now the United Way had, in the words of its chairman, "a rather considerable problem."

In August, the United Way withheld $11,000 from its grant to Legal Services, using the pretext that Legal Services had a surplus of funds at the end of the previous year. There were several flaws with that stated reason. First, any positive fund balance we had that year had been in LSC funds earmarked for extending service to five rural counties, whereas the United Way funded only our services in Davidson County, and in that account, we had a deficit of $40,000. Second, there was no United Way policy against a charity carrying a positive fund balance. Otherwise, some of the larger, more established charities like the Boy Scouts or Red Cross would not have received United Way grants. Third, the United Way encouraged responsible fiscal management, and it is only good practice for an organization with uncertain funding to carry a positive fund balance, if it can. Although we objected to the United Way's pretext, our reasoned response was to no avail.

In early September, the executive committee of the United Way board requested that the Council of Community Support Services (CCS) initiate "an in-depth review" of the Legal Services case acceptance guidelines, case handling, supervision procedures, and the extent of our board's involvement in guiding staff. Later that month, after receiving a "preliminary report" from CCS, which we never saw, the United Way board voted to take the next step by restricting the use of its reduced grant to funding only for our family law section, and it instructed CCS to consult with the Nashville Bar Association in order "to seek a solution to this matter." Perhaps the bar association would stop us.

The hospitals were not alone. In October, William E. Powell, the president of Capitol Chevrolet, sent to William F. Greenwood, the president of First American Bank and chairman of the United Way, a copy of a resolution by the Nashville Franchised Automobile Dealers alleging that Legal Services staff were "interfering with legitimate business concerns and creating unnecessary expense to said businesses by raising issues other than to pay just debts [sic] or other complaints regarding merchandise purchased and services rendered." There were no specifics included in this inartfully worded complaint, but the dealers concluded that we were "alienating customers," and by their resolution they requested that the Nashville Bar Association and United Way "make a check into the practices of Legal Services." In his cover letter, Powell, with all subtlety abandoned, fired two shots across the bow of Bill Greenwood's ship. First for himself: "I had all most [sic] decided to give nothing to the United Way because of them." Then for the other dealers, "I have been selected to represent the . . . Dealers . . . to determine whether any of us will give our fair share."

Lester Robb, President of the United Way, and Bob Walther of CCS met with Richard Bird, the President of NBA, and gave him an earful about the "overzealous handling of various matters by the staff attorneys at Legal Services." In addition to the hospitals and car dealers, Robb voiced the concerns of banks in Gallatin about attorneys in our office there raising Truth in Lending defenses, the same complaints that Legal Services board member Hal Bigham had encountered and scornfully dismissed earlier (Chapter 5). Bird agreed to look into the complaints, but, in fact, using Occam's razor, he limited his inquiry to an examination of the role of the NBA-appointed board members at Legal Services, including their oversight of cases. While he was doing that, another complaint from another source, not involving the United Way, came to Bird. A lawyer from Franklin, representing an automobile dealer there, in a case that also involved First American Bank, sent a letter to Bill Greenwood claiming that Greg Sperry in our Murfreesboro office was representing a woman who was not eligible for our services. Greenwood added that to Bird's bundle.

All of this landed in Richard Bird's lap in the last months of his presidency, but he took it on "to avoid delay and leaving another unresolved problem for my successor." By now, he was accustomed to our controversies, having dealt with the Griffin Boyte complaint earlier in his presidency (see Chapter 12). In less than three weeks, he gave a report to the NBA board recounting his interviews and review of relevant documents. He concluded that the Legal Services board members were "well qualified and responsible" and that NBA members had been the "most consistent in attendance" at board meetings. In response to the complaint from Franklin, he found that the board had adopted client eligibility guidelines that it reviewed regularly, and citing the applicable provisions of the Legal Services Corporation Act, he found that questions about client eligibility are not to be raised in a court proceeding, but must be referred to the board or executive director of Legal Services. As to the issue of the board's "oversight" or control over cases handled by staff attorneys, he properly quoted at length from ABA Formal Opinion 324, which ruled that once a staff attorney establishes an attorney-client relationship, the board cannot interfere with the professional judgment of the attorney.

The board of the bar association approved Bird's report and instructed him to forward it to the United Way. In his cover letter forwarding the report, he recognized that his report was not a full response to the broad request from the United Way but stated that while the NBA was willing to assist however it properly could, it was not willing to substitute its judgment for the board of Legal Services. This was a significant moment in the hitherto uneasy relationship between Legal Services and the NBA. Bird's extended investigation, his willingness to hear all sides, and particularly his serious examination of federal statutes and the ABA formal opinion gave him better appreciation for the operation of Legal Services, educated other leaders on the NBA board, and was a step toward a better understanding.

The United Way was not so sanguine. CCS issued its report in January, and like the bar association, it found no grounds to condemn us. It concluded that Legal Services was "providing a needed, non-duplicatory service to an economically disadvantaged clientele and merits support from the community," a courageous report considering that CCS received all its funding from United Way and that the United Way board wanted grounds for disciplining us. Undeterred, later that month, the Admissions and Allocations Committee voted to reduce our funding by 48 percent from $38,000 per year to $20,000 and further to restrict the use of their grant not just to the family law section, but to be used only for match money required by a state grant, Title XX, that funded a limited part of our family law practice. Recognizing the problem our controversial cases were causing for the United Way, we did not appeal the restriction to family law cases, but we did appeal the reduction in the grant and the restriction that the grant be used only to match Title XX funding. That restriction effectively reduced our United Way funding even more because the Title XX grant only called for a $15,000 match, at most.

Once again, our patrician board member Joe Cummings, who had been through the same fight with us four years earlier, took the lead speaking on our behalf. In his argument to the United Way committee, he recalled "the Fred Friend incident" when the United Way board had not yielded to pressure, even from a member of the governor's cabinet, and Cummings told them that likewise they should not yield now. He recognized that some of our cases were unpopular, "but you get down to the question, who are they unpopular with? The poor people, the indigents they benefit, or a certain segment of the business establishment?"[1] In the end, the committee was unmoved. We lost the battle, but it galvanized a great deal of support for us in the community.

While the appeal was pending, the Nashville Association of Rabbis, Priests, and Ministers and the Interdenominational Ministers Fellowship issued public statements calling on the United Way to reverse its decision. Before and after the decision, there were letters to the editor in support of Legal Services and urging full funding, including one from Key Plumley, who for years had been the docket clerk in the Fourth Circuit Court and had watched us in action. In her modest way, she wrote, "I realize that I am only a 'small voice' and my contribution to United Way would hardly be missed, but I am hopeful that if enough 'small voices' make themselves heard . . ." There were other less public expressions of support, but the most gratifying was from Louis Farrell, our old nemesis of a couple years before.

Farrell wrote directly to Bill Greenwood immediately after the decision had been finalized, calling the action "inexcusable" and "an unworthy gesture." He averred that Legal Services was created to represent "indigents in their controversies with landlords, industrial insurance companies, hospitals, conditional sellers and others who have for years gotten away with murder in dealing with little people." He recalled, "I resigned from the Legal Services board a year ago because I didn't think it was doing an adequate job of this sort of representation. Perhaps I was wrong in my judgement. . . . It appears it is precisely this group . . . who are insisting that United Way stop funding legal services."

A week later, the *Tennessean* added its editorial condemnation entitled "Legal Services Loss No Gain for United Way." It recounted that in the past, despite complaints, the United Way had withstood pressure and stood by its member organizations, and it hoped that the principle of serving those in need despite criticism had not been lost.[2] What the editorial did not point out was the irony that, given the nature of things, even the retreat into funding only family law cases would not shield the United Way from donor criticism. In our adversarial system there always would be someone on the other side of our cases, whether that were a hospital executive or a working guy, and as often as not, there would be hard feelings about our client's claims. The United Way would continue to receive complaints about us, and although now they would come from individuals rather than automobile dealers or hospital associations, they still would be inflated, conflated, and more based on passion than on fact. Indeed, a temporarily unsettling complaint came only a few months after the funding reduction and after a change in the administration at United Way.

I received a call one morning from the new United Way executive, John Goessman, about a problem their fundraising had encountered at the Ryder truck facility in town. After the volunteer United Way solicitor had given his pitch to the assembled workers, one man in the crowd stood up to urge that no one give any money to the United Way because the United Way supported Legal Services and Legal Services was representing his no-good ex-wife in her bogus petition for an increase in child support. Much to the embarrassment of the unexpecting volunteer, the facts as described by the irate worker to his coworkers made the ex-wife's petition sound entirely unjustified and an example of our representing someone who was well over our income guidelines. John gave me the names and dates for the Ryder employee and his ex-wife, plus other information that had been relayed to him with great concern by the volunteer, and he asked me for a response that might help quell what had turned into a full-scale uprising with potential to sink any hope for United Way fundraising at Ryder.

I told John the facts sounded strange because we rarely handled child support cases, but I agreed to look into the matter and call him back with whatever information I could give him without violating client confidentiality. I looked through our client list and could not match the name John had given me. I asked for help from the staff in family law. No one could make any connection. Finally, Gayle Squires, the institutional memory of the section, came up with an idea. She looked in our "turn-down" files and found that we did have an intake sheet with a name that matched. The woman had called and asked us for service roughly within the time-frame given by the Ryder worker, but we had declined her case because we did not handle child support cases. Then why had the Ryder worker been so emphatic that we had represented her?

Gayle had a clue for that too. When we would decline to take a case, more as a sop to our conscience than as any hope for the caller, we would tell her that she might try to hire an inexpensive lawyer through the NBA Lawyer Referral Service (there was not yet a pro bono program in Nashville) or as a last resort call the legal clinic at Vanderbilt. The staff at the clinic accepted a limited number of cases each semester for third year students to handle under their supervision. Gayle skipped the lawyer referral program and went straight to the most likely suspect: someone could easily get the clinic confused with us. One telephone call and the riddle was solved. It was their case. No connection to us or the United Way. I called John back and told him I hoped this not being our case would save the campaign at Ryder, but, of course, both he and I knew that once a story like this poisons the well, facts are rarely an antidote.

As John's phone call to me illustrates, the relationship with the United Way already had improved considerably. Instead of launching an investigation employing the CCS and the NBA, he simply picked up the telephone. Things have continued along those lines over the years. Less than two years after the turmoil, our allocation was restored to $45,000, and in 2020 Legal Aid received $93,000 from the United Way in Nashville to fund work on housing and Social Security disability cases. In addition, LAS now receives more than $40,000 in allocations from six other United

Ways: in Anderson, Franklin, Rutherford, Sumner, and Williamson counties, plus the Greater Clarksville Area.

—————

The improving relationships and understanding on a local level beginning in the early 1980s came just in time. That support was sorely needed as we entered into a most difficult time on the national level, as detailed in the next chapter.

CHAPTER 15

Doomsday

1981-1991

This is my work; my blessing, not my doom.
—Henry van Dyke, "The Three Best Things"

The election of Ronald Reagan to the presidency in 1980 was a great victory for those who opposed comprehensive legal aid for the poor and federal funding of the Legal Services Corporation. As governor of California in 1970, Reagan had vetoed the Office of Economic Opportunity grant to California Rural Legal Assistance (CRLA), which he had authority to do under the then OEO grant provisions. Just as we in Nashville in 1979 drew the ire of the automobile dealers, hospitals, and banks, CRLA in the late 1960s by its representation of poor people, including migrant farm workers, had generated a great deal of opposition, principally from agribusiness interests, especially the California Farm Bureau and other political allies of the governor.

The man the governor had cynically appointed to head the OEO office in California, a longtime member of the John Birch Society, drew up a list of 127 charges against CRLA to justify the veto, but under OEO procedure, CRLA had a right to defend itself before an impartial commission. When CRLA asserted that right, OEO headquarters in Washington appointed a commission of three supreme court justices from other states, all of whom had been appointed by Republican governors, to hear the charges and determine the fate of CRLA. After extended hearings and testimony from 165 witnesses, the commission issued its unanimous report to OEO finding that the charges "were totally irresponsible and without foundation," after which OEO renewed its grant to CRLA, and CRLA continued its work. As one might expect, the animus of the governor and his allies only grew.

Even before Reagan's election to the presidency and his inauguration, the long knives were out. Howard Phillips, head of the "new right" Conservative Caucus, whom President Nixon had appointed to dismantle OEO and abolish Legal Services back in the early 1970s, more recently had organized a "National Defeat Legal Services Committee." Among those who joined his effort, not surprisingly, were small loan companies, and now that the drama was on the national stage, the American Farm Bureau. Other members were less predictable. For instance, appearing as part of the organized opposition for the first time were the boards and executive directors of many public housing authorities.

At first blush it seemed aberrant to have one group that was established to help the poor seeking the abolition of another group established to help the poor, but it is understandable when one appreciates that until Legal Services came along in the 1960s, housing authorities in many parts of the country had been run as paternalistic projects, at best, and outright fiefdoms, at worst. In some parts of the South, they seemed like a continuation of the old plantation system, with stern overseers and arbitrary rules. When Legal Services began representing tenants of those housing authorities in landlord-tenant disputes, the dynamics changed. The Legal Services lawyers would raise statutory claims and constitutional rights that never before had been raised, and often they were successful. Many housing authority managers and boards could not abide these challenges to their authority and jumped at the opportunity to encourage the new administration and Congress to get rid of this nuisance.

The executive director of the Knoxville Housing Authority, who was a recruiter for that opposition in the Southeast, called Legal Services a "predator" and complained about lawsuits and informal hearings handled by Legal Services lawyers on behalf of public housing tenants. In his impassioned recruitment letter, he solicited examples of Legal Services lawyers "engaged in tactics that are clearly designed to harass and intimidate housing authority executives."[1] To its credit, Nashville's housing authority would not join. "We are not going to be a part of that," George Barrett, MDHA's attorney, responded to an inquiry from the *Tennessean*. He called the effort embarrassing, and ever the ready litigator, George added, "We have disagreements with Legal Services, but there's nothing the matter with that."[2] The attorney for the Lebanon Housing Authority, Bob Rochelle, in response to an inquiry from David Ettinger at our Gallatin office, wrote that the accusation of the Knoxville director "certainly does not express the situation in Lebanon. I have always found you and the other attorneys who I have worked with in regard to the Housing Authority to be very responsible, ethical and practical."

Howard Phillips's national campaign proceeded at a furious pace. Less than a month after the inauguration, David Stockman, the new head of the Office of Management and Budget, published a "working paper" that proposed abolishing the Legal Services Corporation, then the source of nearly 90 percent of our funding in Middle Tennessee. Administration spokespeople, headlined by Edwin Meese, counselor to the president for policy and later attorney general, argued that legal aid work should be handled by law school clinics and judicare systems funded by social services block grants to the states, if the states wanted to have legal aid. It was the same ruse senators Brock and Helms had sought to advance seven years earlier.

Many of our staff members, for quite understandable reasons, became alarmed about job security and family income and began looking for other employment. By June, we had lost nine of our thirty-three lawyers and eleven other staff, as well. Anticipating layoffs for some remaining staff, I proposed to our board that we set aside part of our fund balance to cover unemployment compensation payments (we were self-insured) or else enroll in the state plan. The board appropriated $70,000 as a reserve for possible payments.

We were not without allies in our fight for survival. On the day in March that the administration presented its budget to Congress with zero funding for LSC, the president of the American Bar Association, Reece Smith, a corporate lawyer from Florida, held a press conference to condemn the administration's proposal, saying it "would undermine a commitment to equal justice under law and destroy a cost-effective program . . . that has made real progress in meeting the needs of the poor."

He immediately mobilized the ABA and three weeks later 120 prominent attorneys representing bar associations from around the country participated in a highly organized "March on Washington" to lobby members of Congress.

Locally, strong support emerged. The Nashville Bar Association board of directors voted unanimously to oppose the administration's proposal, and the president, Bob Walker, sent copies of its resolution to all members of the state's congressional delegation. Referring to complaints about Legal Services from the automobile dealers and others that the NBA board had dealt with just a few months before, he said, "We have found that all those complaints resulted from Legal Services doing a dad-gum good job of working for the people they're representing."[3] In April, the deans of three law schools in Tennessee joined 140 other law school deans from across the country in a letter of support for LSC. In an unusual political action, seventeen Nashville judges sent a letter of support drafted by Chancellor Robert Brandt to the Tennessee congressional delegation.

Editorial endorsement from the *Tennessean* came early and often, sometimes twice in a month, and editorials also appeared in the *Clarksville Leaf-Chronicle* and the *Dickson Herald*. The *Nashville Banner* did not editorialize, but early on it did publish a fulsome column by one of its top writers, Mark Howard, that conveyed a favorable picture of our work and articulated its importance. Many individuals wrote senators and representatives on our behalf, and again, as in the United Way struggle, one of the dearest was from Key Plumley. The gracious and motherly courtroom clerk sent me a carbon copy of the letter she wrote to Senator Howard Baker, "I personally am in a position to observe the work. . . . The quality of representation is excellent, and I know beyond any reasonable doubt the services . . . *cannot* and *will not* be provided by any other agency or any attorney in private practice" (emphasis hers).

We could not prepare for the worst; it was beyond planning, but we did try to plan for the hoped-for lesser catastrophes. We formed on the staff what Gordon dubbed the "Doomsday Committee." We discussed what criteria we should use for layoffs, what parts of our practice we might abandon, and what parts we could not. We examined how we might work more efficiently given fewer resources. Various staff members took on specific tasks such as looking into possibilities for fundraising and grants, examining ways to save on expenses, and trying to find less expensive office space.

I conducted individual interviews with each person on the staff to gauge each person's tolerance for pain. Whether the person planned to leave or to stay as long as possible, there was a clear understanding of our common crisis and a strong commitment to our work. Evoking the last stand at Masada, some with dark humor projected staying until the bitter end. Others, for quite understandable reasons, financial and otherwise, decided they had to leave. We were making adjustments even as we were planning how to make adjustments.

NLADA, LSC, and the ABA, in addition to their superb congressional advocacy, did a good job of keeping us informed about developments in Washington, and I distributed those communications to anyone on the staff who had the stomach for them. Many wanted to ignore it, keep doing their jobs and let others worry about the drama: "Just tell me when it's over." The bad news is that as we know now forty years later, it is never over. The good news is that the opening scene of this act ended, at last, in November 1981 without a complete disaster. Strong bipartisan efforts in Congress, as detailed in Earl Johnson's history, managed to save the Legal Services Corporation and limit the funding reduction to a loss of 25 percent. We lived to fight another day, and it would be a fight for the next seven years and beyond. (The beyond stretches on. The Trump administration budget for 2020 proposed that LSC be completely defunded.)

Newspaper editorial support for the Legal Services Corporation in 1981 had been strong throughout the country and many had defended it against the attacks, but in December, NLADA singled out the *Tennessean* and made it one of two recipients of its annual Emery A. Brownell News Media Award. The award cited the numerous articles, features, and editorials published by the newspaper that informed the public about the good work of Legal Services of Middle Tennessee and the importance of an independent LSC. While the award recognized the work of the entire staff at the newspaper, it particularly noted editorial writer Jim O'Hara, who had written seven of the eight editorials submitted, and reporter Kirk Loggins, who had chronicled our work in state courts. Kirk traveled to NLADA's annual conference to accept the award on behalf of the newspaper, and at the same conference I was one of two recipients of NLADA's annual Reginald Heber Smith Award, thanks to a fulsome nomination that had been submitted by Walt Kurtz and Andy Shook-hoff. The simultaneous awards to the *Tennessean* and me affirmed a caring community in Nashville and strengthened our resolve for the battles ahead. The battles were not long in coming.

Later that month when Congress was not in session, President Reagan named seven new members of the LSC board, not a friendly crew. The recess-appointed board met immediately on December 31 and cluelessly began by trying to delay the 1982 grants to local organizations like ours. We were saved by the fact that the federal fiscal year had begun in October and the grants had been made already. Undeterred, the board soon reconvened and began in earnest its unsympathetic, destructive operation. The fallout from that operation would dominate the life of LSMT for the next decade, principally in three areas: grants, regulations, and monitoring.

GRANTS

As a grantee of a government corporation, each year we had to submit an application for refunding that consisted of a rather voluminous set of documents in which we were to answer a series of questions describing what we did with the grant during the past year, then what we projected to do in the coming year. It routinely had a financial section, a case service section detailing how we helped people, and a compliance section where we documented our compliance with various LSC rules and regulations. It was a chore to pull all this together, but it was a routine event in the life of any federal grantee, and it gave us an opportunity to take stock of some of our accomplishments during the year. Now, thanks to the hostility of the unconfirmed LSC board, however, that routine bureaucratic process was about to become much more complicated and fraught with danger. Right away, the new LSC let us know that it was no longer a "refunding," but rather a "funding" application. There was no presumption of continuation. At the end of the year for our twenty-lawyer operation and our four thousand clients, we could just fall off a cliff. Each year was to be a new process, a new decision by LSC. No continuity, no stability.

The questions on the application forms increased substantially and became more like hostile interrogatories, questioning activities that were normal and legal parts of our practice. The demand for information became so voluminous that the process was split into two parts, one we had to submit in the fall and the other in the spring after LSC made its "preliminary" decision. It clearly had become a fishing expedition, an effort to gather information that could be twisted against us or construed as violations of some LSC regulation. The process was not for the edification of anyone but our opponents.

Not only did the size of the renamed "funding application" increase exponentially, but also the process for submitting it became more complicated. Now LSC required that the complete document must be reviewed line by line by the grantee board and put to a roll call vote and be approved by a majority of the members, not a majority of a quorum, and that process had to be followed for both Part I in the fall and Part II in the spring. One of the premises advanced by the Conservative Caucus and thus by the unconfirmed members of the LSC board was that the grantees were rogue outfits staffed by young left-wing ideologues with pliant boards of directors that had no control. This cumbersome review process was meant to ensure board control.

In our case, it created board defiance. With each new funding application during those years came not only increased demands for more information but also more onerous grant conditions. One year there were fifty-three new grant conditions we were required to consent to or be disqualified as a grantee. On more than one occasion, our board, suspicious of LSC's intent, had me write contingent letters to accompany our submitted applications. One reserved our right to appeal any reduction of our grant. Another specified that we "would comply with all the rules and regulations [of LSC] which complied with Congressional legislation." LSC already had drawn the rebuke of Congress for some of its departures, and the board suspected that a number of the grant conditions that year likewise were vulnerable.

One device Congress used often to overturn the erratic actions of the LSC board was an "affirmative rider" attached to an unrelated bill. In the last week of December 1988, the LSC board, in a last ditch effort, suddenly and without notice announced that instead of a grant for a year, the grant would be for only four months. The basis for the shortened grant period was that LSC wanted to institute as soon as possible a competitive bidding process that they had talked about for several years, and they did not want to be saddled with yearlong commitments to existing grantees that would delay that disruptive scheme. We were saved from this precipitous action a few months later when Senator Warren Rudman, a conservative Republican from New Hampshire who had been a champion of Legal Services from the beginning, attached a rider on an unrelated bill that prohibited the unconfirmed LSC board from doing that. With the pins knocked out from under them, LSC relented and restored the annual grants.

REGULATIONS

There were constant efforts by the LSC board to change the federal regulations governing us. In each case, during the comment period that was required by federal administrative law, we would prepare comments describing why the proposed changes were unworkable or a hindrance to our representation of clients. Our board minutes during the 1980s are replete with discussions and authorizations for submissions of comments. Sometimes individual board members would submit comments. Others in the community, lawyers and non-lawyers, would do the same. In one case when LSC proposed to change the regulation concerning the composition of our board, the Nashville Bar Association submitted comments in opposition. On several occasions, Congress stepped in to stop the changes or nullify them after the fact, but Congress could not stop them all.

Major targets of LSC included our representation of clients in legislative and administrative matters and our use of class actions to represent a large number of clients in a single case. Another target was our fund balance, which we accumulated when we could in order to carry us through lean years. LSC placed an arbitrary limit on that, which made financial management all the more difficult in these tumultuous times. Other regulations attempted to limit our use of backup centers, complicate our private attorney involvement program, and impose new limits on client eligibility. There was hardly any facet of our operation they did not attempt to mold to their destructive purposes.

The irony of the situation, with the massive number of new and revised regulations arriving monthly, was not lost on us. The people now

at LSC were adherents of a political philosophy that espoused opposition
to federal regulations and centralized control. Yet here they were issuing
regulations in bulk and attempting to impose tighter and tighter central
control from Washington. Practically every one of our board meetings
during the decade had at least one agenda item dealing with our compliance following a new regulation or instruction that had come down
from LSC, and several times during those years our executive committee was authorized to act for the board between meetings specifically to
deal with new requirements that might arrive with deadlines before the
next scheduled meeting.

Toward the end of one meeting in December 1985, at which the board
had slogged its way through several LSC mandated actions, in addition
to wrestling with our precarious financial position and approving two
personnel issues, Bob Thompson raised a very lawyerly concern. The
minutes reflect that he requested that a copy of our "management errors
and omissions insurance policy and/or binder be sent to each member
of the board." In light of all of this federally mandated procedure, he
wanted to be sure they were protected. He may have realized also that
he was about to be elected president of the board for the next year and
as such he particularly might be on the hook.

MONITORING

Another normal procedure gone haywire: monitoring. As a matter of
course, an organization receiving a federal grant will be audited periodically by the granting agency to ensure that the funds are being used
properly and that the grantee is complying with all applicable rules and
conditions. For us that meant that in addition to reports we sent to LSC
and the annual audit by a local CPA firm, we had periodic "monitoring"
visits from teams sent by LSC. Before 1982, the monitors had been people
from the regional office of LSC, joined by experienced folks from other
grantees. Although the teams checked compliance issues, the visits also
were important opportunities for collegial exchanges and suggestions of
better practices, both for management and for case handling.

Beginning in 1982, monitoring became a different matter. It became a
police action. The monitoring teams sent by LSC were made up of former FBI agents, out-of-work CPAs, carefully screened recent law school

graduates, and random other people from politically charged groups such as the Right-to-Work Foundation. They were humorless characters who had no experience with legal aid and no regard for the quality of our service but who were hired specifically to find us in technical violations of LSC's ever-changing rules. Often there were disputes about what we should share with them, particularly personnel and client records. The monitors had little regard for client confidentiality. On more than one occasion we had to consult with staff lawyers at the Board of Professional Responsibility and with other counsel about what we could or could not let them see. Through our membership in an association of LSC grantees and its contract with the Center for Law and Social Policy, we had access to Alan Houseman and Linda Perle, both attorneys with long experience in Legal Services and wide knowledge of the field. They were immensely helpful with compliance issues in normal times as we navigated LSC rules and regulations, but in these highly charged years, they were even more essential.

We prepared the staff for the monitoring visits by reminding them they should treat their interviews like hostile depositions, answering only questions asked and giving the answer succinctly. Board members prepared as well. Minutes several times during the decade reflect that old members would brief new members and share their experiences. We would go over regulations and particular points of concern that monitors might inquire about. At one board meeting in 1987, I was embarrassed to tell the members that in preparation for a visit, the monitors had insisted on having from the lawyer members not only a business phone number, but also a home number. This seemed to me like a needless intrusion on their privacy, but they all gamely assented. Charlie Warfield un-hesitantly shrugged it off, "That's okay. My wife can tell them to go to hell as easily as I can." Needless to say, his assessment was not recorded in the minutes, and mercifully the monitors did not call the Warfield home; Martha Warfield did not have to speak for us.

After the visits, the monitors would send written reports detailing their findings: never complimentary, no mention of significant accomplishments, no praise for effective advocacy, no hint that the federal funds had been spent well, only listing their financial disputes and our regulatory failures. There was no pattern as to when we would receive the monitoring report. Often so much time had gone by since the visit that either the rules had changed in the meantime or our compliance had been modified. The report for a visit in March 1986 did not arrive until April 1987, thirteen months later. Whenever a report arrived, it required that any dispute be filed by a certain deadline. Then would ensue a colloquy in which we would respond, correct their factual errors and misinterpretations, interpret ambiguity, and generally try to convey a sense of reality. Sometimes they actually would bend, most of the times they would not. Sometimes we just folded our tent, complied, and lived to fight another day.

In the end, the whole perverted monitoring process turned out to be a misguided endeavor for LSC, and fruitless. As Congressman Bob Kastenmeier wrote in an October 19, 1988, letter to the *Wall Street Journal*, in the preceding three years LSC had "spent millions of dollars to monitor grantees for alleged abuses . . . but to date not one program has been defunded." The abuses mostly were in the minds of our accusers.

The oppressive actions of LSC did not end right away with the election of the "kinder and gentler" president in 1988. There was a transition, but it was slow, and there was lots of carryover. A few months before the election, a slim but controlling majority of the LSC board had installed as president Terrance Wear, a former legal advisor to Senator Helms. Wear was the latest in an only slightly interrupted succession of zealots who had been hired by LSC boards during the 1980s to carry out their destructive purposes. He stated that one of his top priorities was to combat fraud. In a more informal setting, he once reportedly said that his job was to catch those of us who had our "hands in the cookie jar."

The unconfirmed board was led by its chairman, Clark Durant, who in a defiant speech before the American Bar Association in February 1987, had called for the abolition of LSC. Some of his compatriots on the board filed a federal lawsuit challenging Congress's authority to attach limiting riders to the LSC appropriation bills. When that failed, Durant and Wear, without telling minority members of the board, hired a former high official in the Justice Department to produce a memorandum arguing that LSC was an unconstitutional entity. The attorney's fee for this attempted hara-kiri was nearly $100,000, which they paid for out of LSC funds. By the time the minority members of the board learned of it, the memorandum had been circulated already to a number of like-minded members of Congress and others who would support the bizarre action, including the American Farm Bureau's lobbyist. When the leadership of the House Judiciary Committee learned about this "inexplicable waste of money," the jig was up, the holdover board lost all creditability, and cries went up all around for President Bush to hurry the process for appointing replacements. Finally, in January 1990, two days before the bizarre board was scheduled to meet again, President Bush appointed new members. Six months later, the new board, rather than firing Wear, simply allowed his contract to expire.[4]

The new board would face many challenges as it sought to bring more rational management to LSC and a renewed sense of its mission, but the new chairman, George Wittgraf, a small town lawyer from Iowa who had chaired President Bush's election campaign in that state, was committed to the task and to the cause. He would seek to make peace with the grantees and bring an end to the long years of combat.

———————

Although the 1980s were a time of profound instability for us, with all the difficulties that brought, the phenomenal thing was that the staff who remained were undaunted. By the end of the decade, we had gone from thirty-three lawyers in our four offices to seventeen, nearly half the staff gone; but we continued to represent at least three thousand individual clients each year, and at one point we calculated that we were representing more than five hundred thousand low-income Tennesseans in twenty-one class action cases.

The staff may have been undaunted, but not so the accountant and auditors. They were constantly daunted. From time to time the board appointed special budget committees to work with me and the accountant. There were constant adjustments as LSC funding changed, expenses changed, and staff resigned. Unlike many grantees, we did not have to make any layoffs, but in fear of that possibility we did adjust and readjust our unemployment compensation reserve. We moved the Nashville office out of Parkway Towers into less expensive space in the Stahlman Building.

Despite financial concerns, the board was steadfast about preserving services. At one point in the depth of our despair, the staff accountant,

Jim Adcock, the board president, Dick Lodge, and I proposed closing the Murfreesboro office. Much as we regretted this precipitous action, we were confident it was the right thing to do. The board had more confidence in the future than we did and unanimously rejected our financially reasonable proposal. Their reasoning was that if we left now, the people in our client community and the lawyers in the Murfreesboro area would lose faith in us because of our abandonment, and even if we were able to reopen the office in the future, that shadow of surrender would always be there.

Such was the faith of the board and staff that as the end of the decade approached, we formed what was dubbed the Millennium Committee. Urged by the United Way, for the first time we engaged in long-range planning. By late 1987, Charlie Warfield had completed our first fundraising campaign, which had exceeded its goal by nearly 20 percent, and we were poised for Harris Gilbert to lead the next one. We had started receiving funding from the Tennessee Bar Foundation and were exploring other funding sources. The plan presented to the board in October covered what might be expected: client representation, community education, fundraising, and even new staffing; but most revolutionary of all for those of us who had a hard time seeing beyond being forever young, it proposed that we establish and fund a retirement plan.

In December 1988, the board established that plan, and though that year we could fund it with only 1 percent of salaries, it was a beginning, and a welcomed affirmation for the staff. Even that beginning would not have been possible, however, without the generous assistance of the actuarial firm Bryan, Pendleton, Swats & McAllister, which donated its time to setting up the retirement plan, as well as a cafeteria plan, medical expenses reimbursement plan, and a dependent care assistance plan. For the first time we began to feel like a responsible employer providing comprehensive benefits for our staff. Bryan Pendleton, which later merged into a large national firm, continued to help us administer the plans for many years after that.

Further encouragement along our rocky road: In 1988, the HCA Foundation gave us its Award of Achievement for Outstanding Management, coupled with a $10,000 stipend. The award cited our long-range planning, our local fundraising campaign, our coordination of multiple pro bono programs, and surprisingly, our "increasing revenue by diligently seeking attorney fees." The last item cited became ironic only a few months later when the unconfirmed board at LSC attempted to adopt a regulation that would have reduced our LSC grant by a proportionate amount for any attorney fees we received totaling more than $100,000. Fortunately, our congressional protectors were looking out for us again and stopped that scheme before it started. LSC also tried to offset its grant dollar-for-dollar by the amount of any bar foundation funds we received, but that was stopped as well.

We were still on a financial rollercoaster. I had to suspend the hiring process for attorney vacancies in Murfreesboro and Nashville because it appeared we were facing an $80,000 deficit. We were shifting attorneys around and continued to do that for several years more. The good news was that in every case people volunteered to make the shifts. At various times, David Tarpley and Russ filled in at the Murfreesboro office until we could contract with Gary Housepian to become temporary manager there and then hire Barbara Futter for that position. David Tarpley, Kitty Calhoon, and David Ettinger worked out a schedule by which they would be in Gallatin on alternating days, which meant we did not have to hire a new attorney there until 2002, when Jim Hawkins joined us and returned to his hometown to manage the office.

By 1991 the new LSC board was in place and began requesting increases in funding from Congress. In addition, our campaign and other funding were bringing in more revenue. LSC funding that had been 90 percent of our budget in the early 1980s now was under 60 percent, and would eventually go into the 40s. The board in October voted to give raises that had been suspended at the end of the previous year. Whenever there was any money left at the end of a year, the board would add a percentage or so to the retirement fund. Jim Weatherly, like Cato in the Roman Senate, periodically would raise his insistence that the board should budget an amount at the beginning of the year to fund this important item, rather than using leftovers in December, but with all the uncertainty, it would be several years before we could even pretend we were doing that.

———————

We know now that our optimism and defiance would face another great test in less time than we could have imagined. The 1994 Congressional election brought even greater challenges, but that story will come later.

For now we return to the early 1980s when this chapter began and trace the development of pro bono programs that eventually took up some of the slack from our reductions during this dark decade.

CHAPTER 16

It's an Ill Wind That Blows No Good

> When you volunteer, you vote every
> day about the kind of community
> you want to live in.
> —UNKNOWN

The Reagan administration's attempt to abolish the Legal Services Corporation and pull the plug on federally funded legal assistance to the poor was a transformative experience for the bar. Not only did it need to come to the support of LSC and its local Legal Services organization, but it also needed to get serious about organized pro bono work.

In Nashville, the first discussion had taken place during September, even before the 1980 presidential election. Noting that Legal Services had more applicants than it could handle, George Paine, later a federal bankruptcy court judge, suggested to its board that the Nashville Bar Association start a pro bono program to handle some of the cases that Legal Services could not, and a committee was appointed to look into it. The American Bar Association was actively encouraging local bars around the country to start pro bono programs and was offering grants to help with early expenses, but when the committee reported to the board in January that the ABA was prepared to make a $20,000 grant to the NBA, there was opposition, and the board declined to apply. It was a repeat of the provincial "we-don't-want-your-help" attitude of 1965. The abhorrence of outside influence and the suspicion of national money persisted.

Despite the rebuff, the committee soldiered on trying to come up with an acceptable plan. Seeing that they were having a difficult time envisioning a program that could be operated by the NBA, in the late summer of 1981, I submitted to the committee and the bar president, Bob Walker, a proposal wherein Legal Services would screen cases as a part of its regular intake and refer them to lawyers recruited by the bar association to be on a volunteer panel. I suggested the bar adopt a goal of recruiting four hundred attorneys for the panel. Walker took this proposal to the board at its September meeting with his endorsement, "This is one of the things that lawyers ought to be interested in and ought to do."[1]

That, too, met with resistance. One board member, a trust officer at a bank, is quoted in Kirk Loggins's newspaper account of the meeting as "questioning the 'amount of control' the existing Legal Services staff would have over such a program." Walker responded that the bar had an obligation to do something and that Legal Services could provide a "ready-made administrative set-up" to handle it.[2] Nevertheless, noting the opposition, Walker referred the proposal back to the committee and asked it to report again at a future board meeting.

Bob Walker and the committee tried again at the November board meeting. The committee chair, David Herbert, who later would be appointed by the NBA to the Legal Services board, presented a detailed proposal that still took advantage of the Legal Services intake process, but moved the placement of the cases to the bar association office. This proposal fared no better. One oppositional board member opined, "I don't think we ought to have a plan, period." Another was not so absolutist, but more specifically resistant: "I'm against anything that makes us an adjunct to Legal Services." When Walker insisted that the association had a moral obligation to establish a framework for its members to carry out their individual obligations under the Code of Professional Responsibility, the same board member's suspicions only hardened and broadened. His imaginatively paranoid fear was that the proposed program would make it "almost inevitable that members of the bar association will do work and then be browbeaten for not doing more."[3]

Joe Haynes, who had labored on the committee, and who later would become a federal district judge, spoke in favor of the proposal, as did

Jack Robinson, who would be elected president of the NBA for the next year. Robinson had a practical position, "At least, I'd like to see us try it." A motion to defer any action on the issue failed on a six-to-six tie, and finally Walker got eight votes to send it to a newly constituted committee, but only by including the concession that the structure should be entirely within the bar association.[4]

The committee Walker adroitly appointed with Haynes included Rose Cantrell, who was another supporter, and Michael Miller, who had been one of the most vocal critics. Working off pieces of previous plans and calculating what might survive a vote in the board, the committee agreed on a plan and presented it to the December meeting. Even that provoked "considerable discussion," however, and the resolution that finally passed was that the committee "be charged with responsibility to put into effect the interim portion of the written plan."[5]

The committee worked through the spring of 1982 to come up with an operational plan, which finally was approved by the NBA board in April, leading the *Tennessean* to editorially commend the bar for adopting the program and praise it for offering to supplement the work of Legal Services.[6] The next month, the pro bono program accepted and assigned its first case.

WILSON COUNTY BAR ASSOCIATION

Among the bar associations that responded to the crisis brought about by the funding cuts, not all experienced a prolonged struggle like the NBA. After its bar leaders had attended a 1982 Tennessee Bar Association seminar on pro bono, the Wilson County Bar Association decided that it would establish a pro bono program in which every member would participate. The bar asked that our Gallatin office, which served Wilson County, screen cases and make the referrals. David Ettinger, who at that time was a lawyer in that office, remembers that "most everyone agreed to take pro bono cases." Two years later, it was still going well: 83 percent of the bar was participating and each participant was taking between two and six cases annually.

David was so impressed with their concerted effort that in 1984 he nominated the association for a Harrison Tweed Award given each year by NLADA and the ABA. When the awards were announced that year, they went to three bar associations that were a numerical mismatch: the massive State Bar of California; the commonwealth-wide Puerto Rico Bar Association; and the Wilson County Bar Association of Lebanon, Tennessee. The complexity of the cases handled by the California lawyers, and the volume of cases handled in Puerto Rico may have dwarfed the numbers in Wilson County, but not the spirit. David had explained in his nomination letter, "The relationship between Legal Services and the private bar here is ideal. We don't have to turn any eligible clients away for lack of an attorney to help them." Robert Callis, who was chair of the bar's pro bono committee, explained, "We believe we have an obligation to make sure that the people in our county get the legal services they need. . . . That's why pro bono is the bar's top priority."[7] Other bar associations in Tennessee also responded by establishing volunteer programs that helped fill the gap, including Rutherford and Williamson Counties, but none of them ever had the spirit or commitment the Wilson County bar exhibited during that time.

MEANWHILE, BACK IN NASHVILLE

After operating for a couple of years under the "interim portion" of the plan, in 1984 the NBA pro bono program began to expand beyond that with the appointment of several new members to the committee. Tom Nebel, Riney Green, Mary Walker, Phillip Miller, and Jad Davis each brought a high degree of commitment to the program, and together with Sandra Shelton, a former paralegal, as part-time staff, they began to look for ways to improve the service. In addition to improving the operation of the program itself, the new committee members took a disproportionate number of cases themselves hoping to set an example for other members of the bar. To recognize volunteers and encourage other lawyers, the committee requested that the NBA initiate an annual award to recognize an outstanding pro bono volunteer, and the board approved that in December 1984, initiating what is now the Joe C. Cummings Jr. Pro Bono Lawyer of the Year Award.

When Tom and Mary went to the board requesting additional staff, the board, in contrast to its previous hesitancy, voted to provide the funding even though it created a budget deficit for the NBA. Legal Services allocated $4,000 to the program as a part of our private attorney involvement project. The committee had even greater ambitions, however, that would require more funds, and in order to facilitate fundraising asked the NBA board for permission to incorporate as a subsidiary of the bar association and apply for tax-exempt status. After that was accomplished, they raised $10,000 from law firms and individual lawyers.

When they began talking about applying for United Way funds, the LSMT board and I got nervous. Given our history with United Way, we were concerned that in the future the pro bono program might be seen by the United Way as a safer alternative for their funds, not as likely to get involved in controversial cases. I expressed that concern to the pro bono board and my concern was conveyed to the NBA board, but that did not deter the effort. The NBA board at its next meeting authorized the application, but it did specify that the application must be accompanied by a letter explaining that any pro bono program grant was not meant to be at the expense of LSMT. The application was not successful.

A JOINT VENTURE

In the spring of 1987, NBA board members, including Jim Weatherly, who was a member of the finance committee, began raising concerns about the fact that both the Pro Bono Program and Legal Services were conducting campaigns to raise money from local lawyers and law firms. They also were concerned about "the interrelationship" of the two organizations. Juliet Griffin, former Legal Services lawyer, now clerk of the federal district court, and the first woman elected as president of the NBA, took it on herself to meet with representatives of each organization to discuss this issue and possible ways to prevent problems. When those discussions found no resolution, Juliet appointed Weatherly to chair a committee that would consider the issues raised in the discussions and negotiate a plan that would address them.

Jim was a good choice for this task. He had worked as a lawyer in the clinic at UT Law School, had been Walt Kurtz's chief assistant in the public defender's office, and then had been elected public defender when Walt became a judge. Now in private practice, he understood the legal needs of low-income people, was well respected in the bar, and was a determined advocate. The "Weatherly Committee" began meeting with the parties and quickly expanded its focus to include the question of whether the Pro Bono Program should remain separate or be merged with Legal Services. The pro bono board adopted a resolution stating its opposition to a merger. Nevertheless, the discussions with the committee continued through the summer.

For Legal Services, fundraising was only one of the concerns. The second issue was client confusion. This also was a concern of Jim's. Reflecting the involvement of the bar in both organizations, he said later, "It didn't seem to me to make much sense to be doing virtually the same thing in two different places, particularly as it related to intake of clients." When the NBA board originally discussed beginning a pro bono program in 1981, I had pointed out that one reason for having Legal Services operate the program would be that people needing assistance would have one place to go and not be referred back and forth between two offices depending on case type and availability of assistance. Six years later, despite both organizations having adopted policies attempting to prevent it, the ping pong problem still was present.

Our third concern was entirely defensive, and beyond local. A couple of years previously, groups opposed to LSC, together with Reagan-appointed LSC board members, began urging "competitive bidding" as a way to undercut existing grantees. The plan was to periodically put out invitations to bid in each local community for the delivery of civil legal services to low-income people, purposely preventing continuity and the accumulation of experience, an unnerving prospect for any legal aid provider and its staff. Part of the plan was that representatives of this repurposed LSC would come to local communities to drum up competitive bidders, not only individual lawyers and law firms, but also law school clinics and independent pro bono programs. Although we could not imagine any of the current members of the Pro Bono Program's board wanting to imperil LSMT and its clients by succumbing to the LSC drummers, we certainly did not want that ever to be an option. Better to be together.

Bob Thompson, the president of our board during this eventful year, was a corporate and securities lawyer at Bass. After he and I had participated in several of the talks during the summer, he borrowed a page from his own practice and suggested that we propose as a compromise that the NBA and the two organizations form a joint venture to operate the Pro Bono Program. At Jim's request, I did many drafts of the proposal during the time that followed, and Jim conducted Kissinger-like shuttle diplomacy, adding and subtracting and refining in the process. In October he presented to the NBA board a version of the plan that had been endorsed in principle by our board's executive committee, but lacking pro bono board approval, no action was taken. He presented a revised draft in November, which the NBA board endorsed in concept, and then in December a final version, which was adopted unanimously. Two weeks later, it was signed.

What resulted was an awkward three-party arrangement between the NBA, Legal Services, and Pro Bono, which required many adjustments over the years, but it was a first step. The final draft, at the insistence of the pro bono board, provided that the agreement would have a duration of only three years, unless it were renewed by consent of all parties. That meant repeating the negotiation process more often than we might have wanted, but it did keep all parties accountable. On several occasions over the years, it meant that Jim was called back into service to bring his perspective and to help come up with reasonable solutions. In recognition of his extraordinary work getting this deal done and of his leadership at the bar, in early December, Jim was elected president of the NBA for the next year. In 1991, he was appointed to the LSMT board, where he serves today, having twice been elected president.

BETTER TOGETHER

In January 1988, Victoria Webb moved from the bar office on the third floor of the Stahlman Building to the Legal Services office on the eighth floor as the pro bono coordinator, a position she then held for more than fifteen years. From the beginning, the pro bono board was diligent in trying many techniques for recruiting volunteers to take cases. They submitted articles to the NBA's monthly publication, *The Docket*, and developed their own newsletter, *In Brief*. They made appeals at CLE programs and at the "Bridge the Gap" sessions for new lawyers. Knowing that positive reinforcement and recognition encourages participation, they began recognizing volunteers each month, in addition to the volunteer of the year award. Still, it was difficult to recruit new volunteers and then in some cases to get them to accept referrals once they were on the panel. The program's board minutes often reflect reports from

Victoria on the difficulty of placing cases. At one point she told of having to make twenty-four phone calls to place one case.

One of the most effective vehicles the board hit upon for recruitment and case placement was the "Lawyer for a Day" program. The lawyer would come to the pro bono office and make phone calls in an effort to "sell" a case to the next person on the list of volunteers, a much more effective process than having a pro bono staff person try to get a lawyer on the phone. The process was even more effective when the Lawyer for a Day was a judge. At various times, judges William Faimon, Barbara Haynes, and Marietta Shipley were on the pro bono board and took their turns making the calls. They had no problem getting a lawyer on the phone, and usually the lawyer was more than willing to comply with a judge's direct request.

Some lawyers were hesitant to volunteer because of their lack of experience in the types of cases the program handled. That was addressed by the use of training clinics. There were clinics for unemployment compensation cases and other subspecialties, but the greatest number of them, at one point conducted almost monthly, were held to train volunteer lawyers to do family law cases. The theory was that a good lawyer who did tort defense or corporate litigation could, with training and mentoring, handle relatively simple, prescreened divorce cases. Typically, a pro bono board member would ask the managing partner to recruit a number of lawyers in the firm to stay later one evening, eat pizza in the conference room, watch an instructional video, be tutored by a family lawyer, and then take cases.

The lawyers most often involved as tutors, Lucinda Smith, Jean Crowe, Jackie Dixon, and Mary Arline Evans, in addition to going over the forms and procedure, would discuss the human side, alerting the lawyers to the tension and anxiety their clients would be dealing with in the course of the divorce, which likely would be a bit more personal and certainly different from those they were used to their business clients experiencing. In one clinic I attended at the firm of Stokes and Bartholomew (now Adams and Reese), Jean cautioned the lawyers that they also needed to be careful about some of the things the client might tell them, that heightened emotions often meant the client obscured the truth. At that point one of the lawyers, John Chambers, sitting with his coterie in the back of the conference room, looking up from the leftover pizza and sample pleadings, impishly cracked, "Oh that is going to be very hard for us to deal with. Our clients always tell the truth. We represent real estate developers." Somehow Chambers and his section were able to adjust, and John, at least, became an outstanding volunteer.

There was discussion from time-to-time in the pro bono board of pushing for mandatory pro bono. Thankfully, that never got very far. While it is admirable to imagine that we could have a bar association where everyone did his or her part and fulfilled one's ethical duty, the prospect of placing vulnerable clients with unwilling and grudging attorneys did not inspire in us at Legal Services a vision of equal justice. Better to prioritize the cases and serve as many clients as we could with willing volunteers. Likewise, though under the agreement LSMT was responsible for fundraising, on several occasions there was discussion in the pro bono board about having an assessment added to the bar dues, but our view was that we could raise a lot more money with our campaign for voluntary contributions than we could from a mandatory fee. We feared that any dues assessment would engender an attitude of "I gave at the office" and preclude more generous gifts later.

A SOUND PROGRAM

Many Nashville lawyers contributed an extraordinary amount of time and energy to the success of the pro bono program, and in 1993 their work was recognized when the organization received the initial TBA Pro Bono Volunteer of the Year Award. The next year, that award went to Riney Green individually, and in 1996, he received the ABA Pro Bono Publico Award in recognition of his work building the pro bono program and his continuing service, including by then the presidency of the Tennessee Justice Center board (see more about this in Chapter 20).

In 2003 we were able to put in place one more element necessary for the program's success, the hiring of its first attorney director, Lucinda Smith. It took some persuading to get her to accept the job, but Lucinda was the perfect choice. In addition to having been managing attorney in the family law section at Legal Services for two years in the late 1980s, while practicing at Dodson, Parker & Behm in 1995, she had been named NBA Pro Bono Volunteer of the Year. After being elected to the NBA board, she had been that board's liaison to the Pro Bono board, then had been appointed to that board where she had been an active participant in the sometimes-difficult 2001 discussions around the renewal of the joint venture agreement. She was committed to the work and as director of the program immediately brought order and stability to the operation.

Over the next few years, the number of cases handled through the program increased from 761 in 2002 to over 2,800 in 2013. The Saturday Clinic that had begun in 2001 was expanded and in 2012 was renamed the "McHugh Saturday Clinic" in honor of Bill McHugh and his wife Lou, who bequeathed more than a million dollars to the Community Foundation for the Legal Aid Society's pro bono work. Before his death, Bill had been one of the most faithful volunteers, beginning in 1982 when the program was formed, and there was another connection with us that echoes a consistent donor theme. As was the case with Herman Loewenstein, a major part of Bill McHugh's practice had been as a creditors' lawyer, and as such, his most frequent contacts with Legal Aid had been representing the other side in cases against debtors represented by attorneys in our consumer section. Once again, it was one of David Tarpley's frequent opponents who generously endowed our work.

Lucinda developed specialty clinics that combined the particular interests of lawyers in a law firm or corporate legal department with clients served by various community organizations: refugees served by Catholic Charities and Casa Azafran; veterans at Operation Stand Down; and low-income elderly needing wills and powers of attorney at FiftyForward. This coordination with other service organizations was recognized and rewarded in a dramatic way in 2010. Because the clinics were weaving relationships between law firms, corporate counsel, and community organizations, the Pro Bono Program received the annual Team Building Award from the Center for Nonprofit Management, an award that carried with it a $50,000 stipend.

Since many Nashville lawyers lived and/or practiced in Williamson County, the bar association there sometime before had asked the Pro Bono Program to extend its reach and administer the program in that county as well. The Pro Bono board had approved, and Lucinda operated the programs in the two counties for several years. Then, after Gary Housepian became executive director of Legal Aid, he began exploring possibilities for expanding even further and making pro bono services available to clients in all forty-eight counties we serve. He reasoned that since Nashville lawyers routinely represent clients from all over the Legal Aid Society's service area, perhaps they would represent pro bono clients from outside Nashville as well, particularly if LAS facilitated the clients' communication through Skype or similar technology. With encouragement from the Tennessee Supreme Court, that expansion was implemented.

The operation of a multi-county volunteer lawyers program had institutional implications also. When the periodic discussion began in 2013 about the renewal of the joint venture agreement, questions were raised in the Pro Bono board about whether to continue operating the Nashville Pro Bono Program as a separate entity. The discussions proceeded quickly and within a month there was agreement among the three parties that Legal Aid continue to operate a multi-county pro bono program supported by the NBA and that Nashville Pro Bono, Inc., be dissolved. The next year the newly expanded program opened 279 cases in twenty-four counties outside Nashville; established new clinics in several of those counties; and instituted a project championed by the Supreme Court's Access to Justice Commission that had challenged "Pillar Firms" to take a set number of cases in certain substantive areas.

───────────

Once again this chapter has advanced the narrative far beyond the chronology of our story. Furthermore, we have gone even beyond the temporal scope of this entire history, which was advertised to stop at 2002, but the extension was necessary so that our account could bring up to date the structure of pro bono work that had begun in Nashville in 1982 but today reaches far beyond.

Now we return to the late 1970s to trace the development of our practice in healthcare law, a field we had little awareness of until Callie Mae Newsom asked us to defend her in a suit over an $800 hospital bill. We previously had treated such requests simply as collection cases. That was about to change and go far beyond hospital bills.

CHAPTER 17

Healthcare and Paying for It

The services we received from Pam Wright
and Adinah Robertson were excellent and
very professional. They really cared. There
is no way we could thank them enough.
Some day I hope to send a donation. My
husband passed away October 2, 1990.

—Ms. O. McG., Nashville

When Callie Mae Newsom, a working mother, was hospitalized at Vanderbilt for surgery, Medicaid paid for most of her care, but she was left
with an $800 bill that she could not pay. She made payments to the hos-
pital's collection agency for a time, but after she fell behind, the agency
sued her for the balance, plus attorney's fee. Gordon agreed to represent
her and tried to reason with the attorney for the collection agency, but
with no success. Then with the court date for this hopeless case only a
few days off, he found a hook. He read an article in the *Clearinghouse
Review* about a possible defense.

The *Clearinghouse Review* was a periodical begun in the OEO days,
sort of a combination of a law review and Bloomberg BNA *Law Week*
for poverty lawyers. With the poverty of the Legal Services programs
themselves, publishing such a review was not an attractive business proposition for a private enterprise like BNA, so OEO and then LSC funded
a nonprofit organization to produce the periodical that contained both

articles and case reports. Practitioners and law professors could submit articles about legal theories that might be applied to address the legal problems of people living in poverty. Local lawyers could send in copies of pleadings from interesting cases they had filed or defended, and the staff at *Clearinghouse* would list them with a short description in the monthly edition that was mailed to every lawyer employed by an OEO/LSC grantee. The lawyer could request a copy of any pleading listed, and it would be mailed to her free of charge.

The periodical and its mail-out service helped educate poverty lawyers in a field that did not receive much attention in other publications. It encouraged creative thinking and vastly improved the practice. And, as one might imagine, it was a prime target of those who opposed federal funding of civil legal aid. In their minds, it was spreading subversive ideas. Opponents in Congress tried for years to strip funding for the *Clearinghouse Review* from the LSC budget; regrettably, in 1996 they succeeded. For nearly thirty years, however, it was a lifeline, as it was in this case for Gordon, Callie Mae Newsom, and many others.

The article Gordon read described a 1946 federal statute, the Hill-Burton Act, that authorized large loans and grants to hospitals for construction and modernization, requiring in return that the hospitals provide a reasonable volume of free services to low-income people unable to pay for their care. As pointed out in the article, this obligation was more honored in the breach than the observance, and though the legislation had been enacted in 1946, for all the intervening years there had been no systematic enforcement of the obligation. A hospital often would write off bad debt and count that as satisfying the obligation, without any determination as to whether the debt was owed by a low-income person truly unable to pay or just a guy with enough money who cynically was avoiding the bill.

Gordon figured that Callie Newsom was just the sort of person who should have benefited from the Hill-Burton obligation, or at least should have been screened by the hospital as a potential beneficiary. He raised this with the collection agency's lawyer and asked him to take this into consideration, but the hospital and the collection agency would not back down, so just before the collection suit was to be tried in general sessions court, Gordon preempted them by filing in federal district court against the collection agency to stop the suit; against Vanderbilt Hospital for its violation of the Hill-Burton Act; and against the state health department and the US Secretary of Health, Education, and Welfare (HEW) for their failure to enforce the Hill-Burton requirements.

The case fell to Judge Clure Morton, who granted right away the temporary restraining order to stop the collection suit. Then began eight years of discovery fights, litigation, contempt procedure, and appellate practice. Gordon was fortunate in securing some good help along the way, most significantly from the National Health Law Program (NHeLP). That program, known as a backup center, was another effort by OEO and then LSC to provide support to local lawyers struggling with cases in unfamiliar areas of the law. One of the young lawyers at NHeLP in 1975 was Andy Schneider, just starting out on a career in health law that would lead to significant congressional staff appointments and federal administrative positions. Andy became Gordon's co-counsel and brought to the case the insights and experience of other lawyers at NHeLP. They worked easily together, subtly challenged each other to dig deeper, and thereby developed a friendship that led to lifelong collaborations.

While the case was pending, HEW in an administrative hearing found that Vanderbilt was, in fact, in compliance with Hill-Burton, but that finding was not an impediment; just the opposite. That merely strengthened Ms. Newsom's case against HEW and its inept enforcement. Tellingly, the HEW finding missed or ignored the fact that Vanderbilt had recently certified in a bond prospectus that it had provided no charity care. At one point during discovery in the court case, a Vanderbilt document surfaced entitled "Weekly Summary of Patients Denied Admissions to Vanderbilt Hospital for Financial Reasons," which gave no indication that anyone on the list had been screened for Hill-Burton eligibility. When the case was tried in September 1977, testimony from hospital staff revealed that Vanderbilt's notice of and screening of patients for Hill-Burton benefits was spotty, at best.

Judge Morton received much more evidence than HEW had considered at the administrative hearing, and he reached a very different conclusion. In a break for Vanderbilt, he found that the hospital could not be held responsible for noncompliance before 1972 because the negligent federal administrators had not promulgated any rules for the hospitals to comply with, despite the clear intent of the 1946 statute. Vanderbilt got a bye on that, but not for the years after 1972 when HEW finally had established some rules.

In the course of the case, Gordon discovered that Vanderbilt had employed a couple of devious accounting schemes in order to claim satisfaction of its Hill-Burton obligation. Though the hospital had contracted with Medicare and Medicaid to provide services to patients in those programs at a set price, it then charged against the Hill-Burton program the difference between that agreed upon price and what it would like to have charged, its "full charge." In other cases, it was crediting against its Hill-Burton obligation charges for services to Hill-Burton patients that were more than its "reasonable costs," jacking up the bill to get more Hill-Burton credit. The court prohibited both of these practices.

To compensate for its failings after 1972, the hospital was ordered to render free care to future eligible patients in an amount equal to what it would have rendered had it complied, and it was enjoined from claiming credit for providing uncompensated care unless its records showed specific compliance with the Hill-Burton Act and regulations, including screening for patients who qualified. As a further check, the judge enjoined the hospital from bringing a collection action against a patient who would have qualified for free care but for the failure of the hospital to properly determine eligibility. The federal defendants, in turn, were enjoined from finding Vanderbilt in compliance unless the hospital's records clearly demonstrated that it had done everything it was supposed to do under the Act and regulations.[1]

Vanderbilt and the government appealed to the Sixth Circuit Court of Appeals, and in that court they got some relief.[2] The district court had held that because Vanderbilt was administering a federal program, it must afford applicants due process, and that HEW must issue new regulations specifying the elements of that due process. While the Court of Appeals did not disturb the finding of Vanderbilt's noncompliance with Hill-Burton, it did reverse on those due process issues. The Secretary, however, following Judge Morton's ruling, in the interim had already issued regulations that provided most of what the judge had ordered, and the leniency of the Court of Appeals did not at all disturb that.

Callie Mae Newsom was not the only beneficiary of the outcome. Because Gordon filed the case as a class action, the case benefited hundreds of other low-income people who would have been treated by Vanderbilt the same way she had been if the hospital's practice had continued. And the case had a multiplier effect beyond Vanderbilt. Not all hospitals had taken Hill-Burton funds, but those that did had the same obligation as Vanderbilt. Consequently, when low-income people were sued by a Hill-Burton hospital and came to us, we were able to raise that in defending them, and it was effective. The hospital did not want to end up in federal court like Vanderbilt had. Often a phone call to the hospital's lawyer would solve the problem. The lawyers in our Gallatin office found this particularly effective. But there was an even larger multiplier effect. The regulations HEW promulgated in response to the district judge's order specifying requirements for compliance with Hill-Burton made the program a benefit for thousands of patients nationwide.

CHARITY CARE?

If the hospital was not a Hill-Burton recipient, and the client had been sued, we would defend the client as best we could, usually questioning the charges (e.g., the $4 aspirin tablet) or raising some factual dispute in an effort to reduce the bill. When we failed to get the needed relief, we would file slow pay motions and/or help our client claim exemptions from judgments. When all else failed, we would file bankruptcies, or try to get a private lawyer to file for our client.

Then Gordon came up with an additional arrow for our quiver. If the hospital suing our client were a charitable institution and as a result was exempt from taxation, then we should argue that it ought to have a charity care policy with a fund set aside in lieu of taxes for charity care and our client ought to be evaluated to see if he met the qualifications in this putative policy. Of course, Gordon was making it all up. If a hospital had a charity care plan, which in itself was a big "if," it commonly did not want that plan to be public, preferring to administer the program secretly and selectively so that it could determine who might be worthy. At the same time, anyone could predict that collection lawyers and general sessions judges would not spend court time making such a determination. They just wanted to get through their docket and dispose of the list of warrants as expeditiously as possible. They did not want to deal with any charity theories. They were not social workers.

Mary Walker was a social worker. Before she went to law school at UT, she had earned her master of social work degree there and worked for ten years in child welfare and as a supervisor for human services departments in North Carolina and Tennessee. During law school she clerked with us in the family law section, and after finishing her coursework in early 1979, came to work with us full-time. While waiting to take the bar examination, she could practice under the third-year practice rule, and she did that under the guidance of our then student supervisor, Russ Overby. Gordon said he needed some help, so Russ let Mary work for Gordon.

As Mary recalls, she would dutifully trek over to general sessions court and try to defend our clients who had been sued for hospital bills. She would "pick at" the bills; she would try to demand proof of the services; and when it was appropriate, she would insist her client's charges should be taken care of under the hospital's charity program. All to no avail. She then would come back to the office and report her humiliating defeats to Russ. Finally one day, Russ had heard enough of his student being treated as cannon fodder. Mary remembers that on that fateful day he left her in his office and stormed down to Gordon's office at the other end of the hall. Although they were several offices away, she could hear Russ yelling at Gordon and demanding that he "stop sending Mary over there on these no-good cases with these bullshit defenses."

Russ was not the only person upset. Mary must have had more of an impact than we realized. It was just a couple of months later that I. E. Lowrey Jr., the executive vice president of Baptist Hospital, wrote to the United Way to complain about our "harassing" the hospital (see Chapter 14). With Mary's futile trips to defend our poor clients and her questioning the financial arrangements of tax-exempt, church-sponsored hospitals, we had not only struck a nerve, we had attacked a sacred cow. Russ's anger had been "friendly mad"; I. E. Lowrey's was not.

As it turned out, within a year after the United Way had sided with Mr. Lowrey, Gordon and his quixotic theory were vindicated. Dana Dye, a lawyer in our Murfreesboro office, was in Davidson County general sessions court representing a client who had been sued there by Baptist Hospital for a bill the client could not pay. Dana, just over a year out of Duke Law School, raised all the Gordon-inspired defenses in general sessions, and predictably she lost. But she did not stop there.

She appealed the adverse judgment to circuit court, where the case was tried before Judge James M. Swiggart. After the collection lawyer put on his proof, Dana put on her client and established that with her annual income of $3,000 she could not pay the emergency room bill while at the same time buy food and pay her rent. Dana then argued that the hospital had a duty to render charitable services, based on a 1928 Tennessee Supreme Court case holding that the city of Nashville could not levy taxes on property at Baptist Hospital because that property was used for charitable purposes. She was not challenging the tax-exempt status of the hospital or its property. She simply wanted her client to receive some of the charitable services for which the hospital purportedly used its tax-exempt property.

When the judge asked the collection lawyer about the hospital's charity program, the lawyer had to plead ignorance. In response, the judge continued the hearing and ordered the hospital to come back the next week with a description of its program so that he could determine how he should rule. If the hospital did have a charity care program, then he said he would determine whether or not Dana's client qualified. If it did not have a charity care program, then he said he would give it one.[3] Faced with this dilemma, a couple days later the hospital dropped its suit against our client and the case was over. Unfortunately, the case had no binding precedential value, but we were able to cite it later on occasion to some effect in other collection suits by tax-exempt hospitals.

HEALTH PLANNING AND ACCESS

Paying for medical care was one thing, a problem for many people in our society, and the chief cause of individual bankruptcies, but for our clients, there was a prior problem: access to medical care.

The National Health Planning and Resource Development Act of 1974 and its amendments in 1979, like Hill-Burton, Medicare, and Medicaid, was an incremental measure aimed in part at increasing access to healthcare in the United States. Because universal access to healthcare had not been a possibility due to consistent opposition from the American Medical Association, Congress from time to time passed these partial measures that provided access to some low-income people. The 1974

Act was designed to implement the shibboleth in vogue that if we could control duplication, waste, and abuse in the "system," we could thereby make healthcare more economical for all and ensure greater access for vulnerable populations.

The bodies established by the Act to carry out these idealistic purposes were state and local commissions, in our area the Middle Tennessee Health Systems Agency (MTHSA) and the Tennessee Health Facilities Commission (THFC), which were to study the needs and resources in their areas and issue permits called Certificates of Need. If a medical provider wanted to make major changes to its operation, such as build a new facility or purchase expensive equipment, it was required to apply for a certificate from the local and state commissions. The commission staff and panel were to examine the proposal and determine, first, whether or not it was needed in the area and, second, whether the applicant was providing access to women, minorities, low-income people, and people with handicaps. That second test was particularly important for our clients.

Neither test was being applied correctly by the MTHSA and the THFC, in part because of two failings. One, the commissions' panels were stacked in favor of the industry. Despite federal requirements for diversity, they included few, if any, low-income people, only a token number of people of color, and no representatives from primary care clinics located in low-income communities. Two, the application form that facilities were required to complete, while intricately testing many aspects of their proposal, failed to test for access. When our lawyers, Bob Ray and Mary Walker, challenged the commissions on behalf of three clients, they had mixed success with the MTHSA correcting these failures. Though the MTHSA agreed to comply with federal regulations and be more inclusive in its membership, it was decidedly indifferent in carrying out that agreement, requiring constant prodding by our lawyers. The resolution of the application issue was more definite. After only a few months, Mary was able to persuade the MTHSA that it must require the applicant to answer a civil rights survey, furnish a copy of its admission policy, and specify its criteria for staff privileges. Using these would give the staff and panel a basis for making its judgment about access.

The compliance of the local agency was not duplicated by the state commission. The THFC was recalcitrant on both points and the ramifications of that resistance soon became obvious in an individual case, an application by Baptist Hospital for a certificate of need. Once again, as with other matters involving this hospital, the case turned into a public controversy. In addition to an uncompromising defense, the hospital mounted a spirited public relations campaign and even involved the state Baptist newspaper. Two congressmen got involved: the one from the district that included the hospital was helpful; the congressman from a neighboring district was not. Both the *Nashville Banner* and the *Tennessean* followed the proceedings from beginning to end, each paper with sophisticated and well-informed coverage.

The hospital filed an application in September 1980 to do substantial renovation of existing facilities and to expand its obstetrics unit by thirty-three beds. The MTHSA staff reviewed the application and recommended that the renovations be approved, but that the expansion be denied. The basis for the denial was that there were already too many hospital beds in Davidson County and that other nearby hospitals had obstetrical beds that were not being used. Over-building by hospitals was a problem in the county according to a previous study that found there were about eight hundred more beds in the county than were needed, even when factoring in out-of-county patients. The MTHSA panel agreed with the staff recommendation, approved the renovation, and denied the certificate for the expansion. The hospital appealed to the THFC.

The THFC staff, consistent with the MTHSA staff and MTHSA panel decision, recommended approval for the renovation and denial for the new beds. Before the commission panel was set to consider the application, Bob Ray wrote to the THFC requesting that the panel postpone its decision until it had considered the application in terms of access to health facilities by minorities, handicapped, and the poor. He pointed out that because the THFC had not made the needed changes to its application, it had no basis for assessing access of these groups, and thus it was violating federal law. The THFC panel ignored Bob's request, ignored its staff's recommendations, and ignored the MTHSA staff and panel's decision. It voted ten to one to approve both the renovation and expansion.

The Health Planning Act provided that citizens who were aggrieved by a health facilities commission decision could petition for a reconsideration and a public hearing. Bob, Mary, and Stewart Clifton filed a petition on behalf of their clients, pointing out that Baptist, despite its tax-exempt status, had no apparent charity care policy, delivered very little charity care, had strict financial conditions on admission, and admitted very few Medicaid-eligible patients. These practices, they pointed out, each and all together constituted discrimination against minorities and the poor. The defiant THFC panel set the case for hearing, and our lawyers began discovery. They also began discussions with Tom Schlater, the lawyer for the hospital, in an attempt to work out an agreement that would settle the matter. After much discussion, the lawyers for the two sides came to a resolution that was agreed upon all the way up the line at Baptist. Then it got to David Stringfield, the executive vice-president of the hospital who, after all that, reportedly said, "If the terms are okay with Legal Services, then they are not okay with me."

The hearing began on April 22, 1981, with testimony supporting our petition from, among others, the director of community medicine at Meharry Medical College and from Louanne Kennedy, a national expert in the field of health planning and hospital administration at Mt. Sinai Hospital and the City University of New York. Dr. Kennedy compared Baptist's charity care, which was 0.3 percent of total revenue, unfavorably with the generally accepted national practice of 3 percent. The hospital countered that with its bad debts, reduced payments from Medicare and Medicaid, and charity care, it delivered $6 million in "free care." It was the same contrivance Vanderbilt Hospital had tried unsuccessfully to use to satisfy its Hill-Burton obligation a couple of years earlier, but the fact remained that when one stripped away those irrelevant factors, the charity care delivered by Baptist the previous year had been $174,513, against $50.3 million total revenue. The other large religious hospital in town, St. Thomas, with only slightly more revenue, delivered five times as much charity care.

The THFC, not accustomed to having its decisions questioned, was openly hostile to the petitioners and their witnesses from the beginning to the end. The administrative law judge who was presiding at the hearing struggled to keep proper order as several panel members, rather than functioning as impartial decision makers, cross-examined our witnesses, made accusations against our clients, mocked our experts, and even gave speeches during the hearing about what they thought about our claims. Because proof was not completed in one day, the hearing had to be continued until the commission's next scheduled meeting the following month.

At that first day of the hearing, a public relations spokesman for the hospital announced that for the current year, the hospital would set aside $375,000 for charity care. During the month between the two days of the hearing, David Stringfield upped the ante in an internal memorandum to the medical staff, writing that the "current annual budget" for charity care was "in excess of $500,000." Then at the reconvened hearing, Mr. Lowrey, the senior vice president for fiscal affairs, testified that there was a new charity care program budgeted at $325,000. It clearly was a moving target. Mr. Lowrey also testified that the program was never publicized because hospital officials feared the program might be abused by indigent patients. He added, "I personally feel that would be disruptive." Apparently, it would have been disruptive also to inform staff who talked with incoming patients. A financial counselor at the hospital, called to testify by our lawyers, said he never received any written notice of the new charity policy.[4]

The THFC panel, unmoved by any testimony, voted unanimously to uphold its prior decision and issue the certificate of need. The Legal Services lawyers had asked that the certificate of need be conditioned on (1) increased charity care, (2) more accommodating admission policies, and (3) reestablishing a prenatal clinic that Baptist had closed soon after it was forced to abandon its Whites-only policy in 1966. One commissioner, a hospital administrator who had been particularly vitriolic in the hearings, opined that our proposal amounted to a "tax" on the hospital, "no question," and such a tax would be "outside the law."[5]

The next step up the ladder for us was to file a petition in Davidson County Chancery Court, which had jurisdiction to review decisions of the THFC. The petition alleged that the THFC, among other failures, had made its decision without regard for federal rules requiring a showing of access. In response to our filing, David Stringfield requested help from Robin Beard, the congressman in an adjoining district. Congressman Beard obliged quickly and enthusiastically. On August 18, 1981, he sent a letter to the president of the Legal Services Corporation threatening that "unless something is done to stop what I see as pure harassment . . . I will be in the forefront of those seeking to abolish LSC." This was during the Reagan Administration's effort to do just that. The congressman charged that "After being unsuccessful . . . by using the tax law," we then had been unsuccessful twice before the THFC. His charge falsely flipped Judge Swiggart's favorable ruling in Dana's charity care case, and he conveniently omitted the fact that the MTHSA staff, the MTHSA panel, and THFC staff consistently had agreed with our position.

In the race-baiting style of the day, Congressman Beard further charged, "Legal Services attorneys acknowledge they received aid . . . from the NAACP Legal Defense Fund," as if that were a count against us. He also pointed out that our proof included testimony by a health planner whose "credentials . . . included being a Civil Rights organizer in the South during the early 1960s." In fact, Dr. Kennedy's extensive resume and credentials did not include her civil rights experience. That experience had come to light in questioning after her testimony when an embarrassingly provincial member of the commission challenged her by asking her if she had ever been in the South before. When she responded truthfully that she had and why, he scornfully denounced her as an "interloper."

The president of our board at the time, Dick Lodge, was asked by the *Banner* for a response to Beard's letter. After expressing regret that the Congressman would attempt to use political influence in "a judicial matter, which involves legitimate legal issues and which is outside his congressional district," Lodge lamented, "I'm sorry Beard would raise race as an issue. That is absolutely absurd, irresponsible and demagogic."[6]

The Congressman for the district in which the hospital was located took a different approach from that of Representative Beard. Representative Bill Boner called me to say that his friend Paul Durham, a Baptist pastor who was on the board of the hospital, wanted to talk and might be able to break the logjam. After our lawyers and Tom Schlater had spent "two solid weeks," according to Stewart, trying to settle the case back in the spring, only to be squashed by David Stringfield, and after Stringfield had just written in the hospital's staff *Bulletin* (June 4, 1981) that Baptist was resolved "to resist all efforts by [Legal Services] to interfere with the operation of the hospital," any discussion looked pretty hopeless.

As it turned out, Paul Durham had a much different attitude than that of the hospital administrators, and he was a longtime board member with not a little influence. He was candid and reasonable and anxious to get the matter settled. And he was a character, an old-school evangelical Baptist preacher who was politically connected and quite an entrepreneur. I enjoyed our visits. It probably helped that I had taught for two years in a Baptist mission school in Bangkok before becoming a lawyer. After several visits at Radnor Baptist Church, we worked out some general agreements, and six weeks later, the Legal Services lawyers and Tom Schlater settled the case.

This time, thanks to Paul Durham's power on the board, the agreement stuck. The hospital agreed, among other things, to establish and staff an obstetrical clinic to provide free care for expectant low-income mothers. It announced it would increase its surgical and its internal medicine residency programs, which would provide "more clinical services for needy patients." In his announcement of the settlement, Stewart said, "we are satisfied that the level of services to needy patients will increase to the extent that a continuation of litigation is not appropriate."[7] The next month a spokesman for the hospital announced that the hospital had increased its charity care budget to $800,000.

Although unrelated directly to our challenging the practices at Baptist, there were two other telling developments that followed close to the same time. First, a spokesman for St. Thomas Hospital said its charity budget would be increased from $900,000 to $1.2 million. Second, the city-owned General Hospital took a stand. It began to cut off the avenue other hospitals had used for transferring nonpaying patients to it. General adopted a policy of refusing to accept patients from other hospitals after they had exhausted their fourteen days of Medicaid-funded care. The well-publicized testimony of our clients had hit home. In making the announcement of the new policy, the spokesperson for the hospital proclaimed its new stand, "General is not the dumping ground for other hospitals."[8]

During the time the other lawyers were settling the case, I was preparing a response to an inquiry from LSC concerning Congressman Beard's letter. The staff member in the congressman's office who drafted the letter to LSC had not checked any of the allegations with me before sending it. I pointed out to LSC that though the letter charged that the hospital "experienced continued and unjustified harassment" from us, this chancery lawsuit, in fact, was the first lawsuit we had ever filed against Baptist Hospital. Other than this case, the only involvement we had with the hospital had been to defend clients who had been sued by the hospital. In the end, LSC concluded that we had not violated any of its restrictions and took no action against us, even in the face of the congressman's threat "to try to abolish the LSC totally."

LSC was not the only funder that came under pressure to stop our advocacy. Banking on their success from the year before, the hospital once again complained to the United Way in Nashville. This time, however, the new president, John Goessman, unlike his predecessor and unlike Congressman Beard, contacted me and asked for an explanation. I sent to him brief paragraphs about the experiences of seven of the thirteen clients whose testimony we had presented to the THFC, including these two:

- One was a pregnant woman whose doctor had arranged to deliver her baby at Baptist, but then her husband lost his job and thus his insurance. Her doctor agreed to a payment arrangement, but the hospital would not, and told her she would have to go to General.

- Another was a woman from outside Nashville who suffered from diabetes, arthritis, and anemia whose local doctor had arranged for a Nashville specialist to see her and for her to be admitted to Baptist Hospital. When she arrived, however, the hospital refused to admit her without a $600 deposit. She did not have it. Although her relatives offered to pay a portion of it and then make the long trip home to bring back the rest of the money, the hospital refused to admit her, despite her rapidly deteriorating medical condition.

I explained to John that the purpose of our representation before the THFC was to persuade it to place appropriate conditions on the approval of the certificate of need in order to ensure that Baptist would become an accessible facility for low-income people, people with disabilities, women, and minorities. He got the picture. A few months later, the United Way announced its allocations for 1982, including a 166 percent increase for Legal Services, restoring us to the level of what our grant had been three years earlier, before Mr. Lowrey's letter.

The legacy of the case itself turned out to be not so happy. In 1982, with the new administration and congress in Washington, the opponents of citizen participation in health planning were successful in repealing much of the 1974 Act we had relied on, and the rest of it was repealed in 1986. Baptist Hospital, likewise, did not survive for long. Under the management that had resisted our clients' cause so strenuously, it began experiencing financial difficulties in the 1990s, and in 2001 its assets were sold to the same hospital system that owns St. Thomas. The only good news has been that the proceeds of that sale were used to establish a foundation, The Healing Trust, with a laudable mission: "The Trust aims to increase access to quality, compassionate healthcare for vulnerable populations across Middle Tennessee." In recent years, the Trust has given several very generous grants to the Legal Aid Society in furtherance of that mission.

MIXED RESULTS

There were many healthcare cases with mixed results. The US Supreme Court case of *Alexander v. Choate* was unsuccessful in the end, but along the way it saved substantial benefits for Tennessee's Medicaid recipients. Citing overspending and budget concerns, the Alexander administration in 1980 took steps to cut Medicaid services for low-income people rather than reduce payments to hospitals, whose Medicaid reimbursement rates already were among the highest in the country. In response, Gordon and several lawyers with Rural Legal Services in Cookeville filed a class action suit on behalf of their clients and 300,000 other Medicaid recipients to block the cuts. Initially, they were successful when Judge Morton issued a preliminary injunction that enjoined the state from proceeding because it had not followed federally mandated procedure for making the changes. While the state was considering remedies for that failure, the parties entered into negotiations and were able to reach a settlement on several of the intended cuts. The state abandoned its proposed reductions in outpatient services and physician reimbursements, and it reinstated some of the pharmacy services, all of which was aided considerably by the General Assembly's timely restoration of funding to the program that had been reduced earlier.

Judge Morton took up the case again in April to consider the remaining issue, and in June released his decision that the state's proposed reduction of in-hospital coverage from twenty days per year to fourteen did not have a discriminatory impact on Medicaid recipients with disabilities as the Legal Services lawyers had maintained.[9] On appeal to the Sixth Circuit, however, the plaintiffs got a more sympathetic ear. That court held that plaintiffs' lawyers had, in fact, established a *prima facie* case of discrimination in violation of the Rehabilitation Act of 1973.[10] Unfortunately, that victory was short-lived. The state appealed to the US Supreme Court and that court held, in a nine-to-zero decision, that the fourteen-day limitation was neutral on its face and there was no violation of the Act.[11]

The *Jennings/Choate* case was just one of many during the next several years, both individual cases and class actions, that sought to enforce our clients' rights under Medicaid and convince administrators of the wisdom of a more generous reading of Medicaid's limitations. Lawsuits and administrative fair hearings could accomplish only so much, however. If more of our clients were to get access to effective healthcare, it would require systemic reforms, and that could happen only with legislative and administrative changes. The healthcare providers certainly had lobbyists who were looking out for their interests. Our clients would need the same kind of advocacy if their interests were to be served. Fortunately, during this time Gordon and other Legal Services lawyers were gaining the confidence of some legislators and administrators in state government who understood the medical needs of the poor. These relationships would bear fruit as the decade went on.

NURSING HOMES

The elderly poor face special health problems, and one of the most distressing set of problems has been those concerning admission to and conditions in nursing homes. The first problem is getting in the door and staying there. In 1984, Gordon filed suit on behalf of John Doe, a seventy-seven-year-old man with diabetes who had suffered a stroke and had been summarily denied admission to a nursing home, even though he would have qualified for assistance under Medicaid. The state had contracted with E.D.S. Federal, a Texas corporation, to perform the "pre-admission evaluations" (PAE) that were required by Medicaid, and the company had declined Mr. Doe's application on the grounds that he was harmful to himself and others. This was in spite of the fact that the hospital that was treating him had told E.D.S. that Mr. Doe, who had lost one leg and was about to have the other one amputated, was not harmful. Furthermore, there was no legal basis for the ruling: Medicaid had no regulation prohibiting admission based on whether the patient was harmful. The company gave Mr. Doe no opportunity to appeal the denial, and after his second attempt at admission, told him no further evidence would be considered.

Discovery in the lawsuit and negotiations that followed its submission to a federal magistrate revealed that there were approximately five hundred to six hundred people in the same predicament as Mr. Doe, Medicaid-eligible people who had been summarily denied nursing home care without due process. After nearly three years, a settlement was reached with the state. The lawyer for the Department of Health agreed that the admissions process had been "unwieldy, slow, and frustrating," and provisions were included in an agreed order to ensure due process. Those provisions continue to this day to regulate the admission process, protecting the rights of thousands of nursing home applicants every year.

Ah, but wait, the nursing home industry then put in place other admission hurdles. Lobbyists for the industry convinced the Tennessee Department of Health to implement policies that allowed the nursing homeowners to designate only a certain limited number of beds in their facilities as Medicaid beds. That meant they could improve their bottom line by reserving beds for more lucrative private pay patients, while still participating in the Medicaid program and using state money only when they needed to fill the gap, obviously to the detriment of the poor elderly and disabled people who as a result of that designation had fewer beds available to them. Gordon and Pam Wright, together with Legal Defense Fund (LDF) lawyers, filed suit against the state in 1987 to challenge that discriminatory policy and to get beds for two clients who were affected in different ways.

Mildred Linton was severely disabled from rheumatoid arthritis and in a nursing home receiving skilled level nursing care paid for by Medicaid, but her condition had stabilized to the extent that Medicaid officials determined she no longer needed that level of care, so they would pay only for intermediate level care. The nursing home where she lived had eighty-seven intermediate care beds, but under the new state-sanctioned policy only forty were designated as Medicaid beds, all filled, and the nursing home determined that the waiting list was so long for those forty beds there would be none available for her anytime soon. Consequently, Ms. Linton was informed that she would have to leave the place where she had lived for four years, a place close to her family, with no assurance a Medicaid bed would be available for her elsewhere. Too bad, but you have to go. You cannot have one of these vacant intermediate care beds we have here. We are saving them for rich people who can pay us more than Medicaid will pay.

Belle Carney, the other client, was eighty-nine years old and suffered from Alzheimer's disease. After a two-week hospitalization she was to be discharged to a nursing home, but no Medicaid-designated beds could be found. Consequently, Ms. Carney, who was Black, was shunted around among a series of unlicensed facilities. The federal class action suit on behalf of these two and thirty-four thousand other Medicaid recipients who potentially could be treated the same way, went through multiple hearings in district court, three trips to the Sixth Circuit, and an unsuccessful petition for *certiorari* to the US Supreme Court filed by the nursing homes.

The district court, after trial in the initial round, found that, as the Legal Services lawyers had alleged, the state's limited bed policy violated several provisions of the Medicaid Act and because of the way Ms. Carney was treated, violated Title VI of the Civil Rights Act of 1964.[12] The court ordered the state to submit a remedial plan, which it then did after negotiations. The plan, among other things, required first-come, first-served admissions in facilities that accept Medicaid; prohibited involuntary discharge based on payment source; provided protections for patients if the facility decided to withdraw from Medicaid; imposed a two-year exclusion from rejoining if a facility withdrew; and promised rules for civil rights compliance and enforcement. The court adopted the plan without amendment.

Then twenty-five days after the court's final order, five nursing homes sought to intervene. The district court ruled the nursing homes and their large Washington, DC, law firm came with too little, too late, but the

Sixth Circuit reversed and said the district court must hear them.[13] Hoping to appease the intervenors, the plaintiffs and the state modified the remedial plan to make the penalties less onerous, and after a hearing for all the parties, the district court approved the revised plan, but the nursing homes still were not happy and appealed again. The state and the plaintiffs, having labored to devise a plan that met the complaints of the industry, moved to dismiss the nursing homes' appeal, but as before, the circuit court allowed it. It let them in the door, but then after hearing the case, held against them, finding that the remedial plan was not overbroad, was consistent with the Medicaid Act, and was not an impairment of contracts. The court never got to the question of the bed designation policy's disparate impact on Black patients, reasoning that the approved remedial plan took care of that.[14]

It was a dramatic victory with a wide impact, but because of that, and predictably so, the battle was not over. After failing in the courts, the nursing homes' lawyers then sought to have the Tennessee General Assembly pass legislation that would have circumvented the court's rulings. This legislative effort neatly corresponded with the time in Washington when various opponents of LSC were successful in having Congress prohibit LSC-funded lawyers from handling class action lawsuits and legislative advocacy. That would have left our clients without representation at this pivotal point had it not been for the brave decision of Gordon and Michele Johnson to leave our LSC-funded organization and establish the Tennessee Justice Center. They took Mildred Linton and Belle Carney's case with them, waded into the legislature, and with the help of sympathetic members were able to stop the industry's bill from being passed.

The Linton case highlighted but did not resolve one significant issue. Developing the proof of disparate impact on Black patients in the case had been especially difficult because the US Department of Health and Human Services (HHS) lacked data that linked racial identifiers to medical treatment records. That lack of linked data was a persistent problem, and Gordon raised it specifically in a 1993 case on behalf of Vareda Madison-Hughes, this time joined not only by the LDF but also by nearly thirty other civil rights groups. Unfortunately, both the district court and the court of appeals ruled that while the 1964 Civil Rights Act required data collection, there were no standards in the Act specifying what data was required, and in that situation the courts must defer to

HHS's administrative discretion as to what was sufficient.[15] Case over, but all was not lost.

Several years later Gordon learned from former Surgeon General David Satcher, an acquaintance from when Satcher had been president of Meharry, that in fact the claims raised in the *Madison-Hughes* case had prompted conscientious people at HHS to reexamine its responsibilities under the Civil Rights Act. Satcher, who himself had highlighted health inequality based on race and criticized healthcare disparities, told Gordon that HHS had begun making available to health researchers Social Security and Medicare eligibility records that contained racial identifiers, which the researchers then could cross-match with treatment records. That had the effect of advancing research and understanding of racial disparities in health status and racial discrimination in patient treatment. The research documented what previously had been only anecdotal: the sharp racial differences in the treatment of patients with identical medical conditions. It revealed such discrepancies as, one, much less pain relief being afforded to Black patients with identical diagnoses as White and, two, much more frequent amputations among Black diabetes patients than White. Belle Carney's treatment in Memphis, being shuttled around among a series of unlicensed facilities without access to a licensed nursing home, did not happen in a colorless vacuum.

The significance of the *Madison-Hughes* case in the development of the data is recognized to this day. One of the leading researchers, Sara Rosenbaum, founding chair of the Department of Health Policy at the George Washington University School of Public Health and Health Sciences, did so in a recent piece for the journal *Milbank Quarterly*. Arguing that more complete and current data is needed now in order to spur effective corrective action, she reminded her readers, "this is not a new issue." She credited previous calls for useful information, including reports of federal advisory panels, and then specifically credited the "equal justice advocates" who brought the case of *Madison-Hughes v. Shalala* more than twenty-five years earlier.[16]

———————

Nursing home access issues are frustrating, but they pale beside the horror of conditions that have existed inside some of the facilities. In 1987, one of the people in Tennessee most concerned about this issue was himself a nursing home owner, and he was in the singular position of having just been elected governor. Ned Ray McWherter had been Speaker of the House for fourteen years, and famously claimed in his campaign that if elected governor, all he would need to get started on the job would be a cup of coffee and three vanilla wafers. It was not an empty boast. Two items that were included in the governor's initial legislative package are of special interest to our story. He proposed a major initiative to match local dollars with federal Medicaid money in order to increase indigent care, the subject of the next section in this chapter, and he proposed to levy civil penalties against nursing homes for any health or safety violations. This was a reversal by McWherter, who as Speaker had repeatedly killed nursing home reform bills.

The issue had been brewing in the General Assembly for years, pushed most vigorously by Representative Pam Gaia of Memphis and the Coalition for Nursing Home Reform, with occasional collaboration from Gordon and Linda O'Neal at TALS working on behalf of our clients. With McWherter's election and new perspective, the industry's Tennessee Health Care Association, which had opposed any reform, now saw the handwriting on the wall and modified its opposition somewhat, but the two sides still were far apart.

Two months into the legislative session, the increasingly impatient governor charged Representative Tommy Burnett with finding a solution and coming up with a bill that would pass. In prototypical style, Burnett brought the major players together in a room, including Gordon and the three lobbyists for the industry, and he kept them there. Jim O'Hara's story in the *Tennessean* several days later dramatically described the process employed by the colorful Burnett, who for a few years at that point was between terms in federal prison:

> For two marathon nights and a morning last week, Rep. Tommy Burnett played preacher, poker player, and psychiatrist for nursing home representatives and reformers.
>
> The cast of characters was jammed around a conference table littered with papers and empty Coke bottles as they tried to negotiate civil fine legislation for nursing homes violating health and safety standards.[17]

O'Hara goes on to describe quite vividly several of the characters around the table and the strain of the negotiations on them, including this gem: "As the nights wore on, the wings of hair on the balding head of Gordon Bonnyman . . . took flight, standing out like the wings on a B-1." More substantively, he also describes the progress that was made in the negotiations, which by then had stretched over more than a week. At that point, Burnett called on Mike Engle, the lawyer for the Department of Health, which regulated nursing homes, to draft a bill that reflected the status of the negotiations. Mike skillfully did that, incorporating much of what Gordon had advocated, reworking it, and making it more palatable. The result was a bill that easily passed the House and the Senate and became law. It provided, among other provisions, fines and admission freezes against substandard homes, fines for violations of patient care, and a private cause of action to enforce state standards.

As it turned out, the benefits of that legislation were not limited to Tennessee. In the fall of that year, Gordon had a significant role in helping convince Congress to take steps to improve nursing home conditions throughout the nation. Sometimes state enforcement is not a sufficient remedy and federal enforcement is needed as well. To emphasize the need for congressional action, Gordon brought to Washington for testimony a Nashville woman whose mother previously had suffered horribly from neglect and mistreatment at what was then Belmont Healthcare Center. As a result of her graphic testimony before the House Committee on the Budget and the advocacy of many others around the country, Congress was persuaded to act. Andy Schneider, formerly co-counsel with Gordon in the *Newsom* case, now staff for a key House subcommittee chaired by Representative Henry Waxman, was involved in the drafting of legislation. Consequently, a number of provisions modeled on the Tennessee Act were included in the broad nursing home reforms that Congress adopted as a part of the Omnibus Budget Reconciliation Act of 1987.

HEALTHCARE FUNDING

The other commitment of the McWherter administration that was important to our clients had grown out of the governor's visit to the

Regional Medical Center ("The Med") in Memphis during his election campaign. At that large, county-owned hospital, he came face-to-face with inadequate medical care for low-income people and the plight of a major hospital trying to provide care to them but itself being in a perilous financial situation. He said then and there he was going to do something about it. What he quickly did resulted from the initiative of an alert number-crunching state Medicaid official who seriously studied federal regulations, not only during office hours, but at night as well.

Steve Reed and Gordon had developed a respectful relationship when they were on either side of several lawsuits. They had met in negotiations and established trust in one another. One night in November 1986, soon after the gubernatorial election, Reed was reviewing administrative rulings by a board of HHS when he came across reference to federal regulatory amendments allowing the use of donations to satisfy the state's match for its Medicaid grant. The impetus for the amendment, adopted a year earlier, had been the Reagan Administration's insistence on private charity rather than government funding for any program serving the poor.

Reed called Gordon and told him about his discovery. Sometime before that, Gordon happened to have been at a conference in Tallahassee while a fight was going on in the Florida legislature to repeal a tax on hospitals. The two Tennesseans put together the Reagan Administration's charity contention with the forsaken Florida tax and came up with a funding mechanism that could substantially enhance Medicaid in the Volunteer State. The mechanism they devised would mean that funding would increase at the same rate as medical cost inflation and Medicaid would stop cannibalizing the state budget, while the state would be enabled to provide much-needed payments to hospitals that served a disproportionate number of low-income people.

Instead of a tax, the proposal they submitted to the governor's staff called for donations. The governor adopted the plan, sent legislation to the General Assembly, and it was put into effect less than eight months after Reed's phone call. Not all hospitals participated, but those that did, particularly The Med and General Hospital in Nashville, reaped the benefits of increased Medicaid funding for their services. Their initial donations of $19 million were matched by new federal funds and produced $63 million of increased Medicaid funds for the state. In addition to the grants to hospitals serving a disproportionate share of indigents, the increased funds were used to finance expanded coverage for pregnant women and infants, and the balance was used to restore the annual inpatient hospital coverage back up to twenty days, thus reversing the decision of the previous administration that had been allowed by the Supreme Court in the *Jennings* case.

One year later, in a cynical negation, the same federal Health Care Financing Administration (HCFA) that had adopted the amended regulation authorizing the donations disallowed Tennessee's donation plan. The state appealed to the HHS Appeals Board, but fearing losing the appeal, Finance Commissioner David Manning, Gordon, and the governor's task force on indigent healthcare began looking for a fallback position, alternative ways of coming up with the needed match money. A hospital gross receipts tax, similar to the one Gordon saw in Florida, was floated for a while, with predictable apocalyptic opposition from the providers. The governor remained publicly neutral on this explosive tax issue, but his budget staff warned the hospitals that if the disallowance of the donated funds plan were upheld by the appeals board, the resulting shortfall would force a major cut in payments to hospitals. This got the attention of the industry and brought forth a compromise that was not a tax but a "hospital license fee." Seizing the day, not waiting for the HCFA appeal, and illustrating the alacrity inspired by the financial office's warning, the legislature passed the license fee plan. When after ten months the appeals board reversed HCFA and approved the donation plan, Tennessee used both the donation and the new fee, generating enough federal match to liberalize its already most-generous-in-the-nation hospital payments and removed any annual limit on inpatient coverage for Medicaid patients.

With that success, the next step was to move to the other large healthcare cost center: nursing homes. A nursing home license fee was instituted in 1990, resulting in $112.5 million new funding that was used by the homes to cover the additional cost of complying with the congressionally mandated reforms and by the state to expand home- and community-based care. By July 1991, Tennessee's funding mechanism was raising more than $350 million from all providers, and when combined with federal matching funds, it generated over $1.1 billion, or 48 percent of the state's total Medicaid budget. Consequently, the state was able to extend coverage to more people than ever, increasing the number of those eligible from 508,000 people before Steve Reed's call to 879,000 at this point. And the significance extended beyond Tennessee. Within a few short years, forty-eight other states had adopted donation or provider assessment plans similar to what Tennessee had pioneered, increasing the availability of healthcare for millions more low-income people across the nation.

When HHS in 1991 tried amending its 1985 regulation to, among other things, limit the amount of provider revenue that could be used as Medicaid match, Senator Jim Sasser and Representative Jim Cooper, working in tandem with the governor's office, played important roles in opposition. Finally, negotiations between the National Governors Association and the Office of Management and Budget, with significant Tennessee involvement, resulted in amendments to the regulation that modified the provider revenue limit but grandfathered in Tennessee at its higher current rate.

The next struggle came as a result of federal legislation, effective January 1992, that banned provider-specific taxes on medical facilities being used as Medicaid match. The industry, led by the Tennessee Hospital Association (THA), seized this occasion to try to escape paying the licensing fee or anything at all for the millions of dollars its members were receiving. In response, at a press conference in March, more than forty groups, including the American Cancer Society, AARP, the Catholic bishops, and the Tennessee Healthcare Campaign (THCC), emphasized the gravity of the situation and the threat to the health of people in the state. With Gordon's help, the state developed a compromise proposal that met the strictures of the new federal legislation and spread some of the pain by establishing a privilege tax not only on healthcare facilities, but also modestly on other entities. Finally, after more public pressure, THA voted to modify its position. There still was much haggling and mutual recrimination to come at the legislature, but in the end, the privilege tax was enacted and went into effect July 1, 1992. Even then, as long and as difficult as that fight had been, the governor's efforts and Legal Services' involvement were not over.

TENNCARE

David Manning and Medicaid director Manny Martins knew that even with the privilege tax and other funding mechanisms, the Medicaid program in Tennessee was not financially sustainable. At some point soon they would need to begin making cuts in a number of the services it provided. In addition, the hospitals and THA continued to vigorously oppose the privilege tax that was funding the program, even to the point of filing a federal lawsuit seeking to undo it. Manning began looking for alternatives and found one in an obscure part of the Medicaid Act, Section 1115, which provided for the possibility of a waiver that would allow states to develop "innovative solutions to a variety of health and welfare problems" deviating from some Medicaid rules and requirements.

With the governor's blessing, Manning and Martins in discussions with Gordon, apart from the Medicaid Task Force, came up with the beginning of an innovative plan that would use managed care to serve not only people eligible for Medicaid, but also be available to other uninsured and/or uninsurable people in Tennessee on a sliding fee scale based on their income. The plan would use savings from managed care and be funded, one, by shifting disproportionate share funds from hospitals like The Med and General; two, by capturing local and state healthcare funds that had been used for a variety of previously uncovered medical issues that now would be covered by the state plan; and three, by eliminating various subsidies to hospitals. Other revenue would come from a slight increase in federal funding, plus premiums, deductibles, and copayments from people who chose to be covered but were above Medicaid income limits. One great advantage of the plan was that it would enable the administration to put an end to the constant carping about the tax.

When Manning and Martins presented their plan to the governor in early 1993, he was interested, but not convinced. He said he would come to the next meeting of the Medicaid Task Force where Manning and Martins would unveil it. The morning of that meeting, Manning called Gordon to say that all their technical discussions about the plan might not carry the day, "The governor's heart is in the right place, but he cares about stories. We need stories by this afternoon." He knew Legal Services had the stories; clients and their stories were our work every day.

Gordon turned to Pam Cardoso. Pam was in her late twenties when she came to work as a paralegal with Gordon, Linda Narrow, and other lawyers in the Nashville office. Her principal responsibility was helping our clients navigate the Medicaid maze to get the services they needed for themselves or for family members. She was an advocate, and she came to that role with experience herself. Her ten-year-old son Sammy had developmental and intellectual disabilities, plus he was blind, and she had been an advocate for him all his life, as well as for others. Because of limited family income, Sammy received services from Medicaid that helped him and freed up Pam enough that instead of caring for him 24/7, she could work outside the home for part of the day. She had been president of the Association for Retarded Citizen of Davidson County, had been named volunteer of the year by the Community Rehabilitation Agency of Tennessee and parent of the year by Middle Tennessee Association for Persons with Severe Handicaps.

Pam agreed right away to go to the Task Force meeting that afternoon, and she took with her two other mothers whose children had special healthcare needs. At the meeting she talked about Sammy's difficulties, his blindness and developmental disabilities, the Medicaid services he received, and the devastating effect losing those services would have on him and their family. If the cuts being discussed had to be made, it was a very real possibility that Sammy would have to be put in an institution. As Pam sat there in that meeting with Sammy cradled in her lap, she told the panel and the governor she could not stand the thought of doing that.

Not many days later, on April 8, 1993, at a joint session of the General Assembly, the governor announced the new plan, now called TennCare. He could ask for the Section 1115 waiver without legislative action, and he could institute the plan by executive order, but he needed the legislature to make one change in the state statute concerning Medicaid eligibility in order to satisfy one requirement of the waiver application. As he announced his plan and made his plea to the legislature, he did not do it alone. He had invited Pam, Sammy, and their family down to the well of the House to be with him, and they sat on the front row as he spoke.

The required legislation passed quickly in the House, but the hospital association mounted a concerted effort to block it in the Senate and almost succeeded. The determined governor, however, by a combination of realistic threats and a three-month early cessation of the hated hospital tax, ended their resistance. The Senate approved the needed change, and the application for the waiver was sent to HHS in Baltimore. And there it sat for months, its inertia aided by the concerted efforts of the highly-paid lobbyists for the medical industry to derail it at HHS. In an attempt to blunt their sabotage, the governor asked several advocates to follow them to Baltimore and present the case for the plan. Charlotte Collins, general counsel at The Med who had arranged the visit that so moved McWherter during his campaign, Tony Garr of the Health Care Campaign, Gordon, and a client of his made the trip in a rented van, which, in a mocking reference to the travel style of the industry's lobbyists, they dubbed "The People's Learjet."

In spite of the inaction at HHS, Gordon and David Manning had begun working through a checklist of what needed to be done before the governor's ambitious start date of January 1. Manny Martins and his department proceeded full steam ahead as if it were a done deal, enrolling people, signing up managed care organizations, and setting up the procedures that would be needed to run the program. Adinah Robertson, our community education coordinator, was enlisted to make sure communications from the state to potential enrollees were in plain English they could understand, not government jargon. It was a concerted effort to meet the looming, though unapproved, start date.

In truth, approval of much less consequential changes had routinely taken a year or more of bureaucratic consideration before being granted, but for Governor McWherter this was not routine. He had started this daring venture even at a late date when he was a self-declared lame duck, and he was going to see it through before the end of his flight. When no waiver had been received by early November, impatient and resolute, he went not to Baltimore to haggle with HHS, but to Washington to see his young friend from next door in Arkansas, President Bill Clinton. They had been friends for a long time. The waiver arrived a few days later on November 18, six weeks before the massive innovation was to take off.

Thanks to devoted state employees working extra hours and through Thanksgiving and Christmas holidays, and even the governor himself staffing the phones and enrolling eligible people, it did take off on January 1, 1994. It was an innovation that, though it would have many difficulties along the way, at one point insured healthcare for more than a million people in Tennessee, including almost four hundred thousand previously uninsured. The effort also built strong personal relationships.

The governor later said that more than any single individual, Pam had influenced his decision to enact TennCare, but as it turned out, Pam would live to see only the first ten days of TennCare. She had leukemia. When the governor learned of her illness, he began calling the hospital to check on her. A later newspaper article reported on his commitment to her: "I called her the night before she died and made her a promise to do everything I could to make TennCare work so it would be there for her little boy."[18]

Several years after McWherter left office, Gordon was nominated to receive a national award from Families U.S.A., for which the former governor wrote a letter of support. He joked about how many times and for how many different things Gordon had filed lawsuits against him as Speaker and as governor, and he mused that one of the nicest things he could say about Gordon was that since he had left office Gordon had not sued him once. He then went on to write,

> On many occasions during my time as Governor of Tennessee, my Administration sought Gordon's advice, support and assistance on a variety of important issues. This was especially true of our efforts to improve the Medicaid program where our work together finally resulted in healthcare coverage for almost 400,000 uninsured Tennesseans. I am proud of my Administration's work with Gordon and I am convinced that we were able to do more as a result of his able leadership.

Governor McWherter's signature program was a landmark in the delivery of healthcare in this country. Subsequent governors and legislatures, often for ill-informed reasons, chipped away at its benefits and limited its eligibility, but it remained a model. Many of its improvements anticipated by more than fifteen years advances on the national level with the adoption of the Affordable Care Act in 2010: expanding Medicaid to low-income people beyond the narrow eligibility categories, raising the income limits for Medicaid, instituting a sliding scale for moderate income people to buy into Medicaid coverage, and insuring people with preexisting conditions.

TELL IT SIMPLY

A chapter about healthcare advocacy would not be complete without a section on community education, a vital part in every area of our practice, but particularly effective here. Beginning in the early 1980s, that was the responsibility of Adinah Robertson, who brought her rare combination of intelligence, enthusiasm, creativity, and hard work to the job. A Phi Beta Kappa graduate of Vanderbilt, with a master's degree in social work from Tulane, she had worked in several social work positions, including a time at Vanderbilt Hospital, where she went in each morning charged with the mantra she and her husband had devised, "Humanize the hospital." Her empathy with our clients and their difficulties may have been informed by her own dealing with a disability as results of an injury at birth, but whether that is true or not, it is most certain that her empathy and her commitment were motivated by a deep religious conviction.

The previous section of this chapter mentions in passing her part in the launch of TennCare, but that involvement was not insignificant and deserves more than a mention. One of the talents Adinah had developed and honed in the more than ten years with us at that point was the ability to take complicated legal issues and translate them into plain English. Her goal was to publish pamphlets, brochures, and even longer publications in language a person with a fifth-grade education could read and understand. This meant particular attention to vocabulary, the number of syllables in a word, the length and syntax of a sentence, and the size of paragraphs. She had limits for each and would not go above them.

The initial communications from the state to its target population for TennCare did not meet those standards and predictably fell flat. One letter from the governor evoked only a 14 percent response. Gordon volunteered Adinah to help, and she did, working through Thanksgiving to improve this and other communications. As was her practice, after she finished her first draft, she took it to a group of low-income people to review. She found a social agency that was open over the holiday and offered to bring food if they would gather a group for her. After the folks ate, she distributed copies of her letter, which was half the length of the governor's, assured the group, "don't be worried about hurting my feelings," and they responded enthusiastically. She took their criticism and questions, reworked her draft where necessary, and gave it to Gordon to take up the Hill. This time the letter from the governor evoked an 82 percent response.

For Adinah, it was not always a matter of writing; community education also involved gimmicks and shameless acting. She would dress up in outlandish costumes and tell corny, very corny, jokes at gatherings of low-income people to explain legal solutions, opportunities, requirements, or rights. She was and is naturally shy, but one would not have known it when she was dramatizing a legal issue for a group.

Gimmicks also worked. One of the most effective gimmicks she and Gordon came up with was a wallet card a person could use if refused emergency treatment at a hospital. The citation to the emergency care law was printed on one side. On the flip side there were two short forms, one to be signed by the hospital representative refusing care and the other by the physician authorizing the refusal. Gordon claimed that in a medical emergency "it may be the next best thing to having your lawyer in your hip pocket." The *Hastings Center Report*, a journal of bioethics, printed a replica of the card in an essay entitled "Adam Smith in the Emergency Room" and the *ABA Journal* mentioned it in an article "Dumping the Poor—Private Hospitals Risk Suits."[19]

The largest project Adinah undertook was the research and writing, with attorney Beverly Fisher in our Clarksville office, of the *Guide to the Medicare Supplement Insurance Maze*. The supplemental policies were relatively new in the early 1980s and largely unregulated. Bev had several clients who had encountered problems with the product: uneven coverage, surprise billings, agents' false promises, and cancelation after claims. In response to these and other problems, the Department of Insurance drafted proposed rules and held a public hearing for comments on them. Familiar with inept regulation of insurance from her previous work on industrial insurance, Bev testified at the hearing on behalf of three clients and argued for stricter controls. When the rules as adopted did not go far enough, Bev determined that we needed to educate seniors about the policies and the pitfalls before others got into the situations her clients had faced.

Together with Leslie Creech, a paralegal in the Nashville office, Bev developed the first *Guide*, which was very well received in the community. By the time Adinah came to work with us, it needed to be revised and updated, and the result was a 190-page booklet, in plain English, with charts and pictographs, explaining the product and comparing in detail each policy sold in Tennessee. We printed a couple thousand copies of the *Guide*, distributed them to senior centers, medical facilities, and other likely places. The national financial magazine *Changing Times* called it "the best we've seen on medigap insurance" and the *Clearinghouse Review* featured it as the cover story for its June 1985 issue.[20] The HCA Foundation gave us a grant to print seven thousand copies of the next edition.

Because insurance companies occasionally changed their policy offerings either due to new regulations or for business reasons, it was necessary to publish updated editions from time-to-time. Adinah and Bev published nine editions over the years, and by 1990 expanded the scope of its information to include Medicare itself, so that the title then became *The Legal Services Guide to Medicare and Insurance.* They printed forty-one thousand copies, funded in part by AARP, and still ran out.

Not all of Adinah's publications covered subjects regulated by the state, but when that was the case, her practice was to verify the accuracy of her information with someone in the responsible department. If they could convince her and the lawyer she was working with that she was wrong on a particular point, she wanted to correct it. We did not want it to come back to bite us later. This care built trust, and in some instances became a form of advocacy. An example of that was her development with Gordon of an eight-page pamphlet about an extremely complicated and generally unknown program, Medicaid Spend Down, a program designed to help families who suddenly have been pauperized by large medical expenses.

In the drafted pamphlet, using pictures as well as words, Adinah listed the bills a family could use to establish eligibility, and in addition to the big expenses, she included medical supplies and over-the-counter medicines. The state's eligibility director, while reviewing the draft, flagged this as incorrect. It was not their policy to count those expenses. When Gordon and Adinah showed her that federal regulations allowed them, the state promptly changed its policy to follow suit. No fuss, no federal class action lawsuit, just good collaboration to help our mutual clients.

By the time Adinah retired in 2018, there were nearly sixty publications listed on our las.org website that she had produced and updated over the years, eighteen of which had been translated into Spanish. Some were self-help instructions, some were informational only. They covered a wide range of issues, with titles like "Are You and Your Baby Safe?," "Unemployed Because of a Military Move?," "Bill Collectors," "Renter Rights," "Behind on Your House Payment?," and "Earned Income Tax Credits."

Two of her pamphlets, complete with color illustrations and calendars showing deadlines, dealt with Social Security issues, the subject of the next chapter.

CHAPTER 18

Social Security Disability

> Give justice to the weak and the
> fatherless; maintain the right of
> the afflicted and the destitute.
>
> —PSALMS 82:3 (RSV)

David Ettinger still remembers the first Social Security disability case he handled as a new Legal Services lawyer in Gallatin. It provoked an embarrassing rebuke from a federal magistrate, temporarily. His client, a widow who lived in Wilson County, had a condition that caused severe adhesions in her stomach. She had applied for disability benefits because she no longer could work due to the complications associated with those adhesions, and the administration found that she qualified for partial benefits, but because of the finding as to the onset date, she was not qualified for the full amount she had anticipated. On her own, she appealed the partially favorable decision, seeking full benefits. That backfired. In its reconsideration, the Disability Determination Section, in a complete reversal, decided that she never had been disabled.

Frustrated and desperate, the woman came to Legal Services. Jane Fleishman, a talented paralegal in the Gallatin office, took her case before an administrative law judge. She lost. Then Jane petitioned the appeals council, but was unsuccessful there as well, despite having submitted supportive evidence, including narrative reports by the client's physician describing the laparoscopies she had performed and the extent of the adhesions. The physician's reports confirmed the client's abdominal pain and was fully supportive of a finding of disability, but to no avail. At this point the only option remaining was to go to federal court.

David took over the case, and coached by one of his colleagues, filed an extensive complaint with attachments seeking review of the appeals council's ruling. The case was assigned to Magistrate Kent Sandidge, who soon thereafter issued an order requiring that both parties, represented respectively by David and the US Attorney, file a motion for summary judgment and supporting brief within thirty days. "Being a bit nervous, I think I spent sixty hours on the brief," David remembers. Reflecting further insecurity, he personally delivered his motion and brief to the clerk's office in Nashville and had the clerk stamp his copy as filed, a wise move as it turned out.

Several months later, the magistrate completed his review and issued his report and recommendation, which, shockingly, began with a damning statement about the young lawyer's work: "This case is pending on the Defendant's [the government's] motion for summary judgement, the Plaintiff having failed to file any motion or any brief." Fortunately, after that inauspicious beginning for David, the tone of the magistrate's findings changed and the rest of the report was favorable for his client. The magistrate recommended to the federal judge that the decision of the administration be reversed and that the case be remanded for payment of benefits.

David had won for his client solely on the basis of the laboriously produced complaint and the overwhelming evidence he and Jane had submitted, including the strong support from his client's treating physician, even without the required motion and brief. And he had won a recommendation calling for an immediate reversal and payment. Looking back now with more than forty years of experience, David notes that rather than a reversal it is much more common for a judge to remand a case to the administration for a new hearing: "I did not receive another reversal for several years after that." Even with the resounding victory, however, the young lawyer did not want to leave the case without setting the record straight and clearing his name. He hand delivered to the magistrate copies of his stamped motion and brief to prove his innocence. Recognizing the mistake in his own office, Magistrate Sandidge then issued an amended report and recommendation exonerating David and reiterating his favorable decision.

The importance of cases like this for our clients cannot be overstated. For most people whose cases we handled, the success in the case was the difference between having an income and not having any at all. Furthermore, qualification for Social Security disability benefits or for Supplemental Security Income (SSI) benefits could mean eligibility also for Medicare and/or Medicaid, and thus be the difference between having healthcare or not. It is life-changing.

Another case illustrates dramatically how life-changing it can be, not only materially but also emotionally. This was a case handled not by David, but by his spouse, Kitty Calhoon. Kitty, a graduate of Swarthmore, had been a high school history teacher before she went to law school at Northeastern, a school renowned for its internships in poverty law and public interest, which is where she met David. She graduated a year earlier than he did, and in 1978 we recruited her to come work in our Nashville office. David followed. Their initial plan was to be in Nashville for two years and then move to the Northwest, where David is from, but now he says, "We stayed in Nashville because we both loved our jobs."

Kitty did not specialize in Social Security as David did eventually, but as was the case with most lawyers in the general section and the branch offices, it was one of the many types of problems she handled over the years. Her description of the general section illustrates our wide-open practice in those days, "I did name changes, expungements, utility cut-offs, hospital bill cases, legitimations, paternities, dependent/neglect cases, Metro Social Services benefits, private landlord/tenant (which mainly meant trying to reduce the amount of back rent owed using uninhabitability claims or recouping a security deposit), and of course public and subsidized housing evictions." And Social Security cases.

Kitty inherited Ms. Wilson's case soon after arriving at Legal Services and remembers nothing special about the facts or the law involved. What was special to Kitty was the countenance of her client when she met her, "She looked very run down and rag tag." It was as if she had given up on life, but Kitty did not give up on the case. Previous advocates had not been successful at the administrative level or in federal district court, but at the Sixth Circuit Kitty was successful and won a judgment that not only resulted in future benefits, but because the case had been pending so long, also resulted in Ms. Wilson being awarded more than $30,000 in back benefits. Kitty called her client with the good news and sent her a copy of the order. Shortly thereafter a grateful Ms. Wilson came to the office to see Kitty to thank her and to bring her a small gift. Recalling that visit now years later, Kitty can still picture her client, "She was transformed. She wore a nice (but not fancy) dress, had her hair done, and carried herself with dignity." She had a new lease on life.

Later on, David was able to use the possibility of recoveries of back benefits like Ms. Wilson's to entice more private lawyers to take Social Security cases. Recoveries like that left room for them to get a decent fee. In the early 1980s, he organized an all-day continuing legal education (CLE) seminar at Volunteer State Community College in Gallatin attended by about forty attorneys, introducing them to the practice and teaching them the procedures. One of the speakers he brought in was Nancy Shor, executive director of the recently formed National Organization of Social Security Claimant Representatives. A few years later, he organized a similar but more advanced CLE program at Tennessee State University, this time attracting about one hundred attorneys, reflecting the growing interest in the field.

One of the hindrances for private attorneys handling disability cases was the inability of the client to pay for medical exams and other necessary evidence. Likewise, the attorneys understandably were hesitant to invest their own money in this new and uncertain undertaking. In 1984, David persuaded our board of directors to set aside a revolving fund of $3,000 to make available to private attorneys to pay for evidence development in cases we prescreened and referred to them. David would approve the use of money from the fund to pay for such things as psychological or medical consultations, and if the case were successful and there were substantial enough back benefits, the lawyer and client would repay the fund. David also would be available to consult with the attorneys and from time-to-time he would conduct training sessions for them. By doing this, he was able to build up a list of lawyers who were competent in this singular field and were willing to handle cases that otherwise we either would have taken or been compelled to turn down for lack of staff.

For several years after he moved to the Nashville office, David compiled and wrote a review of Social Security and SSI cases decided in the Sixth Circuit. He was a one-person reporting service. We published the review, sent free copies to other legal aid organizations, and sold copies to private practitioners, for a nominal fee to cover our costs, and at the request of a clerk of the court, we sent copies to be distributed to judges throughout the Sixth Circuit. In 2008, the Social Security Administration, recognizing David's expertise, and fulfilling the prophecy of his longtime assistant, Melba McNairy, appointed him to be an administrative law judge, first in New York City, and later, following his and Kitty's preference, back in Nashville, where now he presides over appeals brought by advocates he encouraged and trained in earlier days.

While David was responsible for bringing many more practitioners into the field, they could not reasonably be expected to take on cases that involved major challenges to the administration of the program or that involved similar procedural complaints common to a large number of people. In those cases, we still were uniquely in a position to help. The prime example and the largest case of that kind we handled was the *Samuels* case.

The problem the case addressed first surfaced in 1980 when Legal Services lawyers around the state began to notice that a disproportionate number of people who came to our offices after being denied Social Security disability benefits had in common that they had been evaluated by the same group of doctors. A state agency, the Disability Determination Section (DDS), which made the determinations of who qualified for the benefits, had in turn contracted with an organization of doctors named Suburban Internal Medicine Group to perform the medical evaluations of the applicants. The group, which had contracts in several states, consisted of two Nashville brothers and three Louisville doctors who flew into Nashville once a week to conduct the evaluations.

In many cases, DDS would rely solely on the report of these contract doctors, disregarding completely the diagnosis and evaluation of the applicant's treating physician. John Vail, an attorney with Legal Services in Johnson City, interviewed by the *Tennessean*, called the group "a factory."[1] US District Judge John Nixon cited problems with their evaluations in several cases that came before him for review and ordered that the cases be reopened. Nevertheless, the program administrator for DDS praised the group saying they were "excellent," mainly because they completed their reports so quickly.[2] In July, a US district judge in Virginia ruled that examinations conducted by one of the group's doctors were fraudulent, and he prohibited the group from operation in his district. The Social Security Administration was not as charitable as the

Tennessee administrator had been. After the ruling in Virginia, it suspended the doctors' group from performing examinations in any state.

Regrettably, getting rid of those doctors did not solve the underlying problem. Even with different doctors, DDS continued its practice of giving undue weight to reports from consultative examinations rather than honoring the reports from of the treating physicians. And other problems came to light. In some cases, DDS failed to obtain any report from the treating physician. When considering the reports, DDS used standards that did not properly evaluate severity of pain, failed to consider the cumulative effects of non-severe impairments, failed to assess the severity of impairments, and failed to assess "residual functional capacity." Lawyers from around the state filed a class action suit in the US District Court for West Tennessee in October 1982 on behalf of nine named plaintiffs who either had been denied benefits on an initial application or had been terminated from the program after a review by DDS's consulting physicians. They alleged that DDS had "systematically denied benefits by using policies and procedures never intended or authorized by Congress." Frank Bloch, whose specialties as a law professor at Vanderbilt included Social Security, originally was lead counsel, but when his father died and Frank went to California for an extended period to manage his affairs, Russ assumed that role.

Russ's client, Denzil White, a fifty-eight-year-old disabled steelworker, was one of the named plaintiffs. He had begun receiving disability benefits in 1978 because he suffered from diabetes, heart disease, advanced osteoarthritis, and a displaced vertebra, which prevented him from working, but in 1982, after a routine periodic review, an examiner at DDS said that he was able to return to work, despite the fact that his conditions had not improved. White explained the situation that left him in, "I needed my disability payment to live on and pay for my medications. After my check was cut off, I had to borrow money from my brother and my two sons." One son gave him a pig so he would have meat to eat. "My doctor told me I needed to go to the hospital because of diabetes, but I couldn't go because my disability benefits had been terminated." Losing disability benefits, he also had lost his eligibility for Medicare.

In 1984, Senator Jim Sasser of Tennessee and others in Congress became aware of the disability determination problems and passed legislation, first, setting new national termination standards and, second, directing federal courts to remand pending disability cases to SSA for evaluation under the new standard. The next year, US District Judge Robert McRae, who was presiding over the *Samuels* case, went a step further. With the agreement of all parties, he ordered the SSA to notify all Tennesseans whose disability benefits had been terminated between 1981 and 1984 that they could be reexamined under the new standards. The notice went out to seventy thousand people.

David, who became involved in the case while it was pending, was quoted in the *Tennessean* urging anyone who had been terminated to go to the Social Security office and apply for reinstatement even if they did not receive a letter from SSA: "A big concern we have is that some of the addresses will be three or four years out of date [a common problem for people who do not have the income to pay their rent] and people may never receive [the letter]."[3] With Adinah's help, David and Russ by publications and otherwise tried to get the word out in the community about the ruling. They set up a toll-free telephone number for people to call us from anywhere in the state for a determination as to whether they might be covered by the ruling.

In 1986, responding to the claimants' motion for a summary judgment, Judge McRae issued a final order in the case in which he found that instructions and practices used by DDS had violated Social Security regulations, that medical opinions of treating physicians must be preferred unless there are questions about the doctor's qualifications or the duration of relationship to the claimant, that DDS policies on pain and impairments were invalid, and that a number of other policies must be changed. He ruled that members of the claimant class were entitled to reevaluation, and if reevaluation showed that benefits had been improperly denied, then they were entitled to full retroactive benefits.[4]

We tried to come up with a rough estimate of the dollar value of the ruling for members of the claimant class. Calculating retroactive benefits and future benefits for the rest of their lives or until retirement benefits began for some, allowing that some may not be qualified after reevaluation, and recognizing that some would never hear about the ruling, we estimated that over the years, total value for class members who benefited would be around $750 million.

One attorney in private practice, who himself by then had handled a large number of individual disability cases, with gratitude wrote to Russ after the case was over, "This order obviously results from many hours of thorough preparation, as well as skillful advocacy. You have accomplished a feat that those of us in private practice would never have been able to undertake."

And it was not only fellow lawyers who were impressed and grateful. After Denzil White was approved and reinstated for disability payments, he invited Russ and his spouse Sara to his house for dinner. One of White's sons and his wife were there, as well as two granddaughters. The pig meat was long gone by then. "We had steak," Russ reports. "Sara usually didn't eat red meat, but she did that night. After dinner his granddaughters played the violin for us."

Gratitude came not only from the clients we knew, it also came from class members we never met. One evening as I was reading my mail, I opened a small envelope, hand-addressed, with the unlikely return address of Finger, Tennessee, a mysterious place I had never heard of and could not find on my state map. Inside was a handwritten note on a small piece of paper that thanked us for our work on the *Samuels* case. The writer explained that her husband's Social Security disability benefits had been terminated some time ago, but thanks to the work of our lawyers and the judge's ruling, he went for a reevaluation, was approved, and received substantial back benefits. He was not one of our named plaintiffs. He was just one of the thousands of people in the class, a previously anonymous beneficiary. And there was more than a letter in the envelope.

She enclosed a check for $125, saying she wanted to contribute to us so that we could help other people like them. Out of their poverty and their suffering, she wanted to give for others. It was one of those glorious moments that makes a person feel connected to The Good. It was an affirmation of all the effort Russ, David, Adinah, and others had spent on this case and all the hopes they had for their clients. In addition to the warm feeling, the check also gave me a clue to the mystery of Finger, Tennessee. The check was drawn on The Bank of Adamsville, a town I recognized only because the previous governor, an unsavory character who had been removed from office, was from Adamsville, a small town in West Tennessee. No wonder I could not find Finger on my map. A more detailed map than I had access to then later helped me locate the village of Finger in the northwest corner of rural McNairy County. She had gone to all the trouble to reach out to us from that remote place a long way away.

I wrote to her and thanked her for her generous gift and told her we were grateful that we could help her husband. I did not tell her about the other gift she had given us because my full appreciation of that gift was still inchoate. That contribution of $125 had sparked my thinking that perhaps people of more means might contribute money to us to help us with our mission. She gave; perhaps others would give. But I had no idea how to begin to ask. Then one day Ann Starr came to see me.

CHAPTER 19

Justice Is Everybody's Business

I . . . pay homage
To the One . . .
Whose presence is felt
In acts of kindness
By one person to another.
—CHARLES H. WARFIELD, 2010

Ann Starr was, and is, an impressive woman, bright and energetic, daring and outspoken. She had been involved in community organizing and raising money for progressive organizations, first in Chattanooga and more recently in Nashville. At this point, she was between jobs and looking for someone to help. She came to see me toward the end of 1985 saying she was willing to volunteer part-time for a couple of months. We chatted for a while and I mentioned various places where we might well benefit from her talents, like assistance with community education or investigation of cases. She said she was more interested in administrative matters like fundraising. Helping with this had been her mission all along.

I was apprehensive. Even though I knew times were changing and that nonprofits were going to have to start taking fundraising more seriously, I doubted that we would have sufficient appeal to make it work. We were lawyers; we sued people; we defended poor people; we represented them sometimes in extremely unpopular cases, often against some of the same moneyed interests we now would be asking to give us money. The staff would think we were selling out. Our board was not composed of people who had been chosen for their fundraising connections. But we had to try or be left in the dust. Ann and I agreed that this would be her project, to try to figure out if and how we might start a bona fide annual fundraising campaign.

The Reagan Revolution had a profound impact on nonprofit organizations that help the poor. Along with the disparaging speeches about "welfare Cadillacs" and the mantra of "government is the problem," came a resolve to dismantle whatever was left of the War on Poverty and make sizable cuts in federal funding for anything of that kind. We no longer could rely on that funding. We either would have to find new funds or we would wither away, and if we ever hoped to expand services and help more people, then we would need radically new funding patterns.

Also rising in the popular mind at this time was a heightened sentiment of individualism, and that had a profound impact on the United Way, which up until that time had been the major local funder of social services. The communitarian principle behind the United Way since its founding by businesspeople as the Community Chest in the early twentieth century had been that rather than having each charity conduct its own fundraising, it would be more efficient and less confusing for donors to have one annual campaign for all of them, "One gift does it all." Following that principle, member organizations that received funding from the United Way had been severely restricted as to what fundraising they could do and when they could do it. Now in the new era, with donors more inclined to make idiosyncratic choices rather than contribute to a common fund, the larger, more popular United Way members (e.g., Boy Scouts, YMCA, etc.) that had been doing their own fundraising on a smaller scale with a wink and a nod from United Way, began to ramp up their efforts, and they were so powerful, with such strong support in the community, that the United Way could not stop the tide. For a couple of years, the United Way tried to keep up the charade by requiring member organizations to submit any fundraising plans to them for their approval, but that soon fell by the wayside, or into the tide. In this more relaxed and at the same time more competitive situation, even those of us who were slower on the uptake began to realize that it was a matter of sink or swim. At Legal Services we first had to learn how to swim.

We had made some asks beyond the usual government grants and contracts. In early 1984, we had approached Nissan for funding of word processing equipment but were unsuccessful. Later that spring, the HCA Foundation gave us a grant to pay for the printing of our Medicare supplement insurance publication. We received a generous individual gift later that year from Cliff Probst, who had volunteered with us a couple of years before, and we had received a gift from one law firm. From time-to-time we would receive a small gift from a client, but like the gift from the sweet lady in Finger, Tennessee, it was all quite random.

Ann said we needed to do a feasibility study. We did not hire a fund-raising consultant. It was not a very sophisticated feasibility study, and the results were not very encouraging, but they were instructive. We chose to interview several people who had been involved with Legal Services and/or were in a position to know about the giving habits of people in the city. Two of our visits stand out in my memory. Joe Cummings had retired from our board after serving for nearly ten years, including one year as president. He knew about the desperate fundraising effort in 1968. In 1971, he had been one of the board members who called on a number of law firms asking them to contribute and came away with under $2,000. In 1975 and 1980, he had been our staunch defender when we had problems with donors to the United Way. Based on those frustrating experiences, "Vinegar Joe" acidulously concluded, "People aren't going to give money to Legal Services. We tried that before, and it didn't work."

The other equally blunt assessment was from Albert Werthan, who with his family had been generous contributors to many educational and charitable organizations in the city. We had written Albert a letter asking for an interview, and he invited us to his office at the large manufacturing facility his family owned and operated in Germantown. Very early on in the visit, he graphically introduced us to one of the guiding principles of fundraising: people give best to people they know. Our stationery on which we had written to him listed all our staff lawyers and our board of directors. Our staff, if known at all to the business community, would have been known only as adversaries. Our board was made up of one-third clients, certainly unknown, and the rest were lawyers who were good souls appointed by bar associations to our board, not because of their connections in the giving community, but because they were supportive of our cause. There were a few exceptions, but for the most part that was who we were.

The experienced philanthropist barked at Ann and me, "I can't give money to an organization when I don't know the people. Who are the people on your board? I hardly know any of them." Properly chastened, we politely withdrew, but Albert Werthan had not seen the last of us, and we had not heard the last from him and his family. They would be a key to our success.

Armed with new knowledge and undaunted by negativity (Joe and Albert had not been the only ones), Ann prepared a memo for the executive committee of the board describing what a fundraising campaign might look like. Ann and I met with that committee twice in April 1986 to discuss the possibilities, and they approved our going forward. Later that month, the board authorized me to spend $9,000 "to explore the opportunities for fundraising and formulate a program." I was authorized to employ staff "within that budget." Ann would get paid at last. We kept working and came back in August with a proposal; the executive committee approved it; and the full board followed in September.

The next step would be critical: the selection of someone to lead the first campaign, someone known and respected not only in the legal community, but beyond that in the wider community as well. Rachel Steele was vice president of the board and a member of the firm of Farris, Warfield & Kanaday. She came up with the idea of asking Charlie Warfield to head the first campaign. We never considered anyone else.

Warfield had not been involved previously with Legal Services in any way. My only contact with him had been in Fourth Circuit or Probate Court where I had spent quite a bit of time on divorce cases in the 1970s, and he had too. His clients were all on the opposite end of the economic scale from ours, but he had always been kind and generous to me and to Dot Dobbins who followed me in the family law section. In casual conversations, he often told us we were doing what he had envisioned doing when he entered the practice of law in 1949. Now he had a varied practice, and his firm represented Third National Bank, but it was not only his cordial manner and his standing at the bar that made him the ideal choice. He had been deeply involved in the community and in the fabric of the city.

Warfield had been a member of the Metropolitan Charter Commission that put together and campaigned successfully for Metropolitan Government in 1963, and he had managed the election campaign of its first mayor, Beverly Briley. Among his many civic involvements, he had been president of the Nashville Chamber of Commerce and the Junior Chamber before that. He and his friend Nelson Andrews, the real estate developer, had established the Better Business Bureau in Nashville. He had raised money for the Red Cross and Vanderbilt Law School. While he was on the board at Fisk, to which he had been recruited by Albert Werthan, he gained some notoriety for an unusual fundraising gambit. When the university was in difficult financial circumstances and fell behind on its utility bills, he and a couple other board members, joined by representatives of the NAACP and John Seigenthaler of the *Tennessean*, went down to Church Street with buckets like the Salvation Army to collect contributions. They raised a fair amount of money, but more significantly, several national publications published stories about their begging, resulting in several substantial contributions from Fisk alumni and friends in other cities, which relieved the crisis.

When we asked him to head our campaign, Warfield was still head of the executive committee of the board at Fisk and chairman of the board at Battle Ground Academy, so it took him several weeks to give us an answer. In the end, his commitment to the law and his commitment to our cause won out, and he added this challenge to his list. It was a precisely organized and executed campaign. He set deadlines and expectations right away, and he recruited a strong group of division leaders to help, including Joe Cummings. Given his wide experience in the city, he had the vision that this should be not only a lawyers' cause, but also a concern for the whole community. Although Legal Services was little known in the wider community, it was time for us to get known. The person he chose to head the community division had been not only a generous donor and supporter of a number of good causes in the city, but also a worker in the vineyard, May Shayne.

This would be the first of May's several significant contributions to Legal Services over the next twelve years. After the successful campaign, she stayed in touch, referring clients, offering advice, making connections, contributing to the campaign, and even appearing in a public relations video developed for us by Opryland Hotel. May was trained as a clinical social worker, and in the video she told the story of a person she had brought to us for help. She recounted not only the specific relief David Tarpley had been able to provide to the client, but also the sensitive way in which David had interviewed her.

In 1991, when the person slated to head the campaign became gravely ill and had to resign, we had to reorganize at the last minute. May recruited her parents, Albert and Mary Jane Werthan, to head the community campaign. Albert could no longer say he did not know people in our leadership. In 1999, May and Anne Roos, our great supporter and Advisory Council member, organized our thirtieth anniversary celebration at the Parthenon. It was a grand event that even included an imaginative song written by May and her cousin recounting the names of dozens of people who had been significant in our history. Tragically, May was not there to lead us in singing it. During most of the planning we had been unaware of her terminal illness. That night at the Parthenon, her friend John Seigenthaler, who was presiding, had to announce that she had died that afternoon at a hospital in Boston where she had gone for treatment.

With Charlie Warfield and May Shayne leading the campaign in 1987, we should not have been apprehensive, but we were. The negative predictions and all the people we had irritated over the years haunted us. Warfield set the goal at $50,000, and we kicked off in January with a luncheon for the campaign leadership at the Cumberland Club. Harris Gilbert recounted the history of Legal Services, I told about a couple of cases, Warfield gave a pep talk, and everyone agreed to do their best to raise the money. We were encouraged by supportive articles in the *Tennessean*, and even an editorial in the *Nashville Banner*, and Warfield and I visited anywhere we could get an invitation. Ann Starr must have arranged an appearance for us on the Ruth Ann Leach radio talk show.

Ruth Ann, later Ruth Ann Harnisch, now lives in New York, but she maintains Nashville connections and through the Harnisch Foundation has been a significant financial supporter of the Tennessee Justice Center. In those earlier days she was a challenging interviewer on WLAC radio and WLAC television (channel 5), and she wrote a column in the *Banner*, so she was a force to be reckoned with. During the radio interview she challenged us on several points. She brought up the common view that legal aid is a lawyers' issue, something lawyers should take care of and not ask other people to help. We had coined a motto to counter this idea soon after we decided to have a community campaign, "Justice is everybody's business." We explained pretty effectively that justice is a concern for the whole community and not just a lawyer issue.

Another challenge from Ruth Ann, however, left us dumbfounded. I don't remember if this was on the air or after the show. She said that when Warfield and I walked in, she did not believe we were from Legal Services. Why? Because, she said, every other person she had met or interviewed from Legal Services had been either a woman or Black. That was the first and only time I ever had to defend the fact that, yes, we have White males on our board and staff. In any case, it spoke well of the women and Black attorneys who were or had been on our staff like Dot Dobbins, Floyd Price, Jimmie Lynn Ramsaur, Richard Jackson, Susan Short, Judy Bond McKissack, Robert Greene, and others who had been out doing community education on domestic violence, housing discrimination, and various topics of interest in the media. It also highlighted the fact that at a time when jobs for women and Black lawyers were scarce, LSMT was hiring.

In the end, that first campaign raised $59,837, nearly 20 percent over our goal, and we were building confidence for the years to follow. During the year, the Tennessee Bar Association appointed Warfield to our board, and he soon was elected to the executive committee, a position he served in for nearly twenty-five years, continuing as an inspiration and guiding force for each subsequent campaign. The second campaign chair, appropriately, was Harris Gilbert, who in 1968 had made the motion in the NBA board to establish our organization and who had been the first president of our board. That was the first campaign under the Joint Venture Agreement to fund both Legal Services and Pro Bono, an added incentive that propelled the total raised to $99,088, which was an increase of over 25 percent more than Legal Services and Pro Bono had raised separately the year before. The third campaign chair also had a significant place in our history. Jack Robinson's firm of Gullett Sanford Robinson and Martin in 1968 had been the first to pledge financial support for the fledgling Legal Services of Nashville; in 1982, it was Jack who made the motion in the NBA board meeting to give the pro bono plan a try; and in 1985, even before our first campaign, his firm had sent Legal Services, unsolicited, a nice contribution.

After the third campaign, we lost our instigator and innovator, Ann Starr. Ann moved to Atlanta where she became executive director of a charity devoted to helping troubled adolescents, which she built from nearly nothing into a strong and effective organization. Sherrie Knott ably took her place and staffed the campaign for several years. The first one she staffed was led by Woody Sims, who had been president of the TBA and had contacts all over the state. He set as one of his goals increasing the contributions from other counties. He and I made several trips to bar association meetings outside Nashville to raise money and encourage support for our cause. The campaign in Nashville continued to improve, now up to more than $140,000.

The next two campaigns had rocky starts. In both years, the campaign chairs had to resign before the campaign got off the ground. In 1991, Warfield persuaded David Herbert, who was treasurer of our board, to step in and lead the campaign at the last moment, a rescue that for years after earned for David the title of "Hero Herbert." The next year Byron Trauger gamely took over a couple of months before the kickoff, and thanks to a sizeable anonymous gift, substantially exceeded the campaign goal. Byron also recruited two lawyers to head the large firm division who would lead the campaign in following years: Matt Sweeney and Jim Cheek. Among the successes of Matt's year was that his community chair, Colleen Conway-Welch, solicited a contribution from her friend Ruth Ann Leach and obtained for us not only the first of many gifts from her, but also a column in the *Banner* urging others to give. Not one to miss a chance at a punchline, Ruth Ann entitled her column "It's no lawyer joke: many need legal help."

When Jim Cheek led the campaign in 1995, he brought innovations that changed both the campaign and our organization. We had been soliciting routinely individual lawyers and law firms alike and never had concentrated any special effort on the firms. We had giving categories in which we recognized levels of giving by individuals, but we had not thought to have any such category for firms. Jim said we needed to go "where the real money is," in the large firms, and he instituted a campaign category called the "Leadership Cabinet." A firm could become a member of the Leadership Cabinet by donating as a firm gift, in addition to any individual members' gifts, an amount calculated at $200 per law-yer in the firm. Jim predicted that peer pressure would come into play because when we publicized the names of the firms in the Leadership Cabinet, no major firm would want to be left out, and that would propel the campaign to new heights. He was right. In the first year twenty firms signed on. Initially, Jim's firm of Bass, Berry & Sims led the way as the largest single contributor to the campaign, only to be edged out later by Waller, Lansden, Dortch & Davis when it became the largest firm in town.

Jim's other idea was that we expand the role of the community cam-paign committee and have it also be an advisory committee that would meet with the board of Legal Aid twice a year. It did not happen during his campaign year, but the next year our board authorized a modified version with the creation of a separate advisory council composed of twelve to eighteen community members who were neither lawyers nor clients, who could bring their experiences and insight to the Legal Aid Society and help build wider community support. The advisory council would help expand our key contacts in the community as well as advise us on issues of organizational effectiveness and fundraising. Aubrey Har-well, the 1996 campaign chair, recruited John Seigenthaler to be head of the council, and they recruited a stellar group of members. John con-tinued as chair for several years thereafter, long after Aubrey's campaign was over, and his leadership made it easy to recruit other members as people rotated off. When he retired from the position after three years, Vic Alexander, the chief manager at KraftCPAs, agreed to step up, and he led with distinction for several years thereafter.

Among the many good ideas generated by the advisory council, none was more significant than their advice that we engage professional help with public relations. I soon came to understand that, like the advisory council itself, a public relations firm could give us ideas and help us develop a standing in the community that could, in fact, help our advo-cacy work and our fundraising as well. Howard Stringer, a retired cloth-ing executive, guided us in that new venture and helped sell it to our board. After interviewing several firms, we hired The Bradford Group, now Dalton Group, which has generously worked with Legal Aid for more than twenty years.

I did have some sense of public relations even before we hired Jeff Bradford, and I had initiated one change in 1994 that reflected my concern:

I proposed that we change our name to the Legal Aid Society. I recognized that in some quarters the term "legal aid" had been discredited by the rather perfunctory representation rendered by many organizations with that name earlier in the century. When OEO in 1965 began funding poverty law organizations and insisted on more sophisticated representation, one may recall that it was opposed by traditional legal aid groups. OEO specifically avoided the term "legal aid" and preferred the title Legal Services to distinguish its purposes. We needed to be mindful of that history, and certainly did not ever want to reflect the former connotation in our practice. At the same time, some older organizations in New York, Atlanta, Cleveland, and other cities had retained "legal aid" in their titles without detriment. In fact, they were among the most prominent in the country at providing effective advocacy.

For us, the pluses outnumbered the minuses. My initial motivation had been to aid in fundraising. The title was more specific than the generic "legal services," which could be rendered by any lawyer for a fee. "Legal aid" set us apart, spoke of our purpose, and would make us more appealing to donors. But actually an equally compelling reason for the change was apparent every day as our receptionists answered calls from prospective clients. The receptionist would answer, "Legal Services. May I help you?" and inevitably the first-time caller would ask, "Is this legal aid?" That was the term most recognizable in our clients' communities, as well as in the general public.

Adding the affiliative term *Society* to our title also would help defuse the assumption on the part of many people that we were a government agency. That mistaken assumption had led to many misunderstandings about who we were and what we do. We had anecdotal evidence that some people would not contribute money to us thinking we were a government agency instead of a charity. The term "society" in our name would help clarify our status and reinforce our position as a community effort. The executive committee agreed, and at its October 1994 meeting, the board followed suit. As of the next January, we had a new name.

It cannot be said that the name change resulted in an immediate doubling of contributions to the campaign, but it did help. The campaign had its own momentum. Each year would build on the one before. There were a couple of years in which because of economic conditions or other factors, it has not done as well as we might have hoped, but each leader has gamely taken on the challenge and in the process not only raised significant money for Legal Aid and Pro Bono, but also improved our visibility and support in the community. This is in large part because each person who has been asked to head the campaign has been a recognized leader in the bar, but it also is because of the legacy of the lawyer who led it first and who was identified with it for years after.

Every September for nearly twenty-five years, Charlie Warfield would make the phone call to the leader selected by the executive committee and would set up the appointment for me, and in later years Gary Housepian, to go with him to make the ask. More often than not, early in the conversation our target would confess, "I knew when I got the call from Charlie what this was going to be about, and I am honored to be asked," and invariably the answer would be "yes." It helped that we almost always were asking for a year or two in advance, but it also mattered who was asking, and that the lawyer would be joining such a distinguished list of colleagues.

———————

Unfortunately, such commitment and support on the local level did not prevail in Washington. While our campaign succeeded and the effective advocacy of our lawyers representing their clients proceeded apace in Middle Tennessee, there were those operating on the national level who once again wanted to put an end to it all. That, regrettably, is one of the subjects of the next chapter.

CHAPTER 20

High Hopes, Doomsday II, and Then Consolidation

1992-2002

> To withhold the equal protection of the
> laws, or to fail to carry out their intent
> by reason of inadequate machinery, is to
> undermine the entire structure.
>
> —REGINALD HEBER SMITH, 1919

This is a chapter of contrasts. The whole unlikely saga told here was
driven by political events in Washington that had a profound impact on
our local organization. In the years from 1992 to 2002, we rode the rollercoaster up with increased national support and funding, then down
with reduction in federal funding, clamps on our practice, loss of staff
(again), and the tragic rending of our organization. Toward the end of
that ride, we labored through the climb of putting together the rem-
nants of three very different legal aid programs. The good news was that
through it all the staff kept the faith, the board kept its steady hand, the
campaign doubled, other funding came our way, and new staff from the
other programs brought strength and experience.

HIGH HOPES

The year of 1993 was a time of high hopes. There was a new, even friendlier administration in the White House, headed by a lawyer. The First

Lady, also a lawyer, was a former president of the Legal Services Corporation. The board of LSC that had been appointed by President Bush
in 1991 continued to look for ways to advance the cause and reverse the
hostility toward grantees that had built up under previous boards; they
encouraged good bipartisan support in Congress, which increased funding each year. The LSC board chairman, George Wittgraf, visited grantees to learn about the work and show his support. He pushed the LSC
staff to streamline the refunding process, make the application forms
more reasonable, and conduct the monitoring visits in such a way as to
improve performance rather than emphasize surveillance. For us that
meant we could concentrate on representing clients and delivering services without constant interference from LSC or apprehension about
loss of funding from Congress.

At the end of 1993, the *Nashville Scene* named Gordon "Nashvillian of
the Year" and cited a variety of cases he and other colleagues had worked
on: the design and implementation of TennCare; the reform of Tennessee's prison system; and the ruling by the US Court of Appeals forbidding
nursing homes from discriminating against Medicaid patients in admission decisions. In Washington, the LSC board appointed a new president
of LSC, Alex Forger, who at age seventy had just stepped down from
being managing partner at the New York law firm of Milbank Tweed.
Forger then chose as his vice president Martha Bergmark, a veteran legal
aid lawyer from Mississippi who had been a leader in a national advisory
group as well as in the administration of LSC. Forger and Bergmark
began assembling a staff of people with a vision for improving civil legal
services, and for the first time since 1980, LSC began long-range planning.

DOOMSDAY II

Then came the congressional election of 1994, and we were right back
in the stew. LSC was one of the organizations targeted for abolition as a
result of Georgia representative Newt Gingrich's victorious "Contract
with America," a campaign very much akin to Nixon's Southern strategy. This time the opponents of LSC had a new partner, the Christian
Coalition, a group with its own allied contract: "The Contract with the
American Family." It maintained that LSC should be abolished because
we represented poor people seeking a divorce, and this was anti-family,

disregarding that in most divorce cases we were representing abused women seeking to escape violence.

Once again, the American Bar Association rose to the occasion and rallied lawyers to go to Washington in an effort to try to educate members of Congress, correct misunderstandings, and contradict unsubstantiated charges that were lodged in various congressional committees. Harris Gilbert, who was president of the TBA that year, led a delegation from our state that included Howard Vogel, the president elect; Riney Green, chair of the TBA pro bono committee; Chuck Fleishmann of Chattanooga, who himself would be elected to Congress a few years later; and me. Although we were well received by our congressional delegation, the prospects were not good. The long knives were out; opponents of LSC were in control of both houses of Congress, and they were moving quickly.

At the April 1995 meeting of our board, I had to report that Congress already through a rescission action had reduced the LSC funding that had been appropriated for that year by an amount that would cause us to lose $18,000 from our grant; and for the next year the most optimistic proposal in the House would mean a loss of $400,000 for us. At the same time I told the board that our Nashville United Way grant would be $26,000 less in the year beginning July 1. We discussed buying into the state unemployment insurance plan.

At the May meeting of the executive committee, we began discussing "possible budget adjustments for 1995 and 1996." Frank Bloch, who was president of the board, volunteered to attend the managing attorney meeting and discuss "specific concerns of the staff." Our specific concerns were not only the loss of funding or the abolition of LSC altogether, but also what by then had developed in Washington as the fallback position for those trying to save LSC. That position acquiesced to the complaints of many critics in Congress who objected to the more controversial cases handled by LSC-funded lawyers, but who could be persuaded to continue funding LSC, albeit at a reduced amount. The price of that support would be severe restrictions on our practice, including the following: no class action lawsuits; no representation of clients in legislative matters or administrative rulemaking; no requests for attorney fees; no prison condition cases; no challenges to welfare policies or law. These restrictions, and several more, including restrictions on representing certain immigrants, would apply not only to our LSC funds, but to all funds regardless of the source if we took any grant from LSC. No more LSC funding would be allowed for the state support centers like TALS, or for the *Clearinghouse Review*, or the national support centers.

Once again, we formed a board-staff committee and discussed our prospects. It was a dilemma. The limits on our practice would mean a severe reduction in the number of people we could help through class action cases and legislative and administrative advocacy. The loss of revenue from attorney fees would deprive us of significant supplemental funding that in some years had saved us from laying off staff. The application of the restrictions to all other funds was the most cynical of all. In their determination to hamstring lawyers for the poor, the hostile members of Congress wanted to control not only the money they appropriated, but everyone else's money, as well. And they would succeed. And that is still the law.

On the other hand, choosing not to accept a grant from LSC did not seem like a viable option. We received more than a million dollars each year from LSC, and though because of our other funding it was a declining percentage of our income, it would be impossible to replace, at least in the foreseeable future. That would mean drastic reductions in staff and capability, right away. Finally, in one meeting Frank asked us to list all the kinds of cases we handled and the community education projects we conducted, and then he pointed out to us that despite the restrictions, if we accepted the grant, we still would be able to do more than 90 percent of what we were doing for clients. Immodestly, we reasoned that if we declined the LSC grant, any successor grantee that might be formed to receive the restricted LSC funding would not be in a position to deliver services as well as we had. We began to adjust to the likely future, and we began to consider how we could conclude responsibly or refer the class action cases we were handling.

Alex Forger at LSC, seeing what was coming from Congress, the restrictions on our representation and reduced funding, required that all the grantees in each state institute a planning process with bar associations, law schools, and others, to determine who could take up the slack, and how. The goal was to develop a comprehensive, integrated system of legal aid for the state, including not only LSC grantees, but all the possible players. TALS and the pro bono committee of the TBA convened several meetings that began planning how we might meet the crisis.

Meanwhile, others had been taking remedial action on a different level. Early in the spring, seeing what was happening in Congress, Mike Murphy and Stewart Clifton started looking at the possibility of obtaining state funding for legal aid in Tennessee. Mike and Stewart were the TALS government relations team that had been so effective in helping our lawyers communicate our clients' concerns to the General Assembly and various state agencies. Mike, a Father Ryan High School alumnus, had been a legislator in the 1970s and still had lots of friends in both the Senate and the House. Stewart, a member of the city council, had moved over to TALS after several years at Legal Services.

Mike and Stewart came up with a funding mechanism and named the bill the Tennessee Access to Justice Act. They had lots of help, first from the strong sponsors they persuaded to carry the bill: Democrat Mike Kisber and Republican Randy Stamps in the House; Republican Curtis Person, Chair of the Judiciary Committee, and Democrat Douglas Henry in the Senate. Senator Henry, who had talked of securing state funding for legal aid as long ago as the early 1970s, this time would make it happen. The TBA lent its weight with both executive director, Allan Ramsaur, and the chair of its legislation committee, former representative Steve Cobb, on the Hill. Riney Green, along with Jim Delanis and others on the TBA pro bono committee, contacted hundreds of lawyers across the state, recruiting them to contact their senators and representatives. By May, the bill had passed and was signed into law. We would not begin receiving any funds until the next year, and it would not come close to making up for the reductions in funding from LSC, but the prospect of any funding was comforting, and the fact that our state legislature had stepped up to support us was especially encouraging.

The action in the US Senate that September was not encouraging. At one point it had been hoped that the Senate would be a bulwark against the passion of the House, but it was only minimally so. It rejected the "glide path to oblivion" from the House and preserved LSC, but accepted the restrictions and reduced funding. The final legislation would not be signed until early the next year owing to the many conflicts between Speaker Gingrich and President Clinton, resulting in what at that point was the longest government shutdown in US history. Even with that impending delay, however, by the end of September 1995, the handwriting was on the wall.

In October, Howard Vogel, president of TBA, convened a statewide "summit" in Nashville, and as result of discussions at that meeting, three things happened. Gordon already had decided that he had no choice but to leave LAS when the restrictions became effective. He had too many complex class action cases that ethically could not be transferred to another lawyer, or even several lawyers, and furthermore, there was no one in Tennessee who would or could take them. He needed a place to go, a structure that perhaps someday might support his work and hopefully the work of others. The first thing that happened after the summit was that Stewart asked Harlan Dodson to draw up a charter and incorporate an entity known as the Tennessee Justice Center (TJC), and it was done before the end of the month. There now was a structure in place to use when it became necessary.

The second and third steps after that October summit were related to each other and involved getting some operating income for the nascent TJC. The only immediately available source of revenue that the people in that meeting had connections with was the Tennessee Bar Foundation (TBF) with its IOLTA funds. (IOLTA is defined and explained in the next section of this chapter.) The directors of the eight LSC grantees, which all received IOLTA grants from the TBF, realized that although we were facing a desperate financial situation in 1996, losing 30 percent or more of our LSC grants, we were in the fortunate position of being able to anticipate the receipt of some state funds in the next year, and in the spirit of state planning, we should do something to help the funding of TJC. We decided to suggest to the TBF that it might reduce our IOLTA grants in order to free up funds for a grant to TJC.

Howard Vogel, Harris Gilbert, and Riney Green began discussions with TBF board members. They were fortunate in its leadership: Lowry Kline of Chattanooga was president and David Herbert, the long-time treasurer of the Legal Aid Society board, was president-elect of the TBF. They were receptive and in short order came up with a plan. They would reduce the next year's IOLTA grants to the LSC grantees by a total of $120,000 and hold that money in reserve for a possible grant if and when TJC began operation. At Howard's suggestion, Riney, the corporate lawyer in the group, drafted bylaws for TJC that provided ample representation on its board for members appointed by the bar association and the foundation. As a result of that assignment, Riney became more involved with TJC, and in fact became the first president of that board, a position he held for ten years thereafter, nurturing the young organization to maturity and earning for him a special place in the history of legal aid to the poor in Tennessee.

The time came for making TJC operational. A feature article and picture in the Sunday *New York Times* documented Gordon's decision and planned move.[1] The next day, the last Monday of January, the LAS staff formed a bucket brigade from the Stahlman Building to the office of Williams and Dinkins a few buildings down Second Avenue. We transferred banker's box after banker's box of files up into the back attic "office space" that Richard Dinkins, a former president of the LSMT board, had offered to Gordon one day when they happened to be crossing the street at the same time on their ways to the courthouse. The firm of Senator Avon Williams and later Court of Appeals Judge Dinkins, prominent in civil rights advocacy throughout the state, was an appropriate first home for TJC.

The good news on that sad day was that Gordon was not going alone. He had a willing cofounder for this brave effort, Michele Johnson, who had been with us for three years. A graduate of Father Ryan, she had spent a year before law school at UT working at a Jesuit Service Corps project in upstate New York. When I conducted the interviews for my article on law and religion described in the introduction to this book, Michele seriously thought about it for a while, then wrote to me, "Faith gives me the context to more clearly hear my calling and the courage to answer it every day." She had a profound commitment to equal justice and came to us as a part of a Lyndhurst Foundation project "to educate low income families about their children's legal rights and to help them obtain the medical care the law and their doctors said they should have." In her short time with us she had great success in fulfilling the purposes of that project, and she wanted to continue to learn about and practice healthcare law with Gordon as her mentor.

Gordon tried to talk her out of it. It was a chancy endeavor with very little funding prospect, but Michele had an answer to Gordon's scare tactics: she had a grant. In fact, for the first couple of months that Lyndhurst

Foundation money was the only income there was for TJC, and when that grant ran out, Michele was awarded another, this one from Equal Justice Works.

Gordon's recollection is that I filled out the IOLTA application for him because he was too busy with the General Assembly and the Governor's Office trying to help deal with other fallout from the Contract with America. The grant application was approved, and in March, as the LSC restrictions were becoming law, TJC received the first installment of its IOLTA grant. In July, Gordon filed the first quarterly report with the foundation detailing how its grant had funded cases that helped more than 1.2 million Tennessee citizens, many with severe health problems, who now were able to get medical attention. Bringing TJC and legal aid in Tennessee to that point had been a lawyerly process, facilitated by a number of bar leaders who were committed to the idea that poor people in our state should still have access to comprehensive legal assistance without the hobbling restrictions. It was a milestone. We had come a long way. It had been thirty years exactly since "Et tu, Brute!"

The progress in Tennessee contrasted with the stark realities of what had happened in Washington. Alex Forger, the former Wall Street lawyer, reflecting on the fruitless efforts to communicate with Congress about what good LSC and its grantees were doing for equal justice in this country, remarked that his experience at LSC had been "totally different than one would see from the vantage point of a law firm in New York City when dealing with Congress on matters of banking or tax. When you're representing people who lack influence or clout, the door generally is closed."[2]

The Wall Street lawyer had learned firsthand the lesson of the day. It was a setback, but it was not new. Things always had been difficult for people without means, without influence. The 1960s and 1970s had breathed some hope into the idea of equality under the law: the Voting Rights Act, the Fair Housing Act, other civil rights legislation, the empowerment of the War on Poverty. The 1980s, however, had brought retrenchment, and the 1994 election brought a concerted effort, a contract with the elements of our society that wanted to make America like it had been again, before racial minorities and low-income people began asserting their rights and claiming equal protection under the law. Some of us who had been in the struggle much longer than Alex Forger initially took it as normal, just another setback, but it was not normal; it was profound.[3]

Julie Clark, the long-time lobbyist for NLADA, during the legislative process had it expressed to her quite succinctly by a friendly senior staffer for Senator Ted Kennedy. The senator, who could count the votes, with great regret was going to go along with the compromise and the restrictions because it was the only way to save LSC. Julie was arguing desperately for some alternative, but finally the sanguine staffer laid it out, "Julie, the two most unpopular groups for this Congress are poor people and lawyers. You represent lawyers for poor people. Figure it out."

IOLTA

The alacrity of the Tennessee Bar Foundation response to funding for TJC illustrates why IOLTA grants have been so important for the delivery of legal services to the poor in Tennessee and throughout our country. These programs, operated by bar foundations in each state, total the second-largest source of funding for legal aid in our country behind LSC. That explains why the IOLTA programs were a litigation target of some of the same groups that attacked LSC in Congress, with lawsuits that began just about the same time that Representative Gingrich began touting his Contract with America. Following the seesaw theme of this chapter, the present section will deal with the ups and downs of IOLTA: first a brief explanation of its ingenious origin; then its early history in Tennessee; and finally, the multiple lawsuits that sought to bring down the whole arrangement.

The odd acronym IOLTA stands for Interest on Lawyers' Trust Accounts. When a lawyer receives money from a settlement, court order, business deal, or whatever, that ultimately belongs to and will go to a client, the lawyer must deposit that money in an account separate from her own, a trust account. If the amount is too small or the time it will be in the trust account is too short to justify opening a separate account for the one client, the lawyer places the money in a common trust account, a pooled account she maintains for all such receipts. That account traditionally had been a noninterest-bearing checking account because of the impracticality of trying to unscramble the small interest entitlements of each client in the common pot. About fifty years ago, however, astute and civic-minded lawyers in Australia figured out that instead of having the bank receive the windfall free use of that money, the bank could figure the gross interest attributable to the entire trust account and pay that interest amount to a charitable foundation to be used for legal aid and other appropriate causes.

The idea spread to Canada, and then it was imported to the United States by the chief justice of the Florida Supreme Court. A bar foundation was established by court order in that state, collected the interest from lawyers' trust accounts and, in 1983, began making IOLTA grants. The good news traveled fast. Sometime that year, I received a call from Joe Cummings inviting me to come meet with him and Woody Sims to talk about some possible funding for legal aid in Tennessee. Woody was the first president of the newly formed Tennessee Bar Foundation and had heard about the IOLTA program through the bar foundation network. He saw this as a worthy undertaking, and with great appreciation for his initiative, I encouraged him to proceed. When the TBF filed a petition in our Supreme Court asking that an IOLTA program be established here, TALS filed an *amicus* petition joining the request. With little hesitation, the court granted the foundation's petition in 1984, and by 1988 the bar foundation had accumulated enough income to make its first IOLTA grants. Since then, the TBF IOLTA grants have totaled more than $21 million, mostly to legal aid and law-related nonprofit organizations.

It has not been an unhindered history for IOLTA in this country, however. The lawsuits attacking the plan began in 1994. The Washington Legal Foundation, with a jaundiced eye toward how the money was being used, first challenged the Texas IOLTA program in federal district court there, claiming it constituted an unconstitutional "taking" of interest from the client without "just compensation" in violation of the Fifth Amendment to the US Constitution. Similar suits were then filed in Florida, Massachusetts, and the State of Washington. As detailed by Earl Johnson in his history of LSC, the decisions of the various federal courts were not uniform. Some upheld IOLTA, some did not. The most harrowing time was when the Texas program lost in the Fifth Circuit Court of Appeals. The only good news was that in each case while the lawsuits were pending, no foundation was enjoined from collecting the funds or making grants, and the TBF continued making grants to us.

Finally, nine years after the attack had begun, after cases had gone up and down from district courts to circuit and back and at one point up to the US Supreme Court and back down, the Supreme Court granted *certiorari* again. In March 2003, that court held that indeed there was a "taking" from each client who had money in the trust fund, and that the taking required "just compensation," but since there was no practical way to isolate and deliver one client's share of the interest, the compensation in each client's case would be zero, and therefore there was "no violation of the Just Compensation Clause of the Fifth Amendment." IOLTA could continue unabated, and it has.

STATE PLANNING–HEAVY DUTY

When Alex Forger wisely decreed in 1995 that we should begin planning in each state how to deal with the funding cuts and restrictions, one of the items for consideration he specified was consolidating grantees for greater efficiency. As we in Tennessee proceeded along over the years with our planning meetings, we assumed this directive would not apply to us. States like Virginia with sixteen grantees or Pennsylvania with twenty-four would have to look seriously at consolidations, but we were not in that category. There were only eight LSC grantees in our state, so we ignored that part of state planning. Our confidence was premature, however, for we could not see all the twists and turns in the road ahead, particularly the selection of a new president of LSC after Forger's second retirement in 1997.

John McKay was a forty-one-year-old commercial litigator from Seattle whose brother had been appointed US Attorney there by the first President Bush and who himself later would be appointed to the same position by the second President Bush. He had been active as a pro bono attorney and had been the head of the Washington State Equal Justice Coalition, in which role he had lobbied Congress in support of LSC two years earlier. Because of his political connections, his zealous advocacy, and his commitment to the cause, he was an ideal candidate for the presidency of LSC, though he did not seek the position. A search firm, much to his surprise, recruited him, an enthusiastic LSC board offered him the job right after his interview, and as Earl Johnson recounts it, that night, "somewhere during [a] stroll on the Mall, his parents' lessons and his Jesuit upbringing came to the fore," and he accepted.[4]

From his experience in the state of Washington, where all of the LSC grantees had consolidated into one organization, McKay had a specific view on the best way to provide more economical access to justice: consolidate. He was convinced that LSC was funding too many grantees and that having fewer and larger recipients would lead to more efficiency. He steadfastly persisted in this belief despite resistance from most grantees, NLADA, and a few members of the LSC board. One of his advantages was that as president of LSC, he had the particular authority that allowed him to implement his plan: he could define the geographical service area of a grant. It followed that regardless of how many grantees had been previously within his newly defined area, now there could be only one.

McKay moved quickly to impose his will on the states that were obvious candidates, and we persisted in our belief that we would be exempt. Each of the Tennessee grantees had a rational geographic definition and important local identities: Memphis, West Tennessee in Jackson, South Central in Columbia, Rural on the Cumberland Plateau, Knoxville, Upper East in Johnson City, Southeast in Chattanooga, and us. The local connections and the geography were significant in each case. For our part at LAS, we did not want to dilute the strong staff we had assembled, the supportive board, and the significant local financial support from the campaign, foundations, and other funders.

In August 1998, with TALS coordinating the drafting, the grantees in Tennessee developed a state plan and submitted it to LSC. It did not include consolidating any of the grantees, but instead defended the existing structures. Our plan emphasized our good cooperation and expansively described our actions and our successes. LSC staff at that point clearly was concentrating on other states, and we were benefiting from their bureaucratic overload because we did not hear anything official in response for a year after that. Then in September 1999, a letter came approving our plan in part, but adding further requirements, including that we examine consolidation.

A few months later, on its own initiative, LSC gave TALS a grant for $10,000 specifically to hire a consultant "to facilitate state planning." The consultant was to come from LSC's approved list. LSC sent messages to us and sent messengers to TALS statewide meetings who were very cordial, very collegial, but very insistent. They tried to convince us that consolidation would be all for the best, and it would be exciting. In each case the consultants and messengers were long-time legal aid lawyers now on the staff at LSC or on contract, good people and trustworthy, but we were not buying their line.

The LAS board minutes for the year 2000 reflect several reports from me and from Jim Weatherly and Charlie Warfield, who also attended several TALS meetings. These meetings were attended by not only people from the grantees, but also representatives of the TBA, TBF, Administrative Office of the Courts, UT Law School, Tennessee Commission on Aging, and Tennessee Conference on Social Welfare, all concerned about coming up with a workable plan that would please LSC and at the same time cause the minimum of disruption for us. I brought several drafts of plans to our board and executive committee during the year, and finally in August the one we would submit, still with no consolidations. LSC responded quickly this time, with objections. We submitted another plan extoling further the cooperation between our organizations that we thought would answer the objections.

By that time LSC must have lost patience with all the formal back and forth, and one of its messengers laid down an ultimatum. We had to come up with a plan that had only three or four grantees in Tennessee. Our tactics of delay had run their course. The message was respectful and cordial, but it was firm: LSC did not want to impose a plan, but it would if we did not propose an acceptable one. Facing that, it was Bob Cooper (later attorney general of Tennessee, 2006–2014) who came up with a solution for our organization. He knew the good reputation of the lawyers at Rural Legal Services in Oak Ridge and Cookeville, and he proposed that we seek a consolidation with them, with the condition that I be the executive director. He pointed out that the resulting organization would serve thirty-three counties, one-third of the state, and opined that such a plan ought to satisfy LSC for our part. The board did not consider what the plan should be for the rest of the state. Its back against the wall, and exercising its specific corporate responsibility, state planning fell by the wayside. The board simply was trying to do what it deemed best for our organization.

Although the practice at Rural was like that at Middle in many respects, there were distinctions as well due in large part to its location, its origin in the coalfields of the Cumberland Mountains, and its determination of what should be its priorities. Unlike Middle, Rural had a precursor, the East Tennessee Research Council (ETRC). Neil McBride had come to the Cumberland Mountains in the mid-1970s after graduation from the University of Virginia's law school and after an internship with the Law Students Civil Rights Research Council. He and a couple of other lawyers founded ETRC in Jacksboro. The small legal aid organization, funded with foundation grants, concentrated mainly on the environmental impact and personal impact of the coal industry on the low-income people in the hills and hollows north of Knoxville. They handled black-lung cases and surface mining runoff issues. They represented the regional environmental advocacy organization, Save Our Cumberland Mountains, as well as several local community groups attempting to improve life around them.

When LSC began receiving additional funding during President Jimmy Carter's administration, Neil saw the opportunity to broaden their work, established a new organization, Rural Legal Services of Tennessee, and applied for a grant. When the grant came through in 1978, RLST began operation with offices in Oak Ridge and LaFollette. The next year, with additional funding from LSC, another office was opened in Cookeville. As mentioned several times in this narrative already, and with two more described in the next chapter, lawyers from Rural had been co-counsel with our lawyers on numerous cases from the beginning, each having clients with the same problems.

True to its name, RLST handled many more specifically rural cases than Middle. In addition to the environmental cases and community development issues, the lawyers and paralegals had a remarkable number of cases against the Farmers Home Administration (FmHA), which provided loans to low-income rural homebuyers and as a part of that process was responsible for supervising the construction of the houses. One of Lenny Croce's cases involving a defective house went to the US Supreme Court, where he won with an impressive nine-to-zero decision.[5]

Rural had developed expertise in other areas as well. Bill Bush, a former Reggie, successfully litigated one of the first private enforcement actions under the Family and Medical Leave Act of 1993 (FMLA).[6] As a member of the ABA Section of Labor and Employment Law, he became an editor-in-chief of the section's treatise, "The Family and Medical Leave Act," published jointly with Bloomberg BNA. Theresa-Vay Smith and Marla Williams had numerous cases involving TennCare and other benefits, and Mary Gillum had developed a nationally recognized practice in tax law for low-income people, which was funded by the Internal Revenue Service.

After our board made its decision, I called Neil. We quickly agreed it was the best thing for both organizations. The next month I reported that to the board. Losing no time, Gif Thornton moved that the president, Dan Eisenstein, appoint a committee of Dan, Jim, Warfield, and me to enter into negotiations with Rural to construct a merger between the two organizations. It was a natural. There were no disputes. Neil, who for several years had taught a seminar at UT Law School on legal issues of nonprofit organizations, took the lead in drafting documents, and we made good progress through January and into February.

We thought we were doing well and making the best of the situation when I received a call from a long-time friend at LSC who told me that our "ideal" plan, covering one-third of the state, was not enough. LSC had other ideas about the geographical boundaries of our service area and was going to require us to take more. The administration and board at Legal Services of South Central Tennessee (LSSCT) in Columbia had made several overtures to consolidate with other grantees, but none had been successful. Now LSC, exercising its prerogative, was going to add the counties covered by that organization into our service area. We were under no obligation to merge or otherwise consolidate with that organization, just include the counties in our grant proposal. I discussed it with Neil and then put in a call to David Kozlowski.

David had gone to practice at South Central when it was established in 1980, after having worked with Junius Allison at the Vanderbilt clinic and serving as interim director when Junius retired. He had been co-counsel with our lawyers on numerous cases, had authored practice manuals for TALS, and like Russ and Lenny on occasion had been asked by TJC to take a leave and come work on a specific case there. His most prominent reputation was, and is, as an appellate advocate. He had won several significant cases in the Tennessee Supreme Court and federal Court of Appeals. A justice on the Tennessee court once told me, quite unsolicited, "David Kozlowski is one of the best appellate advocates in this state." Neil and I wanted his counsel. He would be an important part of the new organization.

I took the new development about LSSCT to the board committee dealing with consolidation. Not having any choice at this point, we agreed to comply with LSC's mandate and apply for the entire territory. Dan announced that to the full board at its February meeting; there was no motion, no vote; it was part of the deal if we wanted to continue receiving LSC funding.

Neil and I decided that when the time came we would hire only selected members of the staff at LSSCT and none of the administration. Given that decision on our part, it is understandable that the transition would not be easy. Seeing the difficulties ahead, Bob Cooper enlisted Barbara Mayden, then at Bass, to counsel us and draft documents for us. We met with the board leadership at LSSCT, but with the exception of one member, that was difficult and unproductive. Houston Parks was the exception. A leader in the bar at Columbia and in the state, from the outset of the process Houston was cooperative and helpful, and in the new structure, he became a vice president of our board. Several years later, he was elected president of the LAS board and still is the only person from one of the new areas to serve in that position.

As we labored during 2001 to put all the pieces together, most of us still longed for simpler times and a separate peace. At one point, we actually saw a ray of hope that our burden might be lifted. In May 2001, John McKay announced that he would return to Seattle at the end of June. At the same time, there began to be rumblings of resistance to consolidations from some members of Congress who were responding to the laments of their aggrieved constituents. Learning of these developments, at the May executive committee meeting, Dan Eisenstein instructed me to contact LSC to determine whether or not our consolidation must go forward.

It was a futile attempt. Large institutions do not pivot that quickly, not with the departure of an effective chief executive, not even with the complaints of a few Congressmen, and certainly not with the plea of a lone grantee. I must have reported the results of my quixotic inquiry at the board meeting the next month, but the report did not merit even a mention in the minutes. Rather, the minutes, among other business, reflect that Gif and I were authorized to sign the application, certifications, and grant assurances necessary on the application for funding to serve the forty-eight-county area defined in the LSC request for proposals.

The process went on. We met with the executive director and some board members of LSSCT, but while it was civil, we were not successful in persuading them to execute a transfer of assets agreement. Six weeks later, their board president wrote to us requesting that we enter into mediation, but our board, while expressing a willingness to continue discussion, unanimously declined to enter into mediation. Barbara drafted a transfer of assets agreement between Rural and LAS and a successor in interest agreement. Bryan Pendleton prepared revised benefits documents. Neil drafted a restated charter and amended bylaws. They all were duly adopted; LSC awarded us the grant; and we began our new operation on January 1, 2002. Matters with LSSCT were not resolved until six months later when the president of that board, apparently prodded by LSC, sent to David a quitclaim deed for the office building in Columbia, together with a bill of sale for all personalty, and David forwarded them to me.

The long, unwieldy name we chose for the consolidated organization, "Legal Aid Society of Middle Tennessee and the Cumberlands," reflected the wide service area stretching from Cumberland Gap on the Virginia line to the border with northwest Alabama near Florence, and from Land Between the Lakes to Sewanee on the Cumberland Plateau. More significant than the name or the geography was the fact that within that forty-eight-county area there were more than 350,000 low-income people eligible for our services, and each one, according to a UT School of Social Work study, had an average of 1.2 legal problems each year. The challenge for each of our three organizations before consolidation had been great, but now in the aggregate, it became even more daunting.

———————

The first paragraph of this chapter foretold contrasting stories of ups and downs resulting from national events. The next chapter, the final one, will discuss a substantive area of the law, welfare law, a part of our practice unique to us, that had provoked much of the opposition to Legal Services. Such was the anger over our advocacy in this area that Congress, as it cut our funding and restricted our practice, went one step further

and attempted to shut down our effective practice of welfare law altogether. Once again, as with the attack on IOLTA, the US Supreme Court
was persuaded to step in and declare that this too shall not pass.

CHAPTER 21

A Unique Practice of Law

> The poor will always be with you in the
> land, and for that reason, I command you
> to be open-handed with your countrymen,
> both poor and distressed in your . . . land.
>
> —Deuteronomy 15:11 (NEB)

Welfare law is a field unique to legal aid lawyers. Many other attorneys handle landlord-tenant cases, domestic relations, or consumer disputes as part of a general practice of law, albeit for a fee, but for understandable reasons, no lawyer in private practice would undertake to become conversant in and represent clients in matters involving government benefits for the poor. Being poor, the clients by definition are unable to pay a fee, and because the benefit amounts at stake are so small, hardly sufficient for subsistence, any recovery would not yield enough to fund a reasonable fee. A practice in this area could not be sustained financially.

Welfare law is a complex of ever-changing government regulations, policies, and instructions generated by both federal and state agencies. It involves an alphabet soup of programs: Supplemental Security Income (SSI) for aged, blind, and disabled people; Aid to Families with Dependent Children (AFDC), which was replaced in 1996 by Temporary Assistance for Needy Families (TANF), known in Tennessee as Families First; Supplemental Nutrition Assistance Program (SNAP), otherwise known as food stamps; and Employment and Community First (ECF). It also includes dealing with medical programs such as Medicaid, known in Tennessee as TennCare, which includes TennCare Standard and Tenn-Care Kids; Standard Spend Down (SSD); CHOICES for long-term care; Qualified Medicare Benefits (QMB); Specified Low-Income Medicare Beneficiary Program (SLMB); and Early Periodic Screening Diagnosis and Treatment (EPSDT). Each one has its own eligibility standards and income limits, and its own peculiarities.

Unfortunately for many, it is not enough to be poor and needy in order to qualify for these programs. A person has to be poor and fit within the restrictive category for the particular program, such as single parent, child, blind, elderly, or disabled. To complicate matters even further, each program requires dealing with the specific department of government responsible for its administration and interpretation. Sometimes that means dealing with both a state department and a federal agency since each one of these programs is a joint state and federal program administered by the state, except SSI, which is administered by a federal agency only. There are many knots to unravel.

The practice takes many forms. It may involve simply advising an individual client about programs she may qualify for and how to apply, together with advocating at a department on that client's behalf. That was the case with Shirley, a woman from Fairview who was featured as a Williamson County United Way "poster person" in 1995 because of the comprehensive relief Russ Overby was able to fashion for her and her family. She had been the sole support for her invalid husband and four children, and until illness struck, they had been getting by on her income as the renowned biscuit-maker at Loveless Cafe. First, one daughter developed pneumonia and the cost of that medical care took all their savings. Then another daughter needed expensive medication. "We might have managed except my husband started blacking out. I was afraid to leave him, afraid he was going to die." She had to stop working.

Without her income, the bills started mounting up and things went from bad to worse. They were in danger of losing their home and becoming homeless when a social worker, who had done all she could do, referred her to Russ. Shirley later said, "I felt like giving up, but Russ said, 'You can't,' so I didn't." Russ was able to help Shirley get TennCare, food stamps, and AFDC for her family. He also was able to save their home from foreclosure by negotiating with the Farmers Home Administration (FmHA).

"Russ, you knew nothing about FmHA; how did you do that?"

"I called the housing law backup center, and they told me what to say."

This is another example of the salutary effect of OEO's decision to establish the centers in the 1960s and the detrimental effect of Congress's decision to defund them in 1996, the year after Russ's productive call. What Russ was able to do in obtaining the welfare benefits and mortgage forbearance stabilized the family's situation and enabled Shirley to go back to work. Her assessment of Russ's advocacy: "Nobody on earth had ever done as much for us. He saved us."

Another important part of the practice is communicating with administrators of the various programs and urging policies or practices that would improve, or preserve, the benefits for the participants. From the late 1970s until the early 1990s, Russ met almost monthly with Department of Human Services (DHS) administrators to talk about problems facing our common clients. From time to time, Stewart Clifton and Linda Narrow also participated in those informal conversations that took place through the course of several administrations. Some commissioners were more receptive than others. Sometimes there was agreement, sometimes not, but the frank discussions avoided many misunderstandings and prevented lawsuits.

Not infrequently, however, more formal contacts were required. In 1982, Russ and Allan Ramsaur at TALS petitioned DHS to raise its standard of need for recipients of AFDC, which at that point was forty-ninth lowest in the country. Allan is quoted in a newspaper account, explaining, "If we had a realistic standard, we might realize how little we are paying in AFDC grants."[1] After the commissioner authorized a study by a business center at the University of Tennessee, Russ provided data and analysis to the center that resulted in a recommendation for an upward adjustment, which then was approved by the legislature. While the increase in the standard did not increase the shamefully low amount of the grants, it did mean that some families that previously had been above the standard now would qualify for the grant and with that be eligible for Medicaid coverage. The next year, Russ and Allan, together with Stewart and Adinah Robertson from our staff, worked with Linda O'Neal, then at the

Institute for Children's Resources, to convince the legislature to institute the free breakfast program for schoolchildren.

During a fiscal crisis in 1991, the state proposed to reduce the already low AFDC grants. When Russ showed up at a hearing before the General Assembly's finance committees to present testimony from his clients, Commissioner Bob Grunow welcomed him, even though they were on opposite sides. After Russ's testimony and the passionate plea of Senator Douglas Henry, the committee voted not to reduce the grants, and the proposal died. On other occasions, we were able to help the department accomplish its purposes. When DHS wanted an exception from the federal Department of Health and Human Services (HHS) allowing it to treat modest one-time payments a child on AFDC might receive (e.g., from Social Security or a will) in such a way as not to deprive the child of ongoing health benefits, Russ helped negotiate with the federal administrators. He could provide stories from his clients illustrating the unfair penalty required by the rule. In most cases, the child would have been better off never to have received the modest sum. The joint effort by DHS and Russ in the end was successful, and HHS granted the exception.

The trust Russ was able to build with DHS was reflected in a letter to him from Michael O'Hara, the assistant commissioner for family assistance, when O'Hara retired after thirty years. The two of them had been adversaries on some occasions and accomplices on others. Mike looked back on "a number of meaningful accomplishments . . . and many great associations" and credited Russ for their work together on "many key issues": "You helped make our programs, policies and procedures better, and I thank you for that, and for getting my attention when I was looking elsewhere. I think our teamwork helped a lot of people—and that's the most satisfying thing of all."

Inevitably, things were not always that friendly, and not everyone at DHS had the grace of Mike O'Hara, so there were times when neither informal nor formal means of persuasion could carry the day, and lawsuits were necessary. The narratives of Chapters 3 and 4 contain many accounts of federal lawsuits we filed against DHS in the early years of LSON, beginning with the 1969 case Sarah Green filed challenging a state regulation. The lawsuits did not end with the early years, however; there was, and is, just too much that could go wrong in this complex area, including a conflict between federal child support law and AFDC law.

A federal statute enacted in 1984 required that for the purpose of determining a family's eligibility for AFDC, any monies received by one child
must be deemed available to the whole family. On the other hand, the federal child support legislation enacted several years earlier provided that
it is a felony to use money collected under that program for the benefit
of any family member other than that one child. This created a Catch-
22. Earline Gibson, who with her three children received AFDC, was
caught in the conflict between these two laws when the federal child support program prosecuted the father of one of her children and he began
paying the court ordered support for that child. DHS, which dutifully
had adopted a policy it judged to be consistent with the AFDC statute,
deemed the one child's support to be available to the whole family, consequently making the family no longer eligible for AFDC and Medicaid.

Russ, David Ettinger, and Alex Hurder filed a class action lawsuit on
behalf of Ms. Gibson and several other mothers who had come to them
with the same problem. After the case was briefed and heard, Judge
Thomas Wiseman ruled that DHS had misread the AFDC statute, and
he enjoined the state from counting the support of the half-sibling as
available to others in the family. Dilemma resolved for our clients and
thousands of other families statewide, at least for a while.

Unfortunately, it was not a permanent victory. Three years later,
the US Supreme Court in a similar case from North Carolina ruled the
other way, holding that the government could constitutionally create
such a cruel dilemma.[2] Reflecting back more than thirty years later, Russ
remembers that he was not surprised. He thought the case might likely
be a loser when he took it.

"Why did you take it then?"

"I only took it because Adinah begged me to, but I'm glad I did; at
least we got those families benefits for three years. And besides, if you
are winning all your cases, you're being too picky."

As with many legal disputes, AFDC cases often involved parsing out
definitions: What is an "absent parent?" What is an "incapacitated parent?" The AFDC program was designed to give aid to poor families with
"dependent children." The federal statute governing the program defined
a dependent child as one deprived of parental support due to the death,
incapacity, unemployment, or absence of a parent. In 1991, Russ, Gordon, and Linda filed the Sebastian case in federal court on behalf of four

families that had been denied AFDC because of DHS workers' faulty interpretation of those qualifying terms. In one case, the child had been terminated from AFDC because according to DHS records, the child "shows a strong emotional bond between himself and [his absent parent]" and because the child's paternal grandparents had taken him to church. The parent and grandparents were not absent enough. The three other families had similar claims based on DHS's interpretation of one of the qualifying terms or because the DHS worker failed to check for eligibility under all applicable categories.

DHS corrected its errors for these four families and moved to dismiss because the case then was moot, but although Judge Wiseman denied class certification, he allowed the case to go forward, ruling that "voluntary cessation of alleged illegal conduct . . . does not make a case moot." The department had changed none of its definitions, policies, or practices; thus the illegal actions against our plaintiffs, which it corrected only under duress in this case, could, if left unchecked, easily be repeated and imperil other AFDC recipients. Judge Wiseman proceeded to rule favorably on one of the plaintiffs' charges, ordering that DHS in future "must check all bases of eligibility for . . . AFDC before rejecting an application," an important correction, but he found he could not rule on the disputed definitions and other matters still pending without further hearings.

Rather than going back to court, the attorneys agreed to try to come up with a settlement, and after many months and many meetings, they did, partially. Only two matters remained. At a stalemate, they jointly moved the court for an order referring the case to a judicially conducted settlement conference. The court granted the motion, the parties entered mediation, and in eight days it was over. In the stipulation and order of dismissal approved by the court, DHS agreed to promulgate the negotiated changes to its rules regarding "absence" and "incapacity," issue further clarifications to its workers, and provide staff training on the changes. DHS further agreed to withdraw the claims of overpayments and to refund the amounts it had collected from our clients.

It had been a long pull for what amounted to an insignificant bit of money for each client, but in their poverty each dollar was significant, and the resulting access to Medicaid is essential. Furthermore, it was not just about the money or the medical care for these four families.

Each case we brought against the department over the years, in its own way, not only helped an individual family, but also helped improve the program and made DHS more likely to respect the rights of the recipients. The recipients had a remedy they did not have before the advent of Legal Services lawyers. An unhappy part of the story, however, is that because of the recalcitrance of later administrators, some of those victories did not stay won. In several cases, we had to go back and enforce the orders. We could do that. One of the advantages of the long years in the same practice was that we still had the old pleadings.

In a 1973 class action case Walt Kurtz and I filed on behalf of Carole Newsom, the welfare department entered into an agreed order binding itself, among others things, to comply with federal promptness regulations and to process all AFDC applications within the forty-five-day deadline. Over the years, the department took on a new name, Human Services (DHS), but its application practices slipped back into its old ways. By the early 1990s, there were hundreds of cases with illegal delays, 617 counted in one month. When clients came complaining about the delays, Russ and Linda pulled out the nearly twenty-year-old order and filed a motion for contempt.

This time the department was not so agreeable. In a two-day hearing before Judge John Nixon, the department admitted the facts but argued that because of budget cuts, it could not comply with the order and the federal regulations. The court was not persuaded by DHS's "impossibility of performance" defense and found that it had "not taken all reasonable steps to comply with this Court's [previous] order." In fashioning a remedy, the court ordered DHS to begin AFDC payments and issue Medicaid cards to all pending applicants on the forty-fifth day following the date of application, whether it had made an eligibility determination or not. At Russ and Linda's request, the court went one step further and ordered DHS to provide several detailed monthly reports to them to ensure compliance. One of those reports was designed to prevent a scam they had seen before where the department, knowing it could not act on applications by the deadline, would simply deny them on the forty-fourth day. The court ordered DHS to report to Russ and Linda any cases denied benefits between the fortieth and forty-fifth day.

The contempt action in the *Caruthers* case, heard in 1980 before Judge Clure Morton, later stirred up more ire. The original case, filed in 1974 by

Lucy Honey and Gordon, had resulted in an order from Judge Morton holding that the welfare department's procedure for reducing or terminating AFDC grants violated both the federal statute and its regulations. The court enjoined the state from implementing rules to the contrary or otherwise making arbitrary deductions from children's grants. It certified the case as a class action on behalf of not only present "dependent and needy children," but also those who in the future qualified for AFDC. In 1980, six years after the *Caruthers* order, a woman who had the care of her niece and nephew came to see us because DHS had terminated the children's $97-per-month AFDC grant and their Medicaid after a relative had sent her a $200 check to be used for the children's Christmas gifts. Both the department's arbitrary action and the provisions of its service manual it had followed were in violation of the *Caruthers* order.

Russ, together with Lenny Croce at Rural, filed an enforcement action, and when Judge Morton ordered the defendants to show cause why they should not be held in willful contempt of the *Caruthers* order, their counsel had no good answer. After a hearing, Judge Morton decided the case based on the pleadings, affidavits, and statement of counsel. His memorandum recounted the heartless story, including the aunt's effort to do the right thing by showing the check to the children's DHS worker. During that meeting, the worker had given the aunt no indication that the children would lose their AFDC and Medicaid because of the Christmas gift and did not explain to the aunt that if the check were made out to her, instead of to the nine-year-old boy, there would be no problem. Clueless, the aunt cashed the check and bought a bicycle and clothing for the children. Then the department sprang into action. To recoup its "overpayment," the department terminated the children's benefits in January without advising the aunt of their right to reapply. When the boy needed medicine, there was no Medicaid coverage to pay for it.

The court found that what the department had done was "exactly what the defendants did in the regulation struck down by this court in 1974," and that their attempts to differentiate between the 1974 order and their present practice was "juvenile." Judge Morton was not finished, "These defendants are sophisticated, knowledgeable, trained persons. They are capable of understanding the English language. The order of May 3, 1974, was couched in simple terms. . . . Their assertion . . . is absurd and an insult to a person of less than normal intelligence."[3] He found that the department officials had willfully and deliberately violated the order and held them guilty of contempt. In addition to the contempt order, the judge ordered the department to identify all AFDC recipients who had been victims of the illegal terminations during the past year, and at a later hearing he ordered that they be reimbursed for their losses.

Sammie Lynn Puett, who had been the newly appointed commissioner of DHS at the time of the case in 1980, by 1992 was vice president for public service and continuing education at the University of Tennessee, and she had been appointed by President Bush's secretary of agriculture to head a committee to "streamline" federal welfare programs. The *Knoxville News Sentinel* reported on her appointment and related that "she has seen firsthand some of the worse examples of welfare bureaucracy run amok." The example she chose to relate to the newspaper is telling:

> Still clear in her mind is a hearing before a federal judge over the reduction in a welfare mother's benefits. Cause: A cash gift of about $100 accepted by the welfare mother so she could buy her child a Christmas bicycle.
>
> Fighting in court over that bicycle were a federal judge, assistant attorney general, lawyers from legal services, Puett, her staff attorney and others—all paid directly or indirectly by the federal government at costs far exceeding the gift.
>
> Puett remains rankled by the case a decade later—she still refers to "the absurdity of it all."[4]

Rather than an example of a bureaucracy "run amok," it is a criticism of judicial efforts to clean up the muck. We do not know whether or not the former commissioner was remembering the *Caruthers* contempt proceedings, but her description sounds familiar. A few of the details she remembered a decade later were slightly different from the facts of the *Caruthers* contempt proceeding. She remembered a reduction in benefits rather than a termination of benefits, a "cash gift of about $100" instead of a $200 check, and she remembered that it was accepted by the "welfare mother" rather than accepted innocently by the aunt and cashed only after checking with DHS.

For former commissioner Puett, the court fight was about "that bicycle." For the two children in the *Caruthers* contempt proceeding, it was about subsistence income and paying for needed medication. In his ire, Judge Morton described the department officials' attempts to defend their actions as "juvenile" and "absurd." A decade later, Ms. Puett, still "rankled," had her own complaint. She recited the involvement of a federal judge, an assistant attorney general, lawyers from Legal Services, herself, and her staff attorney, and she bemoaned "the absurdity of it all." For her, the former commissioner whose duty it had been to ensure the welfare of the poor and disabled in Tennessee, it was not the "juvenile" defense of the officials that was absurd, but rather it was the involvement of all that legal talent in the picayune petitions of the poor.

Unfortunately, similar sentiments, striking in a nation pledged to ensure justice for all, are prevalent among many powerful politicians, and in 1996 we saw that reflected in the action of the 104th Congress when it restricted lawyers for the poor employed by an LSC grantee. Most of the punitive restrictions applied to all areas of our practice, but in addition to those general prohibitions, Congress added one that was specific to welfare law, the area of practice exclusively for poor people and least likely to attract private representation as a substitute.[5] It prohibited LSC from funding any organization "that initiates legal representation or participates in any other way, in litigation, lobbying, or rulemaking, involving an effort to reform a Federal or State welfare system . . . [or] an effort to amend or otherwise challenge existing law in effect on the date of the initiation of the representation."[6]

It prohibited not just class action litigation, but participation "in any . . . litigation . . . to reform . . . a welfare system . . . [or] challenge existing law." Congress did not want any more complaints from welfare recipients, or applicants, or their lawyers about inequities in the welfare system or deficiencies in existing law.

Fortunately, five years later a slim majority of the US Supreme Court was a bit more sanguine than the callous Congress. A challenge to this section of the law reached the court and the restriction was struck down.[7] While the case was decided on the basis that the restriction constituted "impermissible viewpoint-based discrimination" in violation of the First Amendment, Justice Anthony Kennedy, who wrote for the majority, spent much of the opinion discussing the corrupting influence the restriction had on the legal system.

First, he pointed out that the restriction "distorts the legal system by altering the traditional role of attorneys," which is to present arguments and analysis to a court on behalf of their clients. The restriction prevented the lawyer from doing his job: "if during litigation a judge were to ask an LSC attorney whether there was a constitutional concern, the LSC attorney simply could not answer." Next, Justice Kennedy addressed the "severe impairment of the judicial function," finding that the restriction "prohibits speech and expression upon which courts must depend for the proper exercise of the judicial power." The restriction deprived the courts of "an informed, independent bar." Finally, in response to the argument from defenders of the restriction that the client could find other counsel, Justice Kennedy stated the obvious, "the client is unlikely to find other counsel," particularly regarding constitutional and statutory rights having to do with welfare benefits.

———————————

The *Velazquez* case provided a slight opening, but the other restrictions on our practice persisted, and the problems of our clients persisted. Our lawyers had to find other ways to provide advocacy on issues their clients faced. During the workday they could not represent their clients fully as they had before, but nights and weekends were their own, and the First Amendment was alive then, too. Just as Jean Crowe (Chapter 8) had continued her administrative advocacy on behalf of victims of domestic violence through her extensive bar association activities, Russ, off the clock nights and weekends, was able to provide essential counsel and advice on welfare reform to state government officials struggling with changes made in Washington.

The limitations on legal aid that came down in 1996 were only a part of that year's reengineering of the government's relation to poor people. In an effort to make America harder-edged again, the entire welfare system was "reformed" by the loftily named Personal Responsibility and Work Opportunity Reconciliation Act. The Act replaced AFDC with block grants to states called Temporary Assistance to Needy Families (TANF), and Congress made many changes to the food stamp program.

The states were left to design, work out the details, and administer these programs right at the same time the lawyers for the participants were prohibited from representing them in the process. In Tennessee, however, both administrators and legislators wanted and needed Russ's help dealing with this new reality. Drawing on long-term relationships, Bill Purcell, then Democratic majority leader in the House, and Leonard Bradley, key advisor to Republican Governor Don Sundquist, called on Russ and Gordon for assistance. On his own time, Russ went line by line through the drafted plans, participated in many discussions with Purcell and Bradley, and proposed twenty-five changes, all of which were accepted and incorporated into the plan.

The state's plan was improved as much as possible given the punitive federal mandates, but then came the tribulations of administration. In the four months from September 1996 until January 1997, during the transition from AFDC to TANF, participation in Tennessee fell 23 percent, from ninety-one thousand to seventy thousand families, and it was not because all of these people suddenly found work. The complexity of the requirements for continued participation bedeviled DHS workers and beneficiaries alike. The program was in freefall, and it became obvious that Russ's nights and weekends no longer would be sufficient for the crisis. At that point, Gordon, at the one-year-old struggling TJC, came up with a lifeline, a six-month foundation grant to fund Russ's working there. Russ took a leave of absence from Legal Aid and began full-time representing clients who had flooded TJC with their TANF problems. The six-month leave would last for eight years.

The first problem he had to address was the enormous number of erroneous terminations under the new program. Russ meticulously documented the experiences from scores of his clients, "welfare reform's casualties," and took them to DHS administrators and legislators. When DHS was slow to respond, he threatened litigation. Quickly, they entered into productive discussions. First, the department imposed a moratorium on case closures; then Russ helped them design a system of review that must be followed before any family could be terminated from the program. Part of the review required an assessment of whether or not the caretaker might qualify for any of the exceptions to the eighteen-month limit on benefits. If the caretaker had not been able to obtain a job within the eighteen-month limit because of domestic violence, drug treatment, inability to secure childcare, disability, age (over sixty), functioning below a ninth-grade level, or living in a county with an unemployment level twice the state rate, then the family might be eligible for an exemption. The review program Russ and DHS designed stabilized participation and brought a dramatic reduction in erroneous case closures. It was hailed by both federal officials and advocacy groups and became a national model.

Even so, Russ realized there were people on TANF who because of their disability more properly and more advantageously should be receiving SSI instead. That would give them more stability than the time limited TANF. At the same time, having these people off the program and on SSI also would benefit the state. Under TANF, the state could face sanctions and fines from the federal government unless a certain percentage of people on the program were either in job training or employed, and this group of recipients could function in neither. The solution was to have these people apply for SSI, but that was easier said than done. Because of their significant limitations, they would need help negotiating the SSI application process. Immediately, Russ had a strategy for dealing with that: David Ettinger could propose a contract with DHS for Legal Aid to take referrals of likely candidates and help them apply if they seemed eligible. David and I agreed to go along with Russ's scheme, David sent a proposal to DHS to handle these cases for $500 each, and DHS gladly accepted.

David and others on our staff would assemble evidence for the client, get the necessary medical testimony, file the application, and, if appropriate, represent the client in an appeal of any negative decision. Initially, we operated the program only in Davidson County, but when it developed to be so successful there, David expanded it to the other counties we served. After several years, DHS wanted it expanded to the whole state, so we turned it over to TALS to administer it statewide, which TALS does to this day.

While he was at it, Russ saw another opportunity. The dramatic drop in participation had fiscal implications for the DHS budget: a $28 million surplus. Russ did a fiscal analysis showing how the department could use that surplus to improve childcare subsidies and increase the TANF grants, still low at forty-ninth in the nation. The state was persuaded and that happened. Then, invoking the Americans with Disabilities Act, Russ also was able to persuade DHS to provide masters level social workers to families with needs related to mental disabilities, addiction, or domestic abuse. That program too was recognized as a national model, this time by the Health and Human Services Office for Civil Rights.

━━━━━━━━━━━

The food stamp program, since 2008 the Supplemental Nutrition Assistance Program (SNAP), is authorized under the Farm Bill and operated by the US Department of Agriculture. Although one of its purposes was to create a larger market for producers of food, it generally is regarded as a welfare program because of its other beneficiaries, low-income people. Certainly Congress regarded it that way in 1996 when it took several swipes at food stamps in its vaunted Personal Responsibility and Work Opportunity Reconciliation Act. While we have had many fewer cases involving that program than AFDC over the years, it has been an important part of our community education program, has been the subject of some administrative advocacy, and occasionally has required litigation.

Adinah and Stewart were actively involved with MANNA, a community advocacy group concerned about hunger issues, and were particularly knowledgeable and helpful to clients. Adinah published pamphlets and flyers touting the availability of food stamps, how to apply, and the rules of the program. She gave enthusiastic presentations to community groups to educate them about food stamps, the school breakfast program, the commodities supplement program, and other food sources. Unfortunately, the Department of Human Services, which administers the program in Tennessee, was not always so enthusiastic or competent in its administration.

We had filed a federal class action suit against the department in 1974 on behalf of several clients addressing many problems in the administration of the program that prevented eligible people from getting food stamps. Stewart finally achieved a settlement in February 1979 that we hoped would lead to improvements, but that hope did not last long. By July, he and Russ were back in court charging the department with violating the agreed order. During a two-day trial, they presented testimony from numerous clients who variously had not been told by DHS of their possible eligibility for food stamps, had been denied emergency service, had not been allowed to file an application when they contacted a DHS office, and/or were told they would have to wait two weeks before they could apply. One former employee testified, "I was advised not to tell clients when they were eligible for expedited service." DHS clearly was systematically violating the order, and Judge Wiseman told department officials they were "headed for contempt," but he indulgently did not find it was "willful" yet. He gave them sixty days to submit a plan that would ensure compliance and allowed Russ and Stewart to conduct discovery to assess their progress. With that pressure, the case was settled before the next scheduled hearing.

The indulgence of the judge was not so successful for the DHS administrators a few years later in the case of *Lynch v. Lyng*. Gwendolyn Lynch was permanently disabled and had very little income, thus she was qualified to receive food stamps, and she did receive stamps worth $13 each month. Due to a quirk in the law, however, if she had been only temporarily disabled, she would have received more than twice as much, $30 per month. Congress, having been made aware of this inequity, in December 1985 amended the Food Stamp Act to correct that and made the corrections effective immediately. Nevertheless, USDA did nothing to implement this correction until the next May and, consequently, neither did Tennessee.

Finally, USDA issued regulations requiring the state to implement the correction by August 1, but even then it took Tennessee another six weeks to get it done, another month of limited food for Ms. Lynch. She came to see Russ asking to get the benefits she had been entitled to nine months before but had not received. When he contacted DHS, the department did give her benefits retroactive to the incorrect federal start date of August 1, but declined to go back to the effective date of the legislation. Russ, joined again by Lenny, filed suit against both USDA and DHS on behalf of Ms. Lynch and other permanently disabled food stamp recipients. USDA took the position that the phrase "effective on the date of enactment" did not mean what it said, but implicitly allowed for administrative discretion. With deference to the administrators, Judge Wiseman agreed. Incredulous, Russ and Lenny appealed to the Sixth Circuit. That court quickly pointed out that "the most basic tenant of statutory construction holds that courts are required, where possible, to give words their plain, unambiguous meaning," and it reversed.[8] Ms. Lynch and hundreds of other people at last received the amount of food stamps the law required.

Ms. Lynch's case was a fine illustration of the singular role of Legal Aid.

First, experience. Russ and Lenny had experience in food stamp law. It was part of their everyday practice, certainly not the case for a lawyer in private practice. Because they kept up with the law, they knew Congress had corrected the oversight and that USDA was disregarding the legislation. They knew what needed to be done for their clients.

Second, affordability. Except for a dedicated lawyer in a large firm with a strong pro bono commitment, no private lawyer could have afforded to take this case to federal district court and then to the Sixth Circuit. Such a commitment of time and resources is substantial and beyond the ability of most to carve out from a paying practice. The reality here is the same as it was in the *Samuels* case when the lawyer wrote to Russ, "You have accomplished a feat that those of us in private practice would never have been able to undertake."

Third, cost/benefit analysis. A lawyer in private practice, if she considered taking Ms. Lynch's case as one of her own, would have to do a cost/benefit analysis. Is it worth it to go to district court and then the appellate court in Cincinnati, one step away from the US Supreme Court, over the difference between $13 and $30 in monthly food stamps for just a few months? Does it help that if you win you may be benefiting another several hundred people you never met? Not likely. Still not enough economic gain to justify taking the case.

Fourth, relativity. In many legal aid benefits cases, the amounts seem small, laughable even, to a person who does not depend on those benefits for food, medicine, shelter, and other basic necessities of life. It's all relative to one's circumstance. For a person on a limited income, $17 a month can indeed make a proportionate difference in the amount of food she can buy. For attorneys dealing with much larger numbers in our economy, it is difficult to appreciate the value.

Fifth, the sentinel effect. The presence and persistence of legal aid lawyers is important beyond the benefits of one case. A case like *Lynch* functions as a reminder to the government agency that someone is there to stand up for the recipient. When agencies pinch the recipients with administrative discretion or disregard for legislation, there will be a heedful lawyer there to call their hand and challenge their harm, even to the point of taking it to an appellate court. That reminder is not nothing.

It is essential to the equitable functioning of our government. We have seen since the beginning of OEO Legal Services in the 1960s much more regard for the rights of low-income people and much more recognition of due process and equal protection in the administration of programs that are designed to help them. The progress is uneven. There have been significant setbacks, and certainly issues continue to come up, but because the heedful lawyer is there, the arc of justice is toward a more equitable society that protects the rights of each person every day, regardless of means or poverty.

Epilogue

Now twenty years on, beyond the end of our narrative, the challenges remain. In the intervening time, the recession of 2008 and the pandemic of 2020 through 2022 have been especially difficult for low-income people, creating more problems with healthcare, housing, financial issues, domestic violence, and difficulties in dealing with government agencies designed to help. Even the eventual recoveries have not distributed their blessings equally. The legal problems of the poor persist and compound.

We are, however, in a different place now from when our story began nearly sixty years ago. There is a different attitude in the bar and in our society. We have come a long way since the days when a committee of the bar brought charges against Legal Services lawyers for daring to represent developmentally disabled wards of the state, and it has been more than forty years since the hospitals and automobile dealers persuaded the United Way to cut our funding. No longer is it the head of a legal aid organization who must be the chief spokesperson for access to justice. Now the chief justice of our state Supreme Court and the Access to Justice Commission established by that court in 2008 are carrying the banner, and there is increasing emphasis on pro bono in the state and local bar associations.

As some of the chapters in this book have extended beyond 2002, they have told already of advocacy and accomplishments at the Legal Aid Society (las.org) since then. That was particularly the case in the chapters on family law, Social Security Disability, and the pro bono programs. In addition to those and the carrying on of the everyday delivery of legal aid, my successors Gary Housepian and DarKenya Waller also have developed several targeted programs. These include special services for immigrants who have been victims of domestic violence, a medical-legal partnership with Vanderbilt Shade Tree Clinic, and a reentry program assisting people who formerly were incarcerated in jails or prisons. Continuing a connection that dates back to the beginning of our story, the reentry program, which was originated by a recent Skadden fellow, Vidhi Joshi, is now funded by a gift from Harris Gilbert, who in 1968 was the first board president of Legal Services of Nashville. The bar and community continue to provide generous support for the annual campaign, and new grants and contracts have enhanced various services LAS provides.

In the years following the end of our story, the Tennessee Alliance for Legal Services (tals.org) under the direction of Ann Pruitt capitalized on the potential of computer technology for providing brief advice and referrals to low-income people. After George T. "Buck" Lewis and his law firm of Baker Donelson developed a web-based program through which low-income people can pose questions to volunteer attorneys around the state, Buck asked TALS to administer it. That program became a national model and has been adopted by bar groups in nearly every state. In addition, TALS operates a free senior legal helpline funded by International Paper and a general access hotline, 1-844-HELP4TN, for callers to talk with an attorney about their problems. On the TALS website, there is a Legal Wellness Checkup for users to assess their legal needs; it provides helpful information and referrals.

The Tennessee Justice Center (tnjustice.org), founded on a shoestring and amid adversity twenty-seven years ago, continues its essential work for clients throughout the state thanks to generous individual and foundation support. It has collaborated with healthcare providers and social services organizations not only in Tennessee but also nationally in order to advance the interests of its clients. During this time, through both individual and class action cases, as well as through advocacy with legislators and administrative agencies, TJC has obtained for its clients over $2.5 billion in healthcare benefits and $300 million in food assistance. Even so, there is greater need that cannot be met. Lacking vital government funding, TJC's work is largely limited to representing clients with health and public benefits problems, which are only a fraction of the many complex legal difficulties that burden the poor in our state.

Despite positive notes and the progress we have seen, access to justice still faces many hurdles. The legal ethicist Deborah Rhode described the irony of our situation: "'Equal justice under law' is one of America's most proudly proclaimed and widely violated legal principles."[1] We violate that precious principle by insufficient government funding. We violate it every time an understaffed legal aid office turns away an eligible client with a legitimate problem. We violate equal justice by cynical congressional restrictions that exclude whole groups of people from representation and limit the tools available to lawyers. We can and must do better.

When Congress in 1974 adopted the Legal Services Corporation Act, it found that "attorneys providing legal assistance must have full freedom to protect the best interests of their clients in keeping with the Code of Professional Responsibility, the Canons of Ethics, and the high standards of the legal profession."[2] As we have seen, a much different Congress in 1996 eviscerated that inspiring declaration of purpose. Lawyers employed by an LSC-funded organization today no longer have that "full freedom to protect the best interests of their clients." They are bravely laboring under multiple handicaps. That continues as a blot on our systems of law and justice every day.

Nevertheless, regardless of the limitations or other frustrations today, the duty of the legal aid attorney, in whatever setting, is still the same as it was for that Legal Services attorney many years ago. First, it is to stand by one's client, listening attentively and speaking respectfully, appreciating her plight and according to her the dignity so often denied to the poor and dispossessed. Second, following the admonition of Judge William Wayne Justice, the lawyer must, in whatever forum, tell the stories, present the revealing facts, convey the realities of poverty, advance the interest of the client, and prod the system toward justice. In that regard follows the third imperative: to devise creative legal solutions, challenge the way things are, and when necessary, be that burr under the saddle.

ACKNOWLEDGMENTS

Many people have helped me along the way since I began this project in April 2016. The first was Katharina Herring, then the librarian of the National Equal Justice Library at Georgetown University in Washington, DC, who encouraged my undertaking. Significant along the way were the two peer reviewers, anonymous to me, who offered detailed criticisms and important suggestions for further consideration that enriched and enlarged my story.

In my research I read the minutes of the Nashville Bar Association and its Board of Directors from 1912 to the present, and I refer to them often, especially in early chapters. I appreciate the assistance of Ken Seith and his staff in the Metropolitan Government Archives at the Nashville Public Library where the older minutes are housed. Thanks also to Monica Mackie at the NBA for access to more recent minutes.

The NBA minutes from the late 1960s starkly revealed the central role of Nashville attorney Lewis Pride, the hero of Chapter 2, whose persistence finally brought the OEO Legal Services funding to Nashville, despite staunch resistance in the bar. After his much too early death in 1978, his family graciously sent to our office the file he had kept documenting that struggle. His sharp letters and insistent messages have informed and enlivened this story, but they also brought regret that those of us who came only a few years later had not been aware of his pivotal role. He should have been honored in his lifetime. This recognition is a small tribute.

Letters and papers from the files of the late Thomas O. H. Smith Jr. provide many details of the deliberations of NBA in the late 1960s. Tommy was the only member who was on all three successive committees of the NBA that dealt with whether or not we would have an OEO-funded Legal Services program in Nashville. Then he twice was on the board of Legal Services, once in the early 1970s, appointed by the NBA, and again in the 1980s, appointed by the Council of Community Services. He thus was the institutional memory of the early years, a role he enjoyed. Whit Stokes, who as a young lawyer appears twice at crucial points in Chapter 2, was helpful filling in details of the time.

Former and present staff members of the Legal Aid Society have been helpful with information, reminders, and citations. My thanks to Maria Arvizu, Jerry Black, Whitney Blanton, Gordon Bonnyman, Bill Bush, Kitty Calhoun, Stewart Clifton, Dot Dobbins, Dana Dye, David Ettinger, Norm Feaster, Pete Frierson, Paul Geier, Rita Sanders Geier, Grayfred Gray, Juliet Griffin, Iska Hoole, Alex Hurder, David Kozlowski, Walter Kurtz, Neil McBride, Carol McCoy, Judy Bond-McKissick, Russ Overby, Adinah Robertson, Janet Rosenberg, Patricia Rulon, Andy Shookoff, Lucinda Smith, Greg Sperry, David Tarpley, Mary Walker, Marla Williams, and Allston Vander Horst. I appreciate the encouragement and assistance I have received in this endeavor from my successors as executive director, first Gary Housepian and then DarKenya Waller.

Five former presidents of the Legal Aid Society board helped by clarifying details of various actions: current board members Susan Kay and Jim Weatherly and former members Bob Cooper, John Pellegrin, and Bob Thompson. In addition to the help, I am grateful for the leadership of each one and their support.

Steve Christopher, a Deputy Chief Disciplinary Counsel at the Tennessee Board of Professional Responsibility, and formerly managing attorney for our Gallatin office, straightened me out with a detailed memorandum on the chronology of Tennessee's adoption of the various revisions of the ABA Code of Professional Responsibility. That saved me, I hope, from anachronisms and mistakes.

In Chapter 20 I make good use of Neil McBride's several compilations of "Significant Cases and Activities of Rural Legal Services of Tennessee." Useful there, as well as in other chapters, was David Kozlowski's 2018 memorandum "Notable Legal Aid Society Cases," in which he highlights twenty-one of the more than two hundred reported cases handled by Rural, South Central, and Middle lawyers in state appellate courts and federal courts over the years. The minutes of the meetings of our Board of Directors, all intact except for a couple of gaps in 1969 and 1973, gave structure to the story of the organization.

Special thanks to Karen Piper in the Special Collections Department of the Nashville Public Library and Bess Connally, Reference Librarian at the Knox Country Public Library, who each tracked down an essential newspaper article the citation to which had eluded me. Thanks also to Julia Wilburn, the new editor of the *Tennessee Bar Journal,* who provided cites to articles, one very old, in that publication, and to Vicki Bailey, chief deputy clerk, and clerks in the Davidson County Chancery Court Records Center who resurrected forty-year-old cases for me to read.

Don Saunders, longtime vice president at the National Legal Aid and Defender Association, gave me helpful perspective on national events and shared important contacts, for which I am grateful.

———————

And now to the mother lode.

This history would be a mere shadow of itself if it were not for Kirk Loggins's reporting for the *Tennessean.* The scrapbook of the Legal Aid Society kept by Maggie Thompson and then Cindy Durham is full of Kirk's articles about us and our cases, and searches on Newspapers.com brought even more. I have relied heavily on the hundreds of articles Kirk wrote, and have expressed my gratitude to him.

Even before Kirk, reporters from the morning paper including Rob Elder, Tom Ingram, Marcia Vanderburg, and Pat Welch covered us well. Throughout the years, the *Tennessean* gave us eloquent support with well-timed editorials by John Siegenthaler and Jim O'Hara, for which the newspaper appropriately received the Emery A. Brownell News Media Award from the National Legal Aid and Defender Association in 1981.

———————

My indulgent scribe for more than four years was Angela Edwards Smith, who lives on Yellow Creek in Houston County where this project began. She patiently deciphered my scratchings on legal pads and endured repeated re-drafts to produce digital copy. Her interest and good spirit enhanced the project. And thanks to Patricia Rulon, formerly my assistant at Legal Aid for nearly twenty years, who, after I moved back to Nashville, labored through several more drafts, offered helpful suggestions, and produced the final version of the manuscript. Her technical ability and commitment to the project were essential for bringing our product to the publisher. Thanks also to Zack Gresham and Joell Smith-Borne at Vanderbilt University Press for their work in guiding this project along to publication.

I am grateful to the following people who have read all or parts of this work: Margaret Behm, Gordon Bonnyman, Kitty Calhoun, Dan Cornfield, David Ettinger, Hal Hardin, Walter Kurtz, Russ Overby, Bill West, and especially Susan Ford Wiltshire. I'm grateful for their suggestions, corrections, and encouragement. In the end, however, to acknowledge again that the writing of history is always personal, I quote in translation the first person ever to write a history in prose, Hecataeus of Miletus (550–476 BCE): "I write these words as they seem to me to be true."

ABBREVIATIONS

AARP	American Association of Retired Persons
ABA	American Bar Association
ACLU	American Civil Liberties Union
AFDC	Aid to Families With Dependent Children
CRLA	California Rural Legal Assistance
CCS	Council of Community Services
CSA	Community Services Administration
DDS	Disability Determination Section
DHS	Tennessee Department of Human Services
DOC	Tennessee Department of Correction
HCFA	Health Care Financing Administration
HEW	US Department of Health, Education And Welfare
HHS	US Department of Health and Human Services
HUD	US Department of Housing and Urban Development
IOLTA	Interest On Lawyers Trust Accounts
LAS	Legal Aid Society Of Middle Tennessee (1995–2001); Legal Aid Society Of Middle Tennessee and the Cumberlands (2002–)
LDF	NAACP Legal Defense and Education Fund
LSC	Legal Services Corporation
LSMT	Legal Services of Middle Tennessee (1979–1994); now Legal Aid Society

LSON	Legal Services of Nashville (1968–1977); now Legal Aid Society
LSONMT	Legal Services of Nashville and Middle Tennessee (1977–1979); now Legal Aid Society
LSSCT	Legal Services Of South Central Tennessee
MAC	Metropolitan Action Commission
MDHA	Metropolitan Development and Housing Agency
MTHSA	Middle Tennessee Health Systems Agency
MTSU	Middle Tennessee State University
NAACP	National Association for the Advancement of Colored People
NBA	Nashville Bar Association
NHeLP	National Health Law Program
NLADA	National Legal Aid and Defender Association
NOW	National Organization for Women
OEO	Office of Economic Opportunity
OLS	Office of Legal Services of OEO
RLST	Rural Legal Services of Tennessee
SCLAID	American Bar Association Standing Committee on Legal Aid and Indigent Defense
SNAP	Supplemental Nutrition Assistance Program
SSA	Social Security Administration
SSI	Supplemental Security Income
TALS	Tennessee Alliance For Legal Services (previously TALSLAP, Tennessee Association of Legal Services Legal Aid Programs)
TANF	Temporary Assistance for Needy Families
TBA	Tennessee Bar Association
TBF	Tennessee Bar Foundation
THA	Tennessee Hospital Association

THCC   Tennessee Health Care Campaign

THFC   Tennessee Health Facilities Commission

TJC   Tennessee Justice Center

TRO   Temporary Restraining Order

TSU   Tennessee State University

UGF   United Givers Fund; now United Way

UT   University of Tennessee

WHAC   Wherry Housing Action Committee

WHC   Wherry Housing Cooperative, Inc.

YW   Young Women's Christian Association;
or YWCA   recently changed to simply YWCA

NOTES

INTRODUCTION

1. W. L. Grandberry in the minutes of the Nashville Bar and Library Association meeting, November 1915.
2. See Harmon L. Smith and Louis D. Hodges, *The Christian and His Decisions* (Nashville, TN: Abingdon Press, 1969).
3. See Abraham J. Heschel, *The Prophets* (New York: Harper and Row, 1962), especially 27–38, 212–13.
4. See "Charles Sherrod, Civil Rights Pioneer in Rural Georgia, Dies at 85," *New York Times*, October 17, 2022, https://www.nytimes.com/2022/10/15/us/charles-sherrod-dead.html.
5. See Joseph T. Howell, *Civil Rights Journey* (Bloomington, IN: AuthorHouse, 2011), 87–156. The pages cited contain a diary Joe kept describing our time in Georgia. The earlier part of his book describes his growing up in the segregated society that was Nashville. By coincidence, his father, the president of Nashville City Bank, makes an appearance in Chapter 4 of this book, which describes an incident where he was helpful to LSON.
6. Ashley T. Wiltshire Jr., "Religion and Lifework in the Law," *Texas Tech Law Review* 27, no. 3 (1996): 1383.
7. See David Halberstam's description of the longtime owner who had sold to Gannett in 1972. *The Children* (New York: Random House, 1998), 114–21.
8. Felice Batlan, *Women and Justice for the Poor: A History of Legal Aid 1863–1945* (New York: Cambridge University Press, 2015); Shaun Ossei-Owusu, "The Sixth Amendment Façade: The Racial Evolution of the Right to Counsel," *University of Pennsylvania Law Review* 167, no. 5 (2019): 1178–82.

CHAPTER 1

1. Batlan, *Women and Justice*, 17–36; see also Philip L. Merkel, "At the Crossroads of Reform: The First Fifty Years of American Legal Aid, 1876–1926," *Houston Law Review* 27, no. 1 (1990): 1.
2. Merkel, "At the Crossroads," 8–9; Batlan, *Women and Justice*, 81.
3. Reginald Heber Smith, *Justice and the Poor: A Study of the Present Denial of Justice to the Poor and the Agencies Making More Equal Their Position Before*

the Law with Particular Reference to Legal Aid Work in the United States (New York: Charles Scribner's Sons, 1919), 146.

4. See Walter I. Trattner, *From Poor Law to Welfare State: A History of Social Welfare in the United States*, 4th ed. (New York: The Free Press, 1989), 73–101; see also James Leiby, *A History of Social Welfare and Social Work in the United States* (New York: Columbia University Press, 1978).

5. Merkel, "At the Crossroads," 3.

6. Smith, *Justice and the Poor*, 200–204.

7. Merkel, "At the Crossroads," 12; Batlan, *Women and Justice*, 61, 73.

8. Merkel, "At the Crossroads," 11.

9. Merkel, "At the Crossroads," 17–18; see also Smith, *Justice and the Poor*, 214.

10. Merkel, "At the Crossroads," 20.

11. Jack Katz, *Poor People's Lawyers in Transition* (New Brunswick, NJ: Rutgers University Press, 1984), 37–50; Merkel, "At the Crossroads," 35–44.

12. Alan Houseman and Linda E. Perle, "Securing Equal Justice for All: A Brief History of Civil Legal Assistance in the United States" (rev. 2018), Center for Law and Social Policy, https://www.clasp.org/publications/report/brief/securing-equal-justice-all-brief-history-civil-legal-assistance-united-states, 9.

13. Shaun Ossei-Owusu, "Racial Discounting and Self-Help: Blacks, Americanization, and Early Twentieth Century Legal Aid." The article, which received a best paper award from the American Society for Legal History in 2017, is described by Ossei-Owusu in a curriculum vitae at https://law.duke.edu/sites/default/files/centers/clepp/soo_cv_-_4-18.pdf. A more recent c.v. is on the website of the University of Pennsylvania Carey Law School, where he now teaches.

14. John S. Bradway, "Legal Aid Service and Social Work: The Legal Point of View," *Proceedings of the National Conference of Social Work at the Fiftieth Anniversary Session Held in Washington, D.C., May 16–23, 1923* (Chicago: University of Chicago Press, 1923), 188. Cited in Batlan, *Women and Justice*, 162.

15. John S. Bradway to Emmet Field, March 28, 1929, Bradway Papers, box I, vol. 36. Cited in Batlan, *Women and Justice*, 162.

16. Earl Johnson Jr., *To Establish Justice for All: The Past and Future of Civil Legal Aid in the United States* (Santa Barbara, CA: Praeger, 2014), 76.

17. *Tennessean*, February 12, 1937, 1. There is no clue in the newspaper article explaining the surprising existence of the second White bar association. For that see David C. Rutherford, *Bench and Bar* (Nashville, TN: Nashville Bar Foundation, 2003), 35–41. Apparently, a number of lawyers had split from the NBA and formed the Davidson County association several years before because of a dispute about dues payment and the use of the NBA

library. Some seem to have been members of both. Most rejoined the NBA by 1940, and the Davidson County association was disbanded.

18. *Tennessean*, February 20, 1937, 3.
19. *Tennessean*, December 9, 1961, 7.
20. *Tennessean*, August 21, 1963, 6.
21. Smith, *Justice and the Poor*, 162.

CHAPTER 2

1. John 12:8 (RSV); see also Deuteronomy 15:11. Note: The statement quoted by Jesus is only half the story. Relying on that alone neglects the consequential commandment that follows in its original in the book of Deuteronomy (See epigraph at the beginning of Chapter 21 in this book.) Scripture quotations in this book are from either the Revised Standard Version of the Bible (RSV), Division of Christian Education of the National Council of the Churches of Christ in the USA, 1946, or the New English Bible (NEB), Oxford University Press and Cambridge University Press, 1970.
2. Halberstam, *The Children*, 230–34.
3. *Tennessee Bar Journal* 1, no. 3 (August 1965), 11–26.
4. *Tennessean*, "Shriver Relaxes Regulation," August 12, 1965, 34.
5. *Tennessean*, December 17, 1965, 24.
6. *Tennessean*, February 21, 1966, 13.
7. Johnson, *To Establish Justice for All*, 106.
8. *Tennessean*, November 21, 1967, 14.
9. Dewey W. Grantham, *The South in Modern America* (New York: Harper Collins, 1994), 252.
10. *Tennessean*, January 25, 1968, 8.
11. *Tennessean*, January 26, 1968, 28 and 14.
12. *Tennessean*, February 4, 1968, 4B.
13. *Tennessean*, April 24, 1968, 8.
14. *Tennessean*, September 16, 1968, 5.
15. *Tennessean*, December 19, 1968, 13.
16. See Kevin Phillips, *The Emerging Republican Majority* (New Rochelle, NY: Arlington House, 1969).
17. Grantham, *The South in Modern America*, 281.

CHAPTER 3

1. Johnson, *To Establish Justice for All*, 110.
2. *Tennessean*, January 21, 1970, 5.

3. Tennessee, unlike most other states, preserves the ancient English distinction between courts of law and courts of equity. The judges who preside in chancery courts, the courts of equity, are chancellors.

4. In 2006, after having been named distinguished alumnus by the Divinity School (1996) and by the University Alumni Association (2005), Lawson returned to Vanderbilt as a Distinguished University Professor, teaching until 2009. In 2007 the University established an endowed chair in his honor and in 2021 established the James Lawson Institute for the Research and Study of Nonviolent Movements.

5. The ABA Model Code of Professional Conduct was adopted by Tennessee in 1970 as the Tennessee Code of Professional Responsibility. This replaced the ABA Canons of Professional Ethics, which Tennessee had adopted in 1961.

6. *Tennessean*, November 29, 1970, 4B.

7. *Fell v. Armour*, 355 F. Supp. 1319, 1336 (M.D. Tenn., 1973).

8. *Tate v. Short*, 401 U.S. 395, 399 (1971).

9. *Nashville Banner*, December 15, 1971, 18.

10. *Tennessean*, January 15, 1972, 16.

11. *Tennessean*, January 15, 1972, 16.

12. *Tennessean*, January 19, 1972, 31.

13. See David Halberstam, *The Children*, 114–21.

14. As with so many other issues, the unconstitutional practice of incarcerating low-income people because of their inability to pay fines was not stopped everywhere in Tennessee by this case, several similar cases, and even legislative action. Lawlessness endures. See Walt Kurtz's article, "Pay or Stay," in the *Tennessee Bar Journal* 51, no. 7 (July 2015), 16.

15. *Bodie v. Connecticut*, 401 U.S. 371 (1971).

16. With new chancellors, the court did indeed very soon become a learned and respected bench, even designated recently as the "business court" for Tennessee because of the abilities of its chancellors, but alas, this talent has proven to be too much for state legislators who in 2021 wanted to make Tennessee like it was again. They proposed to remove one chancellor because of her ruling in a voting rights case, then proposed to strip jurisdiction of complicated state matters from this court and spread it to Sumner County judges ("why not?") and other unaccustomed judges throughout the state. Finally, the legislature settled on a scheme of using strategically appointed judges from elsewhere and forming special three-judge courts, at a cost of more than $2 million per year, to dilute the power of this respected court.

17. *Shapiro v. Thompson*, 394 U.S. 618 (1969).

18. *Tennessean*, October 27, 1972, 4.

CHAPTER 4

1. *Tennessean*, September 21, 1973, 20.
2. *Tennessean*, December 19, 1973, 22.
3. *Saville v. Treadway*, 404 F. Supp. 430 (M.D. Tenn., 1974).
4. *Saville v. Treadway*, 404 F. Supp. 430, 433 (M.D. Tenn., 1974).
5. *Tennessean*, December 10, 1984, 1B. Sad to say, as we have seen elsewhere, the wheels of justice grind slowly. The implementation of the Saville order did not go smoothly or quickly, and the subsequent story is not entirely rosy. Though Amy Lynn and thousands of others benefited from the ruling in her case, as the years went on and governors' administrations followed one after another, the progress lagged and good intentions withered. Nearly twenty years later, the Department of Justice did get into the fray, bringing its considerable heft and resources. Even so, it was only after nearly twenty-five more years of litigation and the DOJ's persistence that the last of those gruesome institutions were closed and the state went completely to community-based services. Finally in 2017, Governor Bill Haslam was able to announce the closing of the last institution: "We have fundamentally changed the way we serve some of our most vulnerable citizens." *Tennessean*, September 10, 2017, p. 8A.
6. Replevin is an ancient legal remedy by which a person may recover personal property wrongfully taken.
7. *Tennessean*, January 17, 1974, 6.
8. *Tennessean*, January 17, 1974, 1.
9. *Tennessean*, February 3, 1974, 1 and 10.
10. *Tennessean*, May 9, 1974, 1.
11. *Tennessean*, May 9, 1974, 23.
12. *Commercial Appeal*, September 12, 1974, 4.
13. *Tennessean*, May 9, 1974, 23.
14. *Tennessean*, June 7, 1974, 10.
15. NBA minutes, December 1954, 759.
16. 42 U.S. Code § 2996e(b)(1)(B).
17. *Lester v. Gray*, Tenn.Ct.App., Middle Section (January 3, 1975).
18. *Clark v. Thomas*, Davidson Chancery Part I, No. A-6181, (September 19, 1977) 11.
19. *Clark v. Thomas*, Tenn.Ct.App., Interim Opinion (August 2, 1978) 7.
20. *Tennessean*, July 26, 1975, 1.
21. *Tennessean*, April 26, 1976, 10.
22. *Tennessean*, April 22, 1976, 41.

CHAPTER 5

1. *Tennessean*, "Legal Services Often the Last Stop," July 15, 1977, 15.

CHAPTER 6

1. *Tennessean*, January 15, 1978, 2A.
2. *Tennessean*, January 29, 1978, 2B.
3. *Tennessean*, January 15, 1978, 2A.
4. *Trigg v. Blanton*, Davidson Chancery Part I, No. A-6047, Memorandum Opinion (August 1978) 45.
5. *Hanna v. Toner*, 630 F. 2d 442 (6th Cir. 1980).
6. *Grubbs v. Bradley*, 552 F. Supp. 1052, 1057 (M.D. Tenn. 1982).
7. *Tennessean*, November 25, 1981, 2.
8. 552 F. Supp. 1057, fn. 4.
9. *Rhodes v. Chapman*, 452 U.S. 337 (1981).
10. 552 F. Supp. 1087.
11. *Tennessean*, July 3, 1985, 1; *Tennessean*, July 4, 1985. 1.
12. *Grubbs v. Bradley*, 821 F. Supp. at 496, 498 (M.D. Tenn. 1993).
13. 821 F. Supp. at 504.

CHAPTER 7

1. The Skadden Fellowship Foundation, established in 1988 by the global law firm Skadden, each year provides fellowships for twenty-eight selected law graduates to practice public interest law for two years.

CHAPTER 8

Epigraph. The epigraph at the beginning of this chapter and several others are quotes from clients who replied to client satisfaction letters after we had completed their cases. To respect their privacy, I have used initials or pseudonyms instead of their full names and have included other identifiers such as locations and dates if they were preserved in our records.
1. *Tennessean*, November 3, 1977, 25.
2. LSMT newsletter, 1986.
3. *Tennessean*, June 18, 2001, 1B–2B.
4. *Tennessean*, June 9, 2003, 13.

CHAPTER 9

1. See Russell Fowler, "Stealing Children's Lives: Judge Camile Kelley Aided Trafficking of Thousands of Children," *Tennessee Bar Journal* 57, no. 5

(September/October 2021), 36, which cites among others Barbara Bisantz Raymond, *The Baby Thief: The Untold Story of Georgia Tann, the Baby Seller Who Corrupted Adoption* (New York: Carroll and Graf, 2007) and Linda T. Austin, "Babies for Sale: Tennessee Children's Adoption Scandal," *Tennessee Historical Quarterly* 49, no. 2 (Summer 1990).

2. *Tennessean,* August 13, 1977, 17.
3. *Leaf- Chronicle* [Clarksville], September 12, 1985, 15.
4. *Tennessean,* September 29, 1986, 1B.
5. 42 U.S.C. § 1983.
6. *Tennessean,* November 10, 1992, 1.
7. *Davis v. McClaran,* 909 S.W. 2d 412 (1995).
8. *Cookeville Herald-Citizen,* November 7, 1995, 5.

CHAPTER 10

1. *In re Gault,* 387 U.S. 1 (1967).
2. *Batey v. Bass,* Davidson Chancery Part II, No. A-6752 (May 24, 1976).
3. *C. Allen High, et al, vs. Hon. S. Wallace Brewer,* Tenn. Sup. Ct. (May 27, 1977).
4. *Batey v. Bass,* Davidson Chancery Part II, No. A-6752 (October 31, 1977).
5. *Tennessean,* January 13, 1979, 23.
6. *Tennessean,* October 4, 1978, 1.
7. *Tennessean,* October 17, 1978, 1.
8. *Tennessean,* December 27, 1978, 1.
9. *Tennessean,* December 27, 1978, 2.
10. *Tennessean,* January 1, 1979, 1.
11. *Tennessean,* January 2, 1979, 1.
12. *Tennessean,* January 3, 1979, 11.
13. *Tennessean,* January 3, 1979, 1.
14. *Nashville Banner,* February 26, 1979, 1; *Tennessean,* February 27, 1979, 13.
15. *Doe v. Bradley,* Davidson Chancery Part I, No. A-7980-I (December 9, 1981).

CHAPTER 11

1. Matthew Desmond, *Evicted: Poverty and Profit in the American City* (New York: Crown Publishers, 2016), 296.
2. *Ferguson v. Metropolitan Development and Housing Agency,* 485 F. Supp. 517 (M.D. Tenn. 1980).
3. *Goldberg v. Kelly,* 397 U.S. 254 (1970).
4. *Tennessean,* June 19, 1990, 35.
5. *Tennessean,* February 1, 1999, 1B.
6. *Tennessean,* February 18, 1987, 2.
7. *Tennessean,* February 18, 1987, 2.

8. *Tennessean*, January 27, 1988, 1.

9. *Jones v. Mayer Co.*, 392 U.S. 409 (1968).

10. Judge Crenshaw, formerly a partner at the Waller Lansden firm, was appointed to the federal bench by President Barack Obama and took office in 2016. In his Investiture Remarks, he paid tribute to Judge Morton, whose ruling in the *Dellway* case he had worked to overturn as a law student. In a dramatic affirmation of history, the case he cited on this occasion was the school busing case that in 1969 had caused Judge Morton to be rejected by polite, as well as impolite, society in Nashville. With appreciation, Judge Crenshaw recalled that Judge Morton's application of the law in that case "moved me and my South Nashville classmates to Tennessee's largest public school, McGavock Comprehensive High School in Donelson, Tennessee," and he assessed that "Judge Morton's courage set in motion a series of events in my life that brings me here today."

11. *Jordan v. Dellway Villa*, 661 F. 2d 558 (6th Cir. 1981).

12. The Wherry Housing Act of 1949, named for a Nebraska senator, financed the building of housing for families on military bases.

13. Smith, *Justice and the Poor*, 135.

CHAPTER 12

1. Desmond, *Evicted*, 219.

2. *Lebanon Democrat*, February 4, 1993, 7.

3. *Tennessean*, March 8, 1979, 2.

4. *Tennessean*, July 12, 1979, 40.

5. *Tennessean*, July 12, 1979, 40.

6. Kris Shephard, *Rationing Justice: Poverty Lawyers and Poor People in the Deep South* (Baton Rouge: Louisiana State University Press, 2007), 229.

7. *Tennessean*, September 5, 1979, 31.

8. Genna Rae McNeil, *Groundwork: Charles Hamilton Houston and the Struggle for Civil Rights* (Philadelphia: University of Pennsylvania Press, 1983), 84.

9. McNeil, *Groundwork*, 84.

CHAPTER 13

1. Don Doyle, *Nashville since the 1920s* (Knoxville: University of Tennessee Press, 1985), 129.

2. *Tennessean*, August 24, 1978, 9.

3. *Tennessean*, August 31, 1978, 1.

4. *Tennessean*, January 29, 1979, 1.

5. *Tennessean*, April 5, 1979, 1 and 8.

6. *Tennessean*, May 17, 1979, 4.

7. *Tennessean*, May 30, 1979, 15.

CHAPTER 14

1. *Tennessean*, February 14, 1980, 6.
2. *Tennessean*, February 20, 1980, 10.

CHAPTER 15

1. *Tennessean*, February 21, 1981, 4A.
2. *Tennessean*, February 15, 1981, 17A.
3. *Tennessean*, April 9, 1981, 22.
4. Astonishingly, more than twenty-five years after being let go, Wear continued to identify himself as president of the Legal Services Corporation. He did so in March 2018, when he signed a statement of the Conservative Action Project entitled "Congress Must Repeal Obamacare and Protect Life." March 16, 2018, http://conservativeactionproject.com/congress-must-repeal-obamacare-and-protect-life.

CHAPTER 16

1. *Tennessean*, September 2, 1981, 16.
2. *Tennessean*, September 2, 1981, 16.
3. *Tennessean*, November 8, 1981, 32D.
4. *Tennessean*, November 8, 1981, 32D.
5. *Tennessean*, December 6, 1981, 3B.
6. *Tennessean*, April 12, 1982, 6.
7. *Tennessee Lawyer* 33, no. 6 (September 1984), 1.

CHAPTER 17

1. *Newsom v. Vanderbilt University*, 453 F. Supp. 401 (M.D. Tenn. 1978).
2. *Newsom v. Vanderbilt University*, 653 F. 2d 1100 (6th Cir. 1981).
3. *Tennessean*, February 28, 1980, 1.
4. *Tennessean*, May 29, 1981, 17.
5. *Nashville Banner*, May 29, 1981, A8.
6. *Nashville Banner*, September 2, 1981, C5.
7. *Tennessean*, October 23, 1981, 17.
8. *Tennessean*, November 5, 1981, 13.
9. *Jennings v. Alexander*, 518 F. Supp. 877 (M.D. Tenn. 1981).
10. *Jennings v. Alexander*, 715 F. 2d 1036 (6th Cir. 1983).
11. *Alexander v. Choate*, 469 U.S. 287 (1985).
12. *Linton v. Commissioner*, 779 F. Supp. 925 (M.D. Tenn. 1990).
13. *Linton v. Commissioner*, 937 F. Supp. 1311 (6th Cir. 1992).
14. *Linton v. Commissioner*, 65 F. 3d 508 (6th Cir. 1995).
15. *Madison-Hughes v. Shalala*, 30 F. 3d 1121 (6th Cir. 1996).

16. Sara Rosenbaum, "Eliminating Inequity in Health Care Demands Measurement in Real Time," *Milbank Quarterly Opinion*, August 12, 2021, https://www.milbank.org/quarterly/opinions/eliminating-inequity-in-health-care-demands-measurement-in-real-time.

17. *Tennessean*, March 30, 1987, 1B.

18. *Tennessean*, January 29, 1994, 4.

19. George J. Annas, "Adam Smith in the Emergency Room," *Hastings Center Report*, August 1985, 17; Cheryl Frank, "Dumping the Poor—Private Hospitals Risk Suits," *ABA Journal* 71, no. 3 (March 1985), 25.

20. *Changing Times*, October 1985, 88.

CHAPTER 18

1. *Tennessean*, July 16, 1981, 17.

2. *Tennessean*, July 21, 1981, 6.

3. *Tennessean*, December 14, 1985, 1.

4. *Samuels v. Heckler*, 668 F. Supp. 656 (W.D. Tenn. 1986).

CHAPTER 20

1. *New York Times*, January 28, 1996, 8.

2. Johnson, *To Establish Justice for All*, 761.

3. See Brennan Center for Justice, *Restricting Legal Services: How Congress Left the Poor with Only Half a Lawyer* (New York: Brennan Center for Justice, New York University School of Law, 2000), www.brennancenter.org.

4. Johnson, *To Establish Justice for All*, 780.

5. *Block v. Neal*, 460 U.S. 289 (1983).

6. *Bannon v. Oshkosh B'Gosh, Inc.*, 897 F. Supp 1028 (M.D. Tenn., 1995).

CHAPTER 21

1. *Tennessean*, February 23, 1982, 20.

2. *Bowen v. Gilliard*, 483 U.S. 587 (1987).

3. *Eldrozetta Caruthers v. Sammie Lynn Puett*, M.D. Tenn. No. 7188, (May 5, 1980) 7.

4. *Knoxville News Sentinel*, June 8, 1992, A5.

5. See "About Statutory Restrictions on LSC-Funded Programs," Legal Services Corporation, January 2010, https://lsc-live.app.box.com/s/xqhg7qjx8x26zxctafytbbpo3c3frz5v.

6. Omnibus Consolidated Rescissions and Appropriations Act of 1996, § 504(a)(16), 110 Stat. 1321-53 (1996).

7. *Legal Services Corporation v. Velazquez*, 531 U.S. 533 (2001).

8. *Lynch v. Lyng*, 872 F. 2d 718, 720-21 (6th Cir. 1989).

EPILOGUE

1. Deborah Rhode, *Access to Justice* (New York: Oxford University Press, 2004), 3.

2. 42 U.S.C. § 2996(6).

BIBLIOGRAPHY

Annas, George J. "Adam Smith in the Emergency Room." *Hastings Center Report*, August 1985, 17.

Auerbach, Jerold S. *Unequal Justice: Lawyers and Social Change in Modern America*. New York: Oxford University Press, 1976.

Batlan, Felice. *Women and Justice for the Poor: A History of Legal Aid, 1863–1945*. New York: Cambridge University Press, 2015.

Bethel, Billie, and Robert Kirk Walker, "Et tu, Brute?" *Tennessee Bar Journal* 1, no. 3 (August 1965): 11.

Brennan Center for Justice. *Restricting Legal Services: How Congress Left the Poor with Only Half a Lawyer*. New York: Brennan Center for Justice, New York University School of Law, 2000. www.brennancenter.org.

Brownell, Emery A. *Legal Aid in the United States*. Rochester, NY: Lawyers Coop, 1951.

Cannon, Thomas G. *Equal Justice: A History of the Legal Aid Society of Milwaukee*. Milwaukee, WI: Marquette University Press, 2010.

Desmond, Matthew. *Evicted: Poverty and Profit in the American City*. New York: Crown Publishers, 2016.

Doyle, Don H. *Nashville in the New South, 1880–1930*. Knoxville: University of Tennessee Press, 1985.

———. *Nashville Since the 1920s*. Knoxville: University of Tennessee Press, 1985.

Fowler, Russell. "Stealing Children's Lives: Judge Camile Kelley Aided Trafficking of Thousands of Children." *Tennessee Bar Journal* 57, no. 5 (September/October 2021): 36.

Frank, Cheryl. "Dumping the Poor—Private Hospitals Risk Suits." *ABA Journal* 71, no. 3 (March 1985), 25.

Grantham, Dewey W. *The South in Modern America: A Region at Odds*. New York: Harper Collins, 1994.

Halberstam, David. *The Children*. New York: Random House, 1998.

Harrington, Michael. *The Other America: Poverty in the United States*. New York: Simon and Schuster, 1962.

Heschel, Abraham J. *The Prophets*. New York: Harper and Row, 1962.

Houseman, Alan W. "Civil Legal Assistance for Low-Income Persons: Looking Back and Looking Forward." *Fordham Urban Law Journal* 29, no. 3 (2002): 1213.

Houseman, Alan W., and Linda E. Perle. "Securing Equal Justice for All: A Brief History of Civil Legal Assistance in the United States" (rev. May 2018) www.clasp.org/sites/default/files/publications/2018/05/2018_securingequaljustice.pdf.

Howell, Joseph T. *Civil Rights Journey: The Story of a White Southerner Coming of Age during the Civil Rights Revolution.* Bloomington, IN: AuthorHouse, 2011.

———. *Hard Living on Clay Street: Portraits of Blue Collar Families.* Garden City, NY: Anchor Press, 1973.

Johnson, Earl, Jr. *Justice and Reform: The Formative Years of the OEO Legal Services Program.* New York: Russell Sage Foundation, 1974.

———. *To Establish Justice for All: The Past and Future of Civil Legal Aid in the United States.* Santa Barbara, CA: Praeger, 2014.

Justice, William Wayne. "Burrs Under the Saddle." *Texas Bar Journal* 68 (July 2005): 609–10.

Katz, Jack. *Poor People's Lawyers in Transition.* New Brunswick, NJ: Rutgers University Press, 1984.

Katz, Michael B. *The Undeserving Poor: America's Enduring Confrontation with Poverty,* 2nd edition. New York: Oxford University Press, 2013.

Kurtz, Walter C. "Pay or Stay." *Tennessee Bar Journal* 51, no. 7 (July 2015): 16.

Leiby, James. *A History of Social Welfare and Social Work in the United States.* New York: Columbia University Press, 1978.

McNeil, Genna Rae. *Groundwork: Charles Hamilton Houston and the Struggle for Civil Rights.* Philadelphia: University of Pennsylvania Press, 1983.

Merkel, Philip L. "At the Crossroads of Reform: The First Fifty Years of American Legal Aid 1876–1926." *Houston Law Review* 27, no. 1 (January 1990): 1–44.

Miller, Carol Poh. *A Passion for Justice: A History of the Legal Aid Society of Cleveland 1905–2005.* Cleveland, OH: Legal Aid Society of Cleveland, 2006.

Ossei-Owusu, Shaun. "The Sixth Amendment Façade: The Racial Evolution of the Right to Counsel." *University of Pennsylvania Law Review* 167, no. 5 (2019): 1161.

Phillips, Kevin. *The Emerging Republican Majority.* New Rochelle, NY: Arlington House, 1969.

Pride, Richard A. *The Political Use of Racial Narratives: School Desegregation in Mobile Alabama 1954–97.* Champaign: University of Illinois Press, 2002.

Rhode, Deborah L. *Access to Justice.* New York: Oxford University Press, 2004.

Rosenbaum, Sara. "Eliminating Inequity in Health Care Demands Measurement in Real Time." *Milbank Quarterly Opinion*, August 12, 2021. https://www.milbank.org/quarterly/opinions/eliminating-inequity-in-health-care-demands-measurement-in-real-time.

Rutherford, David L. *Bench and Bar: Nashville, Davidson County, Tennessee*. Nashville: The Nashville Bar Foundation, 1981.

———. *Bench and Bar II 2003*. Nashville: The Nashville Bar Foundation, 2003.

Shephard, Kris. *Rationing Justice: Poverty Lawyers and Poor People in the Deep South*. Baton Rouge: Louisiana State University Press, 2007.

Smith, Harmon L., and Louis W. Hodges. *The Christian and His Decisions: An Introduction to Christian Ethics*. Nashville, TN: Abingdon Press, 1969.

Smith, Reginald Heber. *Justice and the Poor: A Study of the Present Denial of Justice to the Poor and the Agencies Making More Equal Their Position Before the Law with Particular Reference to Legal Aid Work in the United States*. New York: Charles Scribner's Sons, 1919.

Summerville, James. *Colleagues on the Cumberland: A History of the Nashville Legal Profession*. Dallas, TX: Taylor Publishing Company, 1996.

Spriggs, Kent. *Voices of Civil Rights Lawyers: Reflections from the Deep South, 1964–1980*. Gainesville: University Press of Florida, 2018.

Trattner, Walter I. *From Poor Law to Welfare State: A History of Social Welfare in America*, 4th ed. New York: The Free Press, 1989.

Wiltshire, Ashley T., Jr. "Religion and Lifework in the Law." *Texas Tech Law Review* 27, no. 3 (1996): 1383.

INDEX

CPSIA information can be obtained
at www.ICGtesting.com
Printed in the USA
LVHW040218241222
735787LV00002B/73